REDRESS

REDRESS

INSIDE THE JAPANESE CANADIAN CALL FOR JUSTICE

ROY MIKI

RAINCOAST BOOKS

Vancouver

Raincoast Books acknowledges the ongoing financial support of the Government
of Canada through The Canada Council for the Arts and the Book Publishing
Industry Development Program (BPIDP), and the Government of British Columbia
through the B.C. Arts Council.

Edited by John Eerkes-Medrano
Text design by Ingrid Paulson
Typeset by Tannice Goddard

NATIONAL LIBRARY OF CANADA CATALOGUING IN PUBLICATION DATA

Miki, Roy, 1942–
Redress: Inside the Japanese Canadian call for justice / Roy Miki.

Includes index.
ISBN 1-55192-650-4

1. Japanese Canadians — Evacuation and relocation, 1942–1945.
2. World War, 1939–1945 — Reparations. 3. Japanese Canadians — History.
4. Miki, Roy, 1942–. 5. Japanese Canadians — Biography. I. Title.

FC106.J3M555 2004   323.1'1956071   C2004-901967-8

LIBRARY OF CONGRESS CATALOGUE NUMBER: 2004092412

Raincoast Books
9050 Shaughnessy Street
Vancouver, British Columbia
Canada V6P 6E5
www.raincoast.com

In the United States:
Publishers Group West
1700 Fourth Street
Berkeley, California
94710

At Raincoast Books we are committed to protecting the environment and to the
responsible use of natural resources. We are acting on this commitment by working
with suppliers and printers to phase out our use of paper produced from ancient forests.
This book is one step towards that goal. It is printed on 100% ancient-forest-free paper
(100% post-consumer recycled), processed chlorine and acid free, and supplied by New
Leaf Paper. It is printed with vegetable-based inks by Friesens. For further information,
visit our website at www.raincoast.com. We are working with Markets Initiative
(www.oldgrowthfree.com) on this project.

Printed and bound in Canada.

1 2 3 4 5 6 7 8 9 10

For my parents

Kazuo (1907-1969) and
Shizuko (Ooto) (1913-2002) Miki

Words cast each by each to weather
avowed indisputably, to time.
— Theresa Hak Kyung Cha

The events surrounding the historian, and in which he himself takes part, will
underlie his presentation in the form of a text written in invisible ink.
— Walter Benjamin

CONTENTS

SIXTEEN YEARS HAVE passed since the National Association of Japanese Canadians (NAJC) signed the redress agreement with the Government of Canada, an event that generated euphoria among Japanese Canadians at the time. Although that event no longer attracts the media attention it once did, the concept of redress continues to spark provocative discussions. Social justice for individuals and groups whose rights have been abrogated by government actions and policies remains an unresolved issue. Indeed, the implications of redress have taken on even greater significance in the context of escalating global unrest.

Our capacity to create models of peaceful coexistence depends on our ability to take critical approaches to past injustices and on our willingness to address — and redress — those injustices by negotiating with the individuals and communities who have endured them. In Canada, redress for abuses in the residential schools set up for aboriginal children has yet to be settled, and earlier redress calls for the head tax levied on Chinese Canadians and for the internment of Ukrainian Canadians during World War I have been denied — at least so far — by the federal government.

In a recently published book, *When Sorry Isn't Enough*, editor Roy L. Brooks presents a range of commentaries in profiling a variety of redress claims: for Jewish victims of the Nazi regime in Europe in the 1930s and

1940s; for "comfort women," young Asian women who were used as sex slaves by Japanese soldiers both before and during World War II; for the Japanese Americans subjected to internment during World War II; for Native Americans, displaced and betrayed first by European settlers and then by various North American governments; and for African Americans, who continue to bear the effects of the enslavement of their ancestors.

In his introduction, appropriately titled "The Age of Apology," Brooks notes that successful redress movements appear to have four main components. Their advocates have chosen to seek redress through a political rather than a legal process. The judicial process is notoriously slow and cumbersome, and all too often a dead end, mainly because judges are reluctant to condemn actions undertaken legally by a government, no matter how unjust these actions may have been. These advocates are also able to exert strong political pressure on the government to establish the legitimacy of their demands. Of equal importance, in demanding redress they speak in a unified voice and "exhibit unquestioned support for the claims being pressed." And, finally, their call for redress is perceived as being relevant enough to be given special social and political attention.

Brooks does not recognize any Canadian examples, but his profile of a strong redress case can be applied to the journey that Japanese Canadians undertook in the 1980s. After years of intense work, the NAJC produced a redress position that was endorsed by the Japanese Canadians who were forcibly uprooted and dispossessed and had their citizenship rights abrogated during the 1940s. With this crucial element in place, the NAJC was in a position to negotiate a redress settlement with the Government of Canada. The agreement reached between the NAJC and Gerry Weiner, then the federal minister of multiculturalism, was made official in the House of Commons on September 22, 1988. By this time, the Japanese Canadian case for redress had become a national story.

This shorthand account of the redress movement implies far too neatly that the movement was the straightforward outcome of a well-choreographed campaign. It does not convey the intricate, convoluted, and all-consuming personal dimensions of the journey. Japanese Canadians were — and still are — a relatively small group. And although they believed strongly in the rights and responsibilities of citizenship, they were inexperienced in the political process and often intimidated by government authority. In creating and sustaining their call for justice, they stretched to the limits their ability to transform their insecurities and anxieties into a national movement that captured the attention of Canadians.

As a writer whose personal life for a decade was overtaken by the issue of redress, I wanted to re-enter the inside history of the movement and to ground this history in the rich body of archival sources I had accumulated on the mass uprooting of Japanese Canadians and their decades-long efforts to articulate their responses to that catastrophic event. The documentary narrative of redress that appears in *Justice in Our Time: The Japanese Canadian Redress Settlement* (1991), a book I co-authored with Cassandra Kobayashi, was completed in the wake of the redress settlement and reflected the perspective of the NAJC. Even then, I wanted to write a follow-up book, one that would move behind the scenes to tell the more "unofficial" story of the redress movement. My research in the early 1990s was directed toward this end, but the form of the story eluded me. I had been so immersed in the language of the movement that I could not get beyond its boundaries to write the kind of book I envisioned. I decided to pull back temporarily and to speculate on the meaning and implications of redress in more open-ended ways.

This distancing process allowed me the intellectual space to study larger questions of cultural and political representation and the role of racialization in shaping the Canadian nation — a nation that had been so instrumental in shaping me. I became more aware of "Japanese Canadian" as an identity formation that had shifted with changes in specific conditions, not just during and after the mass uprooting of the 1940s, but from the time the first Japanese Canadians, including my grandparents, had settled in Canada. Some of this critical thinking in the 1990s was first presented in my essay collection *Broken Entries: Race, Subjectivity, Writing* (1998).

Soon after *Broken Entries* was published, I began to realize how crucially the process of negotiation, which had been the cornerstone of the redress movement, was woven into the entire history of Japanese Canadians as they sought to overcome their alienation from the Canadian nation. The very term "negotiation" brought home to me the provisional and often tenuous relations that Japanese Canadians throughout the 20th century had always had with the nation and with that nation's largely unspoken assumptions about them. Here, too, I began to understand the internal dynamics of my own history as a writer and intellectual whose subjectivity had been deeply bound up in "Japanese Canadian" as an identity formation.

My direct participation in the movement ruled out, for me at least, a standard historical study of redress. A form for a work I had in mind became apparent when I started to think that a complex of sources — archival documents, journals, letters, interviews, tapes, studies of Japanese Canadians, critical theory and even memory — could be incorporated in tandem. This approach opened up a flexible procedure that enabled me to interweave the personal and the historical, the two strands of my own negotiations with "Japanese Canadian" as a shifting frame of reference. *Redress* presents the outcome of this method of composition. My hope is that readers will see within and beyond its pages an exemplary story of a "call for justice" that struck such a resonant chord among so many Japanese Canadians in the 20th century.

ACKNOWLEDGEMENTS

THE REDRESS MOVEMENT was a truly collective effort, and while writing this book I was constantly reminded, often in voices that echoed in words and phrases, of all the people who have shaped my thinking over the past three decades and more. Many of the stories, documents and sources that have been integral to this book's final form have emerged from personal relationships. At every stage of the composition process — but in particular during an extended period of research and reflection spanning the 1990s — I received cooperation and assistance from a number of key players in the redress movement, who generously shared their views on redress and, in many cases, their personal papers.

For invaluable support in doing the research for my book, I acknowledge and thank the following individuals: Harold Hirose, for material on the response of the National Japanese Canadian Citizens' Association to the Bird Commission in the 1940s and for his stories about the mass uprooting; Wes Fujiwara, for lively conversations about redress and for permission to use his large audiotape collection, including his tapes of the National Association of Japanese Canadians (NAJC) conference in Winnipeg (January 1984) and the meeting of the National Redress Committee in Toronto (March 1984); Dennis Madokoro, for taping Wes Fujiwara's collection for me; Roger Obata, for sharing first-hand knowledge of the wartime history of Japanese Canadians; Susan Hidaka, for giving me access to the personal papers of Kunio Hidaka (which are now housed in the Japanese Canadian National Museum) and for permission to use a selection of these; Gordon Hirabayashi, for years of exchanges on social and community concerns and for setting an inspiring example as an advocate of human rights both here and in the United States; Harry Yonekura, for sharing his knowledge of the Nisei Mass Evacuation Group (NMEG) and for allowing me to copy all of his personal papers for the Toronto JCCA Redress Committee and the Toronto Chapter of the NAJC; Jesse Nishihata, for his research files on the resistance movement at Moose Jaw, including his unpublished essay, "Internment of Japanese Canadians, 1941-1946"; Shin Imai and Connie Sugiyama, for material on the Sodan-kai in Toronto; Gordon Kadota, for material from his files as president of the NAJC and for a personal interview; Cassandra Kobayashi, for her files on the Vancouver JCCA Redress Committee and the NAJC Strategy Committee; Kevin Griffin, for passing on to me the material he received on redress through Access to Information; Tameo Kanbara, for copies of documents from his files on the Nisei Mass Evacuation Group and for a personal interview, and his son Bryce Kanbara, for conversations about the Toronto scene in the 1970s; Tatsuo Kage, for translating Tameo Kanbara's essay "The Origin of the Mass Group"; Stan and Marjorie Wani Hiraki, for allowing me to make copies of their audiotape collection, which included tapes of pivotal redress meetings in Toronto in 1983 and 1984; Robert and Jean Okazaki, for letting me read an earlier draft of the manuscript for his book *The Nisei Mass Evacuation Group and P.O.W. Camp 101*, which helped me understand the importance of the work of the NMEG as a precursor of the redress movement; and Jack Murta and Orest Kruhlak, for their interviews on the political aspects of redress.

For permission to cite from unpublished work, my thanks to Michael Barnholden, for "Anti-Asian Riot"; to Andrea Geiger-Adams, for "Writing Racial Barriers into Law: Upholding B.C.'s Denial of the Vote to its Japanese-Canadian Citizens, *Homma v. Cunningham*, 1902"; to Peter Nunoda, for "Co-operation and Co-optation: Nisei Politics, 1943-1950"; and to Victor Ujimoto, for his letter to the Multiculturalism Directorate, June 16, 1983.

The Vancouver redress movement brought me into contact with many hardworking and dedicated community activists from 1984 to 1988. The friendships and alliances we forged in our volunteer work remain the most memorable part of my association with the Vancouver JCCA Redress Committee. Here I acknowledge the vital contribution of a handful whose actions, for me, embodied the very spirit of redress: Yosh Arai, Randy Enomoto, Ruby Foreman, Fumiko Greenaway, Amy Higa, Motoi Iwanaka, Charles Kadota, Lillian Kadota, Connie Kadota, Diane Kadota, Tatsuo Kage, Diane Kage, Sho Kamachi, Jean Kamimura, Walter Kamimura, Gordon Kayahara, Haruko Kobayakawa, Martin Kobayakawa, Kim Kobayashi, Irene Nemeth, Chris Nemeth, Tom Oikawa, Kay Oikawa, Mary Seki, Marilyn Seki, Ken Shikaze, Naomi Shikaze, Sam Shishido, Wataru Shishido, Barbara Shishido, Celeste Sundquist, Tom Tagami, Masue Tagashira, Joe Takashima, Tony Tamayose, Kim Tamayose, Ed Teranishi, Dan Tokawa, Norm Tsuyuki, Irene Tsuyuki, Henry Wakabayashi, Tad Wakabayashi, Aki Wakabayashi and Takeo Yamashiro.

I also wish to acknowledge those whose friendship and encouragement have sustained me over the years — and who have patiently listened to me talk on and on about this "redress book": Michael Barnholden, George Bowering, Pauline Butling, David Fujino, Monika Kin Gagnon, Hiromi Goto, Smaro Kamboureli, Joy Kogawa, Robert Kroetsch, Larissa Lai, Jacqueline Larson, Glen Lowry, Ashok Mathur, Kirsten Emiko McAllister, Scott Toguri McFarlane, Baco Ohama, Linda Ohama, Haruko Okano, Mona Oikawa, Aruna Srivastava, Grace Eiko Thomson, Lola Tostevin, Fred Wah, Rita Wong and Jim Wong-Chu.

In writing this account of Japanese Canadian redress, I have been influenced by many writers and historians, but most especially I have returned time and again to certain voices: Muriel Kitagawa, for her stunning accounts of the mass uprooting in *This Is My Own*; Joy Kogawa, for her justly acclaimed narrative of internment in *Obasan*; Ken Adachi, for his groundbreaking — and still the most comprehensive — history of Japanese Canadians in *The Enemy That Never Was*; and Ann Sunahara, for her impressive use of previously inaccessible government documents in *The Politics of Racism*. Although I have depended on evidence and insights from these and all of the publications listed in the Works Cited, I assume responsibility for the interpretation of Japanese Canadian history and redress offered in this book.

The editors at Raincoast Books have been incredibly helpful in all phases of the publication process. I thank Lynn Henry and Michelle

Benjamin for their confidence that a book on redress was worth bringing out, Derek Fairbridge for shepherding the manuscript through the press, and John Eerkes-Medrano for his impeccable editorial advice. I especially appreciated John's professional yet candid and incisive work on the manuscript as he helped me discover its voice and form. Thanks also to Mary Schendlinger for her perceptive work as a copy editor and for making suggestions that added more precision to the final draft of the manuscript.

I wish to thank the Japanese Canadian Redress Foundation for a grant that enabled me to undertake the initial research for this book and to write early drafts of many sections of the manuscript. I am also grateful for funding assistance from the B.C. Arts Council and the Canada Council that provided me with time away from teaching to work on the manuscript.

During the redress movement I formed a lasting friendship with Cassandra Kobayashi, who never wavered in her commitment to social justice. As I wrote this book, I was reminded of all the remarkable contributions and personal sacrifices that she made to the movement. Her clear and intelligent grasp of difficult issues was often pivotal in formulating strategies to pursue redress. We worked together daily, often until late into the night, and after the settlement we co-authored *Justice in Our Time*.

Art Miki, my brother, was central to the redress struggle, and as president of the NAJC he was instrumental in leading the organization to its 1988 settlement. Our involvement in redress, which stemmed from our family history, brought us together in a common cause that transformed the course of my life. I have benefited immensely by his insights into the movement. I am also grateful to Keiko Miki — herself a major contributor, who sacrificed much to achieve redress — for her close friendship over the years.

Joan Jalmarson has always been a caring and supportive sister, and I deeply appreciated her contributions to fundraising activities during the movement.

In all aspects of my life, I have been inspired by Waylen and Elisse, my son and daughter, who grew up in the seemingly endless commotion of redress that pervaded our home for 10 years and consumed a greater part of their childhood. Their intellectual humour, their hopeful imaginations, and their awareness of the meaning of redress for Japanese Canadians sustained me in times of doubt and gave me the grounds to believe in a transformed future. And through it all, I have been thankful for the companionship of

Slavia, who bore so much of the burden in our daily lives. Without the constancy of spirit, love and meticulous attention to everyday exigencies that she performs with a profound agility and grace, I would not have lasted in the redress movement. And without her care and feedback during the writing of this book, I would not have been able to compose the tale of its unfolding.

APPROACHING REDRESS

Negotiating the Nation

It is not enough just to have a birth certificate, certifying one's birth in Canada. It is not enough to be a native Canadian and expect that mere birth alone is everything: privileges, responsibilities, pride, allegiance. One must grow into citizenship; one must shoulder the responsibilities before there is any real joy in the privileges; one must be vigilant for the honour of one's country, its integrity, else how can one say with pride: I am Canadian.

— Muriel Kitagawa

OTTAWA, SEPTEMBER 22, 1988

I HAD BEEN anxiously anticipating this moment for years. Here I was, with my older brother, Art Miki, the other members of the Strategy Committee for the National Association of Japanese Canadians (NAJC), and a handful of Japanese Canadians from Ottawa. All of us were lined up outside the door to the section of the House of Commons gallery reserved for "special guests." We were present to witness the official announcement by Prime Minister

Brian Mulroney that a "redress agreement" had been reached with the NAJC, the representative body for those "Canadians of Japanese ancestry" whose citizenship rights had been abrogated between 1942 and 1949 and who, as a consequence, had endured mass uprooting, dispossession, dispersal and deportation.[1]

During the roller-coaster years of the redress movement, the very thought of achieving our dream of redress had appeared to slip away so many times. This morning, though, our hopes and fears were about to take on new meanings. I was a member of the Strategy Committee and Art was the NAJC president. Redress had brought us together in a struggle that not only implicated all Japanese Canadians but had its deepest roots in our family history.

In 1942 the Canadian government of Mackenzie King, following a policy similar to that of the United States, ordered the mass uprooting of all people of Japanese ancestry living in the "protected zone," an area that extended along the west coast of British Columbia and 100 miles (160 kilometres) inland. It established the British Columbia Security Commission on March 4 to carry out the incarceration of some 23,000 men, women and children who had been categorized as "enemy aliens." More than 75 percent of these people were either Canadian-born or naturalized citizens. Between March and October their citizenship rights were revoked, their properties, businesses, assets and personal belongings were seized — and, soon after, sold without their consent — and larger groups were scattered to what the government called "resettlement camps" but which in fact were sites of confinement.

---

1   The terminology associated with the wartime history of Japanese Canadians remains somewhat fraught. I consider the term "evacuation," often and normally used to describe their wartime experience, as a government-produced euphemism that misrepresents what was a forcible uprooting. On the other hand, the term "internment," which does more accurately describe what happened to them, also poses a problem. Technically, Japanese Canadians were "detained" rather than "interned." "Internment" properly refers to the incarceration of individuals from enemy countries, not the citizens of a country. My approach to the history attempts to draw attention to the consequences of the violation of the citizenship rights of Japanese Canadians: their mass uprooting, or forced removal from their homes; their dispossession, the confiscation of their properties and belongings; their dispersal or forced movement out of B.C.; and (for some) their deportation or exile from Canada. Since this whole experience encapsulates the more common meaning of "internment," I use this term at times to remind readers of the actual effects of the government's policies. The government's term "detention" allowed for the indefinite suspension of habeas corpus, and this in turn prevented Japanese Canadians from defending themselves in courts of law.

These camps included "ghost" towns in the B.C. interior, sugar beet farms in Alberta and Manitoba, and road camps in Ontario.

But the government actions against Japanese Canadians had begun before March. They had started immediately after the Japanese bombing of Pearl Harbor, on December 7, 1941. A group of 26 men, identified by the government as leaders of the community and potential dissidents, were whisked away to internment camps. All Japanese-language newspapers and schools were closed down, and all fishing vessels owned by Japanese Canadians were rounded up (1,800 boats, up and down the coast), towed to New Westminster, B.C., and soon sold off at bargain-basement prices. The mass uprooting was undertaken after the newly formed B.C. Security Commission was given its widespread powers

> to require by order any person of the Japanese race, in any protected area in British Columbia, to remain at his place of residence or to leave his place of residence and to proceed to any place within or without the protected area at such time and in such manner as the Commission may prescribe in any such order, or to order the detention of any such person, and by any such order may be enforced by any persons nominated by the Commission to do so.

The movements of all Japanese Canadians were controlled, monitored and policed until well after the war ended — in fact, until April 1, 1949. By then, when they were finally able to return to the B.C. coast, nothing remained of their collective lives. With all their properties and businesses gone, and forcibly dispersed all across the country, the vast majority of Japanese Canadians resigned themselves to lives in new towns and cities and began to rebuild their lives, as my own family did in Winnipeg. Even so, the injustices they encountered at the hands of their own government remained alive in memory.

THE YOUNG GOVERNMENT aide who directed us to enter the gallery from the dark hallway advised us of parliamentary protocol — that "guests" were not to stand or applaud. We were to remain seated in silence. To the left and right of us, the seats were unoccupied. The whole upper gallery was almost empty but for a handful of Japanese Canadians, far on the opposite side, who were "spectators," not "guests." Among them I recognized Joy Kogawa, whose *Obasan* had gained prominence as the first novel written about the mass uprooting.

From our aerial positions, we peered down on the politicians. Given the monumental import of this occasion for Japanese Canadians, it was eerie, and somewhat deflating, to see the members of Parliament seated together, among rows and rows of empty seats. It was hardly a full house — though the cameras, as we saw later in the news reports, framed only the occupied seats, presenting the illusion of fullness to the TV audience. After a few moments of solemn silence, Mulroney rose, paused as he looked up at the guest gallery, and then turned to look at the text of his prepared speech:

> Mr. Speaker, nearly half a century ago, in the crisis of wartime, the Government of Canada wrongfully incarcerated, seized the property, and disenfranchised thousands of citizens of Japanese ancestry. We cannot change the past. But we must, as a nation, have the courage to face up to these historical facts.

As the prime minister's voice trailed into history, I thought about my birth in the Winnipeg General Hospital in October 1942. It had occurred only months after my parents, Shizuko and Kazuo, my grandparents on my mother's side, Yoshi and Tokusaburo Ooto, my brothers, Art and Les, and my sister, Joan, had been sent from the Fraser Valley town of Haney to work on a sugar beet farm in Manitoba. With others, they were confined in the Immigration Building in Winnipeg as they waited for farmers to come by and "choose" them as cheap labour.

A document from the B.C. Security Commission papers records my family's uprooting. A. R. Campbell, of the Vancouver RCMP detachment, noted:

> On this date [May 19, 1942] I proceeded by CPR from Vancouver, B.C. to Haney B.C.. At Haney Col. Kemp of the British Columbia Security Commission and Cst. C.W. Robson turned over to me twenty Japanese family groups consisting of 127 persons. I proceeded with the party via CPR to Winnipeg, Manitoba; arriving there without incident at 6:20 PM of the 21-5-42.

The Miki family was listed as a "group of five," with Serial Number 450-A. This little group eventually found itself in a small French Canadian town 40 kilometres directly south of Winnipeg called Ste. Agathe.

Why Manitoba? My mother often recalled that the family had considered moving to Greenwood, B.C., where my father's mother had been sent, but she feared she might be separated from her aging parents. At the time of uprooting the family lived in a house they had built on her parents' property, a 12-acre (4.8-hectare) orchard farm. She knew that she had to care for them, whatever happened. The decision was made somewhat easier when representatives of the B.C. Security Commission approached many families in the Fraser Valley — an area known for its lucrative berry farms, an industry developed by Japanese Canadians — and urged them to accept work on what was called the "sugar beet project," either in Alberta or Manitoba. In the midst of the panic caused by the policy of splitting up families, the Fraser Valley communities were told that the families going to sugar beet farms could remain together. They were not informed that other families, with privileged connections to the B.C. Security Commission, were being allowed to resettle together in certain B.C. towns, such as Minto, Lillooet and McGillivray Falls, in what were called "self-supporting sites," another of the euphemisms liberally produced by government authorities.

All Japanese Canadians were forced to use their resources, including funds collected through the liquidation of their properties, before they were allowed to seek any government assistance. Hence the incarceration sites, from the big ones in the B.C. interior to single farms in Alberta and Manitoba, could all be considered "self-supporting." The so-called "self-supporting" people were those who had agreed to use their own assets to move and to take care of themselves for the duration of the war. That option was not given to my parents. The government wanted to enlist poorly paid workers to relieve the labour shortage on sugar beet farms in Alberta and Manitoba. A number of families in the Haney area decided on Manitoba. Little did they know what awaited them — the harsh living conditions, pitifully low wages and isolation from each other. Many families were confined to the farms they worked on, and all social and political organizing was outlawed.

The Japanese Canadians sent to Manitoba were first placed in the Immigration Building in Winnipeg, near the railway station. Some families remained there for weeks, especially those with small children, as they waited for farmers to come and "select" a family. One man who underwent the process recalled that "it was sort of like slaves in the old slave markets." When my family was relocated to Ste. Agathe, my mother was pregnant, so her closest friend, Nori Hayakawa, came with her to help take care of Art (aged five), Les (aged four) and Joan (aged two). Nori brought her younger brother, Joe, and her father. My grandparents were also expected to provide labour. Along with my mother's single brother, Takeo, they were an appealing "working family," despite having three little children. Since none of them had any significant farming experience, they were a motley crew who barely eked out a living that summer and fall.

My father, Kazuo, had to go up north for the winter to work in a logging camp. The first winter on the beet farm, my mother remembered, was an ordeal — the uncertain future, the loss of homes and belongings, and the atrocious living conditions in a climate so radically different from B.C.'s Fraser Valley. And they felt abandoned, with no "voice" to defend themselves. The following year, the two families moved into separate houses in the town and began to mingle with the French-speaking townsfolk, who spoke only rudimentary English and who were curious about these strange-looking people called "Japanese." The people of Ste. Agathe were friendly and helpful, and even sympathized with the families in the trauma of forced uprooting at the hands of the federal government — seeing Japanese Canadians through their own position as a minority in Manitoba.

The wages from sugar beet farming were not enough to support my family, so after another year they contacted the successor to the B.C. Security Commission representative in Manitoba, the newly formed provincial body called the Japanese Division. It was supervised by George Collins, the assistant deputy minister of public works of Manitoba. The Japanese Division's representative, Frank Ernst, helped my family get permission to move to North Kildonan, just outside the city limits of Winnipeg. By 1944 the city still had municipal policies that made it difficult for Japanese Canadians to live in Winnipeg, but even so, few landlords were willing to rent to them. The area around Edison and McKay streets had available a group of small houses — no more than shacks — that were used to house itinerant farm workers. It was here, during the early 1940s, that a small, tightly knit but very beleaguered Japanese Canadian community formed. We lived at 211 Edison until the summer of 1948. By then, as the restrictions on living in the city eased, we found a house in central Winnipeg, at 631 Alexander Street. My grandfather had died in North Kildonan the year before. And then, a few years later in Winnipeg, my grandmother died.

AS THE SECONDS ticked by, and as these fleeting details of family history passed through my mind, I returned my gaze to this political space — the House of Commons. In his speech, the prime minister had adopted the formal language of political authority to approve the redress agreement that his government had reached with the National Association of Japanese Canadians (NAJC). When he finished, he was given a standing ovation by all the members of Parliament present, a sign that all three national parties — the ruling Conservative government and the Liberal and New Democratic parties — had set aside their partisan differences to share in a rare moment of solidarity. We too spontaneously rose and clapped, despite the admonishment of the government aide. And as we exchanged glances with the politicians from our separate perspectives, the immediacy of the scene struck home. What a relief that the goal of a negotiated settlement had been achieved. What a relief that Japanese Canadians, who had been branded "enemy aliens" so many years before, were at last "officially" exonerated. What a relief that the Strategy Committee had not compromised our demand for both community and individual compensation. What a relief that Japanese Canadians might now be able to resolve their troubled ties to the wartime injustices. Relief, relief and more relief that the lengthy redress movement — and its endless demands — had come to this moment of closure.

Mulroney's statement was followed by responses from NDP leader Ed Broadbent and Liberal multiculturalism critic Sergio Marchi (Liberal Party leader John Turner was absent). Both politicians spoke glowingly about the importance of redress as a human rights issue, but Broadbent, in a show of emotion unusual in the House of Commons, expressed his personal satisfaction with the agreement. Citing some words from *Obasan* — "There are some nightmares from which there is no waking, only deeper and deeper sleep" — he was brought to tears, declaring his close attachment to redress through an earlier marriage to a Japanese Canadian woman.

The "official acknowledgement" lasted only minutes, and its brevity was, for me, quite disproportionate to its significance for Japanese Canadians.

Except for the short passage from *Obasan*, in this hallowed chamber of the House of Commons there was the manifest absence of a "Japanese Canadian" voice that reflected the inner turbulence of the redress movement and its connections to a lengthy history of estrangement from the Canadian nation — a history of Japanese Canadians that reached back to the moment of first arrival from across the Pacific. This absence smudged the edges of what was otherwise a day of empowerment for Japanese Canadians. The language of the redress movement — forged in the heart of the struggle — returned in the heightened language of the prime minister's acknowledgement, the terms of which had been negotiated between the NAJC and the minister of multiculturalism, Gerry Weiner. The wartime trauma of the Japanese Canadian uprooting and dispossession, as inscribed in *Hansard*, was being incorporated into the official history of the nation. From this moment forward, "Japanese Canadians" — "citizens of Japanese ancestry," in the prime minister's acknowledgement — were no longer lacking redress but were now "redressed."

That moment of euphoria, etched in my memory, is now 16 years old. On that day, now a day of remembrance for Japanese Canadians, newspapers across Canada featured the redress settlement as front page news. The *Toronto Star* announced, "Japanese Canadians Win Apology to 'Cleanse Past'," and told its readers in a subhead, "Tears Flow As Historic Deal Signed." A photo showed Prime Minister Mulroney and NAJC President Art Miki smiling at the signing ceremony. The *Vancouver Sun* printed the same photo and proclaimed, "Internees to Share $300 Million," with the subheading, "Japanese-Canadians Get Apologies from Mulroney." For months afterward, there was a flood of media attention as Miki and the NAJC were praised for what they had accomplished on behalf of the Japanese Canadians whose rights had been abrogated during the 1940s. The NAJC had apparently established a major human rights precedent in Canada as the first group of citizens to negotiate a substantial redress settlement for past injustices.

The agreement reached between the government and the NAJC contained all of the elements that the NAJC had called for, starting with an official acknowledgement of the injustices and including both individual and community compensation. The actual terms of the negotiated agreement — to be carried out in the years ahead through the newly established Japanese

Canadian Redress Secretariat — were announced in the Government of Canada's press release:

a) $21,000 individual redress, subject to application by eligible persons of Japanese ancestry who, during this period [from December 7, 1941 to March 31, 1949], were subjected to internment, relocation, deportation, loss of property or otherwise deprived of the full enjoyment of fundamental rights and freedoms based solely on the fact that they were of Japanese ancestry; each payment would be made in a tax-free lump sum, as expeditiously as possible;

b) $12 million to the Japanese-Canadian community, through the National Association of Japanese Canadians, to undertake educational, social and cultural activities or programs that contribute to the well-being of the community or that promote human rights;

c) $12 million, on behalf of Japanese Canadians and in commemoration of those who suffered these injustices, and matched by a further $12 million from the Government of Canada, for the creation of a Canadian Race Relations Foundation that will foster racial harmony and cross-cultural understanding and help to eliminate racism;

d) subject to application by eligible persons, to clear the names of persons of Japanese ancestry who were convicted of violations under the War Measures Act or the National Emergency Transitional Powers Act;

e) subject to application by eligible persons, to grant Canadian citizenship to persons of Japanese ancestry still living who were expelled from Canada or had their citizenship revoked during the period 1941 to 1949, and to their living descendants;

f) to provide, through contractual arrangements, up to $3 million to the National Association of Japanese Canadians for their assistance, including community liaison, in administration of redress over the period of implementation.

During its pursuit of redress, the NAJC had also called on the federal government to rescind the War Measures Act, which had allowed for the victimization of Japanese Canadians solely on the basis of racial categorization. Earlier in 1988, the government had done just that, replacing it with what was called the Emergencies Act (made law in July 1988). The new Act, perhaps influenced by a brief prepared by the lawyer and author Ann Sunahara and submitted by the NAJC, incorporated protective measures to make the government more accountable for its actions and "procedures to ensure that individuals who may have to suffer loss or injury as a result of its application will be fairly compensated."

Even as the redress celebrations were going on, however, the boundaries of the Canadian nation — the nation familiar to those of us who were formed in the crucible of the Cold War years — were beginning to shift significantly. At the moment of the redress settlement in September 1988, the hottest and most contested issue in the House of Commons was the Free Trade Agreement with the U.S.A. When it was ratified that year — in spite of the dire warnings of Canadian nationalists who saw in its capitulation to multinational economic forces a major threat to the country's political and cultural sovereignty — the coherence of the nation that had redressed Japanese Canadians had already begun to unravel. The preoccupation with Canadian identity, so prevalent in liberal markers such as an official bilingualism policy, outlined in the Languages Act (1969), a multiculturalism policy (1971), a repatriated Canadian Constitution (1981) with a Canadian Charter of Rights and Freedoms (1982) and an official Multiculturalism Act (1988), began to lose their urgency when confronted with the new language of globalization. This language introduced an economic agenda in which cultural nationalism was superseded by the power of transnational corporations and global markets.

In the years since the redress settlement was negotiated, the Canadian nation has changed, though the new world touted by proponents of globalization has failed to materialize — except for the ubiquitous reach of consumerism. Rather than ushering in more equitable and inclusive forms of social and political interactions, the processes of globalization have exposed the emptiness at the core of the race to commodify everything, even life itself, in the language of biotechnology. Rather than heralding the end of history, they have made more urgent the need to rethink the historical formation of the nation. Despite the lingo of the fashion industry that says the world is reinvented every shopping season, we continue to be born into highly specific places that are shaped by a network of forces, and we continue to negotiate a network of social and political structures that produce unequal power relations. In this framework, the moment of Japanese

Canadian redress signalled the end of a particular era of Canadian national-ism, a nationalism in which citizenship values gave much more meaning to everyday lives than they do today.

Looking back, I have come to recognize the power that nationalism had in shaping the contours of my life and the lives of the Japanese Canadians who were forever marked by the mass uprooting of the 1940s. While we often perceived ourselves, and were perceived, as outsiders in the Canadian nation, we were always in a process of negotiation with its racialized boundaries. In light of this dynamic, the movement to seek redress was born out of Canadian conditions and placed us deeply inside the language of this nation's democratic values. The high esteem in which "Canadian" citizenship was held, then, accounts for the overwhelming air of celebration that prevailed among Japanese Canadians on September 22, 1988. In their own eyes the NAJC had achieved the dream of "justice in our time," a refrain often cited during the movement. Their aspirations were best expressed by Art Miki when, almost speechless at the press conference following the official signing, he said: "I do appreciate the support that's been expressed by the media, by all of the people who supported redress, because for us this is a great day. I don't know how else to express it but to jump up and to shout and yell — which I won't do, but it's that type of feeling. I'm very proud to be here today and I'm very proud to be a Canadian."

Without denying the spontaneity of my brother's language, which expressed feelings I shared at the press conference, I am struck by the pure force of it. Although the acknowledgement referred to the "Japanese Canadians" who were directly affected by the mass uprooting and the loss of their citizenship rights, it enabled the "Japanese Canadians" who achieved redress — and here Art did speak on behalf of the community — to be "very proud to be a Canadian." In a strange twist, one that haunted me in subse-quent years and has prompted me to return to redress so many years later, Art could see himself as "Canadian" because he had become the "Japanese Canadian" named in the redress settlement.

Seeking the full rights of citizenship, including the right to seek redress, had always been a large part of what "Japanese Canadian" meant, through-out the 20th century. Why was this so? And why had this identity formation been so instrumental in shaping the personal and collective values of the group into which I was born? These questions sparked an investigative and reflective process through which I wanted to unravel why redress was a given in the history of Japanese Canadians. I soon discovered that an understanding of this given would lead me to write about why we were finally given redress.

CHAPTER I

FRAMED BY RACE

A Canadian Knot

Mythologies or national stories are about a nation's origins and history. They enable citizens to think of themselves as part of a community, defining who belongs and who does not belong to the nation. The story of the land as shared and as developed by enterprising settlers [in Canada] is manifestly a racial story.

— Sherene H. Razack

THE FORMATION OF "JAPANESE CANADIAN"

WHILE GROWING UP in Winnipeg, I was saturated with stories of the mass uprooting of Japanese Canadians. Relatives came and went from our home, sometimes staying for lengthy visits, and letters arrived from all over Canada with anecdotes of rebuilding lives. And always there was the overwhelming immediacy of absences in lives so utterly altered by the "exile" from the west coast. These absences turned into gaps in family memory, signified most tangibly in the loss of photo albums that had been stored in a trunk to be kept safe by neighbours but then were sold at one of many auctions. The lost photos became part of my childhood mythos, a mythos that appeared to have everything to do with being called "Japanese Canadian." What could it mean to be born into the historical conditions that produced this identity?

It was a relief to discover, much later, that I wasn't the only one to expend so much energy pondering this question. The nisei educator Ted Aoki, speaking from personal experience, has pointed out that "Japanese Canadian," despite signifying a benign identity for a recognized minority in Canada, is not stable and constant but rather quite "slippery" in the various significations invoked on its behalf.[1] In the early postwar years, on the rough-and-tumble streets of central Winnipeg, the epithet "Jap" was part of a common kid vocabulary, as were "Nazi," "kraut," "wop," and "DP." All of these terms were linguistic residue of the war. But what was this "Jap" that my body, and not my consciousness, called forth when I stepped out of my home?

"Of the Japanese race" was the phrase devised by the federal government to name Japanese Canadians, who, through its deployment, could be equated with "enemy aliens" and thereby reduced to figures who could be uprooted, dispossessed and interned. Living in the shadow of a figure who was "of the Japanese race," a figure that circulated in all the nooks and crannies of my Winnipeg childhood, was always unsettling. One way to resist outright racialization was to default to "Canadian," a term that declared membership in a citizenry — hence a surrogate "family" — and an identity that projected an aura of sameness. The elusive phenomenon known as "assimilation" never ceased to provoke an uneasy tension between my personal awareness and the marking of my body. While social forces encouraged assimilation through language, thought and performance, the movement of my body continued to be tracked as the other — the "Jap" in the midst. "Canadian," in this context, assumed meanings that extended well beyond the mere attribute of citizenship and came to occupy the boundary line between presence and absence — between being somebody and being nobody.

I first consciously encountered the historical (rather than strictly personal) figure of "Japanese Canadian" in an introductory psychology

---

1   Aoki continues, "What does this mean to us? It means that every word has possibilities of multiple meanings and that a choice of which meaning is to count is a legitimating process — a political process — conscious or unconscious."

course at United College (now the University of Winnipeg). The class had reached the section on racism, and the professor had already identified me as the only "Japanese Canadian" in class, an appropriate example for the topic in a predominantly white class. He even identified himself as someone with a stake in the mass uprooting. He was, he said, among the social workers who visited the Immigration Building where Japanese Canadians were housed after arriving from the west coast. Yes, I admitted, my family stayed there, too, before they were moved to Ste. Agathe. The professor encouraged me to write a book report on Forrest E. La Violette's *The Canadian Japanese and World War II*, which had been published in 1948. La Violette, a sociologist, had already published his field work on the Japanese American internment when he was drawn to B.C. to study the uprooting of Japanese Canadians. Included in his account was a section on those sent to Manitoba to work on sugar beet farms.

I was uneasy about being racialized in the class, but I was also curious. I signed La Violette's book out of the library and read what was, for me, the first documented representation of Japanese Canadians. La Violette's access to government documents was limited, but what stood out was his awareness that he was witnessing a major historical event with great implications for the future. Although his liberalism allowed him to acknowledge the harsh and unfair treatment of Japanese Canadians by government officials, he did not — perhaps could not — probe beneath the surface of events to expose their racialization as integral to the formation of Canada as a nation. Even so, without the research sources later available to both Ken Adachi for *The Enemy That Never Was* and to Ann Sunahara for *The Politics of Racism*, La Violette deduced that the internment was a political rather than a military decision, a capitulation to public pressure. "It was," he concluded, "historically the first time that the anti-Japanese groups were able to maintain a concerted drive of such intensity for a period of eleven weeks."

My book report is long gone, even my memory of its contents. Yet it triggered a desire to know more — not only about the wartime dispersal, an event woven into all our family stories, but also the various discourses through which "Japanese Canadian" would be produced by historians, sociologists, government officials and others as an identity formation. "Japanese Canadian" became a kind of Canadian knot that had to be unravelled.

TABULATING INJUSTICES: KUNIO HIDAKA'S RESEARCH

FOR THE NISEI, the second-generation Japanese Canadians, who traced their history back to the prewar years, "Japanese" remained the dominant descriptive term, a stand-alone noun. It was not yet an adjective modifying "Canadian," even though they identified themselves as "Canadian-born," as Kunio Hidaka did in an unpublished study, "Legal Status of Japanese in Canada." I was a graduate student at the University of B.C. when I first came upon Hidaka's work in the card catalogue.[2] The date the study was completed, 1942, is followed by a question mark, and the author's name is erroneously given as Kunio "Hidako." A note indicates that the typewritten copy was made from a manuscript provided by Norman Black in 1946. Many years later, I came to realize that the manuscript had been written by the same Kunio Hidaka who resurfaced in the redress movement in Toronto and became a strong advocate for the National Association of Japanese Canadians. In the early 1990s, I had the opportunity to read through his substantial collection of personal and community documents recording his social and political struggles during the 1940s. In this archive I learned that Hidaka had been a vocal critic of the government's actions and that he had fought for the restitution of losses at that time.[3]

Hidaka probably wrote "Legal Status of Japanese in Canada" during the period from the late 1930s until 1941, while he completed his degree in economics at UBC. When I first read his work, I had recently begun to examine, more out of personal interest than anything else, the policies and the legislation that had enabled the government to strip Japanese Canadians of their citizenship without the right of appeal. I was immediately drawn to the data that Hidaka had compiled and found myself identifying with his determination to produce an inventory of the legal means through which a certain group was excluded from the rights that mainstream (white) Canadians took for granted. Hidaka was part of a maturing nisei generation, Canadian-born and -educated, who were increasingly frustrated by the

---

2   On the card catalogue, the title appears as "Legal Status of Persons of Japanese Race in Canada." Since no explanation is given for this change, I have chosen to use the title on the typescript, on the assumption that it was probably intended by Hidaka. The longer title appears in the Works Cited.

3   Kunio Hidaka died suddenly on June 10, 1985, "the day after he presented the results of the Price Waterhouse study of economic losses of Japanese Canadians at a NAJC Redress meeting."

hypocrisy of a country that espoused democratic principles but ostracized certain groups solely on the basis of race categories — categories that made possible the very language of the discriminatory legislation.

In a brief introductory note, Hidaka says he has been most interested in the "statutory and regulatory restrictions against the Japanese." The sheer listing of such restrictions reveals that Japanese Canadians were categorized as "Japanese." Naturalization and citizenship, as categories of identity, were subsumed by the broader term "Japanese race," which was applicable to any and all circumstances. The barriers formed a dense web of exclusionary policies intended to prevent Japanese Canadians from claiming any part of mainstream public space.

Hidaka's dogged tabulation of laws and regulations that hemmed in his community stands as an early instance of a Japanese Canadian undertaking critical research to resist the official erasure of his personal identity. As he mapped these laws and regulations in all their mundane details, the extent to which Japanese Canadians were produced as outsiders through public policy became starkly visible. As a result, with the exception of those Japanese Canadians who served in the armed forces during World War I, "Chinamen, Japanese, Hindus, or Indians" were unable to have their names placed on the B.C. voters' list. This restriction led to their disenfranchisement in municipal, provincial and federal elections, and consequently, in a domino effect, they were unable to hold or be elected to public office, enter professions such as medicine, pharmacy and law, and secure licences to cut Crown timber or sell liquor.

This blanket exclusion from the public sphere led to more specialized restrictions, one of which was devised to allay the fear that "Asians" and non-Asian women would miscegenate.[4] Hidaka cites Section 3 of "An Act for

---

4   Some examples listed by Hidaka: the "Act respecting the Provincial Home for the Aged and Infirm, Revised Statutes of B.C. (RSBC) 1936, Chapter 228," which prevented "an Indian or an Asiatic" from admission; the "Act to regulate the Working of Metalliferous Mines, Quarries, and Metallurgical Works, RSBC 1936, Ch. 189," which stated that "no male person under the age of eighteen years, nor any Chinese or Japanese person, shall be employed below ground in any mine"; the "Public Works Contract (B.C.), Clause 45," which stipulated that no "Asiatic" could be employed in any public works; the language for "Crown Timber Sales Licenses (B.C.)," which stipulated that licences were issued "on the understanding that no Chinese or Japanese shall be employed in connection therewith."

the Protection of Women and Girls in Certain Cases, Revised Statutes of British Columbia 1936, Chapter 309":

> No person shall employ in any capacity any white woman or girl or any Indian woman or girl in or permit any white woman or girl or any Indian woman or girl to reside or lodge in or to work in or, save as a bona-fide customer in a public apartment thereof only, to frequent any restaurant, laundry, or place of business or amusement where, in the opinion of the Chief of Municipal Police of the Municipality or the Inspector of Provincial Police of the police division in which the restaurant, laundry, or place of business or amusement is situate, as evidenced by a certificate in writing signed by him and posted up in his office, it is advisable, in the interest of the morals of such women and girls, that they should not be employed, or reside, or lodge, or work therein, or frequent the same.

Hidaka also lists laws that indirectly affected Japanese Canadians. For instance, in the granting of naturalization or of fishing licences, federal authorities were given "absolute" discretionary power — which more often than not led to punitive actions against Japanese Canadians.

The intricate network of discriminatory regulations generated a social and political milieu in which Japanese Canadians — even those working in areas where exclusionary laws did not apply, such as teaching and engineering — were unable to find employment.[5] These were the conditions that the issei, the first-generation immigrants, and their nisei children had to negotiate long before the mass uprooting in 1942. In being identified not only as "Japanese" but also as "Asiatics" and "Orientals," they were racialized as external to the nation's identity — a white settler society. Even though the issei were allowed in to provide the cheap labour required by the country's burgeoning industries, all efforts were made to ensure that they would never assume the status of bona fide "subjects" of the Canadian nation. As "Japanese" they were marked as aliens who threatened to contaminate the purity of Canada. As one Vancouver workingman, drawing on prevalent

---

5   The exception to this rule was Hideko (Hide) Hyodo (later Hide Shimizu), who was offered a position in Steveston, B.C., where there was a large population of Japanese Canadian children.

public opinion, testified in 1902 to a royal commission: "My principal objection to them ... is that they do not assimilate, cannot assimilate, with our race, and that our country should be for men of our own race, instead of being overrun by an alien race."

From our vantage point at the outset of the 21st century — 100 years later — it is much more apparent how integral race difference has been in making the Canadian nation. The workingman's reference to "our race" reflected the common belief that Canada was built on the grounds of whiteness, against which Asians came to be identified as "an alien race." His assumption was that his "race," as the norm, was superior to what he constructed as other — those non-whites variously called "Asiatic," "Oriental," "Brown Men," "Mongol," "Jap," "Chinaman" and "Hindoo," social names that stereotyped those outside the sphere of whiteness.

Asian Canadians have always had to negotiate the haunting spectre of the "Yellow Peril," a volatile term that projected the fear of miscegenation and takeover by the "hordes" of "Asiatics" and that resulted in protectionist reactions. Those hordes, including Japanese immigrants, were framed by the dominant ideology as "inassimilable" and subversive. "In the minds of whites," W. Peter Ward comments,

> the Japanese (like all Oriental immigrants) blunted the communal drive for a homogeneous society, one of the fundamental collective goals of west coast whites. At bottom this was a deeply irrational yearning, a fact which made it the more fixed and immutable. As no Asian immigrant group was considered assimilable, all appeared to bar the path to racial and social homogeneity — that condition which nativists meant by the phrase "white British Columbia."[6]

---

6   Although Ward recognizes the racialization processes that formed the core of public attitudes in B.C. at the outset of the 20th century, his qualifying phrase, "deeply irrational yearning," obscures the power relations maintained through race discourse. Far from being irrational, this discourse mobilized the social and political hierarchies that banned non-whites from all relevant public spheres. His phrase leaves the impression that racism — the product of race discourse — is an aberration or simply a matter of social and individual attitudes. This understanding of racism fails to account for the instrumental role played by race in cordoning off those constructed as "alien" from those assumed to constitute the norm.

For my parents and grandparents, who were disenfranchised until 1949 because they were "Japanese," the discourse of race difference had a huge impact on their social lives. Its power resided in the unspoken values of the dominant institutions of their time, but more concretely it shut them out of the public spheres of law, politics and the mainstream media. The most pivotal of exclusionary practices, especially for the nisei, who were educated to revere the principles of democratic rule, was set out in B.C.'s Provincial Election Act. This legislation, singled out by Hidaka, disenfranchised those identified as "Japanese," "Chinese" and "Hindoo" — in effect, all the visible Asian Canadian groups at the time. "Indians," a reference to aboriginal people, were also included, a further sign that the legislation was meant to bar all non-whites from the political process. The prohibition against "Chinese" and "Indian" first entered B.C. law in 1872. With the influx of immigrants from Japan, the prohibition was extended to "Japanese" in 1895. In 1907, with the arrival of the first Sikhs, it was expanded to include "Hindoos" as well.

THE VANCOUVER RIOT OF 1907 AND ITS AFTERMATH

THE YEAR 1907 was notorious for another reason. That year, Vancouver became the site of a "race riot." On a tense September 7, a large anti-Asian rally was organized by the newly formed Asiatic Exclusion League. This group, which had set up a Canadian branch modelled on a counterpart in the U.S., was not merely a radical fringe, but was supported by an influential cross-section of society. The rally was designed, Michael Barnholden writes, to draw "on the participation of trade unions, fraternal organizations, religious groups, veterans' groups and like-minded citizens." Its goal was to push for the complete exclusion of "Asians" from Canada. During the preceding months, anti-Asian groups, dwelling on the arrival of various ships bringing immigrants from Japan, China and India, had issued dire warnings of the "Yellow Peril" that was supposedly motivated by the drive to supplant white workers and to take control first of B.C. and eventually the nation.

Not surprisingly, the immigration figures used by those who pointed to the danger of the "Yellow Peril" were hugely inflated. On the other hand, from a social perspective there was no denying the increased visibility of Chinese and Japanese on the west coast. In 1907 they arrived in large numbers. As Ken Adachi notes, "With the 8,125 Japanese who entered the province during the first ten months of 1907" — 45 percent of whom were on their way to the U.S. — "were over 2,000 Sikhs from India and nearly 1,300 Chinese who were willing to pay the head tax of $500." The head tax had been levied on the Chinese to restrict their entry. First set at $50 in 1885, it rose to $100 in 1900 and to $500 in 1903, an amount equivalent to two years of labour. The pamphlet *It Is Only Fair!*, issued by the Chinese Canadian National Council in its call for head tax redress, states that the government collected $23 million in total, an amount that "would be several hundred million dollars" today. Adding to the drama of the scheduled rally was the news that some 500 Sikhs had entered B.C. after being violently forced out of Seattle.

On September 7, thousands of people assembled at Vancouver City Hall, in what is today the Hastings and Main neighbourhood, near both Chinatown (around Pender Street) and Japantown (around Powell Street). As it was whipped into a frenzy by the speakers — particularly by A. E. Fowler from Seattle's Asiatic Exclusion League, who recounted how Seattle had solved its "Asiatic" problem by expelling all Sikhs — many in the group suddenly broke loose. They rampaged down Pender Street, breaking windows and indiscriminately vandalizing shops on the way. When the rioters headed toward Japantown, though, they found that residents had prepared themselves for a confrontation. They met the rioters head-on and drove them off. "By nightfall," Adachi writes, "when police reinforcements finally arrived, the Japanese had already organized their own patrols to protect their district through the long night."

After the riot, the Japanese Canadian and Chinese Canadian communities protested the violent racist attacks and vandalism. The federal government responded by establishing two royal commissions to deal with each group's damage claims. None other than Mackenzie King, an up-and-coming bureaucrat, and future prime minister of Canada, was appointed to head the commissions. In what was a rare instance of a study that ruled in favour of the two groups, King recommended some compensation for the destruction of properties, but he failed to address the anti-Asian racism that had caused the violence in the first place.

Although the minimal compensation brought some solace to the victims of the riot, Asian Canadians faced further immigration restrictions and Chinese Canadians continued to have the $500 head tax imposed on them. Then, in 1923, the government passed the Chinese Immigration Act (also known as the Chinese Exclusion Act), which closed the door on immigrants from China until 1947. During that period only about 25 Chinese immigrants were permitted to enter Canada. Further, South Asians faced the infamous "Continuous Journey" policy from 1908 on. Only those who travelled directly from India would be allowed into Canada. Since the available ships did not originate in India, this policy was an exclusionary measure. The most devastating instance of its application remains the *Komagata Maru* incident.

On May 21, 1914, 376 Sikhs, Hindus and Muslims from the Indian province of Punjab arrived in Vancouver harbour. The *Komagata Maru*, the ship that brought them, had not sailed directly from India, so the group was not allowed to disembark. The South Asian community in Vancouver hastily raised the funds needed to launch a legal challenge to the policy, only to lose its case in the courts because of yet another loophole for the government: not all passengers possessed the $200 required by immigration officials. After languishing for two months in the harbour, the *Komagata Maru* was forced to depart for India. This event, in the words of Ninette Kelley and Michael Trebilcock, "signalled the virtual cessation of Indian immigration to Canada for many years to come. Between 1914 and 1920, only one East Indian immigrant was admitted. Over the next 25 years, fewer than 650 settled in Canada."[7]

Had there not been an international treaty between Japan and Britain at the time, the government most likely would have levied a head tax on Japanese immigrants. How, then, to restrict immigration from Japan? When Prime Minister Wilfrid Laurier appointed Mackenzie King to head the royal commissions, he also appointed his minister of labour, Rodolphe Lemieux, to the post of Canadian commissioner to Japan. Lemieux's task was to secure

---

7   Sherazad Jamal and Zool Suleman describe the cruel fate awaiting many of the passengers: "The *Komagata Maru* arrived at Budge, India on September 29, 1914. The passengers hoped to raise sympathy for their plight but the Indian government viewed them as agitators. Upon their arrival, police attempted to arrest Gurdit Singh [who had chartered the boat] and some other passengers. During this process, a riot ensued and by the end, 19 of the passengers were killed. While some of the passengers escaped, the remainder were imprisoned or kept under house arrest in their home villages during the course of WWI."

an agreement with the Japanese government to impose emigration limits on its end. He accomplished this through an informal arrangement, a "gentleman's agreement." Even though Japan could have insisted on the free entry of its subjects to Canadian territories, in accordance with its treaty with Britain, the Japanese government "agreed to restrict the number of passports issued to male labourers and domestic servants to an annual maximum of 400."

In a strange twist, the "gentleman's agreement" secured by Lemieux applied only to emigrating males and not to their wives. Until 1908 the overwhelming majority of Japanese immigrants had been men. Now, however, the immigration of Japanese women was unrestricted, a loophole in the agreement that would play a dramatic role in the future of Japanese Canadians in the new country. The very restriction that was intended to exclude emigration from Japan opened the way to the phenomenon of the "picture bride." Through the use of go-betweens and the exchange of photographs, Japanese immigrants in Canada could arrange for women in Japan to become their wives. The "picture bride" system resulted in a large influx of Japanese women, which in turn led to the formation of local communities and a Canadian-born generation, the nisei. They were educated in Canadian schools and came to believe in the democratic values underpinning the nation, particularly the right to vote.

Even while Japanese Canadians began to establish communities in Canada, more exclusionary measures were being devised. In the same report in which Mackenzie King recommended compensation for property damage to Japanese Canadians and Chinese Canadians, he also mentioned the unsuitability of certain types of immigrants. He might have been referring to the supposed inability of Asians to adapt to the Canadian climate, but there is little doubt that he was also referring to their lack of capacity to fit into the cultural and racialized conditions of an assumed white country. This notion of "unsuitability" found its way into the Immigration Act of 1910. In that legislation, the government was granted full discretionary powers — then transferred to immigration officials — to deny entry to those "belonging to any race deemed unsuitable to the climate and requirements of Canada or immigrants of any specified class, occupation or character." The language of "unsuitability" would remain the norm for many decades — indeed, until the removal of explicit race-based categories from the Immigration Act in 1967.

MY PARENTS, KAZUO and Shizuko, belonged to the nisei generation that found itself constantly negotiating with the inhospitable social climate created by anti-Asian agitators. As Canadian citizens who wanted to participate in the democratic process, they and other nisei fixated on the lack of the franchise — a lack that signified second-class citizenship. Without the right to vote, they were not permitted to enter professions such as medicine, pharmacy and law, to hold public office or to work in certain occupations, as Kunio Hidaka made so clear in his report. But the public domain, especially in B.C., offered little hope of change. The Vancouver riot had vividly demonstrated that the racialized language through which they were identified and demeaned as alien Asians was pervasive — not only on the streets but also in the social and political institutions of the province. The B.C. legislature's efforts to pass exclusionary laws against Asian Canadians were relentless. Fortunately its resolutions were routinely struck down by the federal government, the authority in charge of immigration.[8]

Kay J. Anderson, in *Vancouver's Chinatown: Racial Discourse in Canada, 1875-1980*, reminds us that "Chinese" as a race category was constructed through a "race-definition process" that established non-whites, particularly

---

8   The following resolution, passed in the B.C. legislature on December 17, 1924, the year after the exclusionary Chinese Immigration Act was passed, gives us a vivid flavour of the kind of language the nisei would have encountered as they grew up on the west coast of B.C. After noting the number of Chinese and Japanese in B.C., as well as their supposed propensity to multiply, the resolution dwells on the threats they pose to white society:

> And whereas the standard of living of the average Oriental is far below that of the white man, thus enabling him to live comfortably on a much lower wage than our white men:
> And whereas the Orientals have invaded many fields of industrial and commercial activities to the serious detriment of our white citizens:
> And whereas considerable unemployment always exists in British Columbia, partly due to the fact that large numbers of Orientals are filling situations in our industrial and commercial life which could be filled by our white citizens:
> And whereas the Orientals are fast invading the commercial areas of many municipalities and districts ... carrying on commercial and industrial pursuits:
> And whereas many of our white merchants are being forced out of business by such commercial and industrial invasion:
> Therefore be it Resolved, That this House go on record as being utterly opposed to the further influx of Orientals ... and, further, that this House places itself on record as being in favour of the enactment of such amendment to the "Immigration Act of Canada" as is necessary to completely prohibit Asiatic immigration ...

"Asiatics," as outsiders in what were conceived as white Western and European territories. The use of race as a means of marking differences — "them" versus "us" — "gave white groups the power of definition in cultural and ideological terms, as well as more instrumental power in the hands of politicians, bureaucrats, owners of capital, labour unions, judges, police, and other influential members of the 'ruling' sector." Although Anderson focuses on "Chinese," the term "Japanese" was subject to the same assumptions, which placed the "Asiatic" or "Oriental," or more brutally the "yellow races," in the category of "alien." This identity could be invoked at all levels of legislative language to restrict non-whites — including Natives — from playing a significant role in the public sphere.

Even though the "race-definition process" was a powerful mechanism for maintaining relations of social power, it was not monolithic and remained vulnerable to resistance, critical analysis and change. Four pre-World War II instances in the history of Japanese Canadians serve as touchstones in their struggle to achieve the full rights of citizenship: the court challenge of Tomey Homma to put himself on the voters' list; the political efforts of the Canadian Japanese Volunteer Corps during World War I; the quest of Japanese Canadian fishers to gain equal fishing rights; and the major effort of the Japanese Canadian Citizens' League to lobby the federal government in Ottawa. The memory of these events surfaced many times during the redress movement as examples of a vital legacy of activism and negotiation.

THE CASE OF TOMEY HOMMA

IN A COMMENT CITED in *A Dream of Riches: The Japanese Canadians, 1877-1977*, T. Buck Suzuki, a nisei activist, union leader and World War II veteran, recalled the painful impact of disenfranchisement on his generation: "The main thing was this lack of franchise. When you lacked franchise and the politicians were not interested in you, you had nothing to contribute, you had nothing to give them. At the time of election, you were something nice to kick around." This sense of being an outsider, of having "nothing to contribute" to their country, bothered to no end those Japanese Canadians who saw the franchise as the most visible right denied to them. Some of the earliest immigrants, those who were naturalized as "British subjects" (as Canadians were identified at the time), sought to change their conditions. In Vancouver they made a collective effort to have their names placed on the voters' list.

It was as part of this local initiative that Tomekichi (Tomey) Homma sought to gain the franchise, on October 19, 1900. He did so by testing the language of naturalization in the British North America Act, which placed jurisdiction for the franchise in the hands of the federal government. As Andrea Geiger-Adams points out in her analysis of the Homma case, "The *Naturalization Act*, passed by the Dominion government pursuant to its power over naturalization, provided in turn that every naturalized alien was entitled to 'all political and other rights, powers and privileges to which a natural-born British subject is entitled within Canada.'"

Homma applied to have his name added to the voters' list, and as expected, Thomas Cunningham, the collector of voters for Vancouver, turned him down. Homma was no doubt informed of the stipulation in Section 8 of the Provincial Election Act: "No Chinaman, Japanese, or Indian shall have his named placed on the Register of Voters for any Electoral District, or be entitled to vote in any election." But Homma was able to turn this regulation back on itself. Although "Japanese" was defined as "any person of the Japanese race, naturalized or not," in the language of citizenship, as a "naturalized" person, he was no longer the "Japanese" named in the Act. Naturalization had made him a "British subject," a status that was under the jurisdiction of the federal government. In this way, Homma sought to displace the racialized language of the Act by drawing on the broader (British and European) understanding of naturalization as a process through which he had been transformed from one status ("Japanese") to another ("British subject"). He claimed this transformation as a right of naturalization. Once he had been officially refused, Homma could use the denial to launch a court challenge. Well respected in his community and personally outraged by the legislation denying Japanese Canadians the vote, he became a representative for the Gyosha Dantai (Japanese Fishermen's Association), the organization that raised the funds to pay for his legal battle.

Surprisingly, contradicting the entrenched social and political values of privileged white males, the judge who heard the case, Chief Justice Angus John McColl of the B.C. Supreme Court, sided with Homma. McColl concluded that the authority regarding naturalization, and the rights and responsibilities that come with it, rested with the federal government. This meant that the Provincial Election Act of B.C. was outside the authority of the provincial government. McColl went further to issue a warning: "The residence within the province of large numbers of persons, *British subjects in name*, but doomed to perpetual exclusion from any part in the passage of legislation affecting their property or civil rights would surely not be to the advantage of Canada and might even become a source of national danger." On appeal, the Supreme Court of Canada upheld Judge McColl's decision. It appeared that Homma's challenge would be successful, and there was suddenly hope that the Provincial Election Act would be struck down.

Undeterred by the judgements, the B.C. government sought and was given permission to appeal to what was then the ultimate authority, the Judicial Committee of the Privy Council in London. Sadly, in a ruling that paid no respect to the language of the Naturalization Act, the Privy Council resorted to "race" — rather than citizenship — as a basis for enfranchisement. In making their ruling, their Lordships claimed the British practice of class discrimination as a precedent for arguing that naturalization did not include the right to vote. "From the time of William III down to Queen Victoria," they reasoned, "no naturalization was permitted which did not exclude the alien naturalized from sitting in Parliament or in the Privy Council." Moreover, the legitimacy of a policy of exclusion determined by race as a category of discrimination was considered "not a topic which their Lordships are entitled to consider."

The Privy Council's ruling maintained that while naturalization involved the "obligations of allegiance," it did not include "the privileges attached to it," which they deemed "quite independent of nationality." They could then conclude that the B.C. legislature was authorized to determine the "consequences" of naturalization — particularly in cases where the right to vote was circumscribed by place of residence. Ergo, the decision of the B.C. Supreme Court was reversed, and Tomey Homma, along with other Asian-identified citizens — and, of course, white women — would not be entitled to vote in B.C.[9] The challenge to white male power had been defused by "the mother country," and the Victoria *Colonist* could celebrate the return to the status quo:

---

9   Geiger-Adams points out that the Privy Council used as a precedent for their decision an outdated piece of U.S. legislation written during the Civil War. The legislation, which gave southern states control over the franchise to ensure the disenfranchisement of slaves, had no relevance for Canadian conditions but became a convenient legal justification for the Privy Council decision. In doing so, Geiger-Adams says, the Privy Council failed to acknowledge "that the doctrine it invoked

We are relieved from the possibility of having polling booths swamped by a horde of Orientals who are totally unfitted either by custom or education to exercise the ballot, and whose voting would completely demoralise politics ... They have not the remotest idea of what a democratic and representative government is, and are quite incapable of taking part in it.

FIGHTING FOR CANADA

TOMEY HOMMA'S COURT challenge set the precedent for a different negotiation tactic 14 years later — a political rather than a legal manoeuvre. In the midst of World War I, as Canada struggled to provide troops for England, what better way to demonstrate loyalty than through service in the armed forces? In 1916 the Canadian Japanese Volunteer Corps, financed by fundraising in the community, was formed. Their motivation for enlisting was explained in their constitution: "The 200 men go not only as soldiers to fight in the Canadian war. They go to sacrifice themselves in the battle to achieve rights here at home ... The question of franchise in British Columbia is still not settled. The sacrifice of these men is to break this barrier." The assumption was that, as veterans, they would be given the franchise.

Canada accepted the Canadian Japanese Volunteer Corps, and a total of 196 volunteers fought in the war. Of these, "54 were killed, 93 wounded, and only 49 returned home safely." Their high hopes of attaining the franchise were shattered when they returned home. Intense lobbying and a petition from their representative community organization, the Canadian Japanese Association, could not sway the B.C. legislature. The Victoria *Colonist* expressed the standard public position:

We recognize the deadly menace that confronts us for eternity if we open our doors to any alien people with whom we can never assimilate and whose unlimited presence among us can only mean our final disintegration. Therefore, we have stated emphatically our unshakeable opposition to the granting of the franchise to any Japanese for any cause whatsoever.

---

had its origin in the history of the formation of the United States, and particularly the need to accommodate the concerns of slave states that local control over the attributes of citizenship be preserved in order to maintain racial boundaries." The failure to uphold Homma's case helped to "maintain racial boundaries" in B.C.

After another decade of lobbying, the franchise was finally granted to these veterans on April 1, 1931. The law "passed by a margin of one vote." The victory, if it can be described as such, was meagre compensation for the lives lost. And disappointingly, only veterans — not their wives and children — could vote, and that right would die with them. Saburo Shinobu, one of the volunteers, reflected: "I cannot help thinking ... of the future of the Japanese Canadians as a whole. While I write this letter, thoughts of the morrow come, and why, I do not know, but the tears spring unbidden."

GETTING LICENSED

THE 1920S WITNESSED a surge in race-based legislation to corral Japanese Canadians and to divest them of their economic and material resources. Had the B.C. legislature had its way, Japanese Canadians would have had to deal with laws forbidding them to own property, work in resource industries or hold merchant licences. The power to enact such laws, fortunately, rested with the federal government, which could not endorse apartheid-type policies because of Britain's trade relationships with Japan. But specific regulations could squeeze Japanese Canadians out of industries they depended on for their economic security. Regarding fishers, the authors of the *Report on Oriental Activities Within the Province* (1927) were proud of the reduction of Japanese Canadians in fishing achieved by issuing fewer fishing licences to those of the "Japanese race." In his 1925 report, Fisheries Branch Chief Inspector J. A. Motherwell was explicit about the intent of federal actions: "The [Marine and Fisheries] Department's policy of eliminating the Oriental from the fisheries of the Province with a view to placing the entire industry in the hand of white British subjects and Canadian Indians appears to be working out well ..."

Japanese Canadians were the "Orientals" targeted by this policy of elimination. "By 1925," Adachi writes, "... the Department of Marine and Fisheries had stripped close to a thousand licences from the Japanese [Canadians], reducing their control of licences by nearly half." To reduce their efficiency further, the government forbade fishers in the Skeena River region to use gasoline engines with their boats, a policy that remained in effect until 1930. The department made no attempt to address the race discourse that distinguished white "British subjects" from the "Orientals," simply stating that the reductions were part of federal policy. In an effort not to be completely expelled from the fishing industry — the ultimate objective of the federal government — a group of Japanese Canadian fishers challenged the policy in the Supreme Court of Canada in 1928. The court sided with them, concluding that as "British subjects" they had the right to hold licences. The federal government appealed, and when its appeal was rejected through a ruling that the "federal minister did not have the discriminatory power to withhold a licence from a duly naturalized Canadian citizen," the government quickly legislated the power before the appeal was completed.

As Japanese Canadians would discover time and again, even successful challenges to discriminatory policies could be reversed by the federal government's power to script new discriminatory legislation. The lack of the franchise remained the crucial stumbling block. The most organized effort to remove this barrier occurred in the mid-1930s, when the nisei were coming of age.

TREK TO OTTAWA, 1936

THE FRANCHISE QUESTION gained visibility in the 1930s through the efforts of the Co-operative Commonwealth Federation (CCF), a socialist party formed in Calgary in 1932. A year later, in Regina, the party elected J. S. Woodsworth as its leader and set out its platform in the Regina Manifesto, which declared that all Canadian citizens, regardless of race, should have the right to vote. When Woodsworth made this claim in the House of Commons, the Liberals found a pretext to accuse the CCF of being pro-Asian, the "kiss of death" in white Canada. This attack continued in the 1935 B.C. election campaign in the well-publicized slogan: "A vote for any CCF candidate is a vote to give the Chinaman and Japanese the same voting right that you have."

Kept alive by the CCF in the House of Commons, the franchise question was brought to a head in February 1936. At that time Angus McInnis, CCF member for Vancouver East, in a strategic move, proposed a resolution calling on the House of Commons either to support the disenfranchisement of Asian Canadians or to offer equal citizenship rights to all. The resolution did not endorse disenfranchisement but was meant to make visible the double standard for citizenship in Canada. The government avoided a vote by referring the resolution to its Special Committee on Elections and Franchise Acts, a committee that had been formed to review the Dominion Elections Act and to hold hearings to receive recommendations for changes. The B.C. Japanese Canadian community, organized around the newly created Japanese Canadian Citizens' League (JCCL), reacted quickly. It initiated a fundraising campaign to draft a brief calling for the franchise, and to send a delegation to Ottawa.

As recorded in the minutes of the Special Committee on Elections and Franchise Acts, the JCCL brief requested "that clause XI of section 4 of the Dominion Franchise Act, 1934, and amending acts, be repealed, to permit British subjects of the Japanese race to vote in Dominion elections." The repeal, in effect, would override the provisions of B.C.'s Provincial Election Act. By having their names disallowed on the B.C. voters' list, those designated as "Japanese," "Chinamen," "Hindus" and "Indians" were not permitted to vote in federal elections. Achieving the federal vote would pave the way to gain the vote in B.C.

Four JCCL delegates were asked to go to Ottawa to represent the interests of Japanese Canadians in B.C. Clearly they were selected because of their successful "Canadianization": not only were they educated and savvy in current (at the time, Anglo-Saxon) social and political modes of thought, but also they worked in readily identifiable mainstream occupations: Miss A. Hideko Hyodo was a schoolteacher, Mr. Minoru Kobayashi was a life insurance agent, Dr. E. Chutaro Banno was a dentist and Dr. S. Ichie Hayakawa was a university professor. These "normal" nisei appeared before the Special Committee on Elections and Franchise Acts to present their arguments on May 22, 1936. The atmosphere would have been electric for them, made more so by the two B.C. members of Parliament who had been given permission to ask them questions. The two notoriously anti-Asian MPs, well known to Japanese Canadians, were A. W. Neill, an Independent member from Comox-Alberni, and Thomas Reid, Liberal member for New Westminster.

Hideko Hyodo, who later was awarded the Order of Canada and who became a staunch redress supporter in the 1980s, opened the presentation:

> We have come to plead the cause for the Canadian-born Japanese who are disqualified at the present time, not only from exercising the franchise but

also, by this disqualification, are restricted from the enjoyment of certain privileges and also from entering certain lines of work. We feel that the present provincial disqualification of Japanese is not governed by the British principles of fair play and our reasons are stated ... in the brief which we have had prepared to state our case and which, we hope, you gentlemen will find some time to peruse.

Hyodo provided a brief history of her community in B.C., emphasizing the determination of her nisei generation to assimilate through education and to distance themselves from their parents' "Japanese" identity. In their ability to fit in, she explained, "the process of Canadianization is extraordinarily complete, considering the wide gulf that exists between the first and second generation." The nisei were so attuned to Canadian ways that they would "be like fish out of water in Japan. Their ideals are towards being better Canadians, sharing common Canadian goals."

The next presenter, Minoru Kobayashi, dwelled on the consequences of barring Japanese Canadians from certain professions as well as from public life. The lack of the franchise meant that they had not been able to hold public office, become lawyers and pharmacists, or be employed on many public works projects. Such obstacles, he pointed out to the committee members — most of whom knew little, if anything, about his community in B.C. — were demoralizing to the young and discouraged them from contributing to the democratic affairs of their country.

Chutaro (Edward) Banno talked about recent nisei efforts to affirm Canadian democracy by forming an association, the JCCL, to seek the franchise. Its existence as a representative voice was a clear sign that Japanese Canadians were responsible and capable citizens. "My colleagues here and I have been sent here by the Japanese-Canadian Citizens' League of British Columbia to demonstrate to you, in word and flesh, that the Canadian-born Japanese does take his citizenship seriously," Banno told the committee. The JCCL was "anxious to serve Canada with all that we are able to give" and wanted to work toward the integration of Japanese Canadians into Canadian society.

The fourth and final presenter, Dr. S. I. Hayakawa, had travelled not from B.C., as the others had done, but from Madison, Wisconsin. For six years he had been teaching English literature at the University of Wisconsin, from which he had received his Ph.D. the year before. Hayawaka brought a decidedly intellectual, even academic, air to the delegation. He wanted, as he explained, to be "of service to Canada by presenting what I know of the situation in British Columbia."[10] For the most part, Hayakawa reiterated what the three previous speakers had said. Then, drawing on his own experience, particularly in the U.S. and in Japan, he expanded on the Canadian qualities of Japanese Canadians, emphasizing that their modes of perception and thought had grown out of local conditions. "I found in Japan," he explained to the committee,

> that the very basis of their [Japanese] thinking is different from my own — that I am an individualist and therefore philosophically incapable of meeting Japanese thought on its own ground. We Canadian citizens of Japanese parentage are all alike in this respect — we have all been educated on a principle fundamentally different from that which underlies Japanese civilization. And when Miss Hyodo states that the situation of a Japanese in British Columbia is different from that which existed thirty years ago when the ruling against the Japanese franchise was confirmed, she is uttering, it seems to me, a profound truth.

Hayakawa, referring to a key moment in Japanese Canadian history, invoked the Privy Council ruling that had defeated Tomey Homma's legal challenge to the Provincial Election Act, supporting the right of the B.C. government to determine who was deemed eligible to vote — that is, eligible by intellect, temperament and ability — and who was not. "Orientals," the

---

10   Hayakawa later became a U.S. citizen. During World War II he lived in Chicago, teaching at the Illinois Institute of Technology. He was elected to the U.S. Senate as a Republican from California and served one term, from 1977 to 1980. He gained notoriety for his outspoken stance against redress for Japanese Americans. After the 1978 conference in Salt Lake City, Utah, when the Japanese American Citizens League (JACL) voted in favour of a redress package that included $25,000 per individual incarcerated, Hayakawa was interviewed by a local newspaper and his remarks appeared on the national news wire service. Leslie T. Hatamiya in *Righting a Wrong* cites the opening passage of the newswire story: "The Japanese American Citizens League has no right to ask the U.S. government for reparations for Japanese American citizens placed in relocation camps during World War II, according to Sen. S. I. Hayakawa ... 'Everybody lost out during the war, not just Japanese Americans,' and JACL asking for $25,000 in redress for each Japanese American placed in relocation camps was 'ridiculous.'"

government had stated, were so inassimilable that they were incapable of participating in the democratic process. The JCCL delegates constructed their case on "Canadianization," evident in Japanese Canadian accomplishments in sports and music, but they emphasized that behind all this lay an intense drive to get the franchise. To describe just how eager they were, Hayakawa described the community effort required to bring the delegation to Ottawa:

> Hundreds of young boys and girls, some of them even children of grade-school age, have been sacrificing ice-cream sodas and movies, and contributing their quarters and fifty-cent pieces, in order that we might appear before you to secure them the rights for which they are hopefully preparing themselves. Our parent-generation has also been generous of their support. One Japanese-Canadian parent said to me last summer, when I was there investigating this problem, that he could die in peace if his children could have the franchise which he had been denied.

There were signs that some of the Special Committee members were being educated, not only about the unfairness of the restrictions imposed on Japanese Canadians, but also about the ability of Japanese Canadians to represent themselves through the very democratic processes they were denied by legislation. "You all speak English so fluently that if we did not see you face to face we would take you be to Englishmen," a committee member from Quebec said in surprise. The member also commented "that the delegation presented a very excellent case for themselves," and admitted to being surprised "to know that these conditions exist in British Columbia."

This amicable interchange was overshadowed in the question period by an agitated A. W. Neill, who said he was bothered that Japanese Canadians had not taken their case to the B.C. government, as they "should" have done — "Why do you not agitate there?" To which Hayakawa responded: "We have been agitating there for years, sir." Before this verbal sparring could get out of hand, a committee member intervened: "I think that is a most unfair question. I do not think it is up to any member to tell the delegates where they should go to make their protests. It is up to them."

No decisions were made at this hearing. The delegation simply presented the case for the franchise submitted by the JCCL.

The Special Committee did not meet again for another year, at which time both A. W. Neill and Thomas Reid — without the presence of Japanese Canadians — had their opportunity to argue against the franchise. In preparation, Reid even composed his own lengthy brief, "Opposing Oriental Franchise in the Province of British Columbia." He characterized the so-called "Japanese" problem in B.C. in all the familiar language of race that had made possible the exclusions in the Provincial Election Act. While taking issue with what he alleged were factual inaccuracies in the JCCL's brief, Reid focused on the threat to whites posed by the Japanese and other "Asiatics." According to him, the Japanese in particular wanted to infiltrate and miscegenate white Canada. Their ultimate goal — a familiar refrain — was to take over the reins of power. The peril? If they were allowed to vote federally, they would secure the vote provincially. "When that day comes," Reid prophesied, "if it ever comes, we might as well pull up our stakes and seek pastures new, for they will then, by reason of numbers to a great extent be able to control affairs in the Province of British Columbia, political as well as economic."

At this time Japanese Canadians numbered about 23,000 of the 700,000 people of B.C. — hardly a danger to the power structure that Reid was defending. But this simple fact was obscured by his representation of "Japanese" and other "Asians" as, on the one hand, incapable of assimilation, and yet, on the other hand, threatening to assimilate in order to undermine the racial purity of Canadian society. "As a matter of fact," Reid wrote, "the danger is that the Chinese or Japanese by inter-marriage would absorb our own race, and this is simply born [sic] out by the fact that in the few instances where a Chinese or a Japanese has married a Canadian woman or vice versa, the offspring born from the union of these two races have distinct physical characteristics and are unmistakably Oriental in features and appearance."

Reid presented his brief at the March 11, 1937, meeting of the Special Committee. He appeared again at a follow-up meeting on March 16, this time with A. W. Neill. The two men continued to urge the committee not to grant the vote to Japanese Canadians. They brought out all the old arguments — Japanese Canadians' loyalty to Japan and not to Canada, their inassimilability, untrustworthiness and threat to the racial purity of Canada. Neill and Reid used as their support base the White Canadian Research

Society, a coalition of groups opposed to the presence of Asians in B.C. Neill quoted from their report: "This dominion is primarily a white man's country, and the interests of the white man should be paramount, as are the interests of orientals in Asia. This is our interpretation of 'British fair play.'" The reference is a direct response to the notion of "British fair play" that had been raised by the JCCL delegates as a reason for granting the franchise. Neill and Reid then went on to describe the gloomy future of B.C. and Canada if the "orientals" were given the vote. The government would no longer be able to impose restrictions on them, and soon they would multiply and take over the province and the rest of the country. As Neill explained, repeating the theme of Reid's brief, "It is British Columbia to-day but it will be half of Canada to-morrow."

Not surprisingly, the Special Committee chose not to tamper with the existing regulations, and by doing nothing it endorsed the exclusionary provisions of the B.C. Election Act. By 1937, however, other forces were changing the lives of Japanese Canadians in B.C. Soon after Japan invaded China, Japanese Canadians became the targets of an intensified hostility. Their stores were boycotted, and voices rose calling for them to be registered and placed under surveillance as potential saboteurs. The hopeful ray of idealism that had motivated the delegation's visit to Ottawa in 1936 was eclipsed by this ominous turn of events. To mediate the growing antagonism toward their community, core members of the JCCL, including Tom Shoyama and Ed Ouchi, made a concerted effort to educate the public about Japanese Canadians' loyalty to their country and belief in democratic values by founding a newspaper, appropriately titled *The New Canadian: Voice of the Nisei*, in November 1938. The publication became a major vehicle in the formation of a "nisei voice" and the medium through which young writers such as Muriel Kitagawa began to articulate their Canadian perspectives.

A LONG TIME COMING

JAPANESE CANADIANS HAD to wait another decade, until 1949, before gaining the franchise. By then the complex infrastructures of their B.C. communities, which had slowly evolved in the 50 years before the war, had been dismantled by government decree. And by then, Japanese Canadians were emerging from nearly a decade of traumatic events that had dispossessed them and scattered them all over the country. When they were finally allowed to return to the B.C. coast on April 1, 1949, their former lives there had begun to settle into the deeper recesses of memory.

Tomey Homma died in 1945, still not permitted to return to the west coast. When the young nisei student Kunio Hidaka summarized the results of his research into the legal status of Japanese Canadians, he noted the importance of the Homma case. "Discrimination is based on race not on nationality," he concluded, "so naturalization has not accorded to Japanese all the protection that ought to have followed." This condition set the stage for the most cataclysmic event in the history of Japanese Canadians. It would also, four decades later, call forth a movement to redress the injustices inflicted on them.

CHAPTER 2

REGULATING JAPANESE CANADIANS

Racialization and the Mass Uprooting

The sound policy and the best policy for the Japanese Canadians themselves is to distribute their numbers as widely as possible throughout the country where they will not create feelings of racial hostility.

— Mackenzie King

MACKENZIE KING'S ADDRESS TO PARLIAMENT

IN THE HOUSE of Commons on August 4, 1944, Prime Minister Mackenzie King set out the details of his government program to solve (once and for all?) the "Japanese problem": redistribution and assimilation. By this time, the "persons of Japanese race" who were the object of King's comments had been deprived of their citizenship rights, divested of their homes, businesses and belongings, confined in regulated sites across Canada and controlled by a barrage of Orders-in-Council. They had become all but voiceless. There were no outcries in the House of Commons, no challenges to the unquestioned assumptions — and implicit contradictions — in King's speech. Audaciously, King even conceded that resisting the confiscation of one's property was not necessarily an act of disloyalty. "Some may have merely misunderstood their dispossession from their property in the protected zones," he explained to his colleagues in the House of Commons — with no irony intended. But regulated by the War Measures Act, the enabling legislation for the federal government's actions, Japanese Canadians were unable to contest their treatment in any effective way.

King's statement is striking for the manner in which it presented a model of Canada as a fair and democratic country, immune from racism, and an upholder of "principles of fairness and justice." The fact that the rights of Canadians of Japanese ancestry were violated was ignored in his speech. In King's narrative, the presence of "Japanese" on the west coast had "led to acrimony and bitterness" on the part of white British Columbians. So the government found it "unwise and undesirable" — for the benefit of people of B.C. and for the "Japanese" themselves — "to allow the Japanese population to be concentrated in that province after the war." Here the issue had less to do with military security — the official justification for uprooting Japanese Canadians — and more with fostering national unity. Rather than exclusion and expulsion, the desired mode of resolving the "Japanese problem" in B.C. before the war, King proposed the absorption of Japanese Canadians in small doses across the country so that they would disappear as a group.

First, however, to mitigate negative reactions to the resulting miscegenation, a ritual cleansing must take place. The "Japanese" would be required to pass a loyalty test, and those deemed disloyal would no longer have the "privilege of remaining in Canada after the struggle [the war] is terminated." King also appeased the proponents of a white Canada by acknowledging the "extreme difficulty of assimilating Japanese persons in Canada" and declaring that immigration of Japanese would cease after the war.

Once the disloyal had been weeded out, King continued, the remaining loyal ones — "a few thousand persons of Japanese race who have been guilty of no act of sabotage and who have manifested no disloyalty, even during periods of utmost trial" — would be treated "justly." "For the government to act otherwise," King concluded, "would be an acceptance of the standards of our enemies and the negation of the purposes for which we are fighting."

To enact his national plan, the government would establish a "quasi-judicial" loyalty tribunal to isolate and deport those judged "disloyal" and then urge the assimilation of those who remained.[1]

In the social engineering project outlined in King's speech, the racialized are the ones who cause "racial hostility." The visibility of their bodies, their not-whiteness, generates anxiety for Canadians. It is not sufficient to subject these bodies to uprooting and dispossession. They must be dispersed in a process of regulated assimilation that will make the "Japanese problem" — a "vexatious problem" for Canada — disappear. Through a political language that disguises social violence as social efficiency, the narrative propounded by King — and it is just that, a narrative, with the "Japanese" as the "problem" — then represents the Canadian state as an actor that upholds "principles of fairness and justice" and heroically rejects the "hateful doctrine of racialism which is the basis of the nazi system everywhere." The assimilation of the "Japanese" will prove that Canadian liberalism has triumphed.

But fairness and justice for whom? For the "Japanese Canadians themselves," according to the prime minister. In King's narrative of the state as heroic, these individuals, who are publicly perceived as the "Yellow Peril," are able to free themselves from that condition by disappearing as a collective body. This process is made possible by the consciousness that "racialism" is no longer acceptable. What remains — and this too is for the good of Japanese Canadians — is for the "quasi-judicial commission" to "examine the background, loyalties and attitudes of all persons of Japanese race in Canada to ascertain those who are not fit persons to be allowed to remain here."

No doubt the Japanese Canadians remaining in Canada would feel a lot safer knowing that the disloyal among them had been weeded out. But earlier in his speech King had stated: "It is a fact that no person of Japanese race born in Canada has been charged with any act of sabotage or disloyalty during the years of war." *It is a fact* — but what can be the significance of a fact when the state policies within which it is "judged" have already decided that many who were not charged were nevertheless "disloyal" to Canada?

---

1   King's "quasi-judicial commission" was never established, most likely because the government's deportation orders were challenged in the courts.

WHAT THE PRIME MINISTER DID NOT SAY

THE MEMBERS OF PARLIAMENT who listened in the House of Commons on August 4, 1944, were not informed of some basic facts that Mackenzie King, as prime minister, would have known. For instance, King disclosed his government's intent "to maintain a policy that in a sense can be considered as part of a continental policy," which is to say, one in line with the U.S. handling of Japanese Americans. "There is no need for an identity of policy, but I believe there is merit in maintaining a substantial consistency of treatment in the two countries." King did not disclose, however, that U.S. policy differed in significant ways from that of his own government, so that Japanese Americans were not treated as harshly as Japanese Canadians:

- Their properties and belongings were not liquidated without the owners' consent;
- Those incarcerated were not forced to pay for their own incarceration;
- They could return to the coast in January 1945 and were not subject to deportation and dispersal;
- They did not face the prospect of a "quasi-judicial" loyalty commission to deport those deemed "not fit persons"; and
- Their country's constitution protected them from the systematic abuse on the basis of race categories that were legalized in Canada under the War Measures Act.

King's cabinet advisors were aware of U.S. policy and its differences from Canadian policy, so such information would not likely have been kept from him. A draft memorandum dated June 15, 1943, prepared by the Department of External Affairs for an interdepartmental meeting, compares Canadian and U.S. policies: "United States policy appears not to permit sale of property without the consent of the owners." Another document, "Interdepartmental Committee on Enemy Interests in Canada and Canadian Interests in Enemy Occupied Territories," though undated, is apparently related to that meeting and focuses on the liquidation of properties without the owners' consent. Present were officials from the Foreign Exchange Board and the departments of External Affairs, Labour, Secretary of State, Immigration, and Mines and Resources. The representative for the Custodian of Enemy Property in Vancouver, G. W. McPherson — "classified as a 'jap-hater' by the RCMP" — reported to the Interdepartmental Committee that in disposing of properties he was merely following "a decision made in January last by a Cabinet Committee to liquidate all Japanese real and household property in the interests of the Japanese themselves, because it would deteriorate rapidly otherwise."

McPherson referred to the policy authorized by Order-in-Council PC 469, passed on January 19, 1943, under the War Measures Act: "The Custodian has been vested with the power and responsibility of controlling and managing any property of persons of the Japanese race evacuated from the protected area ... such power and responsibility shall be deemed to include and *to have included from the date of the vesting of such property in the Custodian*, the power to liquidate, sell or otherwise dispose of such property." The crucial retroactive qualifier, "to have included," exempted the government from its commitment, at the outset of the uprooting, that the Custodian would manage properties and belongings "as a protective measure only." McPherson also told the meeting: "In property liquidation no distinction has been made between the property of Japanese nationals, naturalized Canadians and Canadian-born Japanese," and one "Mr. Read considered that it was regrettable that our approach to this problem should be on a racial basis instead of restricting our more severe measures to Japanese nationals, as is done in the United States. Mr. Read pointed out further that in the United States no Japanese property was being sold, but all was stored at Government expense."

Behind the scenes, shielded from accountability through the all-powerful War Measures Act, government officials had no problem rationalizing the liquidation policy. Even the phrase "protective measure only" could easily be redefined to their advantage: the properties were deteriorating, so liquidation was necessary to prevent further damage; the action was therefore in the best interests of the Japanese Canadians themselves. A similar logic was applied later to the government's dispersal policy. That, too, was in the best interests of Japanese Canadians: no longer visible, they would no longer generate racial hostility in white Canadians. In King's words, "It is the fact of concentration that has given rise to the problem."

A COMMUNITY DIVIDED

ON THE OTHER side of the social and political divide, the language of racialization and all its restrictions wreaked havoc in the lives of Japanese Canadians. Initially they could do little but call on the government to respect their rights as Canadian citizens, but their voices fell on deaf ears. The only state representatives they encountered were RCMP officers, whose primary objectives were control and enforcement, and government officials who were merely carrying out orders or defending the government's policies. These officials' reports on critiques of government policy reflected a context of surveillance and the assumption that the Japanese Canadians who called attention to abuses of authority simply did not matter. Often lacing armchair sociological interpretations with glaring misrepresentations, these reports were used as supporting documents by policy makers.

For instance, immediately after the order to remove Japanese nationals was passed on January 16, 1942, the RCMP's initial contact person in the Japanese Canadian community was Etsuji Morii. He was a notorious figure in the community, known for providing the RCMP with judo instructors and, along with fellow issei Arthur Nishiguchi and Mitsujiro Noguchi, assisting the RCMP during the registration of all Japanese Canadians from March to August 1941. The RCMP believed that Morii had the authority and stature to assist in getting Japanese nationals to move by April 1, 1942. For Japanese Canadians, Morii was a kind of "godfather" figure who operated the Japanese Social Club, a gambling spot on Powell Street, and whose interests were protected by a loyal group of judo specialists. In any case, at that time most people in the community thought that the government would maintain the distinction between Japanese nationals and "Canadian citizens," so the use of Morii by the RCMP, though not endorsed, was tolerated.

Morii, Nishiguchi and Ippei Nishio became the founding members of the Japanese Liaison Committee, and sent men into the community asking for the first nationals to volunteer quickly to be moved from the coast. It was Morii's position, as he informed the issei nationals, that "only a token uprooting would be necessary." Whether he believed this or was led to believe this by the RCMP, or simply wanted to get the first issei to leave voluntarily as a demonstration to the RCMP of issei compliance, is not known. Nevertheless, at a meeting he convened on February 22, he appealed for volunteers to sacrifice themselves for the greater good of the community.

Many issei were reluctant to leave without knowing what would happen to their families. One issei remembered Morii saying, "'If I fail at this I will commit hara-kiri.' ... He appealed to real Japanese emotion." When only a few issei agreed to leave before the April 1 deadline, and pressure mounted from the RCMP to begin removing nationals, Morii resorted to coercion. As Ann Sunahara notes: "Official notices for removal, enforced by Morii's 'lieutenants,' produced the required hundred men for the February 23 shipment to Rainbow, B.C. However, only half of those notified showed up at the railway station for the February 24 shipment to Red Pass."

The next day, Morii's theory that sacrificing a few would save the community was undermined completely by the passage of Order-in-Council PC 1665, dated February 24, which called for the removal of all "persons of the Japanese race." The Canadian-born and the naturalized, who thought they would be protected by their citizenship, were now subject to dispersal from the coast. Categorization by race, rather than nationality, split open the nightmare of fear and uncertainty. Stunned by what she perceived to be an utter betrayal of trust, the nisei writer Muriel Kitagawa wrote to her brother Wes Fujiwara, a medical student in Toronto, about the devastating personal and social upheaval:

> It has just boiled down to race persecution, and signs have been posted on all highways . . . JAPS . . . KEEP OUT. Mind you, you can't compare this sort of thing to anything that happens in Germany. That country is an avowed Jew-baiter, totalitarian. Canada is supposed to be a Democracy out to fight against just the sort of thing she's boosting at home.

Reduced to the status of "enemy alien," Japanese Canadians like Muriel Kitagawa felt powerless to withstand the government's race discourse. In its final expression of outrage, the *New Canadian*, the community newspaper — which was soon censored by the B.C. Security Commission — spelled out the injustice of the government's actions:

> The first steps taken — immobilization of fishing boats, special regis-tration, parole permits, and detention of certain individuals — were accepted, on the whole, as obviously necessary in war-time.
> More drastic steps emerging from the Ottawa conference in January —

the removal of alien nationals and the banning of short-wave radios and cameras — were likewise accepted. In spite of the fact that almost a quarter of its gainfully employed were affected by the removal order, the whole community was prepared to recognize that government authorities were forced to draw some line between citizens and non-citizens in guarding against the most probable source of danger.

But tremendous public pressure — arising in the first place from very sorry sources indeed — was brought to bear upon the government. In quick order, a whole series of repressive measures, unlike anything before in the history of the nation, have been authorized. In effect, the new orders uproot completely without regard some 23,000 men, women and children; brand every person of Japanese origin as disloyal and traitorous; and reduce to nothing the concept and value of Canadian citizenship.

The process of racialization soon wove its way into the social and political fabric of the Japanese Canadian community.[2] In their initial passivity in response to the RCMP's use of Etsuji Morii and his Japanese Liaison Committee, they had accepted the principle of singling out "enemy nationals" for removal from the protected area. But once race became the criteria for uprooting, Vancouver — the site of convergence for the first groups of Japanese Canadians to be removed from the coastal towns and Vancouver Island — became a vortex of tension, conflicts and oppositional politics.

Overall, though — and this may be evidence of an overwhelming sense of powerlessness vis-à-vis the Canadian state — Japanese Canadians did not resist the government's decision to remove all of them. Perhaps it was here that the lack of franchise came home to roost. Not having the status of "voting Canadians," and excluded from all areas of public life, including the legal profession, Japanese Canadians did not have the resources or the social and political connections to mount a challenge to the racist policies enacted under the War Measures Act. The deep underlying currents of frustration surfaced in demands for a clarification of status, as some Japanese Canadians spoke out against the limbo of non-identification that took over their lives.

---

2   I use the term "community" cautiously here, since those who thought of themselves as "Japanese Canadians" did not have the political infrastructure to represent themselves in any coherent or homogeneous way.

A generational pattern was evident in the formation of two ad hoc organizations that sprang up in the middle of March, shortly after the B.C. Security Commission was established: the Naturalized Japanese Canadian Association (NJCA) for naturalized issei, and the Japanese Canadian Citizens' Council (JCCC) for the nisei, an extension of the Japanese Canadian Citizens' League formed in the mid-1930s. Their initial efforts to organize some representational vehicle for Japanese Canadians involved a coordinated rejection of Morii and his Japanese Liaison Committee as spokespersons for the community. Protests against Morii had been made in February, leading to the addition of some nisei (including Tom Shoyama and Kunio Shimizu) to his committee, but Morii continued to wield considerable power.

The more formal rejection of Morii was articulated in an appeal directed to Austin Taylor, chair of the B.C. Security Commission, on March 29, 1942, the result of a large community meeting of 39 Japanese Canadian organizations. Various resolutions were passed, beginning with a stated "determination to co-operate with the Dominion Government in assisting to expedite the evacuation of those [of] Japanese origin from the protected area." The meeting also resolved "that the present head of the Japanese Liaison Committee, E. Morii, does not represent the Japanese community of British Columbia, and we respectfully request that the Government of Canada make such investigations as may be necessary to have a committee formed who do, in fact, represent the said community." A third resolution asked that a meeting be arranged between the appointed legal advisor for the Japanese Canadian community, Denis Murphy Jr., and government ministers, including the minister of pensions and national health, the notorious Ian Mackenzie. Finally, a resolution asked that Taylor accept a "method of evacuation."

The "method" devised by the NJCA apparently had widespread support from community representatives. Given the unusual circumstances and the internal dissensions in the community, the plan was an effort to enable Japanese Canadians to negotiate a cooperative process that could circumvent, and even contain, the frustration and anger growing among them. The issue of family breakup, rapidly becoming the focal point of resistance, could be resolved (so the Japanese Canadian representatives argued) by the "mass evacuation" of the community to Crown land. There it could assume reponsibility for building a temporary "settlement" for some 21,000 people,

17,000 of whom were part of family units. The government would provide the land, materials and supplies; the community would provide the labour to design and construct the following: 160 bunkhouses (25 x 60 feet/7.5 x 18 metre) to accommodate 25 single people in each; 580 tenement houses (25 x 100 feet/7.5 x 30 metre), divided into five sections, with each to accommodate a family of five. The estimated cost was $1,884,000. An efficient work schedule was also included:

> Under these arrangements, we have planned out to build 100 houses within a month by 1,500 men. At the completion of these houses, about 500 families could be moved into the site, increasing the number of workers to approximately 2,500. In this manner, the building capacity could be reinforced from time to time so that, we believe within four months, all of 21,000 Japanese could be removed.

The NJCA strategy was to have Murphy, their lawyer, present the plan to both the federal government and the B.C. Security Commission. Two days later the JCCC, in a "Statement to the Japanese Public," announced the plan, also reporting that they had retained a lawyer. "Mr. Murphy," their release said, "will also carry a request to the Commission that the departure of Canadian citizens of Japanese origin be delayed until consideration is given to the plan." In the meantime, the JCCC urged all Japanese Canadians who had been ordered to report to the RCMP barracks to cooperate.

The NJCA's important attempt to initiate a process of negotiation, based on the assumption that as Canadian citizens Japanese Canadians should cooperate with their government, was rejected by Austin Taylor. Without consulting community representatives, he had already devised his own "plan" to use various "ghost" towns in the B.C. interior for housing. However, Taylor may have been privately sympathetic to the NJCA's "mass evacuation" scheme. Only a month earlier, just after becoming chair, he had written a telegram recommending the same process as an option. In this March 4 telegram, Taylor noted that he thought he had the cooperation of Japanese Canadians, but this could change if white people's hostility toward relocation was not controlled and if the government resorted to "compulsory internment." He mentioned the possibility of using towns such as Greenwood, Kaslo and Minto, and suggested that men could be sent there first to prepare the houses. At this point Taylor appeared not to favour family breakup. The telegram concluded with the "only other option": "establishment in isolated crown grant areas of communities where these families can reestablish themselves on land and in minor and restricted industrial effort."

But by the end of March, Taylor had ruled out that scheme and settled on the use of certain nearly abandoned towns in the B.C. interior. His decision not to negotiate with the Japanese Canadian community was clear. He rejected the NJCA's proposal and did not act on the request to set up a meeting with the ministers. Taylor did come to recognize that the animosity toward Morii was substantial, but he failed to allow for a more democratic structure of representation in the Japanese Canadian community. Instead, he simply declared that no organization would have "official" status for him. This stance dethroned Morii, but also delegitimized the political process within the Japanese Canadian community. If no organization was to be recognized as "official," any organization could scramble for recognition and power.

Without a representative voice, Japanese Canadians were unable to defend themselves from racialization by the government. No one questioned Prime Minister King's logic that Japanese Canadians generated racism because of their visibility, and no one seemed to care that no one — not even the government — considered them a threat to national security, the ostensible reason why they had been uprooted in the first place. The process of removing Japanese Canadians was officially described as an "evacuation."

"IT WAS AN EVACUATION ALL RIGHT": THE POWER OF EUPHEMISM

A COMPARISON OF PRIME Minister King's representation of Japanese Canadians as a "problem" to be solved and the catastrophic effects of his government's policies exposes the huge divide between the power of the state and the citizens of Japanese ancestry who were identified as "enemy alien" on the basis of race. This left no room for Japanese Canadians to negotiate the conditions of their uprooting, and with both the legal and the political avenues closed to them, they were unable to use the very democratic processes that were being violated in their name.

The shifting of blame is a predictable move in race-based systems of social organization. According to its own logic, racialization is not a manifestation of dominance, but the result of the presence of racialized bodies. Hence the political transformation of "Japanese" into "Japanese Canadian" — the term King used to identify those who were deemed loyal and who had agreed to "assimilation" — ritualized the expulsion of the "enemy alien," which in turn reinforced existing social assumptions. In the subtle adoption of "Japanese Canadian," rather than "Japanese" as the "enemy," King confirmed that the mass uprooting, dispossession, dispersal and deportation were a necessary political solution to B.C.'s century-long "Japanese problem." What was kept under wraps, though, was the question of military necessity. On this point the prime minister of Canada, in the House of Commons, with the Japanese Canadians now having been confined for more than two and a half years, remained silent.

All along, far away from the privileged discourse of the House of Commons, Canadians of Japanese ancestry were aware that national security was never the real issue. If they were so dangerous, why then establish a civilian body, the B.C. Security Commission, to carry out the uprooting? Why not have the military involved, as the United States had done? In fact, the confiscation and sale of properties without the owners' permission — the breaking of custodial "trust" — had little to do with security and everything to do with the larger plan to undo the social, cultural and economic fabric of the Japanese Canadian communities on the B.C. coast.

"Evacuation," the euphemism coined by the government, became the term used to describe the internment of Japanese Canadians. It took root so deeply that to this day many Japanese Canadians invoke the term, not merely to denote the event itself, but also to identify the weight of all its phases — dispossession, deportation, dispersal and assimilation. "Evacuation" in its singularity has taken on the proportions of myth for them, embodying that circumscribed period when each person of "the Japanese race" was subject to the violation of rights without recourse to protective mechanisms. "Evacuation" has come to exemplify the whole Japanese Canadian experience of the 1940s, from the moment of uprooting following Pearl Harbor on December 7, 1941, to the final lifting of restrictions on April 1, 1949. "Evacuation" strikes the chord of a shared "exile" from the coast. The word has been so internalized that many Japanese Canadians use it even when they understand that it is a euphemism for their unjustified forced removal from the B.C. coast, and that it reinforces the government's assertion of power.[3]

For the government, constructing euphemisms was an effective mechanism to whitewash its actions. Euphemisms helped to translate the inherent racism of its policies for Japanese Canadians into the language of bureaucratic efficiency. This way of neutralizing the abuse of power generated a complex of terms that rendered "normal" — in the eyes of the Canadian public — its brutal implications. The representation of Japanese Americans was similar. Raymond Y. Okamura comments on the "euphemistic terminology" deployed by the U.S. government to cover up the reality that their own "citizens" were being incarcerated:

> "Evacuation" is the process of temporarily moving people away from an immediate and real danger, such as a fire, flood, shoot-out, or bomb threat. Similarly, "relocation" is the process of more permanently removing people away from a long-term hazard, such as an unsafe building, earthquake fault, or contaminated environment. Both terms strongly suggest that the movement is for the protection or safety of the affected people. It was precisely for this reason that the government selected such words. There is no hint in either term that people are to be confined, detained, imprisoned, or restrained in any way.

According to the Canadian government, Japanese Canadians who were forcibly uprooted, dispossessed and dispersed were being "evacuated" for the "security and defence of Canada." Many who were shipped into Vancouver from the coastal towns and Vancouver Island during March and

---

3   The word "evacuation" continues to be used uncritically in publications. Ken Adachi routinely used "evacuation" and "evacuees" as if they were normal descriptions of the mass uprooting, and even the photographic history of Japanese Canadians, *A Dream of Riches: The Japanese Canadians, 1877-1977*, compiled by the Japanese Canadian Centennial Project, fails to question the term. During the redress movement, "evacuation" was singled out as a misrepresentation of the injustices suffered by Japanese Canadians, and for a while the more politically conscious refused to use it, substituting terms such as "internment," "incarceration," "mass uprooting," "expulsion" or "exile" and "dispossession." Since the redress settlement of 1988, the term has returned to its earlier use, especially among the elderly, for whom "evacuation" remains the shorthand for an event that shaped their communal lives as "Japanese Canadians." The term is more often than not used without qualification, as it is by Maryka Omatsu in *Bittersweet Passage*, and more recently by Tomoko Makabe in *The Canadian Sansei*.

April of 1942 and forced to live in the livestock barns on the Pacific National Exhibition grounds in Hastings Park — some of them for months — were officially described as being housed in an "assembly centre" or "clearing house." The Custodian of Enemy Property, who took custody of their properties and belongings, did so as "a protective measure only." The "ghost towns" in the B.C. interior, hastily prepared for the "evacuees," were described as "interior housing centres," "relocation centres" and "interior settlements." "But these almost reassuring descriptive terms," says Ken Adachi, "suggesting a cozy picture of a tranquil, sequestered life in the Kootenay Valley, were simply euphemisms for what many Nisei and others preferred to call 'internment' or 'concentration camps'." The Japanese Canadians who were shipped out of B.C. to sugar beet farms on the prairies — my own family were a part of this displacement — were identified as part of the government's "sugar beet projects." The men who were confined to various isolated B.C. sites were working in "road camps."

Use of the term "evacuation" implies an intention to return "evacuees" once the danger has subsided. Among the Japanese Canadians, who themselves adopted the term to explain their experience, there was the assumption that they would return once the wartime danger had subsided. After all, they were "Canadians" and not "enemies," and what better way to demonstrate their loyalty than to cooperate with the government by complying with its "evacuation" policy? For the government's policy makers, its bureaucrats and politicians, however, the question of return never arose. As far as can be determined, no statements or reports seriously considered this scenario. Rather, the documentary evidence points to the fact that the removal was not an "evacuation" in the conventional meaning of the term: there would be no return.

In Joy Kogawa's *Obasan*, Aunt Emily is aware of the double-edged connotations of "evacuation" for the Japanese Canadians expelled from the B.C. coast and confined in the B.C. interior internment camps:

> "It was an evacuation all right," Aunt Emily said. "Just plopped here in the wilderness. Flushed out of Vancouver. Like dung drops. Maggot bait."
>
> None of us, she said, escaped the naming. We were defined and identified by the way we were seen. A newspaper in B.C. headlined, "They are a stench in the nostrils of the people of Canada." We were therefore

relegated to the cesspools. In Sandon, Tashme, Kaslo, Greenwood, Slocan, Bayfarm, Popoff, Lemon Creek, New Denver, we lived in tents, in bunks, in skating rinks, in abandoned hotels. Most of us lived in row upon row of two-family, three-room huts, controlled and orderly as wooden blocks. There was a tidy mind somewhere.

That "tidy mind" worked on behalf of the federal government, producing a lexicon of euphemisms that would effectively hide the social violence experienced by Japanese Canadians at the hands of their own government. Take, for instance, the report submitted by the B.C. Security Commission to Labour Minister Humphrey Mitchell, covering the period from March 4 to October 31, 1942. In a virtual handbook of euphemistic lingo, the report frames Japanese Canadians as the "victims of the cruel action of their [Japanese] race." Their mass uprooting, dispossession and confinement become the "Removal of Japanese from Protected Areas" (the title of the report).

This benign "removal" is then narrated, in an outrageous fantasy, as one of the "colourful pages" of Canadian history. As a "protective measure" and in the "interests of self-preservation, to take the essential precaution against attack from within," this group was being "evacuated" from the coast. The "Japanese" identified in the report become benefactors of the progressive development of Canadian history, as part of a "mass migration ... unique in the annals of this country." Since the desire of these people to live in groups has led to their inassimilability, the report argues that the "Japanese problem in Canada" can be resolved by "relocation in self-supporting family units" — the displacement of the west coast communities. The report concludes:

> It may be said that the foregoing summary of this first episode of the saga of an industrious people lifted from the fields of activity to which they had been accustomed, and placed in comparative idleness in interior towns, depicts no permanent static condition, but is believed to be only the frontispiece to the still unfolding story of the final relocation and rehabilitation of the whole Japanese-Canadian population.

"Final relocation" meant permanent exile from the coast, and "rehabilitation," a term usually reserved for social deviants and criminals, would occur through gradual but irreversible assimilation. Beneath the simplistic appro-priation of narrative forms to repress knowledge of the abuse of Japanese Canadians by racialization lay the broader agenda, a plan to dismantle the geographical, social and cultural spaces they had created and occupied over the previous 50 years. The "Japanese problem," the "cause" that prompted Mackenzie King's statement to the House of Commons in August 1944, had become the focus of the mass uprooting. The threat to "national security" posed by Japanese Canadians was no longer on the agenda.

It is revealing how few references there are in government reports to the security threats posed by Japanese Canadians. Those described as resistant to removal are said to reflect the "unamenable disposition of mind of the Canadian born Japanese" who protested the "separation of families and the alleged discrimination against the Japanese as compared with the treat-ment of persons of other enemy races." That German Canadians and Italian Canadians were not being uprooted and dispossessed is not mentioned. The means for a cover-up was available in that all-purpose and malleable word "race," which could be inserted wherever required to justify dispersal and assimilation.

But some Japanese Canadians resisted the process of racialization. They challenged the hypocrisy of the B.C. Security Commission, which on the one hand claimed to treat everyone equally but then, on the other, manipu-lated the power struggles within the community to the Commission's own advantage. Japanese Canadian informants, for instance, were used to finger "troublemakers," who were targeted for quick removal by the RCMP. In Hastings Park, where thousands were confined in barbaric living conditions, the Commission administered affairs through the Japanese Liaison Committee, a group chaired by Morii. Many Japanese Canadians considered him an untrustworthy person who protected only his followers. Indeed, one of the ways to avoid immediate removal from the "protected zone" was to become a member of Morii's committee. Documents in the B.C. Security Commission archives list varying numbers of members, in one case 112 people, all of whom would have received the Commission's authorization to remain in the protected zone and to have some freedom of mobility in the Vancouver area, even during curfew hours. This favouritism allowed many Japanese nationals on Morii's committee to have greater liberties than did the Canadian-born, a situation that angered to no end the Japanese Canadians who believed their citizenship should have protected them from race categorization.

Morii himself struck a deal with the B.C. Security Commission to take his group, or those associated with him, to "self-supporting" sites where they were left alone to take care of themselves. The term is yet another euphemism. Although the Commission maintained that the policy was based on economic resources, the vast majority of Japanese Canadians were not given the same choice. Then again, the policy of the forced sale of assets so that those interned would pay for their own internment, in fact, meant that all Japanese Canadians were forced into a policy of "self-support."

It was, however, the breakup of families that intensified the perception of preferential treatment by the Commission. For example, those targeted for immediate removal to Schreiber, Ontario, were young nisei men who wanted to stay with their families and aging parents. The government had earlier stated that only Japanese male nationals would be sent to road camps. Why, then, were Canadian-born men being treated as "enemy aliens," many of them placed on trains, while a substantial number of Japanese nationals still remained in Vancouver? Resentment about the breakup of families quickly mushroomed into a resistance group consisting mainly of young nisei men. They called themselves the Nisei Mass Evacuation Group, and their story reveals the extent to which the government would go to preserve the illusion that their "evacuation" was not a gross violation of citizenship rights.

CHAPTER 3

IN DEFENCE OF RIGHTS

The Nisei Mass Evacuation Group

*If Canada is supposed to be such a shining model of "western democracy,"
how can the government justify what it is doing to my community?*
— Robert K. Okazaki

A GROUP OF "RESISTERS" AND "DISRUPTORS"

ONE OF THE LESSER-KNOWN elements of the 1988 redress agreement was the provision to grant pardons to those wrongfully convicted under the War Measures Act. There were cases of Japanese Canadians who had been convicted of entering the 100-mile "protected zone." The most dramatic example was the imprisonment, for one year, of Akihide Otsuji. Even at the time of his arrest, it was clear that Otsuji had no intention of undermining the security of Canada. Frank Scott, a *Vancouver Sun* reporter who covered the trial, noted that "the evidence against him was simply that he was a person of the Japanese race." A number of others may have been arrested for breaking the dusk-to-dawn curfew imposed from February 28 onward.

"On the first night in Vancouver," Ken Adachi writes, "12 offenders — including two milkmen out on their rounds — were caught by police and later given suspended sentences and warnings. Two days later, 66-year-old Sotaro Seki was arrested a block away from his Powell St. home and sentenced to six months in jail with hard labour."

What, then, of the hundreds of young nisei who were confined, many for the duration of the war, in prisoner-of-war camps at Petawawa and Angler, Ontario? The Geneva Convention had expressly forbidden governments to intern their own citizens. Those who broke laws during wartime should be charged with crimes and placed on trial. In other words, citizens should be protected by the legal system from military incarceration. A Japanese Canadian apprehended by the RCMP, placed in the Immigration Building, and then held in a barbed wire enclosed prisoner-of-war camp run by the Canadian military would not be unreasonable in thinking that he (only males were incarcerated in such a manner) had committed some crime against the state. Otherwise, on what authority was he being held?

Harry Yonekura, a young nisei in the 1940s, applied to the Japanese Canadian Secretariat, the office established to handle redress claims, to have his criminal records expunged. For years he had been haunted by the existence of records listing him as a former "criminal," fearing that this information might surface to harm his reputation and that of his children. He was taken aback to learn that after a search of its archives, the government had no record of any convictions. Yonekura had spent over a year in Angler as a prisoner of war, but there were no records, because the government had, intentionally, not charged him with any crime. Had it done so, Yonekura would have been placed on trial and likely released, as would most of the group with which he identified at the time: the Nisei Mass Evacuation Group (NMEG).

The NMEG consisted mainly of Canadian citizens who protested the federal government's policy of breaking up the family unit — hardly grounds for being charged with a crime against the state. In an ironic twist, the government, aware of the power of democratic dissent, countered the challenges posed by the NMEG by circumventing its own system: "detaining" NMEG members like Harry Yonekura "at the pleasure of the Justice Minister" — that is, indefinitely — and incarcerating them without laying charges.

Yonekura could have invoked the right of habeas corpus as protection against unlawful detention, but he was not aware of this right. No legal counsel was provided to him, and the officials who placed him in an internment camp did not inform him of the right to counsel.

The redress settlement allowed many in the NMEG to reconcile themselves to an aspect of the past — their specific experiences — that had been misunderstood not only in historical accounts of internment, but even in the memory of Japanese Canadians. Portrayed by government authorities as militant "resisters" (the "gambari" — or resistance — group)[1] who, it was feared, threatened peaceful relocation, they also came to be perceived by many in their own community as "disruptors," and for this they were criticized and shunned. But it is in the manner in which they were restrained and contained that the government's violation of democratic values becomes most transparent. Even if adequate compensation were given Japanese Canadians immediately after internment, a movement could have been formed to demand redress for the Nisei Mass Evacuation Group alone. How had this group earned so much attention?

ON MAY 14, 1942, the *Vancouver Sun* reported on the disturbance that had erupted the day before at the Immigration Building. The readers, most of them white, who opened the newspaper to the article "Jap Riot" were given this account:

> Japanese began their disturbance about noon. They clamored and gestured at the windows, while about 40 of their compatriots, mostly women, watched from a little distance on the CPR ramp and railway embankment at the foot of Burrard Street.
>
> Shouting grew louder, and the incarcerated Japs set out to take their quarters apart. Top-storey windows were smashed, the glass tinkling into the street. One group wrenched an iron window grating free and hurled it to the pavement.

---

1   The term is used to describe the "mass evacuation" group in the minutes of the Japanese Canadian Citizens' Council report on the Steveston meeting.

While armed guards were rushed to the scene, the Japs smashed furniture, knocked plaster from the walls, floated tissue streamers from the broken windows.

They rushed a fire hose to one window, and turned the jet on the nearest guard and on others when they moved in.

Shouts of "Banzai!" flew between the rioters and the Nipponese audience outside.

Before the riot was quelled with the aid of reinforcements, bed springs and several more window gratings had crashed to the street.

Damage to buildings and contents was considerable, but Immigration officials declined to comment, pointing out that they "merely supply a roof" for the Japanese concerned until they are moved to interior camps.

City police stood by. Since the building is Federal property, they took no part in the disturbance. They did keep a growing crowd of white spectators well back, however. CPR police joined soldiers with fixed bayonets in patrolling all approaches to the building.

"There was nothing malicious about the trouble," said Austin Taylor, commission chairman. "It was more playful than anything else."

"Some of the Japanese just got a little fed up about being kept in the building, and got a little exuberant. There was more yelling than anything else."

In Ottawa, Minister of Labour Humphrey Mitchell assured MPs in the House of Commons that the "Japanese" troublemakers would be "interned" immediately. The *Vancouver Sun*, in turn, explained that those confined in the Immigration Building were men who "failed to report to B.C. Security Commission, and were ordered 'picked up.'" Once they were in that building — federal space — they became the responsibility of the federal government, not the B.C. Security Commission (BCSC), the RCMP or the army. None of the reporters at the three Vancouver dailies who covered the May 14 event — which they dubbed a "riot" — exhibited any investigative curiosity or desire to probe beneath the surface of the disturbance and Taylor's facile explanation. Who, for instance, ordered the men "picked up"? What did "fail to report" mean? Who were these men? What were their motives? The assumption was that the "Japanese" involved were a threat to Canadian security — otherwise why would they be interned? — and that they were the enemy (for which "Japs" served as the shorthand).

The *Vancouver Sun* coverage that did not question the "internment" of Canadian citizens who had not committed a crime was complemented by the editorial "Japs Are Poor Sportsmen, Indeed!" It began:

> Our people have been disposed to overlook small irritations in connection with the Japanese community; little attention has been paid to hunger strikes and similar exhibitions of temporary bad temper. But the incident at the immigration shed yesterday was of much larger calibre and naturally arouses widespread disgust and resentment.
>
> There is no excuse whatever for the wanton rioting staged by many scores of Japanese detained there. The public will rightly conclude that the outbreak was a manifestation of Nazi ideals which these people have absorbed and now have adopted as their own.

The editorial goes on say how lenient the authorities have been and how "the vast majority of Japanese have accepted with reasonably good grace the excellent arrangements made for their removal from coastal areas." But the blame is placed on the Canadian-born nisei who "hotly declined to accept the very generous terms of the government and there was nothing left but to consign them to internment as suspect aliens." The editorial warns Japanese Canadians that their unwillingness to cooperate will mean that they will be sent to Japan after the war, and concludes by invoking the "Yellow Peril": "B.C. has been more than patient tolerating them for nearly half a century with their insolent boring-in and aggressive methods. We certainly won't have them back on any terms at all."

The Japanese Canadians who read this editorial might have pondered the meaning of the italicized line above the editorial, describing the *Vancouver Sun* as *"A newspaper devoted to progress and democracy, tolerance and freedom of human thought."* No longer "Canadian" but now strictly "Japs," they were enmeshed in public and political stereotypes that stripped them of the "freedom of human thought" so valued by the *Vancouver Sun*. Those able to recognize the racism in their portrayal as the "enemy" would have been caught in a complicated bind: cooperation signified loyalty to Canada but also complicity with their identity as "enemy alien"; resistance signified the right — and the responsibility — of citizens to protest the abuse of democratic principles but also confirmed the public perception of their allegiance to Japan.

One nisei inside the Immigration Building on May 14, Robert Katsumasa Okazaki, has written about his experience in *The Nisei Mass Evacuation Group and P.O.W. Camp 101*, a book based on a diary he kept at the time. In a preface, Okazaki refers to the wartime uprooting policy as an action "carried out to satisfy the discriminatory needs of the ruling white majority." The intent of his book is "to show the present and future generations the first-hand truth of what happened during those terrible years, such that they will never, never forget."[2]

In his book, Okazaki lists the names of the 14 persons — 13 nisei, including himself, and one kika-jin (a nisei educated in Japan) — who met at the Hayashi Rooming House in Vancouver on March 23, 1942, to form the "Mass Evacuation Movement." Only shortly before that, the NJCA and the Japanese Canadian Citizens' Council (JCCC), a largely nisei group, had hastily constituted themselves to gain some official standing with the newly established B.C. Security Commission. Another nisei, Yukio (Bob) Shimoda, attended the first meeting and later became, with Fujikazu Tanaka, a vocal member of what became the Nisei Mass Evacuation Group.

What the *Vancouver Sun* story about the Immigration Building disturbance left unsaid, and what the Okazaki narrative clarifies, is that most of the men in confinement were part of the "mass evacuation movement." They were Canadian-born citizens who considered the breakup of families unnecessary and punitive, and who interpreted this policy as proof that the

---

2   Okazaki presents clear evidence that the vast majority of those who were incarcerated in prisoner-of-war camps at Petawawa and Angler, Ontario, as members of the Nisei Mass Evacuation Group thought of their resistance work in terms of justice and human rights. His reclamation of the subjective perspective of Japanese Canadians was one of the legacies of the redress movement and the settlement reached by the NAJC with the federal government on September 22, 1988. The new social and community spaces that opened for diaries, journals, documents and oral histories by those whose subjectivities had been contained and suppressed brought out the extent of the misrepresentations, which had tragic consequences for all Japanese Canadians and even more intensely for a group of men — Canadian citizens — who were "interned" in prisoner-of-war conditions for exposing the racialized mindset of their own government's authority.

uprooting was not primarily a security measure but more a retaliatory action against a group falsely identified as "enemy aliens."

By March 23, uprooted Japanese Canadians were pouring into Vancouver from Vancouver Island and the Gulf Islands, and from up the coast as far north as Prince Rupert. Often given as little as 24 hours to vacate their homes, they were uncertain of their future, fearful of the defensiveness stirred up in white people by the local newspapers and no longer confident that the government would honour their citizenship rights. Now, as well, they had to face the grim prospect of families being torn apart by B.C. Security Commission policy. What would be gained by such a policy? If the men were shunted away to remote road camps, what would happen to the women and children? The anxiety generated by such questions came to a point of crisis when notices were issued to young nisei men to report for immediate departure, by train from B.C. to destinations as far away as Schreiber, Ontario.

Meanwhile, many Japanese nationals, especially those connected to the Japanese Liaison Committee and Etsuji Morii, remained in Vancouver. And in what many Japanese Canadians perceived to be the height of hypocrisy on the part of the government, they were even given authority to "police" those confined in Hastings Park. Morii was not only perceived by many nisei to be acting in complicity with the RCMP to secure privileges for those issei who supported him, he was also suspected of accepting bribes for doing so. An internal memo of the B.C. Security Commission stated: "It is ... alleged that he [Morii] is accepting money and promising that he can use influence to secure a deferment of evacuation."

The final days of March were rife with dissension, anger and makeshift strategies in reaction to the massive internal divisions that had erupted over issues of compliance, negotiation and resistance. Events unfolded at a furious pace.

On March 25, 86 men ordered by the BCSC to report to the CPR station for removal to Schreiber disobeyed. The minutes of the Japanese Canadian Citizens' Council for March 26 noted that the meeting "for this morning was not held in a formal manner" because of this first overt resistance. The men had "stayed at the Tairiku Hall [owned by the Japanese-language *Tairiku* newspaper] for the night. Around 10 a.m. the RCMP officers came to round up these men. 17 other men had been picked up during the night. All these men were detained at the Immigration Building." The following day Austin Taylor, head of the BCSC, resorted to Order No. 5 in PC 1665, which authorized the RCMP to "detain" those who did not comply with BCSC policy and stated:

> That any person of the Japanese race who fails to obey any order of the British Columbia Security Commission directing any such person to proceed to any place within or without the protected area, shall be detained until further order of the British Columbia Security Commission.

That same day, S. T. Wood, commissioner of the RCMP, wrote to Louis St. Laurent, the minister of justice, informing him that "eighty-five were arrested yesterday and confined in the Immigration Shed. They were given until 5 o'clock last evening to divulge the names of the instigators of this action, and at that hour refused to do so." Wood asked what he could do and was assured that the BCSC had the authority to "detain" those who disobeyed its orders. The BCSC's strategy, however, was to avoid "prosecutions and mass appearance in court [which] would give a bad impression to the public, and further complicate the efforts of the Commission in evacuating the Nisei (British subjects) from the protected area."

On March 29, the JCCC took a position of compliance with the BCSC, issuing a resolution calling on the 103 men already in the Immigration Building to leave Vancouver as ordered — "to go to-night." That same day, the JCCC and the NJCA collaborated on a letter to the BCSC stating that Morii did not represent the community, thereby undermining Morii's credibility. Then, on April 1, in response to the anger created by the policy of breaking up families, the NJCA presented to the BCSC a detailed plan for "mass evacuation" of family units to Crown land. When Taylor rejected the NJCA's request, in what would be its last attempt to negotiate with the BCSC, the NJCA said that the men would go to road camps as ordered once their families had been resettled in the B.C. interior towns. Once again Taylor said no.

It was this matrix of intense instability that caused the "mass evacuation movement" that had formed on March 25 to turn rapidly into the Nisei Mass Evacuation Group. Hundreds of young nisei outside the more urban-centred leadership of the JCCC began meeting to organize a resistance movement. Before being sent to Vancouver, Robert Okazaki had lived in a pulp and paper town, Port Alice, on northern Vancouver Island. On March 11 he noted in his diary:

> Out from the next boat load of Port Alice evacuees came more tragic stories of families torn apart by the evacuation. Husbands and sons taken away. Wives and children left behind with no means of support or income. I wondered how will they manage on their own? I realize that I may be sent to a road camp any day now, and my Canadian citizenship is powerless to stop this. My hopelessness and despair are becoming a greater reality with each passing day, and I've begun to question our government's atrocious orders.

Okazaki and other nisei were aware that the U.S. government was removing Japanese Americans on the west coast in family groups. "I am envious of the U.S.," he wrote, "for keeping the families together during the evacuation."

Another young nisei, Harry Yonekura, complied with the confiscation of boats and equipment by the Royal Canadian Navy, but was disturbed by the cruelty of breaking up families. Etched in his memory was a scene that prompted him to tear up his extension pass, join the NMEG and accept internment as a form of protest against the BCSC's policy. Yonekura recalled the moment in vivid detail five decades later:

> An issei woman, whose husband had just entered the train, was down on her hands and knees begging an RCMP officer to take her with her husband. With an infant on her back and a tearful three-year-old by her side, she wept at the feet of this stone-faced officer. The tears were coursing down her cheeks. She was not asking that her husband be allowed to stay. She merely wanted to accompany him to wherever he was being taken so the family would not be split apart. Seeing this public outpouring of raw emotion, I became convinced that something was terribly wrong. How could our community leaders continue to preach conformity to government orders when faced with such inhumane treatment?

After witnessing the crying women, he recalled, "I knew that I could never again blindly accept what I perceived as undemocratic and racially motivated policies."

On Saturday, March 28, Yukio (Bob) Shimoda, soon to emerge as a leading voice for the NMEG, travelled to Vancouver from his home in Port Moody. He noted in his diary that "140 west coast boys were ready to leave for Ontario," and that he "found the town to be in resentment" because of the breakup of families. Soon caught up in the emotional turmoil, Shimoda was drawn into the controversy and wanted to contribute to some form of direct action. He returned to Port Moody with his brother-in-law Tameo Kanbara, and the two of them "worked all night on pamphlet idea of Tameo to be distributed tomorrow." Thirty years later, Kanbara recalled that action, through which, according to his account, the Nisei Mass Evacuation Group was inaugurated. He recalled Shimoda's visits to Vancouver in March 1942 when he witnessed the "state of anxious Japanese families, the repeated sad scenes of family separation when men were leaving for a road camp." While accompanying Shimoda to Vancouver, Kanbara was struck by the idea of organizing Japanese Canadians "by distributing an appeal brochure."

> Shimoda kept quiet for a while, then responded, "Then we may soon be arrested."
>
> I said, "It is very likely."
>
> Again, after a while, he said, "I have parents and younger brothers and sisters ..." Then he said resolutely, "I want to do something, after I saw the sad separation of families, Tameo, let's do it together."

Shimoda wrote the English text and Kanbara translated it into Japanese. The next day they approached Ryukichi Miyaka at the NJCA headquarters, which had been set up in the office of the *Tairiku* newspaper, and asked to use the mimeograph machine. Miyaka supported the contents of the pamphlet, but he cautioned against nisei publishing in Japanese. This would imply an association with Japan that would undermine their Canadian status. Shimoda and Kanbara agreed. The pamphlet, more specifically an "open letter" addressed "To the Niseis," published in English and dated March 29, 1942, was distributed in the Main and Powell streets area of Vancouver in "Little Tokyo" (or, in Japanese, "Nihonmachi"). It was accompanied by a petition addressed to the JCCC urging it to present Austin Taylor with the following resolution: "That we should be evacuated in family groups, providing us with transportation, a decent place of abode, (or materials to build homes), and means of a fair living, (employment or farming), and a written statement promising the same."

The open letter clearly articulated the contradiction in the treatment of Japanese Canadians. If "we" are Canadians, the writers reasoned, then why are we subjected to restrictions and the confiscation of personal belongings (properties at this time were thought to be protected by the Custodian of Enemy Property), and "boycotted, jailed, interned, and also forced to register and thumb-printed. We are being denied every right and freedom of a so-called democracy like any Enemy Alien." And if "we" are deemed "aliens," the government should "intern us." If the BCSC cannot decide one way or the other, then Japanese Canadians should be removed in family units to suitable places and be ensured of adequate employment to support themselves. The letter also asked, "Why are not Canadian-born Germans and Italians treated likewise?" Such double standards showed that "Canada is making a war of race out of her so proudly upheld war of ideals."

On April 7, only days after the BCSC rejected the proposal for the mass removal of family units to Crown lands, both the NJCA and the JCCC appeared before the large meeting mentioned above and confessed their belief that no negotiations were possible with the BCSC. With regret, they advocated full cooperation with whatever orders the BCSC issued. This air of resignation and defeat caused an immediate rift in the JCCC between the core group and the nisei who called for continued resistance until the BCSC should agree to abandon its policy of splitting up families. The putative leaders of the NMEG group, Robert Shimoda and Fujikazu Tanaka, were forced to resign from the JCCC. The nisei, now divided, were pitted against each other.

In the days following this critical community meeting, the NMEG sought to mobilize its power through a more aggressive language of resistance. This change was evident in what was the NMEG's most forceful statement to Taylor, dated April 15, in which it challenged the BCSC to honour democratic rights. Appended to the statement was a chronology of the attempts by various Japanese Canadian representatives to negotiate removal in family units. The language of appeal and supplication was replaced by a harder-edged language that protested the "raced" condition of Japanese Canadians and reclaimed "citizen" as their identity. The first four paragraphs present the case explicitly and without equivocation:

Honourable Sir:

We Canadians have reached a point where we must stop and think deeply regarding our evacuation. For that purpose we have carefully reviewed the development of events which has brought us to this point where we are ordered to part with our families, perhaps never to meet them again for a long time to come ...

As you clearly understand and as it is fully mentioned in our review, we have said "YES" to all your previous orders however unreasonable they might have seemed. But, we are firm in saying "NO" to your last order which calls for break-up of our families.

When we say "NO" at this point, we request you to remember that we are British subjects by birth, that we are no less loyal to Canada than any other Canadian, that we have done nothing to deserve the break-up of our families, that we are law abiding Canadian citizens, and that we are willing to accept suspension of our civil rights — rights to retain our homes and businesses, boats, cars, radios and cameras. Incidentally, we are entitled as native sons to all civil rights of an ordinary Canadian within the limitations of Canada's war effort. In spite of that we have given up everything. In view of this sacrifice we feel that our request for mass evacuation in family groups will not seem unreasonable to you.

Please also remember that we are not refusing to go. Indeed if it is for our country's sake, we shall evacuate to whatever place Canada commands. Yes, it was in that spirit that we obeyed all your previous orders.

The letter ended with a statement of "confidence that British fair play and justice, even in war-time, will manifest itself and grant us our most human and reasonable request."

The articulation of the question of rights — the crux of the government's violation of democratic principles — and the ironic evocation of "British fair play and justice," which the nisei had absorbed through their education in Canadian public schools, did not sway the BCSC. Shimoda wrote in his diary on April 15 that some members of the NMEG had met with Taylor and BCSC Assistant Commissioner (and RCMP officer) F. J. Mead at 2:30 p.m. that day and their request had been rejected. He had the impression that Taylor was "cold hearted doing job & no intention of taking any workable plan," and that Mead could not "be trusted." The two of them, according to Shimoda, "Tried again to scare us into submission by threats & so forth."

The very same day, as recorded in the minutes of the JCCC meeting, Tom Shoyama, editor of the *New Canadian,*

> reported that Commissioner Mead had told him yesterday that the Commission would like to use the *New Canadian* as the official publication of the Commission ... Mead's plan was to have an official spokesman from the Commission edit the news about the Commission's work. There will be a certain amount of independence, according to Shoyama, and the paper can do a certain amount of criticism, if necessary. The Commission is ready to publish its own sheet, if this offer is declined ... The Commission itself, said Mr. Shoyama, did not wish to make public the official connection of itself and the paper. He stated that there would be no outward difference in the appearance of the paper, and thus there will be no danger of the Japanese public assuming a suspicious attitude towards the paper.

In return, the BCSC would pay the publication costs. The offer was approved, with further consultation to be done with the NJCA the following day; the minutes of April 16 confirmed the approval of the NJCA. The power to censor, acknowledged by Shoyama in the minutes of April 16, in effect meant that any criticism of the government's policy could not be published in the only newspaper for Japanese Canadians (all others had been shut down). Kunio Shimizu, who worked with Shoyama on the JCCC, was unsuccessful in getting the NMEG letter published in the Vancouver daily newspapers.

With all avenues of negotiation blocked, and with no access to public media, the NMEG reacted by intensifying its appeal for support from nisei residing in outlying areas. Meanwhile, many nisei continued to defy the BCSC by refusing to turn up at the station for incarceration in road camps. Then, on April 25, the day after 103 men were sent to an internment camp, the campaign for "mass evacuation" switched tactics dramatically. On that day, 66 nisei from Steveston and Vancouver voluntarily gave themselves up for internment, thus setting the tone for more outright defiance by the so-called "gambaru" (translated as "to resist") movement, as the NMEG was identified in the Japanese Canadian community.

SUPPRESSION OF THE NISEI MASS EVACUATION GROUP

DOCUMENTS RELATED TO the government's suppression of nisei resistance — ultimately leading to internment in camps at Petawawa and Angler — show the extremes to which authorities went to sidestep the claims of the NMEG. Breaking up families was both unnecessary and inefficient, even from the BCSC's own perspective. The segregation of able-bodied men from their families meant the loss of the labour needed to build housing in the B.C. interior camps where the women, children and the elderly were to be sent. Indeed, by June, the BCSC realized the extent to which its own policy was slowing down the removal process and reversed direction to plan a family "reunification" policy. The policy was instituted on July 1. By then, hundreds of nisei had been shipped to camps, removed from public view and separated from their families. Of an estimated 766 men of Japanese background who were interned at Petawawa and Angler, 232 were classified as Japanese nationals, 63 were naturalized Canadians, 4 were American-born, and 467 were Canadian-born or nisei. The vast majority of this last group, nearly two-thirds of the nisei, were interned because of their association with the NMEG. How, then, was the government able to contravene the Geneva Convention edict that nations not "intern" their own citizens?

Few Canadians were aware that prisoner-of-war camps existed in their own backyard, and even fewer knew that many of the men interned in those camps were citizens who had done nothing more than protest the violation of their civil rights. The power of language can be awesome in its ability to disguise identities. Most of those who heard of Japanese Canadians being interned in the camps — including many Japanese Canadians themselves — believed that these internees were either "Japanese" enemies of the state or, if not legally "Japanese" because they were Canadian-born, loyal to Japan.

This perception was largely the product of government communications in which the NMEG's opposition to the breakup of families was labelled as disobedience, disloyalty and rebellion. To achieve this make-over from "citizen" to "enemy" dissident, all levels of the government, from the BCSC through the RCMP to the Department of Justice, had to manipulate and sometimes violate their own rules. They had one specific goal in mind: to prevent any group of Japanese Canadians from defending their status as "citizens" in any legal forum. For the federal government to achieve this goal, Japanese Canadians had to be denied the most fundamental legal right, the right of habeas corpus.

There is little doubt, at least from the perspective of RCMP documents and the BCSC's reactions, that the NMEG posed a major challenge to the government's own plans — though why Austin Taylor, the head of BCSC, did not push for removal in family units remains unclear, especially since he was not aware of a policy to the contrary.

Taylor's idea of using Crown lands to move groups en masse matched the proposal offered to him by the NJCA. Why had he flatly rejected this proposal? It may have been the influence of MP Ian Mackenzie, a powerful voice in Mackenzie King's cabinet supporting the mass uprooting of all Japanese Canadians. Mackenzie wanted men moved quickly to appease public resentment toward Japanese Canadians. In a telegram to Taylor, dated March 5, he called for the cessation of "individual movement of Japanese from [the] coast" and the immediate rounding up of "male Japanese of adult years" for shipment away to "work camps farm colonies or whatever type of enterprise decided upon." Perhaps Taylor had bowed to this pressure in formulating the BCSC's policy of family breakup. Whatever the reason, he soon discovered that his decision complicated his relationship with Japanese Canadians. In "interning" the nisei who rose up against his policy, he had to address some slippery problems of jurisdiction and terminology. In *The Politics of Racism* Ann Sunahara explains the situation Taylor had to confront:

> Legally, of course, the Nisei could not be interned. They were Canadian citizens and internment under the Geneva Convention is a legal act applicable only to aliens, a fact Assistant Commissioner Mead quickly pointed out to Ottawa. Accordingly, the Nisei were legally never interned, but "detained at the pleasure of the Minister of Justice," Louis St. Laurent. Their legal status was equivalent to that of a criminal under psychiatric care. None of them, however, were aware of their unusual legal status. Nor were any aware that legally they had thirty days in which to appeal their detention. Isolated, friendless, angry and without legal counsel, the detained Nisei indeed considered their detention "internment" — as did the government, the press and the public of B.C.

Revealingly, the BCSC's inflexibility was not supported by all of the authorities behind the scenes. On May 1, 1942, nearly two weeks before the disturbance in the Immigration Building, S. T. Wood, the commissioner of the RCMP, wrote to H. L. Keenleyside of the Department of External Affairs, calling attention to a report from B.C. that described the nisei opposition "to the breaking up of families." Referring to the U.S. policy of keeping Japanese American families together, Wood said "our policy of evacuating the males to work camps, and thus breaking up the family, is a mistake, and will lead to increasing unrest, if not trouble, in the camps already established."

By then, trouble had been brewing on the streets of Vancouver for at least two months. Back on March 25, the 86 men who disobeyed the BCSC's order to board the train to Schreiber had already prompted Taylor to devise methods of control and retaliation. In his report to Louis St. Laurent, the minister of justice, S. T. Wood described the men as all "British subjects, of Japanese racial origin." He conveyed the view of the BCSC that "prosecutions and mass appearance in court would give a bad impression to the public." To avoid this, he raised the possibility of confinement in an internment camp, "as such action would probably have a beneficial effect on the remaining Japanese males, and it is considered that this action is necessary immediately, before any further evacuation could be ordered." That same day, A. MacNamara, the associate deputy minister of labour, wrote to Taylor that "Section 11 Order in Council P.C. 1665 [the Order-in-Council establishing the BCSC] gives the Commission power to order the detention of any person of the Japanese race and says 'any such order may be enforced by any person nominated by the Commission to do so.'" On that same day, Taylor put into effect "Order Number 5," a section of PC 1665, which stipulated that anyone who disobeyed the BCSC would be detained by the RCMP.

As space was being prepared at the internment camp at Petawawa, the JCCC issued a statement urging the 103 men — who had been confined in the Immigration Building only two days after Order Number 5 — to leave the coast, as demanded by the BCSC. By April 24, when Petawawa was prepared, the 103 had embarked on the long journey by train across Canada. They arrived at the prisoner-of-war camp on April 28.

Behind the scenes, government officials were busy devising terminology to justify the term "internment." On April 14, C. H. Locke, a legal advisor to the BCSC, wrote to A. M. Harper, a lawyer for the BCSC, about the problem with the word. Some officials had apparently determined that use of the term would place the government in an awkward situation. The BCSC had the power "to detain them [in reference to those who called for removal in family groups] so long as it considers necessary" but there was a warning

against the setting up of an advisory committee of the nature referred to in section 22 of the "Defense of Canada Regulations". The British Columbia Security Commission have a large job to carry out in a hurry and I do not think it should be bothered with appeal boards of any kind. We cannot of course prevent any person who thinks he is aggrieved by a detention order from applying for Habeas Corpus: I think however it is improbable that any Japanese will be so ill advised as to make such an application.

Section 22 of the Defence of Canada Regulations laid out the terms of "internment," and since those affected would supposedly be enemy nationals, an appeal process through an advisory committee was required. Had the "internment" of Canadian citizens been contested in an appeal process, the members of the NMEG would have been set free immediately. This outcome, of course, is precisely what the BCSC wanted to prevent.

Not surprisingly, the distinction between "intern" and "detain" underwent further refinement. On April 24 A. M. Harper wrote a memo to RCMP Commissioner Mead, asking Mead whether the Japanese Canadians confined under Section 11 of PC 1665 were "detained" or "interned." The latter appeared to be the case; after all, they had been sent to an internment camp. "If they are interned under the Defence of Canada Regulations," Harper told Mead — and they could not have been interned otherwise — "they *undoubtedly have the right* to submit a Notice of Objection, and under Section 22 of the Defence of Canada Regulations are entitled to a hearing before an Advisory Committee set up under those Regulations." Were this procedure to be carried out, "all this Commission could show regarding these particular Japanese [*sic*] is that they got a verbal order along with a ticket to report at a certain time for evacuation and that they failed to report. I doubt if any Advisory Committee would sustain their detention on such evidence."

On the other hand, the clever-minded Harper advised, if they were "detained under the Military Authorities at an Internment Camp, or otherwise," they would remain "under the jurisdiction of this Commission and the Commission can at any time order their release." In this simple administrative manoeuvre, the nisei in the NMEG could be whisked away to an internment camp by the civilian authority of the BCSC and held there by the military authorities. They were "citizens" on departure and "enemy aliens" on arrival. By the manipulation of regulations supposedly established to protect the innocent, hundreds of NMEG members were imprisoned. They languished in prisoner-of-war conditions, many for the duration of the war, while the government authorities escaped accountability.

CAUGHT IN A TRAP

BY THE END OF April 1942, more than 100 nisei had been interned under the authority of the Defence of Canada Regulations without being given an opportunity to appeal through an advisory board. The wording for an appeal form is contained in a letter dated April 22, to the commanding officer of the RCMP in Vancouver, from D. C. Saul, representing the registrar general of enemy aliens. In a letter headed "Internment of Canadian born and Naturalized Canadians of Japanese Racial Origin," Saul wrote:

> Under Regulation 22, these persons are entitled to make objection to their detention within thirty days. The Official in charge of the Immigration Detention Sheds Receiving Station should, therefore, be advised that each detenu should be given an opportunity to submit notice of Objection.

Then he provided the wording for a form to be used, a duplicate of which should be forwarded to the Minister of Justice:

> To the Minister of Justice
> and to The British Columbia
> Security Commission,
>
> I, _____
> now detained at _____
> having been apprehended on the _____
> day of _____ 19___ , under regulation

twenty-one of the Defence of Canada Regulations do hereby
give notice that I object to the Order of the Minister of Justice
ordering my detention and desire to make an objection in
accordance with the provisions of regulation twenty-two of the
said Regulations.

———————————————

Signature of Objector

Perhaps following through on Mead's request, S. T. Wood, registrar general
of enemy aliens, wrote to the commanding officer of the RCMP in Vancouver
on April 30, 1942. He responded to a list of men to be interned, stating that it
was the BCSC's responsibility to designate which individuals were to be
detained through the authority of the BCSC and which were to be interned
under Regulation 21 of the Defence of Canada Regulations. For Wood, those
detained by the BCSC would only be "temporarily held" for a short period of
time. If they were interned, Wood said, the RCMP, "in collaboration with the
Security Commission, must be prepared to support the order before an
Advisory Committee." For the future, he also asked for a list indicating
which of the three categories an individual belonged in:

a) Detained on the Minister's Order under Regulation 21 of the
Defence of Canada Regulations (in the case of Canadian born or
naturalized); or
b) Interned by the Registrar General under Regulation 25 (8) of the
Defence of Canada Regulations (in the case of Japanese Nationals);
or
c) Detained on the order of the B.C. Security Commission under
Section 11, PC 1665.
With regard to (c) above, the Security Commission should be
impressed with the fact that this Force has not the facilities to take
care of any ordered detained except when such detention is of the
most temporary nature.

There is no correspondence confirming that such distinctions were ever
made by the RCMP who took Japanese Canadians into custody for disobeying the BCSC's regulations. More seriously, there is also no evidence that the

Japanese Canadians who were held were ever given the appeal form. It appears that the two authorities, the BCSC and Internment Operations, were unable to synchronize their operations. This interpretation is supported by a letter dated May 14, 1942 from J. Barnes (writing for C. H. Hill, Assistant Commissioner, RCMP in Vancouver) to Mead. The letter made clear that the men then confined in the Immigra-tion Building, including 80 who had asked to be interned, could not be admitted to the internment camp without an order from the minister of justice. A telegram sent to the RCMP in Ottawa, and cited by Barnes to Mead, said that the Department of National Defence (the Canadian military) would escort them, but "INTERNMENT OPERATIONS REQUIRE MINISTERS ORDER BEFORE THEY WILL ACCEPT." The RCMP in Vancouver was asked to "RUSH IMMEDIATELY BY AIR MAIL COMPLETE LIST OF THESE JAPANESE SHOWING NATIONAL STATUS SO THAT MINISTERS ORDER MAY BE OBTAINED BEFORE THEY ARRIVE." The telegram meant that the minister's order was part of the Defence of Canada Regulations, and was not tied to the BCSC's powers as defined under PC 1665. The nisei, then, in terms of the government's own language, were "interned," not "detained," as the BCSC had intended.

Had the BCSC built its own "detention" camps, it could have acted on its own powers, as set out in PC 1665. But since it was sending individuals to "internment" camps, which were under the jurisdiction of the Defence of Canada Regulations, these individuals had to be "interned" through the order of the minister of justice — despite the assumption that the BCSC, under PC 1665, could simply designate the internment authorities as the "detaining" power acting for them. The governing principle was that no one should have been placed in a prisoner-of-war camp unless he or she had been interned under the jurisdiction of the Defence of Canada Regulations.

The Canadian-born and naturalized Canadians of Japanese ancestry who wound up in Petawawa and Angler were the victims of the government's own regulatory trap. By being "interned" under the Defence of Canada Regulations, they were automatically deemed dangerous to the national security of Canada; yet the RCMP, including Commissioner Mead, knew full well they were not a security threat. Their only "crime" was disobeying the BCSC's order to leave the "protected area." Had they been able to appeal their internment, as they had the right to do under the Defence of Canada Regulations, they would have been released and consequently would have been in a much more legitimate position to negotiate with the BCSC. But it seems to be precisely this recognition that the BCSC, in what can only be construed as its own arrogance, withheld from a beleaguered group so fearful of the breakup of their families. It was the face of a power that had to be maintained, even at the cost of traumatizing innocent citizens.

Nowhere was this power more apparent than in the BCSC's actions after it had finally recognized the inappropriateness of its policy. In mid-June it suddenly started talking about establishing a policy of family reunion, as if it were helping Japanese Canadians to adjust to their uprooting. At the time of this policy switch, many nisei were still confined in the Immigration Building. According to Commissioner Mead, there was no good reason to ship them to internment camps, especially if they were willing to cooperate with the BCSC in reuniting families. The process of release could be very straightforward. The NMEG simply had to agree that it was willing to cooperate. An agreement was made, and individuals wrote letters to that effect to the BCSC. A bundle of these letters, all identical in wording, remain in the BCSC papers in the Library and Archives of Canada, one of them signed by Harry Yonekura:

July 5th, 1942
Immigration Building
Vancouver B.C.

Commissioner Mead
The B.C. Security Commission
Marine Building
Vancouver B.C.

Sir:

I, Hiroshi Yonekura, herewith agree to the terms stated by the Nisei Mass Evacuation Group, and I request my release from the Immigration Detention Building, in order that I may cooperate with the government in Mass Evacuation.

Respectfully Yours,
Hiroshi Yonekura

A. H. L. Mellor, executive assistant to the BCSC, and Commissioner Mead agreed that the nisei should be released. Why pay for their unnecessary internment? Besides, their labour was badly needed in the B.C. interior camps. This position was endorsed by Mead in a letter to A. MacNamara, the associate deputy minister of labour, and in a letter to Austin Taylor dated August 1, 1942:

> I feel that it is useless to keep these people locked up if they are willing to abide by any orders issued by the Commission governing their conduct in future. It costs approximately $500.00 per man per annum to keep each individual interned, and if they are willing to go to work and cause us no more trouble, then it is in our interest to help them get a job. If, on the other hand, they refuse to accept our terms, then we cannot be accused of keeping men locked up who have committed no offense against the state.

This recommendation was categorically rejected by the third member of the BCSC, Commissioner J. Shirras, who was then backed by Taylor and an advisor, W. A. Eastwood. Their reasoning had nothing to do with national security, nothing to do with expediency, and everything to do with maintaining control. In a private memo to Commissioner Shirras, Eastwood opposed the release of the NMEG members because it would "weaken our position." Why? "The Japanese mind does not look on this forgiving spirit in the same light as we do," he explained. Shirras adopted Eastwood's position in his letter to Mead, embellishing Eastwood's views with his own lay sociological theory about the "Japanese," who are "dictatorial" in their attitudes and who can only understand power enforced "without the slightest deviation." Drawing from the historical well of racism for his understanding of "the Japanese," Shirras then noted: "The Japanese are a very cunning and intelligent race and from their actions (at least some of them) they are taking a very passive stubborn stand ..."

During the last week in June, a leading spokesperson for the NMEG, Shigeichi Uchibori, attempted to secure the release of those interned in the Immigration Building. He argued that they could help in the work of preparing relocation sites in the Slocan Valley. The BCSC refused, basing its decision on the argument Shirras had made to Mead. The NMEG members had no idea why their letters that stated their intent to cooperate fell on deaf ears.

THE VIEW FROM THE IMMIGRATION HALL

ON APRIL 24, 1942, from the other side — the position of those who faced confinement in the Immigration Building for protesting the breakup of families — Robert Okazaki noted in his diary: "Life is very tense now. The RCMP is continually monitoring our group's activities. We remaining members of the Mass Evacuation Group never know when we will be apprehended, so everywhere we go, we carry a toothbrush, towel and shaving kit with us."

Okazaki was part of the group of 67 nisei who, on April 25, gave themselves up to internment as a strategy to exert pressure on the BCSC. In Okazaki's terms, they "had agreed to become guinea pigs in the first test against the B.C. Security Commission." At the moment they prepared to force their way into the Immigration Building, he reflected: "Friends and strangers wished us good-luck, and as the excited crowd yelled 'Ganbare!', we waved good-bye and got into about a dozen trucks and taxis ... I could not help but think my future was taking a bleak, foreboding turn for the worse. This would be a fateful day for all of us." They were met by a group of heavily armed soldiers "in full battle gear, bayonets mounted at the ready," and waited through a meal of "Nigiri-meshi" until an official arrived and yelled, "'Let the Japs in!'" Okazaki was struck by the language, which confirmed for him, and for others in the NMEG, that the mind of Canadian authority had already identified Japanese Canadians as the enemy: "It was a shame they couldn't see past our ancestry and realize we were just as Canadian as them!"

Okazaki's first-hand account of his participation in the NMEG provides a rare insider's view of confinement in the Immigration Building. On May 3, 1942, in one of the most poignant passages in his narrative, he wrote:

> I was awakened early by the sounds of a very windy, rainy storm. It was far too early and too inclement for our well-wishers to come out, but as I peered through the barred window, I saw an elderly, white-haired man approaching the building. He had a parcel with him, and I wasn't quite sure who he was at first, but when he called out for me and Mas, I knew it was my father! Before he reached the building, he was stopped and questioned by a guard, and I could see dad shaking his head and talking, probably to get permission to see us. Then, just as dad started to walk by the guard, he was shoved to the

ground, and the soldier pushed his bayonet against dad's chest! I was aghast at what I saw! My father was quite shaken, and as he tried to right himself, the guard again plowed him back to the ground, this time holding dad down there by pushing the bayonet into the back of dad's shoulder! Others in our cell were looking down at this brutish display of unnecessary force, and we shouted at dad to go back before he was hurt more, but I think the heavy rains and harsh winds carried our voices away. My heart almost stopped as I looked at my father, on the ground, dazed, maybe even unconscious, and he didn't move for a few minutes! Eventually, as he slowly got up, I could see the bayonet rip in his coat. Dad struggled to pick-up his parcel, and slowly, finally, walked away.

Okazaki also witnessed the disturbance that erupted on May 13, the event called a "riot" or "revolt" in the local newspapers. The Vancouver *Herald* (May 14, 1942) reported that the BCSC could not comment on the cause of the disturbance because the "Japanese [*sic*] held in the Immigration Building do not come under authority of the BCSC." This explanation was a misrepresentation; after all, it was Austin Taylor, chair of the BCSC, who had authorized their detention under PC 1665. The absence of an investigative journalist on the scene ensured that the "Japanese" were portrayed as social and racial aliens. Had they been identified as "Canadian citizens," someone might have questioned the grounds for their incarceration in a site reserved for "immigrants" who were presumably aligned with an enemy nation.

The report in the *Vancouver Daily Province* claimed that the incarcerated men "turned a fire hose on soldier guards." It failed to match Okazaki's more precise description from the inside: "We grabbed the fire hose and aimed it at the guards outside, but the water only trickled out as the Army had shut off the main valve." Taylor, who was indirectly quoted, "denied that plaster had been pried loose from the walls and thrown out. He said he had visited the building and found no evidence of it." Okazaki, on the other hand, noted:

We obliterated the marble partition in the washroom, and as the men lifted the boom to smash the toilet, somebody yelled out "No stupid, don't smash the toilet! You know we god-damn need it!," so it was spared! We hurled out everything we could bust apart, and continued our rampage by punching out a hole in the concrete dividing wall so big that thirty detainees on the other side crawled through and joined in the demolition!

The *Vancouver Sun* report assured readers that the "riot was suppressed without the use of tear gas," but Okazaki's insider perceptions contradict this: "A tear gas canister was fired into the room, and when a second canister came crashing in, one of the detainees bravely picked it up and threw it back out the window! There was no wind that day, so the gas just hung in the air and never dissipated."

None of the reports on May 13, not even the available documents in the BCSC and RCMP papers in the Library and Archives of Canada, made any reference to gunfire. But Okazaki is precise here:

> Down on the street, the Army brought in reinforcements and surrounded the building. A Major was in charge, shouting out orders when suddenly we heard a gun shot, and we all froze! As we cautiously peered out, we saw the Major had drawn his pistol and fired toward us. The bullet had hit the ceiling and come down on the shoulder of one of the detainees! When more bullets zipped through the air, we dropped to the floor. I don't know how many bullets were fired at us, but we found four very real lead bullets (that we kept as souvenirs!), and judging from all the marks on the ceiling, there might have been about ten shots fired at us. Ten shots which could have killed us, and may have been fired for exactly that purpose. We didn't have any weapons, so how could the military justify using live ammunition?

A few days later, on May 16, the 137 men confined in the Immigration Building were put on the train to the camp at Petawawa, where Okazaki became a prisoner of war, #P 1444.[3]

---

3   The prisoner-of-war camp at Petawawa also held men of German and Italian background, but by July the internment authorities had constructed a camp at Angler specifically for Japanese Canadians, so that the day after Yonekura's group arrived, 287 men were transferred from Petawawa. Another 46 arrived on August 30 and a further 57 on November 12; both groups came from Vancouver.

THE NISEI EVACUATION GROUP: A REASSESSMENT

WITH THE SCARCITY of inside accounts of the NMEG, allegations that its members were simply disruptors and troublemakers, or worse, disloyal to the nation, need to be qualified carefully. One influential publication, *Within the Barbed Wire Fence*, written by the issei poet Ujo Nakano with his daughter Leatrice, bears comparison with accounts of nisei such as Robert Okazaki, Harry Yonekura and Tameo Kanbara.

As an issei, Nakano speaks from the perspective of Japanese nationals who were initially removed from the coast to road camps in the B.C. interior. He was uprooted from the town of Woodfibre on the west coast and sent to "a place called Yellowhead, B.C., some thirty-eight hundred feet above sea level and not far from Jasper, Alberta." After three weeks he was relocated to Descoigne, a road camp a few kilometres away. He was thus far away from the social turmoil in Vancouver and the NMEG's work there during the spring of 1942. Nakano got into trouble with the BCSC when he strenuously objected to his further relocation to Slocan rather than to Greenwood, where his wife and daughter were interned. He had been told at Descoigne that the men would be reunited with their families to help in the construction of housing in the B.C. interior camps. Feeling betrayed, he and a handful of others demanded that the promise be kept. When they were refused, they decided not to go to Slocan. As punishment they were sent first to the Immigration Building in Vancouver, and then to Angler.

It was in the Immigration Building that Nakano, hardly a political activist, first encountered other "resisters." As he explains,

> You see, these inmates were what were known as *gambariya*. They are best described as rebels against the treatment they were receiving in time of war. The Nisei *gambariya* were protesting such unjust treatment of Canadian citizens as they were experiencing; the Issei *gambariya* firmly believed in Japan's eventual victory and looked forward to the Canadian government's enforced compensation to them. These men had actively sought confinement and looked forward to the challenge of internment at the Angler prisoner-of-war camp. The sentiments of us newcomers were quite the opposite: we had absolutely no desire to be imprisoned.

At Angler, Nakano distanced himself from the gambariya, particularly the issei with whom he would have identified more directly. In his account of life in Angler he mentions that the "outspoken gambariya" were the ones who "believed absolutely in Japan's eventual victory and expected personal postwar compensation from a defeated Canada," echoing his earlier comments. But Nakano makes no mention of the position of the nisei who were interned for opposing the breakup of families — a position with which he could have sympathized. In fact, even though large numbers of young nisei were incarcerated for being members of the NMEG, many among them with "no desire to be imprisoned," Nakano does not mention the NMEG by name.

Nakano's account of his internment is, of course, a personal one. His perceptions of daily life are often dominated by his sensory awareness of his surroundings and particularly the loneliness of confinement. He becomes preoccupied with the camp haiku club, an affiliation that allows him to mediate his alienation through poetic texts that incorporate images of nature:

> Primeval forest!
> Feeling as though in violation,
> Cutting down standing trees
> Before watchful guards.
> Cutting firewood.

His inwardness, which is a powerful source of cohesion in his narrative of internment, perhaps accounts for his alignment of the so-called gambariya with those issei he perceives as loyal to Japan at the expense of the Canadian perspective held by the nisei in the NMEG. The term "gambariya" is itself a problem. Translated flexibly, without Japanese nationalist overtones, it can simply mean "those who resist or those who struggle on with a cause." So the NMEG could incite themselves to gambatte, that is, to keep up the struggle for justice. There is no attempt in Nakano's account to probe the social and political complexities of the term, and this oversight has left the unfortunate impression that members of the NMEG were anti-Canadian. Nakano's impression of the camp is shaped in his departure, when one gambariya, identified as M, called him a "traitor" for leaving the camp to accept employment. According to Nakano, "Since gambariya like M numbered in the hundreds at Angler, their views won the ascendancy."

No doubt Nakano spoke the truth as he saw it. In not accounting for the Canadian-based efforts of the NMEG, though, he left out a large part of the story of Canadian internment camps. And when Nakano's personal account is taken as a representative account of what happened to Japanese Canadians during the war, the elision of the NMEG's resistance to social injustice is reinforced, particularly because Nakano's narrative was the first of its kind to be published. Thus, in his afterword to the book, even a historian such as W. Peter Ward can conclude:

> while far from a microcosm of the Japanese immigrant community, those confined at Angler represented two divergent responses to tensions which war created within the minority society. Only a small proportion of all Japanese Canadians felt unswerving loyalty to Japan. Like Takeo, most were ultimately torn between two allegiances. But at Angler the balance tipped in the other direction. There the loyalists were dominant.

In Ward's brief reference to the NMEG, he says that most of those who ended up in prisoner-of-war camps "were imprisoned between March and November of 1942 for resisting evacuation orders. Many were members of the Nisei Mass Evacuation Group, an informal body of second-generation Japanese Canadians who opposed the evacuation order." However, as its open letter to the BCSC clearly stated, the NMEG did not oppose the mass uprooting but the family breakup policy, a policy that for its members crossed the threshold of fairness and justice.

In Tameo Kanbara's recollection, the NMEG were misrepresented, by the BCSC and the Japanese Canadian community alike, as "outlaws and troublemakers," but the "mass evacuation" position they took and fought for was "driven by the ... belief in our struggle to achieve justice." Even 16 months after the first NMEG members were incarcerated, in October 1943, RCMP authorities who visited Angler met with nisei who continued to insist that they be allowed to rejoin their families. The RCMP was considering using the blanket release order signed by Justice Minister Louis St. Laurent a year before. But RCMP Inspector D. C. Saul, sent to Angler to assess the mental state of nisei men, reported that they "are carefully nursing what they believe to be a sore grievance — they say the authorities have unwarrantably distrusted them, broken up their families, sold their homes and businesses and generally pushed them around or interned them." Saul concluded that once out of Angler, they would attempt to rejoin their families. His assessment led Mead to conclude that he "would not care to see a lot of Japanese turned loose in Ontario who would probably prove themselves a nuisance and detract from the good name the Japanese-Canadians are acquiring in Ontario."

The supreme irony, one not lost on the interned nisei, was that Japanese nationals could appeal to the Protecting Power, at that time Spain, under an international agreement to protect interned enemy nationals. When Jose Margueirat, representing Pedro E. Schwartz, consul general of Spain in charge of Japanese interests, visited Angler in October 1943, some Japanese Canadians attempted to air their grievances to him. They were warned by internment camp officials that they were jeopardizing their Canadian citizenship by approaching him for help. As Canadian citizens interned by their own state, Japanese Canadians had virtually nowhere to turn for mediation and representation.

THERE IS LITTLE doubt that if Austin Taylor and his BCSC had negotiated a truce by allowing families to remain together, the subsequent incarceration in the Immigration Building and internment at Petawawa and Angler would not have been necessary. Instead, the young nisei "citizens" who organized under the name of the Nisei Mass Evacuation Group suffered the ignominy of becoming "prisoners of war" in their own country — becoming so by the mere fact of their internment behind barbed wire. They became, in this translation process, not legally but by categorization the "Japanese" among the Japanese Canadian community who were portrayed as disloyal to Canada.

In the broader sweep of history, and in light of the documentary record, the members of the Nisei Mass Evacuation Group can be viewed as casualties in the struggle for justice. For some sansei (children of the nisei), coming of age in the 1970s, the voice of the NMEG emerged as a legacy. It was the voice of protest that set the tone in a decade taken up by the reconstruction of Japanese Canadian history.

CHAPTER 4

DISPERSED

Dispossession and Relocation

We are the billy-goats and nanny-goats and kids — all the scapegoats to appease a damfoolish few who don't figure that our presence here is the best security for this Coast.

— Muriel Kitagawa

Non-Negotiable: The Powers of the War Measures Act

DURING THE YEARS of the redress movement, many reporters and researchers were taken aback when they learned that Japanese Canadians were treated more harshly than the Japanese Americans who were incarcerated during the same period. According to *Personal Justice Denied*, the report of the Commission on Wartime Relocation and Internment of Civilians, "at the end of the year, the centers had the highest population they would ever have — 106,770 people. Over 175 groups of about 500 each had moved, generally aboard one of 171 special trains, to a center in one of six western states [California, Arizona, Idaho, Wyoming, Colorado, Utah] or Arkansas."

Japanese Americans were undoubtedly forced to endure severe conditions, but a simple comparison reveals a number of significant differences in policy between the U.S. and Canada: American properties were not confiscated and liquidated; families were moved together; the costs of their internment were borne by the U.S. government.

In Canada, on the other hand, Japanese Canadians with assets were required to pay for their own internment, primarily from the proceeds of properties and belongings that were sold without their consent by the Custodian of Enemy Property. And after the war the U.S. did not enact policies of deportation and forced dispersal away from the west coast, as Canada did. Japanese Americans were permitted to return to the coast — more than four years before Japanese Canadians were. By December 1944, acknowledging the subsiding military threat, the U.S. lifted the exclusion orders. In this way, the U.S. government pre-empted several legal challenges, thereby avoiding the embarrassment of being forced by the courts to release Japanese Americans. The case of Mitsuye Endo, for example, was settled in her favour when the court ruled "that an admittedly loyal American citizen could not be held in a relocation camp against her will."

How did these differences between the U.S. and Canada come about? The answer lies in the awesome — and non-negotiable — power of the War Measures Act. In a strangely twisted logic, government representatives and apologists could maintain that all the policies and regulations relating to Japanese Canadian internment, no matter how unfair, were legal. And their legality could not be challenged, because the right to do so was withheld by the government, as in the case of the Nisei Mass Evacuation Group. On the other hand, regardless of the technical legality of its actions, should the government not be held accountable for any misuse of the War Measures Act? This, at least, was the position of the National Association of Japanese Canadians (NAJC), whose redress demands initially included the abolition of the War Measures Act. The demand was dropped when the government rescinded the Act in 1987.

The War Measures Act was intended to be invoked during a crisis of wartime in order to provide the governor in council — that is, the cabinet — with the authority to respond quickly to emergencies. Cabinet could pass orders and regulations judged necessary "for the security, defence, order and welfare of Canada." Its powers — which could bypass parliamentary scrutiny — included censorship, the appropriation and sale of properties and, most significantly, the "arrest, detention, exclusion and deportation" of individuals and groups deemed a threat to national security.

Thanks to Ann Sunahara's research of government documents, the dispossession and dispersal of Japanese Canadians can be understood as an abuse of the War Measures Act. Thus, for instance, while the U.S. recognized that citizens could not be held against their will once the military emergency had passed, Canada was figuring out ways to retain control over Japanese Canadians once the war had ended — that is, after the expiry of the War Measures Act. Using its powers under the War Measures Act, the government produced the National Emergency Transitional Powers Act of 1945, an Act that maintained its control over Japanese Canadians. When this Act expired 18 months later, the government passed the Continuation of Transitional Measures Act to extend its control further. Instead of following U.S. policy, Canada prohibited Japanese Canadians from returning to the west coast until April 1, 1949, a measure that had nothing to do with national security. And they made it even more difficult for people to return by liquidating all their properties, belongings and businesses, to erase their collective presence on the west coast.

BECOMING THE ENEMY

IN HER RESEARCH, Ann Sunahara brought to light previously secret documents to demonstrate that government officials, politicians and other authorities knew that Japanese Canadians did not pose a threat to national security. At the critical federal cabinet meeting of January 8-9, 1942, the military and the RCMP reported that they saw no need to uproot the whole Japanese Canadian community. This extreme action had been advocated by the B.C. delegates, who warned of anti-Japanese riots and who were backed by the chair of the meeting, Ian Mackenzie, a politician well known for his desire to expel Japanese Canadians from B.C. The documents showed that the decision regarding mass uprooting was a political move to appease "anti-Japanese" British Columbians rather than a security measure to protect them.

Since Orders-in-Council passed under the War Measures Act could not be contested, government officials were able to craft the language of the orders to create a virtual "enemy alien," one that was more a product of discourse than of actual conditions. Thus when the announcement "To All Male Enemy Aliens" was posted on February 7, 1942, calling for their removal from the "protected zone," Japanese Canadians believed that the term "enemy aliens" was tied to nationality — to citizens of Japan, Italy and Germany, but not to Canadian citizens. They were wrong. Although the order, in principle, applied to nationals of all enemy countries, in fact it targeted primarily Japanese nationals. This was the first premonition of the race categorization to follow, but Japanese Canadians continued to trust the federal government to honour their citizenship rights. After all, Prime Minister King had publicly stated that they would be "justly treated." The political wheels were already turning, however, and working behind the scenes was Ian Mackenzie, the only B.C. politician in Mackenzie King's cabinet and perhaps the most influential voice in the expulsion of Japanese Canadians from B.C.

Mackenzie and his supporters received the boost they needed on February 19, 1942. That day, U.S. President Franklin D. Roosevelt signed into law Executive Order 9066, which ordered the incarceration of Japanese Americans. Just days later, on February 24, the Canadian government passed Order-in-Council PC 1486. The wording of PC 1486, an amendment to the Defence of Canada Regulations, which had earlier established the "protected area," can be seen as the discourse that prepared the way for the legal racialization of Japanese Canadians. Since Japanese Canadians were "Canadian citizens," under the Defence of Canada Regulations they could not be categorized as the "enemy aliens" designated by the earlier PC 365, which had ordered the removal of male nationals only. Policy makers, though, simply replaced the words "enemy aliens" with "any or all persons," an all-inclusive category that then allowed the minister of justice (not the minister of defence) to limit the "any or all persons" to those who could be identified as "of the Japanese race." Two days later, on February 26, such a regulation was issued under the signature of the justice minister, Louis St. Laurent. From this point forward, all "persons of the Japanese race," which is to say, all those designated as such by government authorities, could be treated *as if* they were "enemy aliens."

Japanese Canadians' lack of representation, and the assumption among government officials, politicians, and the media that mass uprooting would solve the long-standing "Japanese problem" in B.C., meant that no one —

not a single influential voice — objected to the government's supplanting of the language of "citizenship" with "race" terminology. The successive Orders-in-Council, accompanied by amendments and interpretations that replaced citizenship with racialization, went unquestioned. Even the Co-operative Commonwealth Federation (CCF) party — later the New Democratic Party (NDP) — long assumed to be the only political party that defended the rights of Japanese Canadians, abandoned them in this crisis.

THE EXPLOITS OF IAN MACKENZIE

IAN MACKENZIE, the Liberal MP from Vancouver who campaigned on the slogan "No Japs from the Rockies to the seas," had no doubt in his mind that PC 1486, which authorized the removal of all Japanese Canadians, not just Japanese nationals, gave him the legal basis to move immediately to appropriate the lucrative and large holdings of berry farmers in the Fraser Valley. On April 14, only six weeks after the order was announced — right in the midst of Japanese Canadian resistance to the government's policy of breaking up families — Mackenzie was already busy with a scheme. Its complexity points to an even earlier date for its conception. As the Custodian of Enemy Property called on Japanese Canadians to place their lands, houses, and belongings in trust with him, Mackenzie contacted T. A. Crerar, minister of mines and resources and administrator of the Soldier Settlement Board. Crerar, acting in cooperation with Mackenzie, assigned Gordon Murchison, director of the Soldier Settlement Board, to assess the farms. Then, on June 29, PC 5523 was passed, forbidding the owners to lease or sell the farms. From that point on, nothing could be done with the farms without Murchison's approval.[1] Mackenzie may have rationalized the takeover as being in the public interest — large quantities of berries, for instance, were needed to produce jam for England, and veterans would need land after the war — but his more political motives are exposed in a letter dated December 7, 1942, to T. A. Crerar:

---

1   Ian Mackenzie, at the time the minister of veterans' affairs, would have preferred to confiscate the farms under the Veterans' Land Act, but the Act would not come into effect until August, so his only political route was through the Soldier Settlement Board, which was under Crerar's jurisdiction.

I believe that from these lands formerly occupied by the Japanese [*sic*], we can establish some very fine holdings for the soldiers of the present war.

I also believe that we can lease them, if necessary, until the soldiers are able to occupy them. I also believe that we should not permit these Japanese to take re-possession of their lands. That is the view of British Columbia and will certainly find expression when the war is over.

Mackenzie's obsessive determination to expel Japanese Canadians from B.C. — even to the point of deportation — may have been pivotal in shaping a policy of dispersal, though it would have been kept secret from the Canadian public and from Japanese Canadians, who were led to believe that the "evacuation" was only a temporary measure. Awareness of such a policy would undoubtedly have made Japanese Canadians far more militant in their resistance. But more of a concern for the government, the policy could very well have been challenged in the courts. After all, permanent displacement to solve the "Japanese problem" in B.C. would have been difficult to justify, even under the War Measures Act. By producing the illusion of a temporary move from the "protected area," the government was able to convince the majority of Japanese Canadians that their cooperation would be seen as an act of loyalty to Canada. Conversely, any lack of cooperation would signify their loyalty to Japan. This psychological and political straitjacket left no room for negotiation: there was no choice other than a "trust" that the Canadian government would uphold the citizenship rights of Japanese Canadians as long as they complied with the mass uprooting.

Ian Mackenzie may have exposed the deeper goal of government policy inadvertently when his own personal agenda spilled out at that time. In "Jap Troubles Here Soon to Be Dispelled," a report on a press conference at the Hotel Vancouver, Mackenzie was cited as making assurances that the "Japanese in Vancouver" would soon be gone. But then he added: "It is ... my personal intention, as long as I am in public life, that these Japanese shall not come back here." This public declaration infuriated Austin Taylor of the BCSC. At the moment, he was trying to defuse criticism by Japanese Canadians of his family breakup policy. Taylor promptly wrote to A. MacNamara, associate deputy minister of labour, to lodge a complaint about Mackenzie's loose tongue:

If it is humanly possible for a member of Parliament to sabotage the interests of this Commission the Honourable Ian Mackenzie has made a very good attempt.

As you know, we have spent two or three weeks arranging places for the Japanese to be evacuated to and have had many difficulties, some of which you are acquainted with, in convincing the Japanese that we are not going to remove the men out of the area so that the women and children can be machine-gunned, etc., etc.

The Honourable Ian Mackenzie's remarks throw these ideas, or suspicions, right back into our lap.

Other documents expose the government's policy of permanent displacement from the coast — a policy that only became apparent to most Japanese Canadians early in 1943, when the Custodian of Enemy Property, without their agreement, sold off their homes and businesses. And to add insult to injury, the liquidation of their assets was justified as a mechanism to pay for their own displacement. An RCMP report, "Japanese Situation in British Columbia," dated March 23, 1943, commented on the "discontent" among Japanese Canadians after "Mr. DesBrisay of the B.C. Security Commission advised the Japanese that their properties are to be sold by the Custodian and that the monies so realized will be used for the maintenance of the Japanese individuals for as long as it lasts." Sick benefits and support for the aged and unfit would also diminish because of the sale of properties and businesses.

Although Japanese Canadians, according to the RCMP report, saw this action as a "means to force them to go to employment in the East and appear to greatly resent it," its writer did not think they would mount an organized resistance, "but it seems that the news is not helping the Japanese to accede gracefully to the proposition for eastward movement contemplated by the Government." That "eastward movement" — a perverse inversion of the "westward movement" that colonized the country — was received with mixed emotions; many people were simply relieved to find employment somewhere.

A politician such as Ian Mackenzie whose reputation was built on anti-Japanese agitation could easily exploit public opinion to bring about the acceptance of the image of the "Japanese" constructed by the government and media, even more so because he was the cabinet minister appointed to handle the "Japanese problem." He also knew that the War Measures Act gave him extremely generous leeway to pursue his objectives. Thus, in acquiring the Fraser Valley properties owned by Japanese Canadians, he could inform his colleague, Secretary of State Norman McLarty, in a private memo: "I am entirely in favour of this purchase ... and we should not be deterred by any representations by Japanese [sic]. Any action we take under the War Measures Act cannot be challenged in the courts."

RATIONALIZING DISPERSAL: THE JACKSON ROYAL COMMISSION OF 1943

A NUMBER OF government documents prove the existence of a "scheme" to use various agencies to pressure Japanese Canadians to leave B.C. for good. One letter of March 30, 1943, from RCMP Commissioner Mead to Arthur MacNamara, deputy minister of labour, made reference to the "Departmental policy to distribute the Japanese population of British Columbia throughout Canada as quickly as possible." Interestingly, Mead acknowledged that Canadian nisei were aware of the U.S. government's recognition of citizenship status in its treatment of Japanese Americans. He pointed to "the more liberal policy being put into effect by the Government of that country." To prevent the nisei from opposing Canadian policy, Mead cautioned the Department of Labour to work less hastily so as not to agitate them. He concluded by recommending that "the original policy be adhered to of quietly and gradually spreading these Japanese throughout Canada through the efforts of the Placement Officers and other agencies rather than force the issue at this time, with possible resistance, which would give the whole scheme a set-back." Quiet dispersal, rather than recognition of citizenship rights, became the "Canadian" solution to the dismantling of the Japanese Canadian collective on the west coast.

Japanese Canadians who accepted "evacuation" as a temporary measure had every intention of returning to their homes once the war ended. Little did they know, at least in 1942, that right from the outset the government was furthering an unofficial dispersal policy — years before the more official dispersal was announced in the spring of 1945. This was so routinely taken for granted by government representatives that no one stopped to question the wholesale destruction of a community whose members had not been charged with any crime against the state. Their racialization as the "enemy" within the nation was so ingrained that most Canadians assumed that the "Japanese problem" was caused by the fact of their collective existence on the west coast. In this way, the erasure of their presence took on the air of inevitability.

However, in an effort to demonstrate that dispersal could even be considered good for Japanese Canadians, the government set up a royal commission, supposedly to investigate conditions of internment. Chaired by Dr. F. W. Jackson, Manitoba's deputy minister of health and public welfare, the commission was created by PC 9498 on December 14, 1943, with the mandate

> to inquire into the provision made for the welfare and maintenance of persons of the Japanese race resident in the settlements in the Province of British Columbia under the administration of the Department of Labour and to report thereon to the Minister of Labour, together with such recommendations as to further measures to be taken with regard thereto as the Commission deems advisable.

The Jackson Commission had the aura of public accountability, but its effectiveness depended very much on its terms of reference, its mandate and the attitudes of its members. Crucially, those serving on this commission were both appointed by the minister of labour and required to report to him. In other words, they served the authority with the most vested interest in the outcome of the inquiry. From the outset, then, the reporting structure ensured a partiality concerning the kind of information gathered and the interpretation of its implications. Under these conditions, no mechanism existed to represent and speak for the Japanese Canadians who were the objects of the investigation.

When the commissioners first met on December 20, 1943, they were briefed by George Collins, commissioner of the BCSC, on the "administrative policy in respect to the care of the persons of the Japanese race resident in the Interior Settlements." Collins informed them that questions of housing, maintenance rates, health and employment were to be assessed only in relation to prewar conditions. This guideline would allow the commission to apply the social conditions of the poorest prewar Japanese Canadians — using data which itself was suspect — to those living in substandard housing and living conditions in the B.C. interior towns used for confinement. Based on this limited frame of reference, the commissioners could argue that Japanese Canadians in the camps enjoyed an improved standard of living, effectively covering over the huge social and economic losses they suffered. Such an attitude, which characterized the overall assessment, is clear in the following statement from the commission's report:

> Your Commission inspected the former Japanese housing on Powell Street in Vancouver, at Steveston and several cannery settlements on the lower Fraser. The new housing as erected by the B.C. Security Commission is superior to that which Your Commission visited. The buildings in the Interior Settlements which are divided into apartments while in most cases unsafe and undesirable are, Your Commission believes, equal to the quarters previously occupied by those Japanese who formerly resided in the Powell Street area.

The commissioners' mental state, particularly vivid in their penchant for glorifying the work of the B.C. Security Commission, did not bode well for the "objects" of their inquiries. In the opening of its report, the commission declared "its admiration for the splendid piece of work executed by the original B.C. Security Commission" and offered congratulations for its "gigantic achievement." They did, however, have one criticism of the administration of the "evacuation": "The office quarters from which the B.C. Security Commission operates, although originally sufficient are, at present, overcrowded. No provision is made for a rest room for the female staff."

In drawing up its conclusions, the Jackson Commission operated under the assumption, using the government's public policy as its guideline, that the "Interior Settlement projects are a temporary means of meeting an emergency." But then the report went on to cite the Department of Labour's approach to these "projects" as "a step in the evacuation process and a training ground for employment ... in the Prairies and the East." The report endorsed this policy (no surprise here) and stated that the assessment of the commission was contingent on the "temporary aspect of the provisions." Clearly, the implication was that this "step" — resettlement in the interior camps — was only the first phase in the expulsion of Japanese Canadians from the west coast. Given this policy, the Japanese Canadians who brought their complaints to the commission, including concerns about the liquidation of their properties, were destined not to be heard. Again, they were spoken for, by a mechanism of representation — this time the Royal Commission — that had been orchestrated by the government. It came as no shock that the commission endorsed the policies that forced Japanese Canadians to pay the costs of their own confinement and to leave B.C.

With no attention paid to the effects of government policies on the welfare of the Japanese Canadians, the work of the Royal Commission proceeded swiftly. From its initial meeting in Vancouver, the commission was in and out of the interior camps with its report written in three weeks — an amazing feat, considering that the schedule included Christmas and New Year's Day. On the other hand, the rubber-stamping mode of proceeding and the uncritical acceptance of government actions meant that pressing issues — family breakup, the abrogation of citizenship rights, the racialization of identity, the betrayal of trust by the Custodian of Enemy Property and the continuing restrictions on movement — would never become public knowledge. The "obedient servants" who placed their signatures at the end of the report were "OF THE UNANIMOUS OPINION THAT THE PROVISIONS MADE BY THE GOVERNMENT OF CANADA THROUGH THE DEPARTMENT OF LABOUR FOR THE WELFARE OF THE JAPANESE IN THE INTERIOR SETTLEMENTS IN BRITISH COLUMBIA ARE, AS A WAR-TIME MEASURE, REASONABLY FAIR AND ADEQUATE." Ask us no questions, and we'll tell you no lies: the report had fulfilled the task of exonerating the government and justifying its dispersal policy. Japanese Canadians would be expelled from B.C.

Mona Oikawa, in her study of relocation patterns in Ontario, draws attention to the administrative and ideological mechanisms devised by federal authorities — often with the cooperation of private citizens — to carry out the dispersal process. "Government involvement," she writes, "consisted of a hierarchical bureaucracy stemming from the Deputy Minister of Labour, down through to the public servants who administered the policy. The interests of Japanese Canadians were clearly non-existent to those who regarded them as mere 'bodies' to be moved." Those with good intentions and those with more suspicious motives worked in tandem to entice or coerce Japanese Canadians to leave B.C. — either to accept menial and low-paying domestic positions in eastern Canada or through deportation to Japan as soon as possible. The wages were so low that many young women in the B.C. camps would not take the jobs offered, and this resistance, Oikawa explains, led to the "policy of firing all women of Japanese origin from employment in the camps in the hopes of forcing them to resettle in domestic positions outside of British Columbia."

These cruel tactics illustrate sharply the fear and anxiety instilled by authorities from the Department of Labour, such as T. B. Pickersgill, who exerted so much control over the daily lives of Japanese Canadians. Foremost in this disturbing social climate was the threat of deportation for any form of opposition to government directives. Pickersgill was known for his view that deportation would be the most permanent solution to the "Japanese problem" in B.C. Oikawa cites a report of a group meeting at Tashme,[2] where Pickersgill was perceived as "another of these Japanese haters" who did not have "the slightest bit of sympathy towards Japanese and consequently his administration of Japanese affairs is dealt with in this attitude ... We felt as though we were facing a Nazi official, a dictator. Momentarily, it gave us an impression of being outside of Canada."

RESISTING DISPOSSESSION

AS KEN ADACHI points out in *The Enemy That Never Was*, the Japanese Canadians who met only briefly with the Jackson Commission during its "whirlwind five-day tour of the interior camps during the first week of January, 1944" were aware that the inquiry was set up to serve the government's interests, not the interests of Japanese Canadians. Two years after the uprooting began, the patterns of deception had become much more visible. The prospect of internment in prisoner-of-war camps — the fate of the Nisei Mass Evacuation Group — was a reminder that those who interfered with administrative efficiencies would be punished through more brutal incarceration. Yet the outright liquidation of properties, businesses and personal belongings aroused indignation that could not be contained.

Muriel and Ed Kitagawa expressed the outrage of many when they wrote to the Custodian of Enemy Property on June 26, 1943, to protest the sale of their home at 2751 Pender Street East. "This house, bought out of

---

2   Tashme was an internment camp constructed just outside of Hope, B.C., a town on the border of the "protected area" 100 miles from the west coast. It was named using the first two letters of the three members of the B.C. Security Commission: TAylor, SHirras, and MEad.

slender earnings, represents our stake in this country of our birth," they explained to the Custodian. They could see no justification whatsoever for the liquidation policy. "We do not quarrel with the military measure but this act can scarcely be in accordance with any war measure. Please hasten to assure us that our house is inviolate." They received a brief response, more a form letter, from F. G. Shears, stating that despite their objections the sale would continue — according to government procedure:

> The proposed liquidation is of course a general one and not only applies to your particular property. The policy has been decided upon at Ottawa and this Office, acting under advice of an independent Advisory Committee, will endeavour to obtain the best possible results.
>
> You are aware I hope that the proceeds of the liquidation will be available to you from time to time as you have need of same.
>
> At the present moment tenders have not been called on your particular property but I am unable to give you the assurance asked for and it will be disposed of in due course if satisfactory offers are received.

The letter did not acknowledge that the "policy" was recommended by the Custodian's office and that the government's policy of making the dispossessed pay for their own uprooting and dispossession ran contrary to the treatment of Japanese Americans by the U.S. government. The indifference of the letter writer, and his utter lack of respect for citizenship values, upset the Kitagawas so much that they responded — passionately. Frustrated and angry, Muriel confronted the Custodian as the face of a government that had completely betrayed its citizens:

> Who would have thought that one day I would be unable to stand up for my country's government, out of sheer shame and disillusion, against the slurs of the scornful? The bitterness, the anguish is complete. You, who deal in lifeless figures, files, and statistics could never measure the depth of hurt and outrage dealt out to those of us who love this land. It is because we *are* Canadians, that we protest the violation of our birthright.

She reminded Shears that the Kitagawas' battle to keep their house embodied the "very principle for which the democracies are fighting." The letter concluded on a note of cynical rage. If the policy were carried out, they wrote, "then kindly send us our 'proceeds' in one sum that we may personally invest in something solid ... Victory Bonds, for instance."[3]

The drive on the part of Japanese Canadians to prevent the loss of their properties led to the first coordinated plan to use the legal system to protect themselves from the Custodian of Enemy Property. Surely, they would have reasoned, the courts would recognize the absurdity of condoning liquidation as a necessary security measure. But while Japanese Canadians organized to protest the sale of properties, the government went ahead on its own. By April 1943, advertisements were distributed for properties to be sold and belongings to be auctioned. Meanwhile, in Kaslo, site of one of the B.C. interior camps, Dr. Kozo Shimotakahara and Saburo Shinobu brought a group of issei together to form the Japanese Property Owners Association. They encouraged the organization of similar groups in other camps, carried out a survey to garner widespread support and raised the needed funds. To begin the legal proceedings, Vancouver lawyer Arthur MacLennan "filed a petition against the Secretary of State in July, asking that he be restrained from proceeding with the sale." It was directed to the secretary of state because the liquidation notice said that the properties were being sold "under instructions from the Secretary of State of Canada, acting under his capacity as Custodian pursuant to the Revised Regulations Respecting Trading with the Enemy, 1943." This phase was delayed for over a year — until May 1944 — to determine the jurisdiction of the Exchequer Court in Canada in lawsuits against the Crown.

Once this hurdle had been overcome, the case was submitted in the names of four individuals representing the Japanese Canadians whose properties were at risk: Eikichi Nakashima, as a naturalized Canadian; Tadao Wakabayashi, as a Canadian-born; and Jitaro and Takejiro Tanaka, as Japanese nationals. The case, heard by Justice Joseph Thorson, emphasized two points: the "trust" between the Custodian and the plaintiffs when they left their properties and belongings in his care, "as a protective measure only"; and property

---

3   To show loyalty to Canada at the outset of the mass uprooting, "incredibly enough," Adachi writes, "the Issei took part in the second Victory Loan Drive and raised, in three weeks, $313,700 from 1,584 subscribers. It was possibly the safest investment they could have made, notwithstanding the irony: 'Buy Victory Bonds to free the oppressed.'"

ownership having no relevance in relation to national security, as defined by the War Measures Act. The judge's ruling — which was stalled *for three years* — went against the plaintiffs on three counts. First, he concluded that no contract existed preventing the Custodian from liquidating the properties; second, the courts could not question any order made by the government under the War Measures Act; and third, the shocking judgement: "the Custodian was not a servant of the Crown but a statutory officer who happened to be the Secretary of State. In other words, the property owners had sued the wrong person." Judge Thorson concluded: "Under the circumstances ... I must hold that the proceedings were erroneously taken. In my opinion, this ends the matter." Judge Thorson, Ann Sunahara writes, was the same "Hon. J. T. Thorson, minister of national war services, [who] had been part of the 1942 cabinet that had uprooted the Japanese Canadians."

In retrospect, the outcome of the court challenge was predictable. After all, even leaving aside Judge Thorson's ruling, Japanese Canadians had to get the courts to assess the question of the government's abuse of the War Measures Act. But the courts were not in a position to pass judgement on the government's actions under the War Measures Act. One of the Act's most insidious aspects was the sacrosanct nature of its powers. This much was known by all Japanese Canadians, who found out, time and again, that their voices — raised time and again — would not be heard.

WEATHERING THE DEPORTATION CRISIS

AT THE END of the war, Japanese Canadians all over Canada still found themselves caught by the administrative machinery of a government that was relentless in its efforts to erase their presence through dispersal (assimilation) or deportation ("voluntary repatriation"). Still dazed by their displacement, no longer able to trust their own government, fearful of what lay ahead after the war, many Japanese Canadians signed the "repatriation"[4] forms that RCMP officials delivered in person to the B.C. camps, ostensibly as

---

4   The term "repatriation" remains perhaps the most outrageous of all the terms concocted by the federal government, especially because the large majority of the nearly 4,000 people who were shipped to Japan, as Canadian-born, had Canada as their patria and, clearly, could not be "repatriated." They were in fact being exiled or expelled from the country of their birth.

a survey of intent, not a legal declaration. Their motives for signing were far more complex than any RCMP officer or administrator at the time could comprehend.

Many Japanese Canadians had lost faith in Canadian democracy; others believed it best to take their aging parents to Japan. Others wanted to remain in B.C. for as long as they could, and signing — so they were told — would prevent them from being forced to move "east of the Rockies." Still others signed because they believed the Canadian government would ultimately deport them all to Japan, and the Japanese government, they thought, would not look kindly on those who did not sign up for "repatriation." These diverse responses to the survey expose how identity had become a trap with no exits for the Japanese Canadians in the camps: racialized as "enemy alien" in Canada, they would also be categorized as a "Canadian foreigner" in Japan. So it was that Irene (Kato) Tsuyuki was deported to Japan as an "alien," only to have her identity card stamped "alien" in Japan. A nisei, born in Vancouver, Tsuyuki had to accompany her aging parents. She recalled that her father gave up his naturalization status because he felt the "government, which he had trusted in, completely insulted him by confiscating his assets and selling everything off without his consent." She returned to Canada soon after restrictions on Japanese Canadians were lifted on April 1, 1949. She planned to bring her parents back to Canada, but both of them died in Japan.

The temptation of "repatriation" was made palatable by the government's offer to pay for passage, to provide a living allowance and to reimburse all funds from the sale of properties. Those going "east of the Rockies" were given no guarantees, only told that they might be considered "loyal" at a later date for cooperating with the government. At least, that was the subtext of the Dispersal Notice calling on "Japanese Canadians who want to remain in Canada" to leave B.C. "as the best evidence of their intentions to co-operate with the Government policy of dispersal." Japanese Canadians were cognizant of the threat implicit in the statement that those who did not "take advantage of present opportunities for employment and settlement out of British Columbia ... may seriously prejudice their own future by delay." Some 10,000 people, including thousands of women and children named by those who signed the repatriation survey, were listed as persons who were, according to the government, destined to be shipped to Japan. On the assumption that the repatriation survey stood as a legal statement signifying loyalty to Japan, the government moved to pass Orders-in-Council to legalize deportation.

The coercive tactics used in the either/or — "repatriation" or "dispersal" policies — prompted the activism of the Co-operative Committee on Japanese Canadians (ccjc), a coalition of some 25 individual organizations formed in 1943 to assist the many Japanese Canadians entering Toronto. Their goal, during December 1945, was to mount a legal challenge to Mackenzie King's imminent use of Orders-in-Council under the War Measures Act — about to expire in January 1946 — that would legalize the deportation of nearly half the Japanese Canadian population. Japanese Canadians in Toronto also quickly formed the Citizenship Defence Committee and raised funds to fight King's deportation orders. The ccjc, having retained Andrew Brewin as their lawyer, were able to convince the government to refer the legality of the orders to the Supreme Court of Canada. In January 1946, Brewin and J. R. Cartwright argued before the court that the orders could not be applied to Canadian citizens and were beyond the powers of the War Measures Act. The government's lawyers, for their part, simply argued that the government had the power of deportation under the War Measures Act.

The decision of the judges was complex: they ruled that yes, the government had the power of deportation, but that power did not extend to the women and minors who had not signed the repatriation survey. What was not so complex — and the reason why the government agreed to a judicial inquiry into the deportation orders — was the exemption from any judicial review of orders made under the War Measures Act. In other words, no matter how unjustly Japanese Canadians had been treated, and even despite the obvious fact that the country was no longer at war, whatever the governor in council (the cabinet) deemed a necessary action was legal. The judges drew the line on their own power, limiting their judgement to the question of the government's authority under the War Measures Act, and not addressing the justness of the deportation orders.

The Supreme Court, in effect, admitted that cabinet, a small group of politicians, had the power to deport and banish from Canada citizens who had not committed any crimes against the state. Racialization alone, or for Japanese Canadians, being designated as "of the Japanese race," was sufficient grounds. The judges refused to discuss the further argument made by the ccjc lawyers that the term "Japanese race" was so vague that the orders lacked legitimacy. Instead, they concluded, their task was to determine the question of whether or not the government had the power to make such orders, not to pass judgement on the language of such orders. The crucial issue of racialization as an identifying process was regarded as irrelevant — "the point whether some words or sentences therein are vague does not fall within that question."

Once again Japanese Canadians were handcuffed by the War Measures Act, the legislation that gave cabinet ministers such as Ian Mackenzie licence to pass Orders-in-Council without being accountable for their actions. These orders, passed with merely the signature of any cabinet minister, became, as the judges stated in their ruling, "the equivalent of a statute; they have the force of law, and, to all intents and purposes, while they stand, they are exactly on the same footing as an Act of Parliament."

While the highest court in Canada could not offer protection against the abuse of rights, one effect was at least salutary: the climate of opposition to the government brought signs of some relief for Japanese Canadians. Perhaps even Mackenzie King, always the pragmatic politician, was relieved that the Supreme Court, in ruling against the deportation of women and children, had opened a useful loophole for him. Without losing face, he could steer clear of a potential public backlash against his deportation orders and the proposed Loyalty Commission, which was to determine whether individual Japanese Canadians were "fit" or "not fit" to remain in Canada. He could also avoid having to deal with the legal ramifications of public hearings and the political fallout from the image of the government as being responsible for the breakup of families. Although these moves were logical extensions of King's uprooting policies, he knew that since Japanese Canadians were now scattered all over the country, their economic and social resources depleted, more and more Canadians were beginning to sympathize with them. The politician in King would have wanted to defuse an embarrassing demonstration of power, one that would so obviously be devoid of compassion. His government had been able to act without being accountable, but now liberal elements were waking to its reckless disregard of citizenship rights.

As the deportation crisis subsided, the government pressed on with its dispersal policy. In 1945 the Japanese Canadian population was distributed as follows:

British Columbia: 15,610
Alberta: 3,550
Saskatchewan: 157
Manitoba: 1,052
Ontario: 2,914
Quebec: 716

By 1947, the demography of the Japanese Canadian population began to take on the shape of the scattering planned by the government's social engineers:
BC: 6,776
Alberta: 4,180
Saskatchewan: 505
Manitoba: 1,186
Ontario: 6,616
Quebec: 1,247

The significant factor for the dramatic decline in B.C. was the government's "repatriation" policy. By the time Prime Minister King rescinded his deportation orders, 4,319 Japanese Canadians had been deported, including 1,954 children. The decline in the B.C. population, 8,834, fed the increases in the other provinces. Ontario's numbers rose by 3,702, coming to equal those of B.C. According to Audrey Kobayashi,

> The government policy of forced dispersal ensured that by the time restrictions were lifted in 1949 the Japanese-Canadian population, formerly concentrated in close-knit communities in British Columbia, was scattered across the country. No single factor is more important in determining the present distribution of Japanese Canadians and, as a result, the fundamental demographic make-up of their communities.

REGROUPING IN TORONTO: NEW ALLIANCES

AS JAPANESE CANADIANS resettled "east of the Rockies," their activities and movements were closely monitored by government officials posted in key centres called "hostels." These hostels were temporary shelters where migrants were housed before assuming jobs at the bottom of the labour pool. This organized distribution assuaged public concerns by making Japanese Canadians non-threatening candidates for the social welfare of liberal-minded Canadians who believed in the government's assimilation policy. Seen less as the monolithic "enemy alien," Japanese Canadians also found themselves having to redefine their lives in new social conditions.

It was out of this historical shift that the nisei especially began to remake themselves as "Japanese *Canadian*," with the emphasis falling on their role in Canada as citizens. This transformation coincided with — and was even stimulated by — a change in attitudes toward them. Once dispersed, they were assisted by social workers, religious groups and civil liberties associations. For the first time in their history, now far away from B.C., the nisei, largely an English-speaking generation, were called upon to reorganize their scattered communities, a process that brought them into complicated alliances with white liberal organizations.

The most prominent of these alliances was with the Co-operative Committee on Japanese Canadians (CCJC), a group that was heavily influenced by individuals with church and social welfare backgrounds, whose values often reflected more of a missionary approach than a collaboration between equals. The titles of two pamphlets written and distributed by the CCJC, for instance, *From Citizens to Refugees — It's Happening Here!* and *Our Japanese Canadians — Citizens, Not Exiles*, implied the social "Canadianization" of Japanese Canadians as they came into contact with liberal values. While no doubt driven by good intentions, the CCJC treated the experience of Japanese Canadians as a "problem case" through which, on the one hand, Canadian democracy could be challenged and affirmed and, on the other, Canadian society could be educated about the plight of Japanese Canadians. Functioning as "missionaries" or "social workers" who sought to speed up this process, the CCJC never questioned the dispersal policy itself. As Edith Fowke wrote, the CCJC appreciated Prime Minister King's policy statement in the House of Commons on August 4, 1944, "and expressed their willingness to co-operate in every way possible to aid in resettlement. They felt that until Canada had conquered her race prejudice it was probably better not to admit any more Japanese, and that dispersing those already here more or less evenly across Canada would help to reduce prejudice." Their logic followed King's: Japanese Canadians could contribute to the reduction of racism in Canada by becoming invisible. Out of sight, so the cliché goes, out of mind.

Nevertheless, the representation of Japanese Canadians as "refugees" who were "ours" increased public awareness of the abuse of Japanese Canadians by the Canadian government, especially in Toronto, where Japanese Canadians saw the possibility of creating a new collective voice. This city, which was a germinating ground of liberal values in postwar Canada, became the magnet for many young nisei. Nurtured on the dream of achieving the franchise and educated to believe in democratic values, they were quick to work with the CCJC. With the CCJC's encouragement, they established subcommittees of the YWCA and the YMCA, which soon merged to become the Japanese Canadian Committee for Democracy (JCCD). Many members of the JCCD had been affiliated with the Japanese Canadian Citizens' Council, the group responsible for sending the 1936 delegation to Ottawa to seek the franchise. Among its many activities, the JCCD took part in the fight against deportation, raised consciousness about citizens' rights through their newsletter of political commentary and community information, *Nisei Affairs* (1945-47), and lobbied the government to allow Japanese Canadians to enlist in the armed forces.

The issue of enlistment demonstrated the drive among the nisei to prove loyalty to Canada. Many were angered because they were not allowed to fight for their country, as the naturalized issei had done during World War I, and they were intent on continuing the struggle for the franchise. In the spring of 1945, ironically under pressure from the British government, the Canadian government lifted the ban on Japanese Canadians joining the armed forces. Many nisei, including the executive of the JCCD, affirmed their loyalty at a volatile public meeting — by vowing to enlist to prove their "Canadianness." Roger Obata, a founding member of the JCCD and the first president of the National Japanese Canadian Citizens' Association (NJCCA) in 1947 — and decades later a member of the National Association of Japanese Canadians (NAJC) committee that negotiated the redress agreement with the federal government — recalled the explosiveness of the enlistment issue at the JCCD meeting in Toronto:

> When the meeting voted against joining up, then we as an executive all resigned en masse, and the whole executive joined up within the next week. And that's how we all got into the army. So you can imagine at that time that people like George Tanaka and I weren't well regarded. When I had to come

up to New Denver from the language school in Vancouver, in an army
uniform, they said you shouldn't go up there, you're going to get tarred and
feathered ... But that was the sort of atmosphere in which we as a group of
nisei joined up, fighting for our principles.

The JCCD was also instrumental in distributing a "survey of 1,800 evacuees
in the Toronto area" and was able to demonstrate that "property estimated
to be worth $1,400,395.66 had been sold for $351,334.86." This proof of huge
economic losses caused by the failure of the Custodian of Enemy Property
to hold properties and belongings in trust became part of a movement to
seek compensation. The disappointing legal decision by Judge Thorson
meant that the political sphere was the only effective forum in which
Japanese Canadians could protest. This approach was made more viable
through the support of non-Japanese Canadian organizations, such as the
CCJC.

In 1946 and 1947, anticipating an official government response to the
compensation issue, Japanese Canadians in the Toronto area began to
organize themselves. In 1946 the JCCD and the Citizenship Defence Committee
collaborated to sponsor a provincial conference to create communication
networks for the scattered "communities." The notion of "communities" (in
the plural) was in its formative state, denoting the new, local conditions of
the Japanese Canadians who had resettled in various places. In a few short
and turbulent years, their identities had been radically altered. The dispersal
had become the dominant event in their lives. With poverty and racism star-
ing them in the face, they were compelled to organize for the sake of their
own survival.

The organizers hoped that the unification of Japanese Canadians into a
more cohesive and coherent national network would open a path to the
articulation of grievances that needed to be voiced. This was the motive
behind the Ontario conference, held in Toronto. Some organizations in
other provinces had set precedents for this meeting. In Winnipeg, as early as
1942, at a time when the government "forbade the congregation" of Japanese
Canadians, underground meetings were held to form what was then considered an illegal organization, the Manitoba Japanese Joint Committee. This
committee later joined with other organizations, such as the Civil Defence

Committee (a counterpart to the Citizenship Defence Committee in Toronto), to form the Manitoba JCCA in March 1946.

The "Report of the First Ontario Convention" (May 25-26, 1946) in Toronto stated the need for "mutual co-operation ... for mutual protection." A motion was passed to form an Ontario organization based on the work and constitution of the JCCD, and discussions began on the prospect of creating a "national federation," a move that was encouraged by the visiting delegate from the Manitoba JCCA, T. Umezuki, who was also the editor of the *New Canadian*. The following year, in September, the National Japanese Canadian Citizens' Association was formed. When representatives from across Canada met to constitute this group, they agreed that the struggle to attain the franchise had to continue and that, in whatever way possible, they had to seek compensation for losses.

The Japanese Canadians who organized themselves in Toronto, initially to challenge deportation but then to respond to the Bird Commission, relied on the backing of the CCJC. The support of a group of respectable white Canadians, mostly from religious and civil rights organizations, gave them the public profile needed to raise their concerns. It was therefore not surprising — given the image of Japanese Canadians as "refugees" who needed to be represented — that the CCJC would also come to speak for Japanese Canadians vis-à-vis government authorities. While Japanese Canadian political groups, such as the newly formed NJCCA, were considered part of the CCJC, their nisei leaders soon found themselves dependent on its advice. There was no doubt that the CCJC's work in mobilizing public opinion had been crucial in the successful fight against deportation. The relationship it had forged with Japanese Canadians in that crisis, however, worked in more ambivalent ways in dealing with the issue that followed: the liquidation of properties and belongings. This matter would arise in 1947, when the federal government announced the formation of the Royal Commission on Property Claims.

CHAPTER 5

Now You See It,
Now You Don't

The Perils of the Bird Commission

Apologists for the government argue that the government, through the Bird Commission, has already compensated Japanese Canadians for injustices suffered. The government's own documents show that, in reality, that Commission was a political measure designed to neutralize claims for redress.
— National Association of Japanese Canadians

BEHIND THE SCENES: THE BIRTH OF THE BIRD COMMISSION

WHEN PRIME MINISTER Mackenzie King finally rescinded the deportation orders in a statement in the House of Commons on January 24, 1947, the issue of compensation for economic losses, including loss of income, moved to the foreground. Many questions could be raised: How could the government have considered property ownership a threat to national security? Why had the Custodian of Enemy Property, entrusted to administer the properties "as a protective measure only," sold off everything? Sidestepping any questioning of the policy itself, King explained that the only concern for the government was to determine a "fair price." Significantly, he cleared the Custodian of any wrongdoing by saying that "a complete appraisal was made before disposition." But then, referring to his earlier commitment to "fairness" in his speech on August 4, 1944, he allowed for a narrow category of possible compensation: "To ensure ... the fair treatment promised in 1944, the government is prepared in cases where it can be shown that a sale was made at less than a fair market value to remedy the injustice."

King's language followed a plan of action carefully worked out in the secrecy of his Cabinet Committee on Japanese Questions (CCJQ), a special committee set up to recommend a continuing policy on Japanese Canadians — on repatriation, relocation and, of course, the claims issue. As it turned out, this group assumed responsibility for formulating strategies that would defuse criticism of the dispossession of Japanese Canadians and in the process, however possible, maintain the appearance of accountability. With the war over and uncensored information about internment becoming public knowledge, the demands for compensation from the Co-operative Committee on Japanese Canadians (CCJC), as well as from individual Japanese Canadians, could not be so easily glossed over. In this context, King's decision to establish a royal commission was a political move, serving simultaneously to appease the public and to close the political door on the compensation issue. The inside workings of the cabinet, where the claims commission was designed, reveal the formidable centre of decision making. Here, questions of justice usually took a back seat to political expediency. For this reason, although members were well aware of the arguments in support of compensation for the violation of rights, at no time in their lengthy deliberations about the claims commission did anyone ever speak for the interests of Japanese Canadians.

On April 17, 1947, just after the first report of claims by Japanese Canadians, the CCJQ recommended that the Special Cabinet Committee on Japanese Claims join it. They planned to address the claims question together. The meeting set for this purpose on April 21 was striking for the range of government departments represented — a vivid reminder of just how deeply the treatment of Japanese Canadians implicated diverse spheres of government authority.[1] A memo from the Department of Justice, signed by

---

1   The meeting was chaired by Humphrey Mitchell, the minister of labour responsible for

F. P. Varcoe, made reference to a cabinet decision to appoint a commissioner under the Inquiries Act "to investigate claims made by persons of the Japanese race in respect of the disposition of their property and also in respect of claims for loss resulting from their evacuation from the protected area of British Columbia."

Of importance in this statement was the acknowledgement that both types of losses must be considered. Claims for the broader area of losses resulting from "evacuation" would include income, business assets, stolen personal belongings, bank interest and perhaps even disruption of education. The preliminary outline submitted to the committee specified that the commissioner would investigate individual claims and advise the government on "the amount of compensation that in his opinion would be fair and reasonable." In the end, however, compensation for "evacuation" losses was deleted and the commission was limited to considering property losses only in those cases "that, by reason of the failure of the Custodian to exercise reasonable care in the management or disposition of the real and personal property ... the amount received by him for such property was less than the market value thereof at the time of the evacuation of the owner." No other losses would be considered, and there would be no investigation into the effects of government policies.

The Royal Commission officially set up on July 18, 1947 — commonly referred to as the Bird Commission after its chair, Justice Henry Bird of the B.C. Supreme Court — was yet another political response to the growing public awareness of the devastation wrought by the government's policies for Japanese Canadians. Despite calls for full compensation, the government stuck with the narrow terms decided upon by the cabinet committee. The vague, all-purpose phrase "reasonable care" placed property owners in

---

Japanese Canadian dispersal. The meeting included the infamous Ian Mackenzie, then minister of veterans' affairs; J. L. Ilsley, minister of justice; C. Gibson, secretary of state; J. A. Glen, minister of mines and resources; D. C. Abbott, minister of finance; H. F. G. Bridges, minister of fisheries; and Raymond Ranger, secretary, from the Privy Council Office. Other key players in the Japanese Canadian saga were present, such as Dr. H. L. Keenleyside, then deputy minister of mines and resources, who criticized his government for its mistreatment of Japanese Canadians; A. H. Brown, influential policy maker on Japanese Canadians from the Department of Labour; A. L. Jolliffe, from the immigration branch; A. R. Menzies, from external affairs; D. H. W. Henry, from the Department of Justice; R. G. Robertson, from the prime minister's office; and K. W. Wright and F. G. Shears, key figures with the Custodian of Enemy Property.

the position of having to prove the Custodian's negligence, a near impossi-bility when all the documents for appraisals and sales were inaccessible to researchers and lawyers. It is no wonder, then, that the secretary of state, in a memo advising the cabinet committee on the formation of the Royal Commission, commented: "It is probable that thousands of claims will be filed, but very improbable that the vast majority could be substantiated in a Court of Law. The Japanese have inflated ideas as to the value of their assets and doubtless their claims will be grossly exaggerated."

The issue of "reasonable care" was a way of ensuring that the rules were fixed in the government's favour. There would be no harm in having a commission and a commissioner as long as it would be extremely difficult, in most cases impossible, to prove that losses did occur. But this time the government was pressured to reconsider its position. The CCJC, for instance, informed the government "that if the terms were not broadened it might have to advise the Japanese Canadians to have nothing to do with the Commission." In response, the government used King's earlier statement — that compensation would be paid "where it can be shown that a sale was made at less than a fair market value." What appeared to be a capitulation of sorts satisfied the CCJC, but hardly boded well for the Japanese Canadians who were anticipating a much broader range of compensation for economic losses.

THE LIMITS OF JAPANESE CANADIAN REPRESENTATION

THE COMMISSION BEGAN its work in the fall of 1947 and continued until June 1948, at which time Justice Bird became aware of the enormous amount of time that would have to be spent in listening to each case. For the sake of expediency, he decided to complete the claims process by determining global compensation by category of properties liquidated. Although this change did speed up the claims process, and perhaps got funds into the hands of Japanese Canadians faster, it also placed their representatives — the young nisei leadership in Toronto — in a much more vulnerable posi-tion as decision makers. Unexpectedly, the categories devised by Justice Bird eliminated individual claims.

At the time, the Japanese Canadian point of view, as represented by the newly formed National Japanese Canadian Citizens' Association (NJCCA), had at least two areas of weakness. First, the NJCCA was an organization made up of relatively inexperienced nisei who worked under the Co-operative Committee for Japanese Canadians and two high-ranking lawyers, Andrew Brewin in Toronto and Robert J. McMaster in Vancouver.[2] Second, the CCJC and the two lawyers were considered "successful" in their public and legal work on the government's deportation crisis, and this reputation added to their authority in taking a leading role in the Bird Commission hearings.

Implicit in the NJCCA's relations with the CCJC was the air of gratitude, and this may have stopped it from criticizing the CCJC more diligently. On its side, the CCJC approached the property issue in a much less strident way; perhaps the question of monetary damages lacked the public drama of Canadian citizens being unjustly deported. Although the CCJC supported the NJCCA's call for fair compensation, it was much less insistent that this demand be met by the government. As a result, when the government refused to negotiate more flexible terms of reference, the CCJC appeared willing to compromise, citing pragmatism rather than principle as its guide. This attitude became evident when some Japanese Canadians advocated a boycott of the Bird Commission until it included a wider range of losses. The CCJC, in a statement dated September 19, 1947, opposed such action, arguing that a boycott would lead the government to disband the commission. Instead, it urged those who were qualified, despite the restricted terms, "to take advantage of the Commission and to present their fair claims as vigorously as they can." In the CCJC's view, the legal defeat of the Japanese Property Owners Association by Judge Thorson had demonstrated that the political route was the only one left. Referring to the three test cases dismissed by Thorson, the statement concluded: "It is our opinion based on the advice of the solicitors who represent the Japanese Canadians in these cases that there is little to be hoped for in the way of legal proceedings in the Courts and those who have based their hope on this means to secure compensation for losses must now abandon such hope."

Even today it is not clear what the effects of a boycott would have been. The CCJC advisors who spoke against the boycott may have been outwitted

---

2   The NJCCA handled 1,100 of the 1,434 claims, so a large majority of claimants relied on its advice. Some 200 claims for Japanese Canadians in southern Alberta were handled by Gladstone Virtue, retained by a mostly issei-controlled group who were suspicious of the Toronto nisei leadership.

by the government. When the terms of the Bird Commission were first announced, both the NJCCA and the CCJC reacted strongly against the requirement that claimants prove that the Custodian did not exercise sufficient "care," a point that would be impossible to demonstrate without access to the Custodian's files. No doubt the government advisors agreed. Indeed, that stipulation might have been part of their own manipulation tactic. The CCJC and the NJCCA had been demanding compensation for a variety of losses, with the key proviso that these be understood as a direct result of the mass uprooting. By opening with the narrowest possible terms of reference, the government cleared some space for a subsequent response that could focus on property sales alone. This diverted attention from general compensation, a subject that would necessarily have implicated — perhaps through a review process — the Orders-in-Council passed under the War Measures Act. Any public scrutiny of the government's treatment of Japanese Canadians would certainly have stimulated public debate on the displacement of citizens on the basis of race categorization. In fact, general compensation for the uprooting would be seen as a tacit admission that Japanese Canadians had been damaged by government policy. This perception would directly contradict the government's argument that dispersal was in the "best interests" of Japanese Canadians (as King had stated on August 4, 1944). However, in removing that first restriction — proof by claimants that the Custodian did not exercise "reasonable care" — the government could project the appearance of conciliation and generosity. This move, if it was planned, was a clever tactic to make the commission more attractive to the Canadian public.

Some support for this speculation is contained in government documents. The change in policy was already an optional policy drafted as early as April 21, 1949, for the Cabinet Committee on Japanese Questions and the Special Cabinet Committee on Japanese Claims. In other words, although the CCJQ appeared to be responding to political criticism of the Royal Commission's narrow terms of reference when it agreed to remove the requirement for proof of "reasonable care," its supposedly new position was already in line with earlier plans. Ann Sunahara's account of the Bird Commission takes into consideration the earlier April 21 draft, and she recognizes that the regulation announced on July 18 was much worse: "Some time between April and July, the draft order-in-council defining the terms of the commission had been inexplicably changed. Under the new terms, compensation would be paid only in cases where neglect or lack of care by the Custodian or his staff could be legally proved, an impossible task."

The government's policy shapers would have recognized the potential political fallout of regulations that made it impossible for Japanese Canadians to prove any claims. Why even have a royal commission? Even worse, lawyers for Japanese Canadians may have been able to argue forcefully that all the records of the Custodian's transactions had to be accessible for legal research. After all, if the onus were on the claimants to prove the lack of "reasonable care," to construct their defence their legal advisors should have access to all of the Custodian's files. Moreover, if the government was confident that the Custodian acted fairly at all times, then the evidence should confirm this. Such a legal scenario would have been avoided at all costs by the government. The much easier route to appear "fair and just" would be to pay out some compensation, but only for demonstrated losses beyond the Custodian's control — in other words, losses for which the Custodian could not be held accountable.

This approach explains why Commissioner Bird would not allow for losses on Vancouver properties. Such a conclusion would have acknowledged that the Custodian had sold the properties at less than market value, a concession that the government was unwilling to make. The five percent across-the-board increase that he allowed was equivalent to the real estate fee charged to the former owners. In taking such a position on Vancouver properties, Justice Bird was not concerned about money; what mattered was the defence of government actions. His action was consistent with his carefully worded exoneration of the Custodian's handling of properties:

> I am satisfied ... that the very onerous task ... was competently performed, with due regard to the interest of the owners, notwithstanding that the task had to be performed in an atmosphere of public hysteria induced by war. The fact that I have found that in certain respects fair market value was not realized in sales ... in no sense reflects upon the work of the Custodian's organization.

REACTIONS TO THE BIRD COMMISSION:
THE CRISIS IN LEADERSHIP

THE MINOR FLEXIBILITY exhibited by the government succeeded, at least for the CCJC and its lawyer, Andrew Brewin, who advocated acceptance after the government removed "reasonable care" from the Order-in-Council establishing the Royal Commission. In their statement of September 19, 1947, Brewin and the CCJC expressed "regret" that the government had "not accepted our representations that in order to do full justice all claims for losses to property fairly arising out of the evacuation orders should be investigated and compensation allowed." Nevertheless, they said, Japanese Canadians who qualified to make claims should do so — and not participate in the boycott advocated by some Japanese Canadians. Furthermore, as Brewin wrote in a letter published in the NJCCA's first bulletin, Japanese Canadians could expect no "public support ... to get the terms of reference further widened at this stage, and I think it would be too much to expect those claimants who may have some reasonable prospective success, to forgo the right to present their claims." Behind the wording of the advice was the assumption that they did not have a strong basis to seek full compensation, so pragmatically, those who qualified for some compensation, however minimal and inadequate, would be foolish not to take advantage of the government's offer. The alternative, it was implied, was no compensation whatsoever. A boycott could easily ruin the chances of those who chose to apply. "Most claimants," Ken Adachi writes, "decided to accept the terms 'under protest' in the hopes that the Cabinet would be amenable, at a later date, to allow further claims. It was also hoped that the Commission would uncover sufficient evidence so that the investigation would indeed be enlarged before its termination."

Up to this point, the dissension among Japanese Canadians in Toronto was held in check by their expectation of further compensation once the knowledge of injustices became public. That carrot, given the government's continuation of restrictions on their movement, was more a rationalized capitulation to the terms of the Bird Commission than a viable means of dealing with its shortcomings. Caught between the recommendation of the CCJC and the discontent of many claimants, the nisei leadership opted for compliance, thus avoiding the more difficult process of seeking a consensus among Japanese Canadians whose emotions were already ravaged by years of government abuse.

The internal divisions surfaced explosively in early 1949, when news came that Justice Bird was to suspend the case-by-case investigations and revert to a formula for losses by categories. Again, the NJCCA agreed with the CCJC and Brewin that this policy change would not jeopardize individual claims — the lawyers would still review each case on its own merits — and even claimed that some 25 percent of the claimants who might otherwise have been excluded by a case-by-case approach would benefit from the application of the formula.

At this critical juncture, the strong influence of Brewin on the NJCCA excecutive — and their dependence on him for decision making — had become apparent. Thus on February 6, 1949, only a few months after the Bird Commission had begun its work, an emergency meeting was arranged by George Tanaka, the NJCCA's National Executive Committee secretary, at Brewin's house. The NEC listened as Brewin informed them that there had been some discussion in Vancouver by his colleagues, lawyers Robert McMaster and Gladstone Virtue, that the Bird Commission's lawyer might propose a method of completing the hearings sooner. The minutes stated that Brewin "desired to know whether the Committee was in favour of the principle of an over-all settlement should it ever be brought to the attention of himself and Mr. McMaster by Government Counsel."

The NEC did not endorse the "basic principle" but it "appeared sound" to them. They were concerned, though, that the commissioner might simply impose low figures for an overall settlement. Brewin's view was that the commissioner could not be lobbied by the CCJC and the NJCCA and that he "would take the attitude that it [the commission] was not a bargaining agent and any proposal made and refused by claimants' Counsel would not in any way influence the Commission to revise any offer made." On the one hand, then, Brewin as legal advisor was seeking approval for an overall settlement, and on the other, he had concluded that any attempt to negotiate with the commissioner was futile. Brewin also informed the executive that he had met with the CCJC "earlier that day" and that it had agreed "that the principle of over-all settlement might be given consideration."

It was soon apparent, then, that an "over-all settlement" — a settlement based on categories of losses determined by the commission, and not based on individual cases — would likely become a reality. By giving the nod to the "basic principle," which Brewin supported, the NEC entered into a process of complicity that would bind them closer to Brewin and the CCJC and distance them from a large number of claimants all over Canada. Brewin, for his part, was convinced that the procedural change would benefit more claimants, including the 25 percent who would likely receive nothing under individual hearings. But when the change was finally announced by the Bird Commission, with the agreement of the claimants' legal advisors, many claimants expressed their disapproval. Two special meetings, on what was understood as a "Settlement Proposal from Commissioner Justice Bird," were coordinated by George Tanaka on April 10 and April 11, 1949. The hierarchical relationship between the NEC and the CCJC and Brewin was evident in the description of the purpose of the meetings. The NEC would first receive advice and recommendations from the lawyers, McMaster and Brewin, as well as from the CCJC, after which it would "formulate" its recommendation to claimants through the executives of the NJCCA provincial chapters.

The minutes of the two meetings, which were drafted together, recorded that McMaster in Vancouver was in favour of the overall settlement offer, except for the mere five percent on the sale price for properties in Vancouver; the 125 percent offered on the Fraser Valley farms confiscated by the government through the Veterans' Land Act was "as much as, if not more than, we could possibly hope to have established." He also admitted that "our evidence on city property is horribly weak," so that it was unlikely that a legal argument would yield a higher percentage — although he thought that some claimants for city properties "are entitled to better consideration." The five percent was designated as a return for the commission taken by the Custodian of Enemy Property for selling the property and not as a concession that the sale price was lower than market price. In addition, Justice Bird was willing to concede an average of 30 percent on claims for personal properties lost, including cars, goods sold at auctions, and some items lost or stolen. The total in additional claims was about $800,000.

In his letter McMaster recommended acceptance, perhaps with some small increases here and there, and advised that the offer was contingent on the costs saved for abandoning further individual hearings. The CCJC also recommended acceptance. The narrow terms of reference, the CCJC believed, could not be changed; further evidence to increase claims was unlikely to be found; and finally, agreeing with Brewin's earlier assumption, Justice Bird's opinion "will prevail as to the fair market price and the amounts to be awarded." From the CCJC's perspective, what was offered was not fair, but Bird would not likely offer any more, and were they to protest further, "it may be considerably less and in some cases nothing at all."

The pressure to endorse the settlement proposal, despite the possibility of a slightly higher percentage for Vancouver properties, placed the NJCCA's National Executive Committee in a delicate position between the powerful influence of Brewin and the CCJC, who represented elements of the dominant white mainstream working for Japanese Canadians, and the claimants, those individuals who suffered the loss of homes, business, jobs and precious personal belongings, and whose lives were destroyed by unjust government policies. It was relatively easy for the NEC itself to understand that an "over-all settlement ... was generally agreed upon as an acceptable method of settlement under the circumstances, on the grounds that it would probably mean a greater number of claimants receiving some award for losses and that the heavy legal expenses required to follow through the hearing of each claim individually would not be practical or a welcome prospect to claimants." What remains much more troubling, however, was the power that had been assumed by the committee, as an "executive body" vested with the authority to represent Japanese Canadians "outside" the community. Such authority was not necessarily endorsed by the claimants, most of whom had to rely completely on advice given them from above, as it were. Relationships became even more tangled because the CCJC, who, in their minds, were assisting Japanese Canadians to assimilate into mainstream white Canada, conducted their affairs exclusively with the NEC.

Brewin himself attended the April 11 meeting to reiterate his opinion that the overall settlement offer from the Bird Commission was the "best" that could be expected from the government. In fielding questions from nervous members of the executive committee about the possibility of pressing for further compensation, Brewin answered in a manner consistent with the boundaries set by the Bird Commission itself. He believed that Justice Bird would not raise the claims figures, and that "he had now stretched his conscience beyond the terms of reference as far as he would go." The sum of approximately $100,000, Brewin said, had been added for losses outside the terms of reference — for instance, the return of the commission deducted by the Custodian for properties liquidated — and this was the limit of Bird's concessions. Brewin therefore warned against non-compliance, in the form of either outright rejection or refusal to formally accept the offer. The government could easily withdraw its offer and close the door on all forms of compensation.

The minutes reveal that the NEC had arrived at a critical moment when they were expected, by Brewin and the CCJC, to decide in favour of the settlement offer, but they remained anxious about their role as mediators. Should they not also consider the offer in terms of a "more all-inclusive basis," in other words, in terms of the claimants' views? Should they not suspend a decision until they had listened to what the claimants had to say? In an awkwardly phrased explanation — cautiously constructed by the note taker — the members of the NEC were portrayed as being in accord with the CCJC, the legal advisors and the NJCCA chapters, and thus not pursuing the interests of claimants as individuals, each with his or her own set of losses:

> It was pointed out [by implication, Brewin is advising] that if an executive member wished to look at the question purely from the point of view of a claimant the settlement offer may be entirely unsatisfactory as far as his own claim is concerned, but as a member of the National Executive Committee and the place of that Committee in relation to Japanese Canadian Claimants, its member chapters, the Co-operative Committee and Counsel and knowledge of the facts and views of each group, he could arrive at a different conclusion for the Executive Committee.

At this point in the meeting, the executive committee passed a motion to make a recommendation. But in deciding what to recommend, the meeting required two motions. The first motion, which died for lack of a seconder, would have required claimants to take a position "giving any indication that they are satisfied with the percentages," and that they would either reject the proposal or simply let the commission act on its own. The second motion, which conformed to the position advocated by Brewin and the CCJC, stated:

> ... although we are not satisfied with the settlement proposal for property claims received from the Government, after hearing and studying the recommendation of Claimants' Counsel, we are of the opinion that there is no alternative than to endorse the recommendation of acceptance as

formulated by the Co-operative Committee with the following reservations:

1. The offer with respect to Vancouver Properties is too low.

2. The Terms of Reference are too narrow.

3. Some special cases which if settled under the proposed formula would be clearly inadequate should be given individual consideration.

The motion carried with seven votes in favour, one abstention and three opposed.[3] The 11 members and George Tanaka soon found themselves caught up in a web of mutual mistrust. In subsequent meetings of the National Executive Committee, as recorded in the minutes, the consequences of the decision-making process unravelled in arguments, accusations and counter-accusations. As the members who voted against the motion aligned themselves — contrary to the advice they were given — with the "point of view of the claimants," the issue of their accountability and responsibility to the claimants, rather than to the CCJC and Brewin, assumed prominence. On May 10, 1949, while reflecting on the April 11 meeting, some members said that Brewin should not have been invited there: "R. [Roger] Obata felt that Mr. Brewin's presence caused them to be torn between loyalties to counsel and claimants and that they were showing lack of confidence in Counsel or acting to the detriment of claimants." Executive Secretary Tanaka responded by explaining the difficult position he often occupied in his dealings with the CCJC: "Sometimes in a Co-operative Committee meeting, he stated that he is placed in such a position that he must second a motion which if he did not would be detrimental to this Committee." Certainly Tanaka found himself in a conflicted situation. When he spoke to claimants in various Canadian centres, he presented himself as a representative of the CCJC and informed claimants that they had to decide on their own, based on the advice and knowledge of the CCJC. "I went out of my way to indicate and state that the JCCA was not in a position to influence or advise the claimants," he reported. Nevertheless, and this knowledge was already circulating among the claimants, the NEC had voted in favour of acceptance.

---

3   The three who voted no — Kunio Hidaka, Jack Oki and Roger Obata — would re-enter community politics some 30 years later, as the redress movement once again revisited the unresolved injustices of the internment.

News of this decision led to a community meeting, at which a petition was signed rejecting Bird's settlement proposal and calling for changes. This action was the focus of the May 12 meeting of the NEC. There, individuals from the claimants' meeting appeared before the committee, taking them to task for not defending the claimants' position, even if that position was rejected by Judge Bird. They were dissatisfied because they had not been given an opportunity to respond to the settlement offer. The decision had been made for them by the executive committee, who were pressured by Brewin and the CCJC. One issei claimant who spoke for the group, identified as "Mr. Shin," stated that Japanese Canadians who applied for compensation did so honestly and conscientiously, and that the figures they gave matched the value of their properties. As the former owners, their assessments had to be taken seriously — but thus far the awards of $800,000 by Judge Bird fell far short of their total claim of $5 million. It was his view that the evaluations were low because the owners had been absent from the assessment process. Hidaka, Obata and Oki agreed that the owner's point of view was crucial in any evaluation; the lawyer who calculated the figures should have consulted with the owners before they made the figures known to Commissioner Bird. Even the percentage increases for the Fraser Valley farms, which both McMaster and Brewin lauded as much more than expected, were inadequate according to the former owners. Mr. Shin gave his own case as an example:

> In 1919, I purchased property at $750 cash. I claimed $3,500. At the time I bought it 3/4 acres were cleared, others in bushes and there was a little house. I built a lean-to, a barn at the cost of $300, a bunkhouse at the cost of $300, 3 1/2 acres were cleared and 2 acres left with standing green timber. Therefore, I considered $3,500 a fair price. (I carried house insurance of $1,000.) The Custodian sold it for $730. 80% of $730 is to be awarded, making a total of $1,300. Therefore, I do not think it fair — I just want to tell the Commissioner and ask him.

The issue of "over-all settlement" was not in dispute here. What stirred the anger of claimants was the perception that their views as former owners were not presented vigorously enough to the commissioner and that the NJCCA was not representing their specific interests.

While the quarrels continued among Japanese Canadians, the Bird Commission proceeded with its overall settlement plans, on the basis of agreement from Brewin and McMaster, the CCJC and, presumably, the NJCCA. When Justice Bird tabled his report in the House of Commons on June 14, 1950, the public learned that he had awarded a total of merely $1,222,829 to the individual claimants who qualified under the narrow terms of reference of the commission. That $1.2 million amounted to about $52 for each of the 23,000 people who had been forcibly uprooted, dispossessed, dispersed and deported without ever having committed a crime. Bird used the term "rough justice" to describe the cash settlement.

The final outrage and insult, aside from the commission's failure to be "fair and just," was the release form that claimants had to sign. Before they could receive any money, they had to agree to waive all rights to make any further claims against the government for any losses. Why had this regulation never been mentioned before? For Japanese Canadians, signing a waiver signified "final" closure on all further claims for compensation. Not surprisingly, the CCJC and Brewin advocated signing the release, so that they could receive the funds. Given the terms of the War Measures Act, there was no possibility that Japanese Canadians could ever launch a successful legal campaign against the government. Better, then — so they were advised — to take whatever money was available. The alternative was nothing at all.

Nothing, that is, in monetary terms, but the release form meant much more to Japanese Canadians who had watched their demands for full compensation fade away as each stipulation of the Bird Commission was first tolerated and then accepted. By 1950, believing that the government held all the power to make decisions, the CCJC wanted closure on the property claims issue. For it, the politics of the issue — with the Bird Commission report now made public — had lost its urgency. The restriction on moving back to the west coast had been lifted on April 1, 1949, and Japanese Canadians had been granted the vote at the same time. They now appeared to be restored as "Canadians." They had gone, to use the language of the CCJC's pamphlet, from "refugees" to "citizens." The CCJC's success in "making democracy work" was evident in its work against deportation and in support of property claims. Token compensation, while admittedly inadequate, was at least some recognition of the losses.

Not everyone shared this desire to capitulate to "rough justice." The most vocal opposition came from a group that split from the National Japanese Canadian Citizens' Association, the Toronto Claimants' Committee (TCC), which pressed Japanese Canadians to reject the Bird Commission's report and continue lobbying for substantial compensation. Initially a part of the NJCCA, the TCC broke its ties once the NJCCA had decided to comply with the CCJC's recommendations. Both Roger Obata and Kunio Hidaka, vocal opponents of the NJCCA's action — and future advocates of redress in the 1980s — were central voices for the TCC.

The TCC position was expressed in a letter sent to the NJCCA's executive committee a few months after the Bird Commission report. Writing as the TCC's chair, Senji Takashima told Tanaka why his group was so disappointed in the NJCCA's failure to say "no" to the Bird Commission. In granting only $1,200,000 when claims had totalled $7 million, and by requiring claimants to sign a waiver agreement, the government had clearly demonstrated that further compensation was off the table. Takashima also reminded Tanaka that the NJCCA, from its founding conference in September 1947 and in subsequent discussions on the compensation issue, had not isolated losses caused by the Custodian from overall losses and that the intent was "to press the Government for all losses for which they were responsible by having ordered the evacuation." When compensation was restricted to those losses "resulting from sales by the Custodian," those who had advocated a "complete boycott of the Royal Commission" had agreed to comply because of the advice of the lawyer, Andrew Brewin — advice that the NJCCA had endorsed.

Brewin, a lawyer working through the CCJC, had argued that the findings of the Bird Commission could be used to press for further compensation. With the report now filed, Takashima said, the NJCCA should mount a campaign to seek full compensation. "We urge that this action be taken promptly before the Government closes the matter of economic losses for all time," Takashima wrote. But even then, the energy required to undertake such action had dissipated. As the new decade began, there was a waning of interest in a "just and fair" settlement and a much stronger interest in rebuilding lives in the rising economic climate of the 1950s.

DECISION MAKING IN POSTWAR TORONTO:
THE PROBLEM OF COMPLICITY

FOR SOME JAPANESE Canadians, the enforced closure signified by the release form became yet another betrayal in a series of betrayals. But now their own organization, the NJCCA, had complied with the expectations of their white allies instead of defending the position of the claimants. Dissension within the leadership reached a breaking point when Roger Obata and Kunio Hidaka, the most vocal critics of Executive Secretary George Tanaka and his NEC, allied themselves with the TCC, a move that caused a major split in loyalties for many in the community.

Would the claimants have been better off boycotting the Bird Commission, as members of the TCC advocated? Could the NJCCA have mounted a protest effective enough to pressure the government to broaden the terms of reference? Was Bird's "rough justice" actually better than none at all? Or would the refusal of the measly sums awarded — again, as the TCC advocated — have left the door open for further negotiations in the future? Would the results have been any different had the CCJC dealt not with the NEC, but directly with a committee formed of claimants? Did the executive secretary, as the main conduit between the CCJC and Japanese Canadians, often get caught in compromising liaisons with the CCJC and Brewin? Would the government have ignored the property issue altogether had the CCJC not taken on an advocacy role for Japanese Canadians?

According to the historian Peter Nunoda, nisei organizations in the 1940s — of which the NJCCA was a prime example — were often overly compliant with government officials and influential white Canadians. Its young nisei leadership just could not overcome an awareness of their subordinate status. Nunoda sees the earlier split between the nisei-based Japanese Canadian Citizens' Council (who advocated cooperation with the government) and the Nisei Mass Evacuation Group (who posed resistance or gambari as a means of pressing the government to change the policy of family separation) replayed in Toronto community politics, though with quite different concerns and allies. In Vancouver, Japanese Canadians acted alone in their turbulent dealings with the B.C. Security Commission. In the largely white Canadian — and more liberal — social milieu of Toronto, the power of the issei and naturalized Japanese Canadians suddenly decreased, and just as dramatically the English-speaking and Canadian-educated nisei found themselves in decision-making roles. With the emergence of the Co-operative Committee on Japanese Canadians, the nisei became the mediators of the new social and political conditions. But given their lack of leadership experience, and given as well their lack of political influence, it was understandable that the CCJC would assume the role of representing Japanese Canadians. And the CCJC did so, as Nunoda argues, on the assumption "that the dispersal and assimilation of the Japanese Canadian community would solve the racial problems encountered in British Columbia."

In other words, despite supporting citizenship rights, the CCJC assumed, along with Prime Minister King, that dispersal and assimilation would solve the "Japanese problem" in B.C. and in Canada. In all their dealings with the NJCCA, they never wavered from this position. This is why they could not be expected to endorse the position of those Japanese Canadians who sought compensation for the injustices of internment. Nunoda argues that a relationship of complicity thus developed between the nisei spokespersons and the CCJC. This relationship, in turn, allowed the CCJC to use its power "to the benefit of some of the Japanese Canadians but at the same time it abused that privilege in its control over the JCCA. Equally, the JCCA were loath to defy the Co-operative Committee because they believed that the power of their organization emanated from their close relationship with the CCJC." The power and influence of Andrew Brewin was pervasive, strikingly evident in meetings with the government. During a presentation to the Committee on Public Accounts regarding a royal commission to determine compensation, for instance, Brewin was the one who spoke on behalf of Japanese Canadians "while Tanaka sat silently by."

Nunoda's reseach on nisei complicity brings out the shortcomings of Japanese Canadians' political awareness at the time, but the consequences of this complicity also need to be measured against the contradictions they faced. The young nisei who found themselves at the centre of a social and political cyclone were so bound up in the trauma of a displaced collective — still reeling from the violence of dispossession, confinement and dispersal — that their own language quickly reached the limits of its grasp. In this state, as they frantically organized to create community mechanisms through which they could speak out against further violations and at the same time remain loyal Canadians, the coalition of white supporters in the CCJC would have been perceived as a gift that could not be refused.

In 1945, with no allies, cordoned off by race categories in a legislative ghetto, nearly half of the Japanese Canadians expelled from the west coast faced mass deportation to a land few of them knew. The prospect of being incorporated into the Canadian nation, especially through a doorway opened by sympathetic white Canadians, offered opportunities of social mobility and political identity that had been impossible in prewar B.C. And the movement east of the Rockies created the conditions for a generational shift in power relations. The English-speaking nisei children of the Japanese-speaking issei, a group that included many young men and women with white middle-class aspirations who had lost little, if any, property in B.C., could see the need to conform to dominant social values. For them, east of B.C. signified access to higher education, the lifting of barriers to certain professions, and new lives distant from the virulent racism of the west coast.

ONE LAST ATTEMPT TO SEEK JUSTICE

DESPITE THE FINALITY implicit in the Bird Commission's report, and perhaps in the faint hope of keeping the compensation question open, the NJCCA submitted a brief to the government in September 1951 — shortly after receiving Takashima's letter from the Toronto Claimants' Committee — pointing out the Bird Commission's narrow terms of reference and the losses it had excluded. The brief was signed by President Harold Hirose and Executive Secretary George Tanaka. The language of the case for further compensation was cautious, polite and careful not to blame the government for property losses. "After a year's experience with the impossible task of protecting all this property," the brief pointed out, "the Government changed its policy to one of 'orderly liquidation.'" Among the losses for which compensation was requested was "a grant of monies to each adult evacuee to compensate for general losses." It was these "general losses," softly inserted in a list of excluded losses, that the Toronto Claimants' Committee wanted to make the cornerstone of a national campaign. "We therefore respectfully suggest," the brief concluded, "a broad appreciation of all the circumstances which shaped the problem into its present form is fully merited, if it is the intent of your Government to provide for a measure of justice which is equal to the standards of a truly democratic, Canadian way of life." Here, the language of appeal sounds like a sigh of resignation: the writers of the brief already have a good idea what the answer to their request will be.

The reply came from a new prime minister, Louis St. Laurent, the former minister of justice, who had signed the order for the mass uprooting of Japanese Canadians. His position was dismissive and final:

> The government appointed a Royal Commission to enquire into the claims of the Japanese Canadians and to ascertain what would be fair and just under all the circumstances to the Japanese Canadians and to the Canadian public generally. The Commission recommended that a certain sum of money be paid to the claimants. The government has concurred in the recommendations and money has been made available to meet the claims. In carrying out the recommendations of Mr. Justice Bird we feel we have discharged our obligations both to the Japanese Canadians and to the general public.

St. Laurent must have been pleased that, once again, the public vehicle of a royal commission — echoing the effects of the earlier Jackson Commission — had absolved the government of responsibility for its "successful" destruction of the Japanese Canadian community on the west coast. He had been displeased when the government decided not to go ahead with mass deportation and had gone so far as to urge King to carry it out despite the public outcry that would ensue, because soon there would be requests that "the Japanese [sic] in Canada be given the same rights as the white population." Clearly, the government that "discharged [its] obligations both to the Japanese Canadians and to the general public" had managed to escape accountability for its systematic abuse of a group of its citizens, solely on the basis of its power to define a person as "of the Japanese race."

The compensation demands of the 1940s focused on the economic losses caused by the mass uprooting and dispossession. The narrow boundaries of the Bird Commission simply reinforced the assumption that material losses were the only basis of compensation. Terms like "injustice" were applied to the experience of Japanese Canadians, but no attention was directed toward the government's own culpability. As a result, the question of the illegitimate application of the War Measures Act, a concept that would have involved a public discussion of citizenship rights, never became part of the property confiscation discussion. The absence of a conceptual approach — indeed, the stripping of Justice Bird of the authority to "judge" the effect of policies — ensured that claims would get mired in calculating the details of monetary value. The more intangible values, in the process, never reached public awareness. For civil libertarians in the white mainstream, the "problem" was solved once the victims had received money for property losses.

The Toronto Claimants' Committee disbanded formally on May 28, 1951, still disappointed that the compensation issue had subsided. In its final report, nevertheless, it placed on record three points of urgency:

a) To bring to the attention of the Canadian public the injustices of the evacuation and the tremendous economic losses which resulted therefrom.
b) To show to the public the total inadequacy of the awards recommended by Mr. Justice H. I. Bird in his report of the inquiry.
c) To show the injustices resulting from exclusion of a group of evacuees from substantial and justifiable compensation; i.e. properties not handled by the Custodian.

Decades later, these concerns resurfaced when Japanese Canadians launched a movement to redress the injustices of the 1940s, including the injustices perpetrated by the Bird Commission itself.[4]

---

4   The dates here are uncanny. The National Japanese Canadian Citizens' Association submitted their brief to the government on September 22, 1950. Thirty-eight years later, on September 22, 1988, the National Association of Japanese Canadians signed a comprehensive redress agreement with the Canadian government.

THE CALL FOR JUSTICE IN MOOSE JAW

THE RECOMMENDATIONS OF the Bird Commission were a tremendous disappointment to Japanese Canadians, who had hoped that the commission would right the wrongs committed by their government. That the government dealt with the injury caused by the mass uprooting, dispossession and loss of freedom by reluctantly awarding people small sums of money did little to assuage the shame of racialization. Instead, it intensified the desire for justice. In 1947, when the nisei writer Muriel Kitagawa asked in her article, "Who Was the Custodian?" she invoked much more than the Custodian of Enemy Property who had sold off her house on East Pender Street in Vancouver. In the much broader framework of the rights of citizens in a democratic nation, she invoked the "custodian" as a figure who represented a nation that is responsible for and accountable to its citizens. She exposed the deep layers of pain in many Japanese Canadians when she answered her own question: "Who is the Custodian of my freeborn rights, if not the government of my native land? Who is the protector of my own chattels from looting, if not the laws of this land? Who is the sponsor of my dreams, of all the hopes and plans, the confidant entrusted with what lies ahead of me, if not my own, native land?"

For Kitagawa and others, the "Custodian" embodied the trust of citizens that their government would protect them from the violation of their rights. It was the betrayal of this trust that accounted for the traumatic effects of internment. The Bird Commission, from this perspective, obscured the deeper consequences that scarred the memories of those directly affected by the betrayal. Nowhere is this more evident than in a marginal but revealing incident in the history of internment. In 1948, while Japanese Canadians coalesced in Toronto to rebuild their community institutions and prepare for the Bird Commission hearings, a small group took a "last stand" in a lonely government hostel just outside of Moose Jaw. Here was a small group — a minority within a minority — who refused to go gently into the frontiers of assimilation and instead raised the question of trust.

For the government's social engineers, the relocation of some Japanese Canadians to Saskatchewan seemed a reasonable plan, given Prime Minister King's dispersal policy. Surveying the vast spaces between B.C. and Montreal (the eastern limit of dispersion), T. B. Pickersgill, an official from the Department of Labour who was perceived by many as cold and cruel, worried about the absence of migrants to Saskatchewan. (The majority of Japanese Canadians favoured Ontario.) Pickersgill's penchant for balanced distribution led him to devise a scheme to force some settlement in Saskatchewan. He set his sights on the government hostel at Moose Jaw, a structure that "consisted of requisitioned buildings at the Moose Jaw Air Force Station," as Jesse Nishihata notes.

Because the Japanese Canadians residing in the B.C. interior towns could not be coerced to move to Saskatchewan, Pickersgill arranged to have most of the remaining 127 men in the internment camp at Angler transferred to the Moose Jaw hostel.[1] His plan was to have their families join them there before resettlement in that province. In a letter to F. J. Mead, RCMP commissioner, dated June 8, 1946, A. H. Brown, a Department of

---

1   According to Jesse Nishihata's figures in "Internment of Japanese Canadians, 1941-1946," there were 427 internees at Angler by the end of the war; of these, 146 left Canada through repatriation and 154 accepted work offered them in Ontario. At that time they were still required to take designated employment and were not allowed to rejoin their families in the B.C. camps.

Labour official, mentioned that Pickersgill wanted to use "this group as the initial group for relocation in Saskatchewan," adding that "we are anxious to get as many Japanese into Saskatchewan as possible so as to balance up the distribution of Japanese in Western Canada."

The Angler prisoner-of-war camp closed in July 1946. The internees and their families were sent to Moose Jaw, supposedly for a temporary period, prior to resettlement in Saskatchewan. One year later, however, 91 people still remained in the hostel. They refused to relocate to Saskatchewan and instead took a more militant stand: to demand either permission to return to B.C. or deportation to Japan and compensation for losses. In the following months, some of the aged and ill were moved to the hospital and sanitarium at New Denver, B.C. By the summer of 1947, the 59 people remaining in the hostel responded to government threats of eviction by adopting a position of passive resistance until their demands were met. By February 1948, the group had split into two: one (33 people) resided in the more comfortable main building and commuted to jobs in Moose Jaw; the other (12 people), a more militant group, stayed in a smaller, unheated building. The militant group was led by Hirokichi Isomura, an issei man whose two daughters were the only women in the group. When they were moved to the larger building, Nishihata says, "the ten men occupied the corridor in a sit down strike that lasted until March 3rd, when the men finally abandoned their protest."

Realizing that the inmates of the hostel planned to remain there indefinitely, officials decided to evict them. After the eviction, 38 people took up residence in tents outside the hostel. They lived in this manner until July 16, when they were given temporary space in a building on the exhibition grounds. Two men, however, refused to leave the tents, and they were joined by another man on the weekends. They were left undisturbed until November 27. "When a sharp drop in temperature was predicted," Nishihata explains, "the RCMP decided to remove the men to prevent them from freezing to death and avoid the 'serious repercussions' which might ensue, as the men had expressed the intent 'to remain in the tent until they died." Two of the men were sent to New Denver, and the third stayed in Saskatchewan.

The demands for compensation in Moose Jaw never received national media attention, nor did the Gandhian strategy of passive resistance generate even a ripple of political support from Japanese Canadians across

Canada. Moose Jaw was hardly a centre of national concern, and perhaps the only politician who became aware of the abuse of power under the War Measures Act was Ross Thatcher, the Co-operative Commonwealth Federation member for Moose Jaw. Thatcher had provided the tents for the last two men to leave the hostel site and had protested the eviction. He told Prime Minister King in a telegram that the "Democratic rights of Canadian citizens [were] apparently endangered by strong-arm tactics," and in the House of Commons he spoke against the continuation (until April 1, 1949) of the policy of not allowing Japanese Canadians to return to B.C.

Hirokichi Isomura was an issei World War I veteran, one of a handful of issei men who, after a decade of lobbying the B.C. government, were granted the franchise in 1932 for having served Canada in World War I. Isomura, then 65, and his son Kunio, then 27, had been sent there directly from Angler. He was joined by his two daughters. On July 14, when the RCMP issued writs of possession on the Japanese Canadians to evict them from the camp, Isomura, so the RCMP report stated, was "alleged to have drawn a knife in the presence of the Sheriff, and refused to give it up when called upon to do so." Isomura was taken into custody, and the eviction proceeded — "and all the property of the Japanese, with the exception of storage belongings, which were stored in another hut, was taken outside the Airport fence, and stacked on a triangle of land formed by the junction of two roads and a road which runs parallel to the Airport fence just west of the gate leading into the Airport."[2]

Isomura, who was born in Aichi-ken, Japan, had been wounded in battle in World War I. He had been a member of the Canadian 50th Battalion and had taken part in the battle of Vimy Ridge. A fellow issei, Sachimaro Moro-oka, recorded an incident during this battle:

> Hirokichi Isomura found a severely wounded German soldier crying for water. Isomura gave it to him from his water bottle. A *hakujin* [white person] pushed Isomura aside and stabbed the German with a bayonet. Isomura cried, "Why did you do that? He would have died anyway!" When we came by, the two were about to go at each other with bayonets. Fortunately, we were able to separate them.

---

2   Isomura received a suspended sentence.

In 1942, Isomura and his son were interned at Angler for not complying with the government's mass uprooting orders. His anger likely stemmed from a sense of outrage. After all, he had fought for Canada in World War I, as did his fellow issei and veteran Masumi Mitsui, who also fought at Vimy Ridge. Mitsui, who was the recipient of the Military Medal for bravery, was also branded "enemy alien," uprooted with his wife Sugiko and their five children, and stripped of his poultry farm in Port Coquitlam by the Custodian of Enemy Property. "Summoned before a Security Commissioner, Mitsui reached into his pocket, pulled out his World War I medals and threw them on the floor. 'What good are these!' he demanded in fury."[3] Then there was the case of Kosho Matano, in the 50th Battalion with Isomura, who was taken by government order from the Essondale mental hospital and deported to Japan. The mistreatment of another veteran, Yasuzo Shoji, was cited in Edith Fowke's *They Made Democracy Work*:

Uazusu [*sic*] Shoji, who was twice wounded while fighting with the Princess Pats in World War I, had purchased nineteen acres of land under the Soldiers' Settlement Act and established a chicken farm. His nineteen acres, a two-storied house, four chicken houses, an electric incubator, and 2,500 fowls were sold for $1,492.59. After certain deductions for taxes and sundries were made, Mr. Shoji received a cheque for $39.32.

As Ken Adachi notes, though, Shoji "promptly declined, claiming a loss of $4,725.02."

Despite the government's labelling of Isomura as one of the "mentally cock-eyed holdouts," it is more likely that as a World War I veteran he was responding to a betrayal of trust, the violation of his rights and dignity as one who had already proven his loyalty to Canada. Although he did not articulate his position in print, he shared the legitimate grievances of other

---

3   Mitsui's family was torn apart and did not reunite until after the war, in Hamilton, Ontario, where they resettled. On August 2, 1985, during the height of the redress movement, Mitsui took part in a ceremonial relighting of the lamp in the Japanese Canadian War Memorial in Stanley Park. This monument had been erected by the community in 1920 to commemorate those who fought for Canada in World War I. Of the 196 men who enlisted, Roy Ito writes, "54 Japanese Canadians had died in battle. Most of the rest had suffered injuries, and only twelve were fortunate enough to return home without a scratch." The lamp had been extinguished since the mass uprooting.

resisters. In a *New Canadian* article published during that time, one of the issei resisters queried: "Who was responsible for the misery I went through behind barbed wire for four years? What did I do to deserve all this punishment? The sooner the government gives me a satisfactory deal, the sooner I will get out of this place. My store has been sold without my consent. My life savings are gone. Is this democracy?" Another Moose Jaw resister, a young nisei, explained his group's position on a local radio station: "The government took us out of our homes, interned us as enemy aliens, and seized our property, all without cause. It may have been legal, but it wasn't justice — and it is justice we want."

In 1947-48, in a remote site in Moose Jaw, Saskatchewan, there were no ears to hear the isolated protestors' cry for justice. There was no public forum in which the issue of responsibility could be addressed. The stand at Moose Jaw and the political expediency of the Bird Commission, though distant from each other, had this much in common: the voices of the Japanese Canadians who were directly affected by dispossession and dispersal could not be heard. Not yet.

CHAPTER 6

SETTING THE WHEELS IN MOTION

The JCCP Redress Committee

What is redress?
• *In general terms, redress is defined as "an act of setting right a wrong."*
• *For Japanese Canadians, "redress" means that all members of our community who were unjustly treated during the war years should now receive some form of compensation.*
— Japanese Canadian Centennial Project (JCCP), Redress Committee

OF JAPANESE DESCENT

IN 1945, JUST as the war was coming to an end and as part of the forced dispersal of Japanese Canadians "east of the Rockies," the Department of Labour hired an independent film company to produce what was ostensibly a documentary, the 22-minute film *Of Japanese Descent*, but which in fact had strong propagandistic objectives. The matter-of-fact and authoritative voice of the film's commentator is distant and aerial. The intended audience, primarily white Canadians, are led to gaze on the figures portrayed as the "Japanese other" who have been moved from the coast as a defensive measure, and who, for the good of the country, are now being resettled east of the Rockies as part of a "rational" federal government policy. The film adopts a pedagogical stance to explain, make sense of or otherwise normalize the government's action. Its approach avoids the obvious question: Why are these citizens — not charged with any crimes against the state, yet uprooted and dispossessed — forced to remain outside of B.C. now that the war is over?

But such an obvious question may not have been all that obvious at the time. Even by 1945, with the movement of Japanese Canadians closely controlled and monitored, Canadians knew little about the political machinations behind the internment. This shattering event did not receive critical attention from the mass media, only an endorsement of official positions. And of course the government acted to hide the knowledge that would have revealed the abuse of its own citizens. *Of Japanese Descent* glossed over the more brutal aspects of the uprooting to offer Canadians a reassuring narrative about "these Japanese," primarily because the dispersal policy meant "they" would soon appear in the audience's neighbourhoods. In this light, the documentary form of the film belied a more immediate ideological intent: to rationalize the displacement of Japanese Canadians as a normal outcome of wartime conditions and to portray their resettlement east of the Rockies as a productive solution to the long-standing "Japanese problem." In short, the film presented in a more popular and consumable way the substance of Prime Minister Mackenzie King's speech of August 1944.

In the film, the "Japanese" bodies — and they are more bodies than persons — are placed in former B.C. "ghost" towns, euphemistically called "resettlement camps," and they appear in various states of contentment. At one point, as the camera pans the lush and primal B.C. landscape, the fact of confinement concealed by the beauty of the wilderness setting. Viewers are invited to appreciate the pristine qualities of the Canadian outdoors, an environment in which Japanese Canadians are likened to participants in a recreational "camp" (not a "detention" camp). The conjoining of nature and the everyday lives of Japanese Canadians implies that they are being rejuvenated and rehabilitated by a government program. In "fact," the commentator tells viewers, the uprooting has raised their standard of living.

Removed from their west coast ghettos — flash to images of an apparently dilapidated house in Steveston, B.C. — these unfortunates are benefiting from the robust and healthy "camp" environment.

"It should be made clear," the voice-over says, "that Japanese in these towns are not living in internment camps." Made clear to whom? Presumably to Canadian audiences, who are being informed that the "Japanese in these towns" are not incarcerated. But more than just functioning as a source of news, the film assures viewers that their country does not have "internment camps," with all the negative connotations of brutality and confinement. Official "internment" was not a viable policy for Japanese Canadians. Under the Geneva Convention, only "enemy aliens" — not citizens — could be interned. This was the situation of the Nisei Mass Evacuation Group members who were wrongfully interned at Petawawa and Angler. Even if the government were to ignore that rule — under the War Measures Act it could perhaps justify such action — it would have paid the costs of building what would then be "internment camps," and would also have provided food and clothing to the internees, as the United States did for Japanese Americans.

The representation of some former "Japanese" neighbourhoods as degraded sites, and of dispersal as a movement into the superior, "clean and wholesome" social milieu of white Canada, draws on the legacy of racialization. In that framework, the figures in the film had already been identified as a manifestation of the unclean "Asiatic." The flash-by shot of a loaf of bread during a section on the supposedly superior living conditions in the camps indirectly denigrates a diet of rice and fish. The implication is that "Canadian" food has made "the Japanese" much healthier and happier. Indeed, the overall impression of the film is that the Canadian government has done Japanese Canadians a favour. Their gardens, through the lens, suggest plenitude; they are filmed hard at work producing lumber to build their homes; and large groups of children smile directly at the camera or are busy at play, including a baseball game and a scouts group, both signs of their successful westernization in the camps.

The film makes no mention of the social, economic and cultural vibrancy of the Japanese Canadian communities in the Fraser Valley, in Steveston, in central Vancouver, on Vancouver Island and up the B.C. coast to Prince Rupert. The patriarchical voice of the narrator determines the meaning of the discourse operative in the film. The "Japanese" bodies remain mute. None of the subjects speaks to the camera. As Christopher Gittings, in a critique of this film's racialization of Japanese Canadians, comments, "the status of speaking subjects is withheld from Japanese Canadians who are not interviewed but transformed into material to be mastered and organized by [filmmaker] O. C. Burritt, the National Film Board and the Ministry of Labour."

A CALL FOR JUSTICE

FAST FORWARD, NEARLY four decades later, to a CBC news documentary. It is the fall of 1982 and the distant, unidentified voice so characteristic of the 1940s is gone. Now the viewer faces the announcer Russ Froese. As he stands on a Vancouver beach with the ocean behind him, he begins a special feature for CBC TV's *Journal, A Call for Justice,* a documentary film prompted by the demand for redress. "They have come from all over North America," Froese begins, "these survivors of Canada's World War II internment camps. Forty years ago these Japanese Canadians were farmers and businessmen near Vancouver. Today they are back for a reunion. They vividly remember the last time they saw each other."

A Call for Justice is constructed through three intersecting frames of reference: clips from a recent 40-year reunion of Japanese Canadians uprooted from the Fraser Valley, the reconstruction of the wartime uprooting using archival photos and film footage (including shots taken from *Of Japanese Descent*), and interviews with a number of individuals, including two Vancouverites who supported the government's policies: former alderman Halford Wilson and former Custodian of Enemy Property Glen McPherson; two Japanese Canadians: Mits Tsuida, a nisei formerly interned, and Reverend Canon Gordon Nakayama, an issei and father of the author Joy Kogawa; and three sansei members of a group identified as the "Sansei Redress Committee."

What stands out in the CBC's representation of Japanese Canadian history is its tacit endorsement of some form of redress for what are acknowledged as injustices. The preface by the host, Barbara Frum, provides a public context for what follows:

We begin tonight with a documentary about one of the most shameful episodes in Canadian history. It's the story about Japanese Canadians who were deprived of their rights, had their properties confiscated and were shipped off to internment camps following the attack on Pearl Harbor.

As a lead-in to the documentary, viewers are told: "Now, after 40 years, the Japanese [*sic*] community is organizing to demand restitution for its hardship and humiliation." Reflecting the more contemporary style of journalism that incorporates the interview mode — in contrast to the omniscient narrator in *Of Japanese Descent* — the feature includes edited snippets of comments by individuals who add a vital, human flavour to the history represented. In line with the feature's sympathetic view of Japanese Canadians, the comments of two apologists for government policy, Wilson and McPherson, are contextualized to expose the limits (rather than the authority) of their perceptions and assumptions. McPherson, for instance, who was likely the one most responsible for Order-in-Council PC 465, legalizing the sale of properties supposedly held "in trust," reiterates the government's rationalization at the time: the sales were necessary to preserve the value of the properties. Of course, he does not address the policy forcing Japanese Canadians to pay for their internment. Froese prods an elderly Wilson to confirm (or not) a summary of his views of Japanese Canadians:

> Let me quote a few things from the times to see if you agree with these statements about Japanese Canadians: They undercut white wages; they monopolized farming in the Fraser Valley, forcing the white farmers out; fished without a care for conservation; broke white fisherman strikes against the canning companies; practised unscrupulous business practices, staying open all hours; their homes smelled; and they stuck to themselves. Do you agree with all that?

To which Wilson responds, without qualification, "I agree with it completely."

Providing the Japanese Canadian perspective are Mits Tsuida, a nisei who talks about the racism of the times that led to the uprooting and confiscation of properties, and Reverend Gordon Nakayama, an issei who is interviewed in front of his former house. He speaks wistfully about trying

— unsuccessfully — to buy back the house from its present owner, adding that it is now valued at around $250,000.

The public desire to understand the injustices suffered by Japanese Canadians during the 1940s — what is presented as the lead story of the CBC TV program — raises the question of redress four decades later. Here the focus narrows to three individuals coming from what Froese identifies as the younger, or third generation, the sansei, those who have a greater sense of entitlement to human rights than their parents and grandparents had. The sansei are calling for redress in the form of compensation to the Japanese Canadians directly affected. One of the three, Randy Enomoto, declares, tensely and emotionally: "A crime has been done. There's been a miscarriage of justice. That's a central fact that cannot be lost sight of. The enormity of that just stands there, and it rankles and festers, it's there, and it's becoming more so there in the Canadian consciousness, and it has to be dealt with ..." Enomoto has summarized the position of the JCCP Redress Committee (erroneously identified as the "Sansei Redress Committee" in the program). Earlier in the film he had pointed to the precedent set by Japanese Americans who had called for $25,000 compensation for each individual. Japanese Canadians, he clarified, experienced more prolonged restrictions: they could not return to the west coast until 1949 — four years later than Japanese Americans.

GETTING DRAWN INTO REDRESS

I WAS ONE of the three sansei appearing on *A Call for Justice*, along with Randy Enomoto and Cassandra Kobayashi. We were part of the Japanese Canadian Centennial Project, Redress Committee (or the JCCP Redress Committee, as it came to be known). The name came from a group project initiated to research and mount a photo-history exhibit, *A Dream of Riches: Japanese Canadians, 1877-1977*. This exhibit, also published as a book, was a national project for the 1977 celebrations marking the first arrival of immigrants from Japan. The more activist members of that group, joined by others with similar concerns, began to meet over potluck dinners in 1981 to think through — in fundamental and often emotionally charged ways — the prospect of redress.

Our most significant projects, beginning with the publication of a pamphlet, *Redress for Japanese Canadians*, included the organization of two large community forums (August 1983 in Vancouver and November 1983 in Steveston). These projects stimulated a whirlpool of conversations on redress in the Greater Vancouver area — in the public media but more crucially in the personal lives of Japanese Canadians. Our final statement was a brief in 1984, submitted to the NAJC at the outset of the redress campaign. We took the position, still unpopular at the time, that redress should include both individual and community compensation.

When our group formed, we were fascinated by the unfolding of the issue in the U.S., specifically in the dramatic series of highly publicized hearings organized by the U.S. Commission on Wartime Relocation and Internment of Civilians. This was the federal commission that had been established by Congress in 1980 with a mandate to review the basis and the consequences of the internment of Japanese Americans and to "recommend appropriate remedies." The commission's conclusions were later presented in the report *Personal Justice Denied*. There were 20 days of hearings in total, mostly on the west coast, and some 750 witnesses appeared. Many Japanese Americans gave deeply personal accounts of the hardships and traumas caused by internment.

The hearings provoked intense discussions among Japanese Americans. Convinced that a similar kind of attention could be drawn to the wartime experience of Japanese Canadians, the JCCP Redress Committee soon changed from an informal study group to an activist collective driven by the belief that the question of redress should be faced by Japanese Canadians. The composition of the group during its most productive period, from early 1981 to 1984, shifted as individuals came and went,[1] but most of us had been influenced by the social and human rights movements in the U.S. during the 1960s — movements born in the new visibility of racialized minorities speaking back to social injustices and inequities. We sympathized with the push for community empowerment advocated by Asian American commu-

---

1   The membership of the JCCP Redress Committee varied over time. During the period 1982-83, from minutes of meetings in the author's personal papers and his memory, the following people were the most active: Charlotte Chiba, Randy Enomoto, Fumiko Greenaway, Gordon Kayahara, Cassandra Kobayashi, Martin Kobayakawa, Lucy Komori, Diane Nishi, Ken Shikaze, Naomi Shikaze, Rick Shiomi, Mayu Takasaki and Tamio Wakayama.

nity workers and artists on the west coast in the early 1970s, in Seattle, Los Angeles and San Francisco. But what drew us together was the possibility of creating a renewed sense of community for Japanese Canadians, and we sought to build on the reclamation of history in the 1977 centennial project, *A Dream of Riches.*

Many of us had been involved in the 1977 centennial — a focal point for celebrating Japanese Canadian history and a sign that we had survived, despite racism, internment and the destruction of the prewar community. A key organizer of the centennial, Roger Obata, in looking back over the whole history of Japanese Canadians, pinpointed the importance of 1977: "The Centennial was a year to confirm our pride in our heritage, to celebrate our 100 year history and contribution to Canada, and to re-establish our bond as a community. It was a year of reunification." This rejuvenation, the members of the JCCP Redress Committee felt, could be taken to another level in the call for redress. We were concerned that the internment of Japanese Canadians had been written out of Canadian history, and we wanted it to be told through the eyes of those directly affected. The catch-phrases of our discussions thus drew on many terms that hinged on the prefix "re-": "reclaiming the past," "recovering identity" and "rebuilding community." The effort, through redress, would be to "break the silence" of our history, to release the "stories of internment" that would help dispel the trauma of victimization and oppression, and to seek "acknowledgement" of the unjust treatment of Japanese Canadians through a "settlement" with the federal government.

In 1982, at the time of the 40th-anniversary Fraser Valley reunion in Mission, B.C., film clips of which were woven into the CBC's *A Call for Justice,* the activist language of the JCCP Redress Committee must have sounded grandiose and impossible to realize. I remember attending the reunion with my mother, Shizuko Miki (nee Ooto). She had grown up in Haney, B.C., in a tightly knit community, and she had come to visit from Winnipeg to meet old friends and neighbours. I circulated among many former friends of the family, listening to anecdotes of the pre-internment community in Haney and Mission. But when I mentioned "redress," I realized the term was so distant and abstract that many laughed at — or simply shrugged off — the idea that the government, the authority that had so relentlessly dogged them in the 1940s, would ever compensate them. "Oh sure, sure, give me a call when you get the offer," was the typical response. Still, no one dismissed the concept outright — for me, a sign that the call for justice was never far from the surface of their thoughts and memories. That such a settlement would ever happen, however, was beyond the borders of the possible. I came away from the reunion thinking much more about the lack of means to talk about the term "redress." This condition, as the conversations I had heard implied, had allowed Japanese Canadians to stow the past away in memory. Could redress transform that past? Or would it place yet another burden on those who had slowly but surely rebuilt their lives during the four decades after internment? Regardless, the issue of redress — even before the memory of the reunion settled — had taken on a public life of its own.

In our conversations with CBC TV contacts, it was clear that they were attracted to a more activist stance toward redress, something that would expose a controversy brewing. Yet when the JCCP Redress Committee was invited to speak on redress, we were reluctant to appear as "spokespersons" for the issue. As a volunteer group, not elected or appointed community representatives, we had no authority to make pronouncements about or to speak on behalf of Japanese Canadians. We were then told that the CBC had been having trouble finding Japanese Canadians willing to speak in public about redress. Our group was appealing because the pamphlet we had just published called for direct compensation to those affected. Our CBC contacts wanted to give the feature more edge and currency by highlighting "voices" advocating redress. The three of us who appeared were not only misidentifed as members of a "Sansei Redress Committee," but viewers were also led to believe that we spoke for the "association representing 45,000 Japanese Canadians" who would be going to Ottawa the following spring "to make their case for compensation." In this strange fashion, a powerful public fiction was generated that would soon have repercussions in the internal networks of the "association" the CBC had referred to — the National Association of Japanese Canadians.

At the time, the JCCP Redress Committee had little awareness, except through minimal exchanges with NAJC President Gordon Kadota, of the NAJC's work on redress. Although the redress pamphlet was distributed widely, our own activities were local in scope. Being featured on *The Journal* on CBC TV gave us a public profile that made us appear larger and more powerful than we were. Almost overnight, the members of the JCCP Redress Committee were identified as "redress activists," and the effects were immediate. The next day I got a phone call from my mother telling me that "redress" was the buzz word among all her friends. Everyone was beginning to wonder, she said, about the prospect of a settlement with the government. The sudden impact of the mainstream media was incredible. It was as if Japanese Canadians were being jolted awake by the public airing of their wartime story — now supported by a respected national institution, the Canadian Broadcasting Corporation.

A Call for Justice ended by issuing a challenge. "Here is what Canada's leaders have to say about redress since the war," Froese said, as he quoted three prime ministers:

> *John Diefenbaker:* "One finds it difficult to forget the wrongs committed in
> freedom's name a few years ago."
> *Lester Pearson:* "A black mark against Canada's traditional fairness and devo-
> tion to the principles of human rights."
> *Pierre Trudeau, speaking in Tokyo:* "The record of intolerance in Pacific
> Canada was not a proud one. No more exemplary was the decision
> taken by the federal government to evacuate Japanese Canadians and to
> deprive so many of their civil rights."

And, Froese added, "at no time has any federal government offered compensation."

GROWING MEDIA COVERAGE OF REDRESS

A CALL FOR JUSTICE was part of a growing public anticipation, particularly in Canadian media circles, that Japanese Canadians, a small minority group, were about to reopen a dark moment of their — and, just as important — Canada's past to seek redress from the federal government. Speculating on what might happen fuelled the drama that made the wartime internment a rich source of media attention. There were immediate follow-ups to the broadcast.

Soon after the CBC report, Michael T. Kaufman came to Vancouver to write an article for the *New York Times* — one that would receive widespread circulation in the U.S. and even in Europe. By singling out the JCCP Redress Committee — mistakenly calling us the "Japanese Redress Committee" in the article — Kaufman reinforced the CBC's portrayal of our small group as a representative body. Redress, through the eyes of the (third-generation) sansei — as we were identified — was presented in a way that was consistent with the CBC feature: the sansei grew up in the silence and shame of their nisei parents and were now taking action to resolve past injustices. Moreover, redress had to include compensation that "would affirm that they were victims of injustice and give them a legacy to pass on to their descendants."

The following spring, in March 1983, Stanley Meisner, a prominent feature writer for the *Los Angeles Times* and chief of its Canadian bureau, flew to Vancouver to interview the JCCP Redress Committee. We met at Kamo Restaurant, a Japanese restaurant on Powell Street, and spoke at length about the mass uprooting and the destruction of the community, especially of Nihonmachi (or "Japantown"), the area right outside the restaurant. After our meal we walked the streets, and Randy Enomoto showed Meisner his grandfather's former pharmacy, still evident in the name, Nimi, set in tiles on the sidewalk entrance. A photo of Enomoto pointing to the name appeared on the front page of the *Vancouver Sun* when Meisner's article was reprinted in Canada. Meisner wrote a major report for the *Los Angeles Times* in which he argued that Japanese Canadians had been treated more severely than Japanese Americans, with the result that a geographically based Japanese Canadian community no longer existed anywhere in Canada. "The trauma of the Second World War," Meisner wrote, "was simply too great in Canada for Japanese-Canadians to want to make themselves so visible again."

It was between the appearance of the Kaufman and Meisner articles that the concept of redress began to receive more in-depth coverage in Vancouver newspapers. *The Province* published a dramatic spread — with historic photos and a profile on Tad Mori, a nisei man from New Denver, a former internment site. On the newspaper's front page, in "Japanese-Canadians Demand Apology and Pay," Steve Berry described the push for redress among Japanese Canadians in terms of a tension between two positions. The more moderate and indecisive position was held by NAJC President Gordon Kadota, who was about to embark on a cross-country tour of 16 Japanese Canadian communities. He intended to survey them "to see what support exists for the move" to seek redress in the form of an "acknowledgement," after which, according to the report, the question of "monetary settlement would have to be discussed." The JCCP Redress Committee (still mistakenly called the "Japanese Redress Committee"), on the other hand, was known to advocate acknowledgement plus compensation — something in the range of the $25,000 for each Japanese American being considered in the United States. As one of its members, Tamio Wakayama, commented, "It's really meaningless, really empty to supply an apology with nothing else."

The issue of redress was given a major boost in the U.S. when, in early 1983, the U.S. commission finally announced its recommendation of "personal redress" in the amount of $20,000 for each Japanese American incarcerated. In submitting their report, the commission members were unequivocal in their assessment of the U.S. government's issuing of Executive Order 9066 on February 22, 1942, to intern the 110,000 Japanese Americans then living on the west coast:

> The promulgation of Executive Order 9066 was not justified by military necessity, and the decisions which followed from it — detention, ending detention and ending exclusion — were not driven by analysis of military conditions. The broad historical causes which shaped these decisions were race prejudice, war hysteria and a failure of political leadership ... A grave injustice was done to American citizens and resident aliens of Japanese ancestry who, without individual review or any probative evidence against them, were excluded, removed and detained by the United States during World War II.

Just as the idea of redress was gaining prominence in the media and simultaneously gaining support among Japanese Canadians, a bombshell hit a new community in the making. The conflicts that arose in the gap between the office of Kadota, the NAJC president, and the NAJC's National Redress Committee became the matrix out of which a national redress movement took formation. And members of the JCCP Redress Committee suddenly found themselves swept up in the forces unleashed by the issue of redress.

SPRING 1983: CRISIS AND RESPONSE

A WAVE OF consternation, which soon turned into panic, was set into motion by a startling announcement. On February 14, 1983, reporter Joe Serge of the *Toronto Star* informed readers that Japanese Canadians were about to seek a settlement for the injustices of the 1940s. The title of his article declared: "Japanese Canadians Seek $50 Million for War Uprooting." Serge, who went on to write about redress in subsequent articles, cited as his main source an interview with George Imai, identified as the representative of the "Japanese Canadian community." Quoting from this interview, Serge became a vehicle for what was a press release that made public a position on redress. According to Imai, Japanese Canadians would seek an "apology" and compensation in the form of a community foundation.

Had such a proposal been issued in the 1970s, for instance during the 1977 centennial year, there might have been cause for excitement, even hope that the trauma of the war years might be resolved. Instead, this mode of going public signalled a crisis in leadership. As the chair of the National Redress Committee — a subcommittee of the NAJC, the national association of which Gordon Kadota was president — Imai chose a mainstream venue to "out" the issue of redress. He did not communicate through the network of Japanese Canadian community newspapers, and more crucially, he acted at a distance from the office of the president. Kadota, who was not mentioned in the *Toronto Star* article, recalled that Imai's announcement "came to me as a surprise." At that time, Kadota was on his cross-Canada tour of local communities to gather information and to get feedback on redress. But alert Japanese Canadian readers of the *Toronto Star* — those who were only then getting involved in redress and who were waiting to learn the fate of the issue south of the border — would have every reason to believe that something was awry.

Some readers might have wondered, as I did, on whose behalf George Imai, named as the chair of the National Redress Committee, was speaking. On the basis of what authority did he become a community "representative"? When, and by what process, did the position — calling for an apology and community fund — come about?

Jim Fleming, former federal multiculturalism minister, wrote an account of the issue, "The Way to Right Wrongs," which was published in

1985 after he had lost his seat as a member of Parliament. He referred to his personal connections with Japanese Canadian representatives in the early 1980s, and he remembered the possibility, at that time, of resolving the question of mistreatment of Japanese Canadians during the 1940s.

> I know this issue well. I was multiculturalism minister back in 1982 when a number of members of the Japanese-Canadian community approached me seeking some kind of redress for their misfortunes at the hands of the Canadian government in World War II. I agreed to fund a national meeting of representatives of the community to see if they could find a common ground to approach the government.
>
> The meeting was held but the moderate leadership that had approached me was overthrown at the conference by a much more militant group. This much more strident core then took up the discussion and has led the exchange ever since.

Fleming did not name George Imai in his reconstruction of the community's history, but it was to the National Redress Committee, chaired by Imai, that the grant was given while Fleming was in charge of the Multicultural-ism Directorate. Most likely, Fleming thought of Imai as part of the "moderate leadership" that was being replaced by a "militant group." He then went on to engage in some armchair sociological observations based on his "insider" knowledge:

> [Art] Miki's militant approach is neither representative of a community that is largely reserved and moderate nor is it practical if a happy solution is to be found. By happy I mean that the Japanese-Canadian community is largely satisfied and the general public feel proud, not wrung out. A bitter public battle that invites further ill-feeling or humiliation for the Japanese-Canadian community is madness!

What is troublesome in Fleming's assessment is the apparent ease with which he presumed to "know" Japanese Canadians, speaking as if he had the confidence of the "reserved and moderate" people in the community. But what are the implications of his phrase "largely satisfied"? What did he mean when he mentioned "further ill-feeling or humiliation"? Fleming's references to the "general public" that wanted to "feel proud" and "not wrung out" by redress could be read as a veiled warning to Japanese Canadians that redress for "individuals" would stir up the public's anger. Is this the implication of "further"? As in the war years? From this historical angle, the language of the article appears to repeat the language of assimilation and accommodation. Public anger, a poor disguise for racist backlash, translates into the dark shroud of retaliation by the white majority, visited on dissidents for being too vocal. Compliance with Imai's position, then, is the way to go — for one's own good, for the good of the community, and for the good of the country. Fleming had nothing to say about public or government accountability regarding the injustices for which redress was sought, nor about the human rights issues at stake.

When Fleming's article was published, the NAJC had just been informed by the current Conservative minister in the Multiculturalism Directorate, Jack Murta, of the government's best offer to Japanese Canadians: a package consisting of an official acknowledgement of injustices and $5-6 million to establish a national, government-controlled foundation "in the name of Japanese Canadians" to combat racism in Canada. The offer was issued as an ultimatum to the NAJC. Either accept it, or the government would move "unilaterally," so the NAJC was told. The recognition of "individuals," according to Murta, was completely off the table.

To former politicians like Fleming, who had perhaps been considering a modest redress settlement, the rise of a more determined Japanese Canadian leadership was a setback. Their desire to negotiate a substantial settlement was directly contrary to Imai's approach — acknowledgement and community foundation — which roughly corresponded to the government's approach. Neither side supported the concept of "individual" compensation. From January 1985 on, public speculation ran rampant on what Japanese Canadians wanted, or should receive, as redress for the wartime injustices. By then, as well, it seemed that they had awakened from a deep slumber. What, indeed, should be done?

The two-year period between 1983 and 1985, during which the NAJC redress movement took on an identity of its own, is difficult to untangle. The emergent language captured a vortex of contradictions, dissensions, fears and apprehensions, and pointed toward the possibility of a transformed future. The word "redress" assumed a life of its own as it became the vehicle for Japanese Canadians to remember — to piece together and bring to the surface — the internalized effects of the mass uprooting of the 1940s. "Redress" embodied a new language that had the power to mediate memories of displacement, of violation, of a buried past. And although Imai and his supporters appeared to speak a language of resolution similar to that spoken by the NAJC, their understanding of the political process was not inclusive enough. This explains why their views were undermined by the voices of those who envisioned a comprehensive process of negotiations with the federal government.

Some significant changes were occurring outside the small enclave of the NAJC. On the west coast, for instance, a non-elected group calling itself the JCCP Redress Committee was attracting national attention for advocating redress in the form of individual compensation to Japanese Canadians whose rights had been violated during the 1940s. In Toronto, a newly formed group, the Sodan-kai, drew large crowds to public events held to address the question of redress.[2] In other cities, such as Edmonton and Winnipeg, interest in redress mushroomed. In the midst of all this rising excitement, the Imai agenda soon came to be seen as premature closure.

THE PRINCE HOTEL CRISIS: DEMOCRACY IN ACTION?

THE ATMOSPHERE WAS electric at the 1983 Labour Day weekend conference called by George Imai and the National Redress Committee. The "Prince Hotel crisis," as it came to be called (after the name of the Toronto hotel where the meeting was held), brought to the surface the fault lines in the NAJC leadership. The new voices calling for a just and meaningful — but as yet undefined — redress settlement erupted in a fairly sedate national organization in which a handful of Japanese Canadians, more or less well known to each other through community work, planned national activities. The drama that unfolded hinged on a federal grant of $103,000 that the

---

2   The Sodan-kai, whose name is a Japanese term that means "arriving at a mutual decision through quiet group discussion," was a small group of lawyers, writers and activists who formed in the spring of 1983 to promote more community discussions of redress. They presented themselves as neutral on the specific forms a redress settlement might take, and instead called for a democratic process to arrive at a community consensus.

National Redress Committee had received earlier in the year from the minister of multiculturalism, Jim Fleming. The monies were to be used to conduct a community survey on redress through a telephone poll and questionnaire, and to sponsor a national conference, where the NRC would come up with a "Japanese Canadian" position. Since Imai had announced the NRC position in the spring, the conference was seen as the occasion to ratify his committee's work.

My own entry into the redress debates at the Prince Hotel came through the JCCP Redress Committee. I was chair in 1983 when the reaction to the Imai position spread through many communities across Canada. In Vancouver, the local Japanese Canadian Citizens' Association (the Vancouver JCCA) was approached for assistance in pressuring Imai to postpone a redress settlement to allow for more discussion time. The immediate concern was this Labour Day weekend meeting. I was asked to attend with Ken Matsune, president of the Vancouver JCCA. Accompanying us were those designated as alternates, Charlotte Chiba (for the JCCP Redress Committee) and Frank Kamiya (for the JCCA).

WHAT WAS AT stake? When the article by Joe Serge appeared in the *Toronto Star* in February 1983, many Japanese Canadians who wanted a Canadian settlement comparable to the one recommended by the U.S. commission were shocked by what they perceived to be Imai's ill-timed action. Even though he characterized his community fund as a kind of wedge for those who wanted to pursue individual claims, the more politically conscious feared that any "official" settlement would likely foreclose further efforts. No government, they believed, would reopen negotiations after establishing Imai's proposed "Japanese Canadian Foundation." They had the precedent of the Bird Commission as a warning. But of more concern, with the issue hardly understood by the vast majority of Japanese Canadians, was the threat of political expediency and compromise. After all, what was the hurry?

Somewhere, one hopes, in someone's archives, are the videotapes made by the filmmaker Arthur Ueyama of the now infamous confrontations between the NRC and their anxious opponents. The meeting had already been postponed twice, and the redress survey that the NRC had asked NAJC centres to conduct had faltered because of uncertainty, indifference and lack of information. Through the summer of 1983, the sense of urgency created by the NRC was questioned, challenged and even rejected by some people. For instance, two large community gatherings, one organized by the Sodan-kai in Toronto (May 1983) and another by the JCCP Redress Committee in Vancouver (August 1983), attracted many vocal Japanese Canadians who until then had heard little, if anything, about redress. They were eager to contribute to the questions of the moment: What should the grounds of redress be? What forms should it take? Why now, so many years after the injustices? How can we reach a consensus? What political process is needed in the NAJC to reach a representative position?

Discontent with Imai's position had escalated. A growing number of nisei, many of whom had lost contact with their community organizations for years, began to talk about individual compensation. In stirring up old memories, the very concept of redress brought the past into a new alignment with the present. In one instance, a group calling themselves "concerned nisei" came to a meeting of the JCCP Redress Committee to speak in favour of individual compensation, claiming that the NRC did not represent them. Outside the NAJC, little was known about Imai, and even less about his Toronto-based committee members, who were appointed rather than elected. As a means of challenging this concentration of power, the JCCP Redress Committee and the "concerned nisei" drafted a statement calling for a more democratically based means of reaching a consensus on redress. Their statement, along with the Sodan-kai's similar approach, helped set the stage for a major confrontation in Toronto. There they would be joined by representatives from other centres, such as Edmonton and Winnipeg, where redress committees had been formed to promote commu-nity discussions and to press for individual compensation as part of the settlement.

The meeting room was abuzz with frayed nerves, unlocatable suspicion and unstable purposes. The agenda had been set by Imai, so he occupied a position of authority. Two members of his NRC sat beside him. Gordon Kadota, president of the NAJC, chaired the meeting. The individuals who were assembled around the table reflected the forum's lack of administrative procedure and accountability. Some identified themselves as the "spokes-person" of their local community organizations; others claimed to have been sent as the "representative" on redress alone; still others came on their own, out of personal interest in the issue. There was even a non-Japanese Canadian from Kelowna who came, as he said, on the request of the Japanese Canadian community there. To add tension to confusion, behind the delegates sat an audience of Toronto Japanese Canadians, many of whom had been drawn together by their common antipathy to what they perceived as Imai's "sellout" of the community's redress claims. Their body language and spontaneous comments added to an already explosive atmosphere, which was reinforced even more by the glare of lights for the video recording of the proceedings.

Since Imai had committed himself to a fall national conference as the occasion to announce a redress position, with politicians such as Justice Minister Mark MacGuigan and Multiculturalism Minister Jim Fleming to be present, the Prince Hotel gathering had been dubbed a "pre-conference" meeting. This was a point of irritation for some participants; they felt that a community consensus required more time. Much of the initial talk by the delegates revolved around the identity of those present, their affiliations and the redress discussions that had occurred in their communities. But it wasn't long before signs of exasperation were expressed in the question: Why had so little been done to further a democratic process in the NAJC? On one side sat an apparently isolated president, who appeared to be acting more as an individual than the leader of the NAJC; on the other side sat the chair of the NRC, a subcommittee, acting as if he were the de facto president. The wide, and at the moment unbridgeable gap between them had weakened the NAJC as a vehicle to represent the grassroots population: those Japanese Canadians all across the country who bore the legacy of dispersal and assimilation. They were the ones who seemed to have been bypassed by the NRC so far.

The problem of representation stirred up some heated questions about the basis of the NRC's position. The telephone poll had never been completed, so the immediate point of reference was the NRC's redress questionnaire. It had drawn few responses, most of them from Toronto, where the members of the NRC resided. What attracted the most attention, however, was the questionnaire's apparently biased language, specifically in the "information sheet" attached to it. Those who filled out the questionnaire were asked to choose either "individual" compensation or "group settlement." As they pondered the either/or, they were encouraged to read the "information sheet." There, "group settlement" in the form of a foundation was favoured over "individual" compensation — the NRC's position. This position was described in detail, whereas the case for "individual" was not explained at all. Further, the form did not contain an option combining individual and group compensation, the position that received assent in the 1988 redress settlement. The either/or limitation restricted freedom of response and, in guiding the choice toward group compensation, prejudiced the outcome.

Imai had publicized the professionalism of the questionnaire through its association with two established sociologists, Wilson Head, from York University, and Victor Ujimoto, from Guelph University. Ujimoto was present at the meeting, seated in the section of the room reserved for observers. When he rose to address the validity of the questionnaire, the room fell into an apprehensive hush. He did not endorse the form of the questionnaire, saying that he had not been directly involved in its construction. He also cautioned the NAJC not to proceed too quickly. Reinforcing critical comments made by Gordon Hirabayashi, a delegate from Edmonton but also, like him, a professor of sociology, Ujimoto felt that a questionnaire would only have representative value when Japanese Canadians knew enough about redress to make an informed judgement. He stated as much in a letter to the Multiculturalism Directorate on June 16, 1983, when the NRC's questionnaire was generating controversy among Japanese Canadians. He wrote that he did not believe "an accurate and meaningful poll of Japanese Canadians concerning their views on the redress/reparations issue can be undertaken by the proposed date of the national meeting in early September." Moreover, there was a need to determine who was directly affected. "Established social science procedures," he said, "albeit time consuming, must be followed if we are to establish an accurate and representative sample of Japanese Canadians." Ujimoto noted a sense of "western alienation," that is, the feeling that Japanese Canadians outside of Toronto had not been fully consulted on redress. Finally, he could not understand the "rush for a national meeting in September given the inadequate preparation for meaningful impetus from the various regions."

Ujimoto's argument that greater participation was required to form a representative position on redress complemented the JCCP Redress Committee's call for a more representative National Redress Committee. In preparation, the JCCP Redress Committee drafted a proposal in which we called for the formation of a more broad-based committee consisting of spokespersons from various local centres, proportional representation according to populations in the various centres, and accountability in the decision-making process.

I presented this proposal on the first day of the conference and was asked to return with a shorter and more clearly defined motion that could be presented to the assembly. Following overnight discussions with others who supported more broad-based representation, I drafted a series of motions that included the establishment of a National Redress Council "consisting of regional representatives (such as the delegates to this assembly) to which the National Redress Committee should be accountable through such means as conference calls, a newsletter, correspondence, and whenever possible, council meetings."

The evening before I presented the motion to form the National Redress Council, in talking with my brother Art, Gordon Hirabayashi and Art Shimizu late into the night, I glimpsed, for the first time, the depth of the psychological and emotional upheavals that were the residue of mass uprooting. The currents of anger, frustration, rationalization — and the desire to contain rather than confront conflict — were all premonitions that redress was volcanic in its implications. The undefined energy flowing in and out of the meeting rooms had yet to find a language in which to make itself visible. Redress was far from over — in fact, the concept was just starting to locate itself through the efforts of the "delegates" who had come from the communities scattered across the country.

The next day the motion to establish the National Redress Council passed. As simply as that — so it seemed — the NRC agenda had been curtailed. But then the unexpected occurred: the passing of the motion prompted the dramatic resignation of Imai who, with his NRC, walked out of the room, leaving a void into which flowed a familiar mixture of guilt, sympathy and anticipation. Voices came to Imai's defence. Had he not devoted many years of his life to the community? Did he not secure the federal grant on the basis of his reputation? Could the NAJC simply let him go? A motion to accept his resignation forced the issue to a vote, and emotions became even more inflamed when the vote ended in a tie. The deciding vote thus fell on the chair of the meeting, NAJC president Gordon Kadota, who had been criticized for indecisiveness.

The irony of the moment was mesmerizing. Imai had been very critical of Kadota's lack of initiative. After three years in his position as president, Kadota had yet to establish his National Executive Committee, and although he had been interviewed on the subject of redress by the mainstream media, he had not addressed the breakdown of accountability in the NAJC. But just as critically, during Kadota's absence from the public scene, Imai had assumed his authority, communicating with politicians and the media as if he were the official NAJC spokesperson. Imai had even managed to secure a major federal grant from the Multiculturalism Directorate. The funds were directed to his committee, the NRC, without passing through the president's office. Kadota recalled that he never saw a copy of the application for the grant. Nevertheless Kadota, perhaps sensing that the collapse of the NRC would undermine the NAJC as a national organization, or perhaps feeling some responsibility for the crisis, voted against the motion. Imai would be asked to reconsider his resignation.

To this day, the circumstances surrounding the large grant to the NRC are still shrouded in mystery, perhaps suggesting closer ties between Jim Fleming and George Imai than were publicly disclosed to the Japanese Canadian community at the time. Though Imai never made public all the details of whatever discussions he had with federal officials on the question of redress, he hinted that something was in works in the "National Redress Committee Report" he presented at the conference. "Since the 1980 Conference [of the NAJC]," he wrote, "we have had informal discussions with the former Minister of State for Multiculturalism, the Hon. Jim Fleming, who was kind enough to initiate our concerns to the Minister of Justice [Mark MacGuigan]. We have also informally spoken to Joe Clark, and other concerned Members of Parliament."

While researching in the early 1990s, I made one attempt to view the files relating to the application in the multiculturalism office. I was informed that for some unknown reason, the file was missing. It had been sent to the minister's office and assessed there, an uncommon procedure but allowable under the minister's authority. Did this mean that Fleming himself had taken a special interest in the file? Under normal circumstances, the grant application may have been rejected by the staff as being too overtly political in its motivations — especially since redress was its objective. Fleming's critical role in securing Imai's grant was confirmed by Art Miki, who remembered speaking about it with an officer in Multiculturalism. This officer, according to Miki, told him that the application "came from the minister's office back down" for approval, and though this person "didn't quite agree with the process" it went ahead because "there was an urgency to approve it, and it came from the minister's office."

A PERSONAL ASIDE

THE FLOOD OF anxieties, uncertainties and enmities unleashed at the Prince Hotel brought to the surface the traumatic legacy of the wartime uprooting. The clashes that flared up in the meeting room were not simply a contest of different points of view but also the noise of a raw language caught in the throes of shifting relations of power. As this process unfolded, the JCCP Redress Committee moved toward obsolescence as many of its members, myself included, were drawn into the rapidly expanding spheres of community politics.

For me, the chance to participate in the political process of Japanese Canadians was new. I had grown up on the edges of community events, and while I knew many Japanese Canadians, I had little interest in the national organization. I had been drawn into the work of the JCCP Redress Committee because I thought redress could have enormous consequences for rethinking our wartime history. Yet the realm of community politics seemed to be a morass of power politics, personal investments and reactionary values. I was very nervous, even afraid, of the prospect of sitting at the council table to "debate" the issue of redress, and to face the NRC with a potentially explosive position paper from the JCCP Redress Committee.

In preparation I even cut my hair and bought a sports jacket, tie and new pair of shoes. I wanted to appear as "normal" as possible to resemble what I then imagined to be the conservative Japanese Canadians of the NAJC. As it turned out, I was the one who was overdressed. Most of the delegates came in casual clothes. Harold Hirose, an old friend of the family, laughed when he saw me all cleaned up. He had only known me to wear jeans and to have longish hair all through the 1970s. I suppose I was already re-dressed — appearances would become crucial during the redress campaign. In any case, after the Prince Hotel crisis, I was attracted to redress as a moth to a flame.

CHAPTER 7

NINETEEN EIGHTY-FOUR

Defining the Redress Movement

So much experience in such a short time, so many memories shared and fears exorcized. We all became a bit giddy as we headed down to Merritt and let our collective hair down. We told jokes, sang and whooped and carried on. I had our people chanting, "What do you want? Redress! When do we want it? Now!"

— Shirley Yamada

WINNIPEG, JANUARY 1984

THE PERIOD BETWEEN the dramatic resignation of the National Redress Committee (NRC) in Toronto in September 1983 and the critical meeting of the National Association of Japanese Canadians (NAJC) in Winnipeg on January 20-22, 1984, was an intense time of accusations, rants and gloomy prognoses for the future of redress. The Toronto-published Japanese Canadian community newspapers, the *Canada Times* and the *New Canadian*, became the outlets for vociferous attacks on those who criticized

Imai and his NRC. Especially targeted were individuals in the NAJC who questioned NRC leadership, such as Gordon Hirabayashi, a respected educator
and human rights advocate, and Art Shimizu, a medical practitioner and
well-known opponent of the War Measures Act. But the most focused attack
was aimed at members of the Sodan-kai and the Japanese Canadian
Centennial Project (JCCP) Redress Committee. The *Canada Times*, in particular, opened its pages to Imai sympathizers, particularly those in Toronto,
who saw Imai as a martyr to the redress cause. On the other hand, the *New
Canadian*, the oldest newspaper in the community — dating back to the late
1930s — had been slumbering for years. For the most part, it had depended
on recycled articles and community news to fill its columns. But the redress
crisis reawakened the *New Canadian*, and with the *Canada Times* clearly
leaning toward the Imai camp, it responded to requests to publish dissenting
voices and to become a national source of information on redress for all
Japanese Canadians. At the time the NAJC, not having its own newsletter, had
to rely on often unevenly distributed community bulletins to disseminate
reports on its work. In contrast to the conflicting points of view appearing
in the *New Canadian*, the *Canada Times* was dominated by voices of outrage
from Imai supporters.

First off, on September 16, 1983, was a series of articles condemning the
Sodan-kai and the JCCP Redress Committee. These groups were accused of
manipulating the democratic process with the express purpose of unseating
the NRC, and specifically Imai. One unknown writer, identified as "MS" or as
"Mark Suzuki" — a pen name — was bitter to the extreme in his accusations. Commenting on the NRC resignation, he said that the committee

> walked out partly to protest against one of the most unethical displays of
> power politics ever seen in the Japanese Canadian community.
>
> It was orchestrated by members of the Toronto-based Sodan-kai and
> the redress committee of the Japanese Canadian Centennial project [JCCP]
> of Vancouver.

Shizue Takashima, an artist and author of *A Child in Prison Camp*, entered
the fracas with "An Open Letter" in the *Canada Times* (November 1, 1983),
which soon after was republished in the *New Canadian* (November 11, 1983).
Singling out the lack of constitutional procedure, she blamed President

Gordon Kadota who, she argued, should have revised the NAJC constitution to prevent what happened at the Prince Hotel. Takashima clearly raised a problem that should have been addressed in the NAJC. On the matter of urgency, though, Takashima sided with Imai. With so many Japanese Canadian seniors (both issei and nisei) aging, there was a need to act quickly. About the Sodan-kai and the JCCP Redress Committee, who wanted a more extended process of reaching a community consensus on redress, she wrote:

> Do they not realize that we owe the Isseis to erase this one blot in our Canadian history before they are all gone? Time is running out, many of the Niseis are dying now too. It is imperative that we settle this as quickly as possible, instead of wasting time, energy, yes, money in quarrelling.

Takashima's desire for unity in seeking a quick settlement was understandable, given Imai's high profile in Toronto, but when her open letter was published, a much wider spectrum of Japanese Canadians was awakening to the concept of redress. The urgency Takashima perceived, and the time line set out by Imai, ran counter to a growing sense that the process had to draw on grassroots Japanese Canadians scattered all over Canada. From this perspective, the disorder at the Prince Hotel and the fast-flying allegations made in its aftermath were not a stoppage; they were, instead, the symptoms of powerful new impulses. The concept of redress was entering the consciousness of both large and small communities, creating havoc and anxiety, but also stirring up positive emotions. The latent memories of the war years began to return with an unprecedented intensity. Bryce Kanbara, an artist, spoke of the Prince Hotel crisis as an "encouraging step" that opened up larger horizons of thought and action:

> There are people who at first felt uncomfortable about raising and even thinking about the issue of Redress, but who have come to change their feelings and their minds — through the developing sense of confidence gained as they became more and more informed. During the process of education their perceptions evolved, gradually crystallizing into convictions. Surely, it does not need to be stated that each of us must regard this learning as a responsibility.

Much of the hot-tempered language around the issue of redress was in the air when delegates from across Canada met in Winnipeg in January 1984.[1] The NAJC opened this auspicious year (made more so by its popular associations with George Orwell's *Nineteen Eighty-Four*) with a meeting focused on an election and a position on redress.

Winnipeg was considered an ideal site for mediation. It was removed from the historically charged polarization of Kadota's Vancouver, the centre of the mass uprooting in 1942, and Imai's Toronto, the city where the most vocal and upwardly mobile Japanese Canadians had resettled and where the National Japanese Canadian Citizens' Association (NJCCA) had formed in 1947. Just as important, of all the local areas where community organizations had been maintained, the Winnipeg-based Manitoba JCCA had greater stability and participation than most. It was here, even before 1947, that the Mannisei (nisei in Manitoba) was established as a political voice for those displaced in the province, despite the dangers of doing so. Since organizing of any kind was banned, the founding members had had to meet in secret — often in Chinese restaurants, where they would not be noticed by the RCMP. With such a strong history of activism, the Winnipeg community was perceived as an effective role model for other communities.

A large contingent arrived from Toronto, including Imai supporters from the Toronto JCCA, both nisei and issei, and some members of the Sodan-kai. The Imai supporters were intent on promoting Jack Oki, their preferred candidate for president. Oki, a nisei, was unknown to most Japanese Canadians outside of Toronto, but he had been active in the NJCCA in the late 1940s. Running against Oki was Art Miki, who had been highly visible during the 1977 centennial and was the chair of the recently formed Manitoba JCCA Redress Committee. Many delegates viewed Miki as someone capable of mediating the dissension threatening to tear the NAJC apart. Whereas Oki backed Imai's position, Miki brought to the issue of redress a more inclusive language of democratic process, of grassroots participation and the need to reach beyond the NAJC's circle, which was small at the time. The vote went in Miki's favour, but only slightly, and Oki became vice-president.

---

1   At the time, 13 centres were represented: Calgary, Edmonton, Hamilton, Kelowna, Lethbridge, Montreal, Ottawa, Regina, Toronto, Vancouver, Vernon, Victoria and Winnipeg. Two centres, Kamloops and Thunder Bay, did not send delegates.

The Winnipeg meeting can be seen as a defining moment for the redress movement. Despite the gulf that had opened at the Prince Hotel, the mood around the Winnipeg council table reflected a desire for conciliation, at least on the surface. Imai's authority had been shaken by the motion to set up an entity called the "National Redress Council" to monitor and control the National Redress Committee. But here the NAJC delegates voted to assume full responsibility for redress. The "National Redress Council," no longer considered necessary, was dissolved. Then a new National Redress Committee (NRC) was formed. In a close election, Imai was elected chair. The Ottawa representative Elmer Hara, who ran against Imai, became vice-chair. To ensure national representation, the NRC was to include members from across Canada. And as chair, Imai was to devise a plan of action and provide recommendations to the NAJC. Once this structural business had been completed, the meeting went on — in a spirit of unanimity — to pass a historic resolution placing on record the NAJC's intent to seek redress:

[T]he NAJC seeks official acknowledgement from the Canadian government of the injustices committed against Japanese Canadians during and after World War II.

Whereas the internment, exclusion and exiling of Japanese Canadians violated individual human rights and freedoms and destroyed the fabric of the community, the NAJC seeks redress in the form of compensation.

Moreover, the NAJC seeks review and amendment of the War Measures Act and relevant sections of the Charter of Rights and Freedoms so that no Canadian will ever again be subjected to such wrongs.

In discussions on this motion, delegates dwelled at considerable length — and with considerable apprehension — on the word "monetary." Should this reference to money be included? Won't Japanese Canadians appear to be selfish, materialistic, interested only in a cash settlement? Shouldn't we appear to be more idealistic in our demands? After all, isn't the acknowledgement of the injustices the important matter? Won't there be a backlash against our resolution? Still, should we not be explicit and open about our point of view? Won't we be seen as "sneaky" (invoking the ghost of a wartime stereotype) when we say later that we meant "monetary" and not just "symbolic" compensation? Aren't we affirming our democratic responsibility in attaching material value to our resolution? Won't the injustices seem inconsequential if no monetary component is mentioned? The ambivalence expressed in the discussions — even though all agreed that the phrase "redress in the form of compensation" certainly implied monetary compensation — recalled the early struggles to articulate the language of redress. Starting from scratch in what would become the most explosive event for Japanese Canadians since the mass uprooting itself, the NAJC council took its first tentative steps to forge the language for what remained a largely unformulated position on redress.

So far, so good. Indeed, by November 21 of the same year, the NAJC had managed to transform the January motion into a formal brief to the federal government. *Democracy Betrayed: Redress for Japanese Canadians* concluded with a call for redress:

> In consequence of the abrogation of the rights and freedoms of Japanese Canadians during and after World War II, the National Association of Japanese Canadians calls on the Government of Canada to acknowledge its responsibility to compensate Japanese Canadians for injustices suffered and seeks a commitment from the Government of Canada to enter into negotiations towards a just and honourable settlement of this claim.

Only three weeks later, on December 15, the NAJC met with a three-member committee of the new Conservative minister in charge of the Multiculturalism Directorate, Jack Murta, to begin what was ostensibly a process of negotiation.

However, not foreseeable in January was another press conference held on the same day that *Democracy Betrayed* was released in Ottawa. There, in a direct affront to the NAJC, Jack Oki and George Imai appeared as the spokespersons of the "Japanese Canadian National Redress Committee of Survivors" and condemned the NAJC. Setting themselves up as a moderate group who spoke on behalf of the "silent majority," a posture playing on the image of Japanese Canadians as the model minority — quiet, unassuming and grateful to their country — Oki and Imai claimed that by opposing individual compensation they wanted to avoid a "backlash" from white Canadians. They asked the government to accept their proposal for an acknowledgement of injustice and some form of compensation through a group or foundation. This had been Imai's position in 1983.

The rift that many NAJC members had tried to avoid was suddenly open to public view. Nevertheless, the national redress movement was at least in motion.

REDRESS GOES PUBLIC

NINETEEN EIGHTY-FOUR was a cataclysmic year for President Art Miki and the NAJC. It also turned out to be the catalytic year, when the NAJC moved into the public spheres of what has been dubbed the "politics of recognition" by the Canadian political philosopher Charles Taylor.[2] Once redress began to infiltrate the consciousness of Japanese Canadians — most of whose connections with community organizations had ranged from indifference to hostility — they found themselves drawn into a web of unresolved memories and reflections. Simultaneously, the term "redress" began to take on urgency as a public issue — even a national issue — and as a result, the story of Japanese Canadian internment gained widespread and heightened media attention. In a welcome burst of TV publicity, Art Miki even appeared as the mystery guest on a popular news-as-quiz show at the time, *Front Page Challenge.*

References to "redress for Japanese Canadians" in popular press and from the lips of politicians, as welcome as they were, were recieved with a certain trepidation. High-profile reports, especially in the mainstream media, put pressure on all parties to arrive at a quick settlement. But for Japanese Canadians, the trauma of the past could not be resolved through a simple political "deal." The situation required a deeper transformation of consciousness, what might be described as a process of empowerment, involving a collective language of negotiation and consensus.

As the movement evolved through the mid-1980s, the NAJC became

---

2   Taylor discusses the negative consequences of "*mis*recognition," and by this he points not merely to the absence of public recognition but more to the effects of distorted, truncated and demeaning representations. Those who are constructed as other than the norm — women, gays and lesbians, and racialized minorities, for instance — may be subject to the internalization of "a depreciatory image of themselves" which may become "one of the most potent instruments of their own oppression." Such misrecognition "can inflict harm, can be a form of oppression, imprisoning someone in a false, distorted and reduced mode of being."

much more preoccupied with the rapidly intensifying language of "redress" that called for some form of articulation. How could this term be read? Who would get to set the reference points for its interpretation? Through what process would Japanese Canadians have the time to think through the implications of redress to determine a meaningful settlement? Answers to such questions were elusive in the psychologically troubled conditions in which they were sought. On the one side were the largely muted voices of Japanese Canadians who had long ago abandoned the belief that the injustices of the 1940s would ever be resolved by the government. On the other side was the appearance of a gesture toward reconciliation on the part of the government. Had it not given a large grant through the Multiculturalism Directorate to come up with a redress position? Then again, what if the process were to dead-end, as the Bird Commission did in the 1940s? What was needed, first, was a brief that would argue the conditions of redress. Is this not the way a grievance is articulated in a democratic process?

But how to proceed? The brief submitted by the National Japanese Canadian Citizens' Association in 1950 — after the Bird Commission had tabled its report — had fallen on deaf ears, because the commission had supposedly settled all of the government's debts to Japanese Canadians. Would a formal acknowledgement of injustices in the House of Commons, prior to the submission of a redress brief from the NAJC, have the same effect? Was the government's apparent interest in issuing an acknowledgement a ploy to use Japanese Canadians, as a model minority, to attract the ethnic vote in the next election? Would a government-choreographed redress settlement then echo the loss of their voice in the 1940s? In short, once the question of redress unfolded outside the narrow network of the NAJC, more and more Japanese Canadians found themselves pulled into a flood of questions that opened the doors to the past.

As a small group with no political clout, Japanese Canadians could be silenced once again by government's control over the language of redress. The NAJC, then, faced a formidable challenge: countering the threat of a politically expedient resolution by the government and at the same time ensuring negotiations with those directly affected by the wartime injustices. In the opening months of 1984, the prospect of fulfilling that task was riddled with dangers, and these were compounded by the lack of cohesion in the NAJC. Just as the new NAJC president, Art Miki, was scrambling to become a voice for a community in apparent disarray, he had to deal with the pressure from within the association, primarily by Imai and his supporters, to immediately seek an acknowledgement from the government and defer the question of compensation for future discussion. Their argument? To seize the political opportunity now, while the government was receptive. For Miki, however, it was more important to work out the meaning of redress, and then to establish a comprehensive redress proposal, one that would include, along with an acknowledgement, a compensation figure and measures to ensure that what had happened to Japanese Canadians would not happen again to other Canadians. The tension between these two positions, which often pitted former close friends and even relatives against each other, set the tone of the NAJC's internal conflicts in 1984. It was out of this discord that a new language of redress was formed, word by word.

WHY ACKNOWLEDGEMENT FIRST?

DESPITE THE SUCCESS of the redress movement, the basis of George Imai's opposition to the NAJC remains a mystery. Imai did not consistently resort to articles and reports to communicate with other Japanese Canadians, and as a result his views were often conveyed through the mediation of others. When he was chair of the National Redress Committee, he usually did not respond in writing to queries, and when discussing redress in public forums, he tended to rely on previously written position papers. As a greater cross-section of Japanese Canadians joined the debate on redress, Imai's resistance to the new voices in the NAJC led to a painful polarization.

Here my positioning cannot be avoided, not only as a brother of the NAJC president, but also as a writer for the movement, a member of the NAJC council and an opponent of the "Imai camp." Yet for those who were puzzled, as I was in 1984, by the strident attacks on Art Miki and the NAJC for failing to seize the "acknowledgement first" moment with the Liberal government, some retrospective considerations might clarify the internal squabbles that nearly destroyed the redress movement. When Imai's actions, which seemed inexplicable to many of those outside his inner circle, are reconstructed, the events of 1984 take on a somewhat intriguing pattern — a pattern that resembles the internal politics of the 1940s.

Even in the aftermath of the Prince Hotel crisis, members of the NAJC and the National Redress Committee, including George Imai, continued to function as if he were still in charge of redress. His election as chair of the NRC at the Winnipeg conference was interpreted, particularly by his supporters, as a ratification of his role as spokesperson. In actuality he was elected chair of a newly constituted committee, but still called the NRC. The new NRC, as the NAJC delegates decided at the conference, would be accountable to the NAJC through President Art Miki and his national executive committee. However, with his most influential Toronto ally, Jack Oki, now the vice-president, Imai strengthened his power base. In a sense, he recovered the status he had had before the Prince Hotel crisis. From this vantage point he could resist the authority of the new president, who, when he took office, knew little of the NRC's history with the government.

In presenting his main NRC report at the Prince Hotel, Imai had stressed the importance of timing, and the need to act "immediately" while the government supposedly was willing to settle. But what was the rush? What about the time required to inform Japanese Canadians, the vast majority of whom were not aware of the implications of redress? The sociologist Victor Ujimoto had said as much in his critique of the questionnaire that was hurriedly being distributed in the spring of 1983. Others, too, worried over Imai's unexplained sense of haste.

In the time line that informed Imai's perspective, however, the work of the NRC was just reaching its climax. In his Prince Hotel report, he briefly outlined the NRC's history, from initial discussions in 1976-77, to the formation of a Reparation Committee in 1977, a questionnaire in 1978, a few public meetings in Toronto and articles in both community newspapers, the *New Canadian* and the *Canada Times*. The NRC position paper was written in the late 1970s and presented to the NAJC at a national meeting in November 1979. Imai himself was not elected chair, but had replaced Naomi Tsuji after she moved to Ottawa. So why must the NAJC decide now?

> After 6 years, the Committee feels it is time for action. Timing is essential. With the Japanese Canadian internment during the war, being used as one of the prime reasons for the entrenchment of the Charter of Rights in our Constitution and the Commission Report from the United States, the political climate is ripe. Politically at the present time we have a receptive govt., who is willing to listen and sit down with us. With the election forthcoming

Family photos from Ste. Agathe, Manitoba, 1942–43. The Miki family —
consisting of Kazuo and Shizuko Miki, their three children Art, Les, and Joan,
Shizuko's parents, Tokusaburo and Yoshi Ooto, and her brother Tak Ooto —
were sent to Ste. Agathe in May 1942 to work on a sugar beet farm. Roy was
born in October. [Photos courtesy Roy Miki]

In the sugar beet field. Clockwise, from lower right: Art Miki, Les Miki, Tokusaburo Ooto,
Kazuo Miki, Tak Ooto, Kunesaburo Hayakawa, Nori Hayakawa, Yoshi Ooto.

From left:
Grandmother Ooto
and Shizuko Miki with
her children,
Art, Joan, Roy and Les.

Tomekichi (Tomey)
Homma, c. 1900. Homma
challenged the regulation
in the Provincial Election
Act that prevented
Japanese Canadians from
having their names placed
on the voters' list. [Photo:
Homma Family
Collection, Japanese
Canadian National
Museum 94/88.3.001]

Delgation to Ottawa, 1936. From left: Dr. S. I. Hayakawa, Minoru Kobayashi, Hide Hyodo (later Shimizu), Dr. Edward Banno. [Photo: Japanese Canadian Cultural Centre, Toronto]

Kunio Hidaka, 1941. Just before the internment Hidaka compiled an inventory of all the legislation discriminating against Japanese Canadians. [Photo courtesy of Susan Hidaka]

Randy Enomoto, March 1983. When Stan Meisner's feature article "Why Vancouver Lacks a Little Tokyo" was published in the *Vancouver Sun,* this photo appeared on the front page. Enomoto shows the name of his grandfather, Toragoro Nimi, who had run a pharmacy in the building before the mass uprooting. [Photo by Bill Keay, *Vancouver Sun*]

DEMOCRACY BETRAYED

THE CASE FOR REDRESS

A submission to the Government of Canada
on the violation of rights and freedoms
of Japanese Canadians during and after World War II

NATIONAL ASSOCIATION OF JAPANESE CANADIANS

Cover of *Democracy Betrayed*, November 21, 1984. The National Association of Japanese Canadians submitted this historic brief, which called on the federal government to redress the injustices of the 1940s.

Redress Forum at the Japanese Language School, Vancouver, August 4, 1984. From left: Tatsuo Kage, Japanese language interpreter, David Suzuki, Tom Shoyama, Roy Miki, Ann Sunahara. Joy Kogawa was unable to attend, but Irene Nemeth, seated behind Suzuki, delivered her speech. This major forum took place in the Japanese Language School on Alexander Street, the only building spared by the Custodian of Enemy Property. [Photo by Ian Lindsay, *Vancouver Sun*]

Wes Fujiwara, October 1992. Wes Fujiwara played a crucial role in developing the redress movement in Toronto. After the settlement in 1988 he moved to Vancouver where he continued to pursue his interest in Japanese Canadian history. [Photo by Brian Kent, *Vancouver Sun*]

Wataru and Barbara Shishido, August 1985. Each year during the redress campaign, 1984-88, large numbers of volunteers promoted the redress issue for the Vancouver Japanese Canadian Citizens' Association Redress Committee. This photo was taken at the redress booth at the Powell Street Festival. [Photo by Roy Miki]

Council members of the National Association of Japanese Canadians with representatives of the federal government, December 15, 1984. This meeting, held in Winnipeg, was supposed to mark the beginning of negotiations with the federal government through its minister of state for multiculturalism Jack Murta, but talks soon broke down. Seated with Art Miki, from left: Orest Kruhlak, Anne Scotton, Doug Bowie. [Photo courtesy of Art Miki]

Ottawa Redress Rally, April 14, 1988. At this large redress rally, organized by the National Association of Japanese Canadians, large numbers of Japanese Canadians from across Canada urged the federal government to negotiate a redress agreement. They placed placards and ribbons around the Peace Flame. [Photo by Gordon King]

National Association of Japanese Canadians Strategy Committee, Montreal, August 1988. From left: Audrey Kobayashi, Cassandra Kobayashi, Art Miki, Roger Obata, Maryka Omatsu, Roy Miki. This photo was taken by Don Rosenbloom, legal advisor for the NAJC. [Photo courtesy of Cassandra Kobayashi]

Art Miki and Gerry Weiner, August 25, 1988. Miki and Weiner shook hands at the moment the redress agreement was reached between the National Association of Japanese Canadians and the federal government. [Photo by Cassandra Kobayashi]

Settlement Day, September 22, 1988. Prime Minister Brian Mulroney and National Association of Japanese Canadians President Art Miki sign the redress agreement. In the background, from left: Don Rosenbloom, legal advisor for the NAJC, Roger Obata, Lucien Bouchard, Audrey Kobayashi, Gerry Weiner, Maryka Omatsu, Roy Miki. [Photo by Gordon King]

in the foreseeable future, the timing becomes critical. If there is another govt. of whatever political party, the lobby process would have to be started all over again and this may take another 2 or 3 years before we can get started. Today the political swing of the major parties are to the "Right," any future make-up of a Cabinet will be to the "right," which will pose greater problems for the Japanese Canadians.

The problem is political; the solution is political.

Imai concluded by arguing the need to act because so many issei and nisei were dying: "For the sake of the victims let us give them some pride before they leave this earth."

To his credit, Imai was attentive to redress during the late 1970s, when support for the issue, especially in the NAJC, was not strong. The general lack of interest, including the apparent indifference of most Japanese Canadians, was a mixed blessing: in the absence of participants, it was easier to draft a position, but then again, the position drafted would lack integral ties to a grassroots points of view. Although NAJC council members had been asked repeatedly to initiate discussions on redress in their local communities, nothing significant had been done.

Despite the NRC's time line, a troubling scenario appeared to have unfolded for the NAJC. For Gordon Kadota, as he acknowledged in his president's report at the Prince Hotel, the NAJC had failed to involve its constituents in redress, and this has led to "the people of our community being left behind." Kadota wanted to ensure that "a democratic process is observed" in producing a representative position on redress. On the other hand, the Imai report did not account for the absence of grassroots representation and the controversial implications of his decision to seek redress in the form of a community foundation. To complicate matters, the Reparations Committee of the National Japanese Canadian Citizens' Association established in 1977 to prepare a redress report was distinct from his own NRC.

Of its three members — Eugene Maikawa (Hamilton), Harge Suga (Ottawa) and Gordon Hirabayashi (Edmonton) — Hirabayashi, who had immigrated from the United States, was the most vocal proponent of individual compensation based on the U.S. model. In a statement critical of the lack of procedural accountability, Hirabayashi wrote: "The current Reparation Paper was prepared by some ad hoc committee, not the NJCCA

Reparations Committee appointed at the Winnipeg Conference," and he took issue with the exclusion of individual compensation: "Individuals were uprooted, deprived of home, treated with indignity, delayed in income and education, confined like criminals. It is therefore the right of individuals to be given reparations/restitution ... Who has authorized the NJCCA or any other group to usurp this right from those who were uprooted and deprived?" His critique, dated April 1980, was attached to the NRC's "Reparations Paper," presented to the 1980 NAJC conference in Vancouver.

Also attached was a statement by George Tanaka, Roger Obata and Kinzie Tanaka, all of whom had been active in Japanese Canadian issues in the 1940s, stating how "unwise and presumptuous" it was "to assume that this committee speaks for the community on the basis of such a meagre poll as the committee indicates." They called for more work to be done in developing a "representative" position. The "meagre poll" was a questionnaire distributed in 1978, at a time when only a handful of Japanese Canadians had information on redress issues. Thus, even by 1980 there were serious reservations concerning Imai's statement that the majority of Japanese Canadians favoured his "foundation proposal."

By 1983, a division had clearly developed between the NRC's perception of its own strategy, based on its position, and the seeds of a widespread community awakening, evident in the initial wave of support generated by two small, non-elected groups formed to promote discussion among Japanese Canadians outside the inner circle of the NAJC: the JCCP Redress Committee in Vancouver and the Sodan-kai in Toronto. In a strangely fatalistic way, though, Imai remained inflexible, and became more so as resistance to the NRC grew.

The question is: why?

When reassembled, the pieces of the position defended by Imai and his NRC take on a pattern not out of line with the political expectations of the government. Imai's 1983 slogan, "The problem is political; the solution is political," while offering little of substance for Japanese Canadians who were trying to empower themselves, does suggest an attitudinal — and to a certain extent, as I shall try to show, accommodational — approach to the resolution of the past injustices. Imai's position hinged on a limited conceptual framework. In asking Japanese Canadians to adjust to the politics of the moment, he presented them with a "Japanese Canadian" subject who could become the recipient of the government's political goodwill at an opportune time; that is, during the time of a Liberal regime interested in using redress as a political gesture. It was a gesture, he must have known, that could not possibly include individual compensation.

This scenario, in part, helps explain why the "Reparations Report" presented by the NRC in 1979 argued that a "foundation" — another way of saying group, and not individual, compensation — would "make the issue of redress politically acceptable in Canada." Only one-third of the imagined foundation's work would be directed toward Japanese Canadians; the other two-thirds would focus on "education, human rights and multiculturalism" and would be used as a "vehicle to develop further cultural and educational relations between Canada and Japan." These goals are consistent with liberal values, and no doubt could be considered worthwhile by the Liberal government in power. The provision to take care of the needs of the elderly through a "nursing home," for the most part the "issei," struck a compassionate note and showed respect for the elderly. The foundation, in gesturing toward Japanese Canadians more in terms of social "needs" than of "rights," would have accommodated mainstream (read "white") liberal values and given the impression that Japanese Canadians were good citizens — even when seeking redress for the violation of their rights. Consequently, the foundation would "signify ... the end of a horrid chapter in Canadian history." In this narrative, the internment is only a "horrid chapter" that finally comes to an "end." Thus the history begun in the 1940s is finally coming to an end in the 1980s. Coming to an end, but not necessarily redressed.

In this way, the rationale for group settlement is consistent with the racialization so pervasive in liberal Canada during the war years. That phenomenon had not disappeared but was latent and ready to re-emerge. In an echo of the 1940s warnings to Japanese Canadians — don't rock the [white] boat, "shikata ga nai" ("it can't be helped"), don't protest — Imai supporters often invoked the spectre of backlash, a spectre that Japanese Canadians had internalized in the postwar years of forced assimilation. In an interview with Joe Serge on August 27, 1983, only days before the Prince Hotel meeting, Imai focused on older Japanese Canadians' "worry" about demanding any redress that involved money. As he explained to Serge, "They fear it may renew resentment against them. They believe no amount of money is worth renewing the prejudice and the traumatic experiences of years ago."

For Imai, the racism was still out there, waiting to renew itself if Japanese Canadians demanded direct and substantial compensation for the violation of their rights. Better to seek a settlement "acceptable" to the Canadian public, to remain model "Japanese Canadians" — compliant, cooperative, non-individualistic.

Imai spelled out his argument for group over individual compensation in a paper, titled "Philosophical Underpinnings of a Reparations Settlement" and distributed at the NAJC conference in Winnipeg in January 1984. In this document, dated November 1983, the NRC says that the "issue is to determine a form of settlement that is agreeable to the majority of the group, thereby avoiding an undermining from within." In doing so, the committee situated itself between the two extremes — no compensation and individual claims — to take a moderate position. The paper's negative assessment of individual claims, however, is misleading because the nature of the option is not clarified. The NRC does not distinguish between "individual compensation" on a fixed per capita basis, using the U.S. case as an example, and "individual claims" for actual losses and damages, including the effects of civil rights violations, calculated on an individual-by-individual basis. The NAJC had never seriously considered the latter route because it believed that such a complicated form of compensation would be impossible to negotiate.

The lack of specificity concerning redress for "individuals" caused some confusion among Japanese Canadians. The NRC's argument that "individual claims" was an avenue too difficult to pursue reflected the dominant view, but it failed to mention compensation on a per capita basis — the form that was eventually endorsed in the 1988 redress settlement. Instead, as an alternative to its notion of "individual claims," the NRC favoured the "foundation approach," based on a group settlement. Although there might be some backlash because money was involved, this option was more likely to be accepted by both Japanese Canadians and the government. To reinforce this conclusion, the paper set out the basis of its defence — but it is here that the NRC's strategy elides the very human rights issues that later became the substance of the NAJC's redress campaign: "The actions of the government were not directed at individuals, although individuals suffered, but directed at a group (Japanese Canadians). The settlement is therefore directed at that level." In treating Japanese Canadians primarily as a group, and not as individuals, the NRC reproduced the logic of the government's decision to uproot individuals according to their association with "the Japanese race." It is ironic that the government was so convincing in its categorization that the NRC adopted it 40 years later.

Aside from obscuring the crucial principle that individual rights were violated because of their putative "race" — a principle that drew many Japanese Canadians to redress — the logic here confirms the bias underlying the guiding notes attached to the NRC's controversial questionnaire. There the "individual claim option" is described as an unresolvable complexity, whereas the "foundation or group option" has clearly stated objectives. Thus, to the question, "What appears to be the best option available to us?" the form answers: "Probably the group-foundation option. This would involve a petition to the Government, which the Cabinet would act upon, without the need of going through Parliament." Yet another irony: informed readers were only too aware that cabinet's power to bypass Parliament was the very means through which the mass uprooting and dispossession had been carried out without discussion in the House of Commons.

In constantly invoking "urgency" in order to pressure the NAJC to quickly seek "acknowledgement first," Imai was perhaps acting in line with his perceptions of the political moment and responding to his exchanges with politicians such as Jim Fleming and officers in the Multiculturalism Directorate. But the question remains: to what extent, if at all, was Imai communicating with politicians and bureaucrats regarding redress? Was he informed that the government would be willing to consider an "acknowledgement" of some kind, but no direct compensation to individuals? In one newspaper article, Justice Minister Mark MacGuigan disclosed that he had engaged in an "exchange of letters" with Japanese Canadian representatives. In the same article, Jim Fleming admitted that he had discussed the issue of compensation with Imai. In his reports to the NAJC, however, Imai did not cite government correspondence. Nevertheless, he was able to secure a large grant in 1983 to establish a redress position to present to the government in the same year. It is unlikely that a government opposed to redress would have provided such funds.

Moreover, in Toronto, in October 1983, Imai had appeared before the federal committee that issued, the following spring, an all-party report, *Equality Now!*, in which Recommendation 33 states: "The Parliament of Canada should officially acknowledge the mistreatment accorded to the

Japanese [*sic*] in Canada during and after World War II and the Government of Canada should undertake negotiations to redress these wrongs."[3] Given Imai's ties with Jim Fleming, the minister who first pushed for a report on the effects of racism in Canada, he would likely have received sympathetic treatment from the committee. One statement in the report seems to bear this out: "Members were deeply moved by the presentation made to them in Toronto by the representatives of the Japanese-Canadian community." But what is even more telling is the paragraph about the January 1984 conference of the NAJC in Winnipeg:

> In late January, 1984, The National Redress Committee of the National Association of Japanese Canadians set out its position in a resolution passed by it in Winnipeg. The National Redress Committee would like an official acknowledgement from the Government of Canada of the way in which it mistreated the Japanese [*sic*] in Canada during and after World War II. It would also like to undertake negotiations with the Government of Canada on the manner in which these wrongs are to be redressed. Although the moral and historical damage done to Japanese-Canadians may be difficult to rectify, the Committee believes that the Government of Canada should make the attempt and, in conjunction with the National Redress Committee, begin to close this chapter in Canadian history.

For a report that would be issued two months later, this paragraph referring to a meeting in "late January" must have been composed sometime in February, in all likelihood after details had been discussed with Imai and the NRC. It may be a coincidence, but the reference to closing a "chapter in Canadian history" echoed the NRC's 1979 "Reparations Report." In this paragraph, the NAJC is misrepresented as an organization whose authority is determined by the NRC. The NRC did not pass the resolution; the NAJC council did. Moreover, it was not the NRC that "would like an official

---

3   The files in the Library and Archives of Canada for *Equality Now!* show that George Imai made his presentation not as a representative of the NAJC, but as the Former President of the Japanese Canadian Businessmen's Association — unless, of course, there is another document not in this archive. In his presentation, Imai does not recommend redress directly, but says that the injustices have not been "remedied" as yet. Significantly, in the list of submissions, the National Association of Japanese Canadians is not mentioned.

acknowledgement." Nevertheless, the writers of *Equality Now!* assumed that the NRC was the representative body for Japanese Canadians. They must not have researched the January conference nor even talked with the NAJC's new president, Art Miki. Whether Imai and the NRC were consulted on this paragraph is difficult to determine.

What its language suggests is the likelihood that Imai had some awareness of the gist of Recommendation 33 by early February or even earlier, perhaps at the time of the January conference. There, while NAJC council members struggled with structure and procedure to ensure a democratic process, Imai pressured them to act immediately to get the acknowledgement first. He urged them to "come up with some kind of consensus tonight." Why? As he argued, going for the acknowledgement right away was "a political thing. Let's face it. It's not because they like us or anything of the sort. And that's the bottom line. And if we can't realize that I think we're really missing something."

David Suzuki, a broadcaster, geneticist and environmental activist who attended the meeting on his own, had called for caution in attempting to politicize redress:

> We are a minority group that is so small that we don't count anywhere. What we have going for us is the moral rightness of the issue. There is a great deal of pressure now to ram through something because this government is tottering on shaky legs. There is no question in my mind that George is right, that this is a very opportune moment politically. Whatever is done is not going to be done by addressing the moral issue involved. It's going to be done for purely political reasons and you're going to be bought out if you don't watch yourselves very carefully.

Even before the conference, there were worries that asking for an acknowledgement first without working out a clear position for a redress settlement could undermine the cause. What if the government then closed the door on compensation, saying that the acknowledgement was sufficient? Moreover, was not the acknowledgement the means through which to seek resolutions on the two other issues? Roger Obata had observed in a memo to the NAJC council: "It appears that the old fable of the bundle of sticks being stronger than each individual stick seems to apply here."

Obata was responding to Gordon Kadota, who was thinking about separating out the acknowledgement and setting aside temporarily the question of compensation and legislative protection. Obata had decided to poll NAJC council members on the three options facing the NAJC: acknowledgement first, with no conditions; acknowledgement "with conditions" that compensation would be considered later; and the "total package," which meant seeking a settlement with three components: acknowledgement, compensation to Japanese Canadians and preventative measures. Obata presented the results of his poll at the meeting. Of the 13 members polled, eight favoured acknowledgement with conditions, four the total package and one took no position. Discussion of the issue, as recorded in the minutes, was inconclusive. Even the substance of the conditions to be attached was left up in the air, and while some thought it would be "opportune" to take advantage of the political scene, no motion came to the floor.

Soon after the conference, however, despite the sense of unity that was derived from the NAJC having passed a historic resolution to seek redress for the wartime injustices, the issue of "acknowledgement first" caused a major rift between Art Miki and George Imai. At that moment, Imai appeared to have considerable backing. With Vice-President Jack Oki and Ritsuko Inouye, president of the Toronto JCCA, both on his side, and with all the former members of his inner circle reappointed to the NRC, Imai's plan to get the acknowledgement from the Liberal government of Pierre Elliott Trudeau seemed to be back on track. Almost.

After being elected president, Art Miki was pulled headlong into the politics emerging around the question of redress. Only a few weeks after the Winnipeg conference, in mid-February, he was off to Ottawa to attend a session of the Canadian Ethnocultural Council (CEC) for presidents of national ethnic organizations. Here he met briefly with David Collenette, the minister in charge of the Multiculturalism Directorate. Collenette expressed interest in redress, but advised Miki to submit a monetary figure with the request for acknowledgement. Whether or not this gesture was a political ploy on Collenette's part, it presented Miki with a major dilemma as the new president.[4] Should the NAJC take up Collenette's advice? Miki was

---

4   In an interview on CBC's "Identities" program, broadcast on January 27, 1984, Collenette was asked about compensation to Japanese Canadians. He responded that compensation "could range

already being criticized by the Imai group for apparently informing the press that the NAJC would be seeking "full compensation," a term used in a *Globe and Mail* news report titled "Japanese Canadians to Seek Compensation," published on January 24, 1984. Although Miki denied making such a statement to the press, some members of the Imai group in Toronto were infuriated because they believed that the news report contradicted the NRC's position of acknowledgement first.

From this point onward, a series of heated memos were exchanged between Miki in Winnipeg and Imai and Ritsuko Inouye in Toronto. Miki was accused of tampering with the NRC's acknowledgement-first plan. The dispute hinged on their opposition to the "and" in a letter from Miki setting out his interpretation of the Winnipeg motion. Inouye claimed that the "and" connecting the call for acknowledgement with the other two parts of the resolution — compensation and preventative measures — implied that the acknowledgement was dependent on a commitment to negotiate compensation. In a memo dated March 15, 1984, Imai went further and accused Miki of advocating a position of "full compensation," which could exceed a billion dollars. Miki said that the NAJC council needed to be consulted on the matter. Imai, however, proceeded by scheduling his NRC meeting for March 17, in Toronto. He did not invite Art Miki. When Miki found out, he decided to show up anyway.

At this time, mid-March, Imai likely knew of the recommendation forthcoming any day with the release of the *Equality Now!* report, though he made no mention of this to Miki. What appeared important to him, and the reason he had arranged a meeting of his NRC, was to get proof of support for the acknowledgement-first position into the government's hands. Following his own advice to take advantage of political opportunism, Imai perhaps did not want to wait any longer.

The critical March 17 meeting, which later became the basis for charges levelled against Miki that he had failed to uphold a motion passed by his council, had Imai as chair, with strong endorsement from Oki. Oki himself appeared to be present as both a member of the NRC and as the NAJC vice-president. All the old members of Imai's NRC attended, along with a

---

anywhere from a few thousands of dollars to well over a billion dollars," so that "it would be premature to make any statement until we have a figure and then I would take it to cabinet."

selection of council members from Montreal, Hamilton, Winnipeg, Lethbridge and Vancouver. Wes Fujiwara, who taped the meeting, attended as an observer. The crux of the meeting, aside from the discussion of various possible forms of redress, was the draft of a letter to the prime minister asking for "acknowledgement now," "with the proviso" that talks on compensation would follow. Imai and Oki wanted committee approval to send the letter "immediately," to be hand-delivered by the president, vice-president, NRC chair and vice-chair. With Henry Kojima from Winnipeg as his only reliable ally, Miki was surrounded by Imai and Oki supporters. He nevertheless expressed his concern, which was informed by his recent meetings with Collenette and officers in the Multiculturalism Directorate, that segregating the acknowledgement from a solid commitment to negotiate compensation seriously jeopardized the compensation issue. The "proviso" could easily be overlooked by the government once the official acknowledgement had been given. At the very least, according to Miki, the letter should not be sent until it had been discussed and ratified at the next NAJC council meeting, in a few weeks' time — early April.

The sense of "urgency" was invoked once again, and the most vocal speakers at the meeting argued that the council members at the January meeting in Winnipeg had approved "acknowledgement first." Those who wanted to send the letter right away also insisted that the three components of the historic redress motion that had passed had to be considered as three separate issues. Despite the inclusion of the "proviso," Miki was torn between his mistrust of the NRC meeting and his sense of responsibility to his council as a whole. After all, Imai had not invited the president of the organization to which the NRC was accountable. There were also signs of collusion that placed Miki on the defensive. No matter what he proposed, he would inevitably be controlled by the majority at the meeting, many of whom were appointed by Imai and hence not elected by the NAJC. Miki decided to go against the prevalent view at the meeting that the NRC represented the full authority of the NAJC and therefore did not have to consult with the NAJC council about the letter. He simply did not believe in the rightness of the action. Not surprisingly, though, a motion to send the letter was passed.

Miki did not send the letter, but chose to wait until the NAJC council meeting on April 7, in Vancouver.

Many questions linger about this unusual meeting. Did Imai, Oki and their supporters know more about the behind-the-scenes machinations of politicians and bureaucrats than Miki and the NAJC council? Was Imai advised, or did he surmise, that the government, or at least Collenette, might issue an acknowledgement as a response to the *Equality Now!* recommendation? Would such a move be part of a larger strategy to court ethnic or minority votes at a time when the Liberal Party's popularity appeared to be declining in the polls? Would a quick acknowledgement be an easy way of containing the issue of redress, even capitalizing on it before the next election, in a post-Trudeau party? Was this why Jim Fleming, the former minister in charge of the Multiculturalism Directorate, would personally endorse a major grant to Imai and the NRC — to get a consensus in favour of a foundation?

But as Imai was pressing for "acknowledgement first," the government's hostility toward the issue of direct compensation to Japanese Canadians surfaced. It took the form of Prime Minister Pierre Trudeau aggressively dismissing redress for Japanese Canadians in the House of Commons. In publicly rejecting Recommendation 33 of the *Equality Now!* report, Trudeau also misrepresented the historical record, designating "Japanese Canadians" as "people whose ancestors in some way have been deprived." Shockingly, he denied the living presence of Japanese Canadians who had been victimized while he, the prime minister, was himself an adult. His obvious lack of compassion for the Japanese Canadians who had been stripped of their rights and dispossessed by the racist policies of a previous Liberal government dismayed many, even in his own party.[5]

From a broader historical perspective, though, Trudeau's attitude conformed to the assumption that the designated "Japanese" Canadians

---

5   John Turner, who replaced Trudeau as leader of the Liberal Party, agreed to reopen the question of redress if he was elected prime minister in the forthcoming September election. He confirmed this position in a personal meeting in front of my house, in the Vancouver riding in which he was running. It was another of the many twists of fate that occurred throughout the redress movement. I was looking out my window one day, and there, moving slowly down our tree-lined street, was the huge Liberal Party campaign bus. I quickly called to my wife Slavia and my kids Waylen and Elisse. As if on cue, the bus stopped outside of our house and out stepped John Turner. A few seconds later, we met on the sidewalk. As we shook hands, I asked him directly to reconsider the question of redress, and he said he would try.

were merely extensions of those "Japanese" in Japan — and not bona fide Canadian citizens. Why else would he, in 1976, apologize to the Japanese government for the mass uprooting of Japanese Canadians? It was also Trudeau who stridently defended his use of the War Measures Act during the Quebec crisis in 1970 to suspend civil rights in the name of the state. It may be that the NAJC's call for changes to the War Measures Act to prevent a future government from abrogating rights on the basis of "race," "ethnicity" or other forms of group affiliation was an affront to Trudeau's federalist political values. Whatever the underlying causes of his statements in the House of Commons, Trudeau's hostility toward the concept of redress placed a damper on "acknowledgement first." David Collenette, as the minister in charge of the Multiculturalism Directorate and the one designated to respond to Recommendation 33 of *Equality Now!*, sought to do some damage control, as other Liberals did, by portraying Trudeau's remarks as not necessarily representative of the government's views. But the die had been cast. Japanese Canadians could expect no compensation from the Liberal government.

What Collenette finally proposed fell far short of NAJC expectations — but not for Imai. A telex from him in the NAJC files, dated April 17, 1984, states:

> The Government will be discussing Collenette's proposal this week to resolve the redress issue by recommending an acknowledgement and a fund to be offered to the Canadian community on behalf of the Japanese-Canadians. This stand of the National Redress Committee Executive is the Winnipeg Conference resolution of acknowledgement now and future negotiations for compensation is confirmed in the Telex letter of April 2, 1984, signed by Art Miki, Jack Oki, George Imai, Elmer Hara and as recommended by the special committee on visible minorities, "Equality Now."

Only 10 days earlier, at its April 7 meeting in Vancouver, the NAJC council had passed a motion to seek a settlement in the range of $500 million and had formed a committee to draft a brief to argue the "case for redress." Imai's telex was his final effort to get the NAJC to accept "an acknowledgement and a fund," which he interpreted as the government's response to *Equality Now!* — despite Trudeau's rejection of redress for Japanese Canadians. This was the position he had been advocating since early 1983. Only now, more explicitly than ever before, he aligned it with the government's response to the *Equality Now!* report.

As it turned out, Collenette and the Liberal government avoided the term "acknowledgement," offering instead the much more lame "regret" as their term of choice. An expression of "regret" absolved the government of any responsibility for the injustices, and in effect amounted to a rejection of redress for the past violations. As a token of this "regret," the government was willing to establish a $5 million "Justice Institute" for all Canadians. Along with many Japanese Canadians and growing numbers of redress advocates, Miki rejected Collenette's response as wholly inadequate for Japanese Canadians.

Imai, however — or so it appeared to many in the NAJC at the time — chose not to reject the government's offer. Acting on his own, without informing Miki, he contacted a select group of NAJC council members and invited them to attend what was to be a special ceremony in the House of Commons. This group was also asked to bring some issei with them. Suspicious of this request, one of those who had been contacted by Imai asked Miki for clarification. Miki, apprised of Imai's plan to have the NRC and a handful of Japanese Canadians present in the House of Commons for Collenette's official response to *Equality Now!*, called an emergency telephone conference of the NAJC council, during which evidence was presented that the Imai delegation would lend an air of legitimacy to Collenette's proposal. Imai did not deny that he had organized the delegation. In a vote taken during this tense conference call, only five months after he was ratified as the chair, his NRC was dissolved.

Removing the NRC from the NAJC triggered a new crisis among Japanese Canadians in Toronto and brought into the open many disputes that had been brewing since early 1983. The resulting turmoil in this major NAJC centre caused splits that struck to the very heart of the emotional turmoil unleashed by redress. It was in this cauldron that new forms of collective identity would emerge.

CHAPTER 8

THE TORONTO CAULDRON

*Community Conflict and the Founding
of the "Toronto Chapter"*

*We have been hurt by what David Collenette said. It's also being perceived by
many people as the end of the issue. It's been dealt with — that's it ... We must
help people to feel that it's not over.*

— Marcia Matsui

SHIFTING POWER RELATIONS

IN LATE JUNE 1984, a week after David Collenette had rejected a meaningful
settlement, Marcia Matsui and other redress activists got together at the
home of Stan and Marjorie Wani Hiraki in Toronto. The group, which called
itself Concerned Nisei and Sansei and included members of the Sodan-kai,
had been meeting informally since March to share thoughts on redress
and to get updates on NAJC activities. Most of the group's members were
estranged from the work of George Imai's National Redress Committee
(NRC) and had lost faith in receiving any assistance from their local

organization, the Toronto Japanese Canadian Citizens' Association, whose president, Ritsuko Inouye, was aligned with Imai. Even though the Toronto JCCA had established its Redress Committee in response to lobbying by local Japanese Canadians, the committee had not been able to develop an effective redress program in the Toronto area. The informal meetings at the Hiraki home thus enabled the group to remain engaged with the national redress movement that was taking shape in the activities of the National Association of Japanese Canadians (NAJC).

Expressing the view of her group, Marcia Matsui confessed the "hurt" caused by Collenette's refusal of redress to Japanese Canadians. Still, given the low profile of redress at the time, his decision to issue only an expression of "regret" for the injustices of the 1940s was not all that unpredictable. What accompanied his bland gesture, however, was much more nerve-wracking. Anger and frustration had flared up in the Japanese Canadian community in Toronto as news spread that the chair of the NRC, directly contradicting the NAJC's rejection of Collenette's response, was cooperating with Collenette. As accusations arose of a redress "sellout" for the sake of political opportunism, many interpreted this situation as a bitter replaying of the community's divided loyalties in the 1940s. Collenette's failure to address the government's role in the racialization that had led to the mass uprooting and dispossession of Japanese Canadians, so tangible in his decision not to use the term "acknowledgement," made the actions of the chair all the more painful.

Instead of resigning themselves to what seemed for "many people as the end of the issue," Matsui and her group were even more determined to speak back to Collenette's actions. Their collective effort to keep redress alive embodied the dynamic energy of the early struggle in Toronto. The Toronto Japanese Canadians meeting at the Hiraki home desperately wanted a more open-ended and inclusive community process for redress than was being offered by the Toronto JCCA. As happened often in the redress movement, resistance to government manoeuvres stimulated new collective strategies. In their frustration that Japanese Canadians such as George Imai and Jack Oki would openly back Collenette, a number of them from the Sodan-kai had "crashed" Collenette's press conference in Toronto, an event that they recalled at the Hiraki home on June 24, 1984. They had been able to undermine the credibility of Imai and Oki, who were at the press conference, and at the same time their audacious action, so uncharacteristic for their community, opened up a way for Japanese Canadians to forge a more collective voice. Their response to the Collenette crisis marked the beginning of a crucial power shift in the redress debates in Toronto.

This change, in 1984, was critical in strengthening the fabric of the national redress movement. Until 1980, Toronto had been the political centre for dispersed Japanese Canadians. Indeed, its historical importance often confused the NAJC's lines of authority and representation, which may explain why the chair of one of its subcommittees, the National Redress Committee, could assume from his perspective in Toronto that he spoke for Japanese Canadians as a whole. Unfortunately, many federal government officials, who themselves considered Toronto the Japanese Canadian centre, sometimes treated the chair as if he were the official voice. From inside the community, however, the centrality of Toronto in Japanese Canadian history — the very centrality out of which the Toronto JCCA derived its power — created the conditions for an uneasy tension between one group maintaining authority through past connections and a new group challenging their power through the more progressive language of the national redress movement. This new group, which evolved out of the "Concerned Nisei and Sansei," became the Toronto Chapter of the NAJC, the community organization that replaced the Toronto JCCA in the NAJC. How did this transformation occur? The answer to this question lies in the history of redress politics in Toronto during the pivotal years, 1983 and 1984.

REDRESS POLITICS IN TORONTO, 1983-1984

AS THE PRINCE HOTEL crisis had made clear, the seeds of the redress movement in Toronto had already been planted in the spring of 1983 through the formation of the Sodan-kai. This small group of lawyers, writers and activists had come together primarily to forestall the quick group settlement favoured by George Imai and his National Redress Committee. The Sodan-kai was instrumental in sponsoring large public meetings that attracted the attention of Japanese Canadians on the sidelines. Their work, which included producing informative and controversial articles for the *Canada Times* and the *New Canadian*, helped to articulate the implications of redress, and simultaneously exerted sufficient pressure on the Toronto JCCA to motivate it to organize a redress committee for Toronto.

Although the Sodan-kai was motivated by a genuine desire to promote a democratic process, the group was soon depicted by Imai backers of the Toronto JCCA as young "dissidents" who did not respect the wishes of the elderly and whose main goal was to undermine Imai's authority. The backers happened to form an influential part of the membership of the Toronto JCCA. The Toronto JCCA also included a number of Japanese-speaking issei who sat on a subcommittee called the Issei-bu. These were issei who endorsed Imai and sided with his NRC when called upon to do so. More honorific than representative, the Issei-bu could be used to dispel criticism of the NRC, especially when they were portrayed as proponents of a group settlement.[1] Their benign image could then be sharply distinguished from that of the individualistic younger generation, who supposedly wanted an exorbitant amount of compensation for Japanese Canadians.

It is truly unfortunate that some members of the Issei-bu, unable fully to comprehend the disputes that raged in English, got caught in the crossfire as resistance to the NRC intensified. On November 1, 1983, for instance, just at the time when a Toronto redress committee was being conceived, the Issei-bu met and passed a number of motions supporting strong positions: an "apology," the "group or foundation option," the Toronto JCCA and the NRC. By committing themselves so soon to the NRC position, the Issei-bu would subsequently be directly opposed to the Sodan-kai and others who wanted more community discussion before coming to consensus on forms of compensation. How could they modify their position without losing face?

These divisions resulted in conflicts among the generations that were eventually played out in strained social relations and personal confrontations. Nowhere was this more apparent than in the brief history of the Toronto JCCA Redress Committee.

---

1   During the redress movement, there was a tendency to assume that all issei were represented by the handful in the Issei-bu of the Toronto JCCA. But this group did not solicit views of other issei from across Canada, such as those in the smaller and remote communities in B.C. — such as New Denver, where many issei stayed after 1949. The Issei-bu members lived in Toronto, and the information they received, primarily through translations, was tied to the perspective of the NRC. Since they viewed the redress movement mainly through Imai's eyes, they came to believe that the movement would die when the NRC was dissolved by the NAJC. They had little knowledge of the NAJC as an organization that could represent the interests of issei across Canada.

THE TORONTO JCCA REDRESS COMMITTEE

PERHAPS THE DEMISE of the Toronto JCCA Redress Committee was already apparent in its origins. Instead of appealing to a broad base of Japanese Canadians in a large urban centre such as Toronto through an election process, the Toronto JCCA sought to manage redress debates by designating the Redress Committee as its subcommittee. Under the signature of its president, Ritsuko Inouye, the organization began by inviting community groups to appoint an individual to serve on its Redress Committee.

Inouye's letter set the date, November 29, 1983, for the inaugural meeting of the Toronto JCCA Redress Committee. The gathering took place in an upstairs private room of the Nikko Gardens restaurant.² Individuals who were not part of the inner circle of the Toronto JCCA suspected that the Redress Committee membership was stacked in Imai's favour, largely because of Inouye's influence. This situation was immediately tested in a motion to change the name of the committee to the Toronto Redress Committee. Removing "JCCA" from its title would signal that the committee intended to reflect the concerns of all Japanese Canadians in the Greater Toronto area. The motion would also establish an autonomous committee, not one under the wing of the Toronto JCCA. The motion was defeated, but its very existence prefigured the rifts to come. Not surprisingly, the Toronto JCCA's favourite for chair, Jack Oki, was ratified by the committee. George Imai and Ritsuko Inouye were also members.

The Toronto JCCA Redress Committee held its first official meeting on December 14, 1983, at the Toronto Japanese Canadian Cultural Centre. There were no serious confrontations. But trouble began to brew at the next meeting, on January 11, 1984, at Nikko Gardens, when the first of several controversial motions was passed. In this one, targeted for the forthcoming NAJC conference in Winnipeg, Imai and his NRC were endorsed "to carry on as the active committee in matters of Redress for the NAJC." Perhaps this was not a critical point to all the members of the Toronto JCCA Redress

---

2   The Nikko Gardens restaurant, once located on Dundas Street West in Toronto, "in the heart of downtown Chinatown," was a popular hangout for Japanese Canadians. Its isolated second-floor room "became the site of some important debates in our community — debates that re-opened old wounds and stirred up new conflicts."

Committee at the time, given the scarcity of accurate information on the NAJC. Those who were aware of the Prince Hotel crisis, however, knew that the endorsement undermined the aim of the NAJC council to assess the NRC's work in Winnipeg. More immediately, the motion could also forestall criticism of Imai, specifically by Japanese Canadians in Toronto who were critical of his handling of redress. With the Toronto JCCA group holding the majority of the votes on the Redress Committee, the minority who disagreed with Imai were made uneasy by what they perceived as political manipulation by Imai, Inouye and Oki.

At the next meeting, on January 15, which consisted primarily of a meeting of the Executive Committee of the Redress Committee, the grounds for future dissension intensified. To prepare for Winnipeg, the Executive Committee wanted to show the NAJC that a process of reconciliation had begun in Toronto. It did so by drafting a "community agreement." Along with a call for an official acknowledgement "of the injustices imposed upon the Japanese Canadians during and after WWII" and a "commitment to compensate for the actions based upon continuing negotiations," the agreement contained a highly restrictive policy statement:

> The Canadians of Japanese ancestry in Toronto have given the Toronto JCCA Redress Committee the mandate to act on their behalf on Redress matters. Therefore all activities including recommendations concerning redress arising from Metro Toronto should be channeled through the Toronto JCCA Redress Committee.

The presence of two members of the Sodan-kai on the working committee to draft this policy, Marcia Matsui and Maryka Omatsu, implied an effort to mediate conflict through a more inclusive process. Of course, had the Toronto JCCA Redress Committee been able to produce a consensus, the policy could have been seen as a visionary tactic at an important moment in the redress movement. But the weakness of the agreement was apparent: the strident tone of decree-making in phrases such as "have given" and "should be channeled" showed the instability of the Toronto JCCA Redress Committee's authority — an authority based more on assumptions than on actions. No substantial grounds were given to show that it had "the mandate to act on their [Toronto Japanese Canadians'] behalf on Redress matters."

Yet, in the language of the chair Jack Oki, because of this assumption, the Redress Committee could declare that "all other Redress groups in Toronto will cease to exist." A decree of this kind could hardly be enforceable. What the rhetoric of the motion reflected, more tellingly, was an unaddressed anxiety over the question of representation.

But it was the contradictory second motion that would soon divide the group. Although the Toronto JCCA Redress Committee was mandated to come up with a community position on redress, this motion endorsed the position already set forth by Imai and his NRC, to seek an acknowledgement first — which had always been Imai's aim — with "a proviso that future negotiations be continued on monetary compensation." This motion was certain to upset many Japanese Canadians in Toronto because, in their opinion, the discussion of approaches to a redress settlement had only just begun. For this reason the minority on the Redress Committee who were already critical of Imai considered the two motions together as an overt tactic on his part to reinforce his authority at the expense of all the Japanese Canadians who did not belong to his circle — the Toronto JCCA.

A further problem was that a motion prescribing a position on redress left little room for the Toronto representatives in Winnipeg to work toward a larger consensus with other local centres across Canada. There, as they advocated the position stated in the motion, Imai and Inouye urged the NAJC council to elect Jack Oki, the chair of the Toronto JCCA Redress Committee, as the next NAJC president. To enhance their representation they were accompanied by an unusually large delegation, which strategically included a number of the Issei-bu who had already sided with Imai in their own motion to seek an acknowledgement and a trust or community fund. Clearly the Toronto delegation, despite minority opposition within the group, came prepared to pressure the NAJC to endorse the work of Imai and his NRC.

Had Jack Oki been elected president, the executive office of the NAJC would have moved to Toronto. The concentration of community power there, with Oki acting in tandem with Inouye, the Toronto JCCA president, and Imai, the NRC chair, would have been formidable. It could very well have led to a quick settlement with the Liberal government along the lines proposed by David Collenette in his response to the *Equality Now!* report.

In retrospect, then, the Toronto JCCA reaction to the Prince Hotel crisis

— the formation of the Toronto JCCA Redress Committee — had appeared conciliatory at first, particularly for those drawn to redress through the work of the Sodan-kai. But disillusionment and outrage were quick to surface once the inner circle of the Toronto JCCA insisted more openly on endorsing the Imai plan. The push for acknowledgement first, with negotiations for compensation down the road — perhaps years down the road — was frustrating for those who wanted negotiations for compensation to form an integral part of the acknowledgement. Otherwise, were they not simply playing into the hands of politicians more interested in votes than in redress? Enter Wes Fujiwara, prominent Toronto physician and brother of the writer Muriel Kitagawa.

Like a number of vocal nisei advocates of a democratic process, Fujiwara wanted redress to speak for all Japanese Canadians affected by the mass uprooting and dispossession. During one meeting, addressing the issue of "urgency" in relation to Imai's advice to take advantage of the political moment or risk getting nothing, Fujiwara said, "I don't think we should confine ourselves to a time frame, to an election, to politics." And he explained further: "When we discuss redress we will discuss it with the government of Canada regardless of whether it's Liberal, Conservative or even the New Democratic Party. I don't care what government it is, we should discuss redress with the government of Canada. And you've got a lot of time to do that." Fujiwara was wary of a quick acknowledgement. Much more important was the need to think through all the implications of redress. He voiced the fears of many when he urged that the process be slowed down so that the complexities of redress could be addressed. What do "we" want from redress? This was the question that seemed to be pushed aside in the headlong rush to accommodate the government's agenda. But just as crucial, perhaps more so, was the question: who, precisely, was this "we"?

THE COLLAPSE OF THE TORONTO JCCA REDRESS COMMITTEE

FOR A SHORT time, the tensions in the Toronto JCCA Redress Committee were contained by the desire for reconciliation. With a different chair this situation might have continued, but Jack Oki already seemed to have too much invested in the NRC position to open up to the alternative approaches that would surely have arisen with broader community participation.

His alliance with Ritsuko Inouye and George Imai was evident in his performance as chair, and this often resulted in actions that were perceived to be compliant with their views. By late March 1984, as Imai battled with NAJC President Art Miki on the NAJC front over the question of "acknowledgement now," the frustration level rose quickly at the Redress Committee meetings.

At the March 28 meeting, perhaps to defuse the tension, Oki brought back (from an executive meeting on January 15) the controversial "community agreement" motion. By doing so he circumvented a discussion of what was far more pressing — the question of "acknowledgement first," which was raging in the NAJC at the moment. As Oki allowed a lengthy discussion on what had already become a non-issue, Fujiwara and others at the meeting waited, their anger percolating. To exacerbate matters, Oki gave precious time to Inouye to present a summary of the NRC's March 17 meeting in Toronto, although members were not informed about the explosive behind-the-scenes power struggle that had developed between Art Miki and Imai over "acknowledgement first."

By March 28, there was a real possibility that the conflict between Miki and Imai would become public. As both the vice-president of the NAJC and the chair of the Toronto JCCA Redress Committee, Oki would have known all about this. Yet instead of addressing this NAJC situation at the meeting, he announced that his executive had added a rider to what was by then an obsolete "community agreement." Not only did the motion decree that Toronto Japanese Canadians had given the Redress Committee a "mandate to act on their behalf on redress matters," but from this point on "any person or group who is a member of the Toronto JCCA Redress Committee must discuss with the Executive Committee of the Toronto JCCA Redress Committee, prior to engaging in any activity of a controversial nature." This prohibition included "media releases."

In presenting this rider, Oki admitted that the term "controversial" made the motion "awkward perhaps." Although he qualified it by saying that its "intent was not to restrict all activities but to undertake that there be unity of purpose and action," the ensuing discussion raised the crucial questions. What negative effects would it have in discouraging the expression of divergent points of view? How would it be enforced? What would the penalties be for violation? How would "controversial," an ambiguous term, be interpreted? If people found themselves excluded because they didn't agree with the Toronto JCCA Redress Committee, wouldn't they simply respond by setting up their own organizations? One member who spoke against the motion aptly argued:

> I don't think we need to have these regulations. And to be very honest with you I don't think you can enforce it. If you try to enforce it, it's going to mean a showdown. You're going to force certain of this organization to leave the Toronto [JCCA] Redress Committee and set up their own. If you're going to put yourself in a corner, then I think it will be very difficult to come out of it.

Another member brought up the need for the "free flow of information and sharing of ideas, positions even, on this issue." Yet another, upset by the lack of open discussion about redress, claimed that an "agreement" was premature until the community addressed in detail all aspects of redress, such as the pros and cons of the foundation, individual compensation and the non-monetary value of redress. "So therefore," he said, "until we have some kind of substantial discussion, a discussion about the substance of what redress is and what it means to us and to our friends and families, how can we talk about an agreement?"

The struggle here was between an abstract unity, declared through committee motions, and a concrete unity arrived at through the much more difficult process of political participation from Japanese Canadians coming from divergent, and often conflicting, points of view. Oki's own distance from the growing alienation of many vocal members of his committee was evident in his comment that he didn't think the motion was "much of an issue. I thought we were stating something that was clearly obvious as to the intent of this committee." Flustered by the strong critical response, Oki said that he would abide by the vote. But then, instead of closing discussions, he solicited one more comment. In a gesture that further alienated members who disagreed with Imai's tactics, he turned to Imai: "George, would you want to say something? I would like to make this the last comment ..."

This privileging of Imai, who as chair of the NRC and the centre of controversy should not have been on the locally based Redress Committee — if not as a matter of policy, at least as a matter of ethics — grated on the nerves of many members. Those who had been associated with the Sodan-kai's work in the previous year had joined the Toronto JCCA Redress Committee hoping to promote open community discussions on the substance and meaning of redress. Like Fujiwara, they did not want to follow Imai, Oki and the NRC down the Liberal political path of a quick resolution that excluded direct compensation. Allowed the opportunity to speak, Imai did not address the motion, but instead dwelled on a comment made by a member on the need for more community discussion on the issue. He went on praising the work of the NRC from the late 1970s on, raising the anger level of those who had lost confidence in him and using up the rapidly diminishing meeting time in his general references to some public meetings, the NRC position paper and articles in the *New Canadian* and *Canada Times*.

Following Imai, Harry Yonekura spoke in Japanese, then provided his own translation. Since the Redress Committee had not been able to unify the varying positions of its members, Yonekura concluded that "we have reached a point of no return." Rather than voting in one bloc on the NAJC council, a practice that had resulted in the control of five votes by Toronto JCCA President Ritsuko Inouye, Yonekura recommended that the votes be distributed among different groups in the Toronto area.[3] After Yonekura spoke, others continued to discuss problems that the community agreement would not resolve and might even aggravate. Then a motion to table the motion was ignored, and Oki called the question: 30 for, 11 against. The Oki-Imai-Inouye nexus may have prevailed for the moment, but the strain among others who considered their leadership to be autocratic and anti-democratic intensified. Meanwhile, the meeting continued with discussion of the forthcoming NAJC conference planned for Vancouver on April 7, 1984.

While the growing antipathy to George Imai and Jack Oki was palpable, an air of restraint kept tempers in check, perhaps indicating a belief that change would eventually overtake the group. After all, the NAJC redress movement at the national level was moving ahead swiftly. There had also been the March release of the federal report, *Equality Now!*, with its recommendation favouring redress for Japanese Canadians. Without a unified committee, Japanese Canadians in Toronto would miss out on the momentum. More urgently, in preparation for an important NAJC conference in

---

3   For an explanation of the NAJC's system of voting, see footnote on pp. 225-6.

Vancouver, only a short time away, Art Miki had distributed a memo calling for input on projected monetary figures for a redress settlement, a subject sure to generate lively debates and motions.

To counter the fear that the "community agreement" would prohibit a full airing of different positions, the Executive Committee of the Toronto JCCA Redress Committee urged its members to adopt three recommendations to take to the NAJC conference in Vancouver: a study of economic losses resulting from the mass uprooting and dispossession, a review of the limits of the Bird Commission, and a brief on the historical grounds for Japanese Canadian redress. These were reasonable recommendations, and in fact they were endorsed at the conference. What was grating to some, though, was the injunction that Toronto delegates to the meeting were expected not to decide on any specific proposals involving monetary figures. As Oki said, "Our position is there's not enough substantive data to prepare a meaningful proposal, and that's it."

As the tensions at the March 28 meeting showed, the Toronto JCCA Redress Committee was destabilized by internal wrangling and the lack of trust. The inability of its members to work together would cause further squabbles among them at the Vancouver conference. By then, moreover, the Imai-Oki-Inouye triangle had more clearly distanced itself from the directions being taken by the NAJC under President Art Miki. The pendulum swung against them as many outside their committee's influence grew weary of their complaints against the NAJC. More Japanese Canadians wanted Toronto to work with Miki in building a redress movement with a strong national scope. The pressure was on delegates from Toronto — a crucial NAJC centre — to get its large Japanese Canadian population on the NAJC's side.

One of the problems was that the Toronto JCCA had not held elections for years, and there was little likelihood of one in 1984. The decision-making powers were so concentrated in the hands of a few, and its president, Inouye, was staunchly loyal to Imai, Oki and the National Redress Committee. With the three of them collectively wearing so many organizational hats, initiating change from within the Toronto JCCA Redress Committee was blocked by one regulation or another. Those who wanted to work with the national redress movement finally became so frustrated that they decided to form another community organization and to seek representation directly from the NAJC.

Conflicts came to a head when the news broke that George Imai, acting as chair of the NRC, was making arrangements behind the scenes — without informing NAJC President Art Miki — to work with David Collenette on an official ceremony in Ottawa. This was the occasion for the emergency telephone conference of the NAJC council on June 17. The motion to disband the NRC and to authorize the president to be the official spokesperson on redress was a severe blow to NRC supporters in Toronto, particularly Inouye and Oki. The situation took on more ominous tones when Imai then announced, through the mainstream media, that he had formed another (as yet unnamed) organization to oppose the NAJC. Brian McAndrew, a *Toronto Star* reporter, wrote that "Imai said he plans to continue meeting today with ministry officials on behalf of the new organization."

In response to Imai's actions, Fujiwara prepared a motion designed to force the Toronto JCCA Redress Committee to decide, once and for all, whether or not it would stand in solidarity with the NAJC:

> Recently there has been an announcement in the Japanese press of the formation of a separatist Redress group in Toronto claiming to represent the whole Japanese Community. In view of this fact, it is essential that before any further business is conducted, the following motion should be considered, otherwise all further business by this organization becomes meaningless.
>
> I move that the Toronto JCCA Redress Committee reconfirms its support of, and its membership in, the National Association of Japanese Canadians.
>
> I request that this vote be a recorded vote by Roll Call.

This was the motion that Fujiwara planned to present to the Toronto JCCA Redress Committee at the Nikko Garden on June 27, 1984 — perhaps the most volatile of all the meetings. A sense that this meeting would become a "showdown" was in the air. Although Imai was no longer in the NAJC, he still sat in the room as a member of the Toronto JCCA Redress Committee. He would have been aware that Fujiwara's motion had major consequences for him. If it passed, the Toronto committee would be endorsing the dissolution of his NRC, and he would lose his power in Toronto. If it was defeated, he and his supporters would be isolated further and the pro-NAJC forces in Toronto would become much more cohesive. Oki's tactic as chair in the face of mounting discontent was to stall the proceedings so that decisions could not be made through motions.

On the night of June 27, tempers were strained to the breaking point. To understand the complexities of this dramatic occasion, it is necessary to track the recent events leading up to it, much of it involving Wes Fujiwara, directly or indirectly. In an unusual pattern of unfolding personal events, Fujiwara's rise to a leadership role in Toronto redress politics typifies the unpredictable community awakening that was necessary to mount a successful redress campaign.

DR. WESLEY FUJIWARA: ONE AMONG MANY

DR. WESLEY (WES) Fujiwara was the younger brother of Muriel Kitagawa and the recipient of her letters, which were written in the heat of the mass uprooting and subsequently published in book form as part of *This Is My Own*, a collection of Kitagawa's writing in the 1940s. A highly respected pediatrician, he was married to Misao (nee Yoneyama), a well-known physician and the first Canadian nisei woman to become a doctor. The Fujiwaras were nearing retirement from their hectic professional careers when their home became the site of many informal gatherings of Japanese Canadians, most of whom, like themselves, were nisei who had become passionate about redress.

By the fall of 1983, the time of the Prince Hotel crisis, Fujiwara had thought little about redress. Following in the tracks of many nisei of his generation, he had been absorbed by the responsibilities of his work, distant from community organizations such as the Toronto JCCA, yet troubled by what was for them an unresolved and painful past. Perhaps the Fujiwaras' distance from other Japanese Canadians was another effect of the postwar pressure to assimilate and to disappear in the mainstream. But a series of remarkable "callings" pulled Fujiwara from the sidelines into the crucible, where he emerged as a leader and vocal redress advocate, not just for Toronto but for the national movement.

It all began for him when one of his patients mentioned Joy Kogawa's recently published novel, *Obasan*. The patient noted that Kogawa had drawn on several letters written by Wes' sister Muriel, who was thanked in the book's acknowledgements. Soon after, Kogawa herself dropped off a copy of the novel at his home, and then Fujiwara read, in this first fictional account of the mass uprooting, many of the letters that his sister had sent him in Toronto during the period from December 1941 to May 1942. At that time he had just begun medical school, and because of his personal connections in the city, including one with the Reverend James Finlay, he was instrumental in assisting Ed and Muriel Kitagawa with their four young children, two of them twins born only months before, to move there.

In the years that followed, Wes and Misao immersed themselves in the medical profession and established themselves as eminent Toronto doctors. Wes dropped by the Prince Hotel meeting in September 1983, not so much to hear about the growing squabbles over redress as to say hello to Kogawa. While sitting on the periphery of the meeting room, though, he was intrigued by the infighting. What exactly was this issue that agitated so many Japanese Canadians? Curious about intellectual matters, and fascinated by the notion of redress for the injustices of the past, he decided to do some basic research by attending meetings and taping them for future reference — a decision ensuring that the records of many crucial meetings would be preserved.

At first, Fujiwara was drawn to Imai and his National Redress Committee, and went so far as to offer his assistance to further their work. Soon after, he was invited to join the Toronto JCCA Redress Committee, becoming one of a handful who were recognized as individuals rather than representatives of a Japanese Canadian community organization. To follow up on his research, Fujiwara decided to attend the important Winnipeg conference in January 1984. He paid his own way and identified himself as a concerned observer, someone who wanted to tape the proceedings so that he could figure out what redress might mean to the Japanese Canadians, like himself, whose rights had been violated in the 1940s. But as the discussion heated up around the council table, he was unable to remain passive and he began to participate. And then, in a strange twist, when Imai had to briefly vacate his place at the council table after being elected chair of the NRC, Fujiwara was asked to replace him. Suddenly he was, albeit temporarily, the official delegate from Toronto.

At the Winnipeg conference, as the debates raged on, Fujiwara suddenly began to disagree with Imai's position, particularly the pressure to seek a quick resolution while the government seemed receptive. He was struck by the energy he saw in those who wanted to "talk through" redress and not accept a token settlement. He attended the March 17 meeting of the NRC called by Imai, again simply to tape the session so that he could learn more, but as he gained a close-up view, he began to mistrust the Imai-Oki circle of the NAJC. A strong believer in the democratic process, he was soon all for a grassroots redress movement.

Then came an even stranger twist in the history of his participation in the redress movement. Dissension was growing over the issue of sending a letter to the prime minister before the next scheduled meeting of the NAJC, in April 1984 in Vancouver. Fujiwara decided to attend — again on his own, and again as an observer. He planned to visit his daughter in Vancouver after the meeting. Since he would be there, some members of the Toronto JCCA Redress Committee thought, Fujiwara might just as well become part of the Toronto delegation. Then, as he was preparing for the meeting, he was approached by some Japanese Canadians who wanted to know how to get their voices heard in the NAJC. Fujiwara suggested an age-old democratic mode of doing so: a community petition. On the day he flew out of Toronto, he was handed just that — a stack of loose sheets containing more than 300 signatures. He was asked to hand-deliver the petition to the NAJC.

This document, directed not to the Toronto JCCA but to the NAJC, posed a major challenge to the credibility of the Toronto JCCA Redress Committee. Here was a substantial group of Toronto Japanese Canadians openly defying the "community agreement" that had just been hotly debated and endorsed. The petition said:

> We, the undersigned Japanese Canadians living in Toronto and vicinity, believe that the Toronto JCCA and the Toronto JCCA Redress Committee did not fully represent the diversity of opinions on redress in our community at the national conference in Winnipeg. We, therefore, present the following position and ask that the Council of the National Association of Japanese Canadians consider this course of action.
>
> 1. Any discussions with the federal government about redress or reparations for Japanese Canadians be accompanied by a brief that outlines the reasons for seeking an acknowledgement of the injustices and monetary compensation.

2. Furthermore, comprehensive research be undertaken to document the losses suffered by Japanese Canadians during and after World War II. The possibility of funding for this research has already been offered by the Secretary of State.

3. Compensation negotiations with the federal government be based upon the research findings.

4. The Japanese Canadian community be kept fully informed about the research findings and the progress of compensation negotiations.

The language of the petition, while carefully non-explicit, asked for an approach different from the one proposed by Imai and his NRC. "Acknowledgement" was now attached to compensation and required an accompanying brief that set out the terms of redress. Imai had recommended a direct deal with cabinet. But more interestingly, the petition also called for negotiations based on the research findings — a point that explicitly rejected the need to react to "urgency." Finally, there was the desire to "be kept fully informed" of redress activities.

On board the flight to Vancouver, Fujiwara looked at the pile of loose sheets and figured that the petition lacked clarity without some explanation of its origins. He decided on the spot to write a note explaining what he understood to be its intent, unwittingly in this way aligning his voice with a group challenging the authority of Imai, the NRC and the Toronto JCCA. In one of the crazy moments of improvisation called for in the early days of the movement, Fujiwara composed the letter on a laptop computer (the first of its kind), but having no printer on hand, he had to copy out in longhand what he had composed on screen. And wanting to present the sheets as one package — and resourceful to no end — he bound the loose sheets using the wire from the "barf bags" on the plane. This was the document he handed to the NAJC Steering Committee shortly after arriving in Vancouver. In that gesture, Fujiwara's note took on the form of a covering letter, creating the impression that he was "representing" (as a political spokesperson) the petitioners, rather than simply "representing" (describing) the intent of the petition. In the flight from Toronto to Vancouver, the messenger became transformed into the spokesperson for a group of petitioners.

Significantly, the petition pointed out the direction in which the NAJC and many Japanese Canadians across Canada were headed. The desire was for a broader national consensus on redress — away from the local politics of community organizations that were trying to manage dissension in order to maintain the status quo. Indeed, with the excitement of "redress talk" spreading, fewer and fewer of the people affected wanted a quick political resolution. The process in development was a move toward what would soon be called, in the language of the redress brief submitted to the government in November 1984, a "negotiated" settlement.

Yet another strange twist in Fujiwara's unlikely rise to prominence in the redress movement occurred during the discussion and vote on the controversial motion that the NAJC seek $500 million for a redress package. When the main Toronto delegate, Rits Inouye, president of the Toronto JCCA — who upheld Oki's injunction not to take a position on a monetary figure — used Toronto's five votes on the council to vote "no" to this motion, Fujiwara supported the motion and argued that at least one of the five votes should be registered as a "yes." Toronto then voted four opposed and one in favour, splitting their vote in defiance of a decision prior to the meeting not to divide the votes. By acting contrary to the wishes of the Toronto JCCA, Fujiwara began to speak for those Japanese Canadians in Toronto who identified with the national movement and not simply with the Toronto JCCA Redress Committee. His move at the council table effectively drove a wedge into the Toronto JCCA Redress Committee that eventually break Imai and Oki's hold on the committee.

On his return to Toronto, Fujiwara had to confront the wrath of Imai, Oki and Inouye. A hostile unsigned article, "Opposition," condemned the motion to seek redress in the range of $500 million, in direct defiance of the NAJC council decision not to go public with the figure right now. Although its author was anonymous, the article clearly portrayed Imai, Oki and Inouye as being in direct "opposition" to the NAJC. The $500 million figure and the motion to submit a redress brief spelled the end of Imai's position of acknowledgement first.

The following week, an unidentified writer singled out Fujiwara, referred to as a "doctor-member of the *Sodan* [Sodan-kai]," for delivering the petition to the NAJC and voting in favour of the $500 million figure. The writer attributed the petition to the Sodan-kai, a convenient scapegoat for the Toronto JCCA group, but by then the Sodan-kai no longer existed as an active collective. Jack Oki also accused Fujiwara of breaking the "community agreement" and described Fujiwara's actions as "surreptitious." These were strong and hostile words — a declaration of open verbal warfare on Fujiwara's character and his belief in the democratic process.

THE LAST STRAW: SHOWDOWN IN JUNE 1984

THE TENSIONS COMING to a head in the Toronto JCCA Redress Committee meeting of June 27, 1984 reflected animosities that had been brewing since the inception of the committee. Now, however, these animosities were out the open. Imai's NRC had been dissolved by the NAJC. The Toronto JCCA Redress Committee's "community agreement" had been defied by a petition circulated in its own community — by a group of "Concerned Nisei and Sansei" not directly affiliated with it — and then submitted to the NAJC by one of its own members. And finally, in the attacks on Fujiwara, the personal enmities among members of the committee had become public.

When the members of the Redress Committee assembled at the Nikko Gardens on June 27, the discomfort among them was palpable. At the meeting Fujiwara openly declared himself in favour of full community participation, and this for him meant an acceptance — even an encourage-ment — of divergent views. Far from being tempted by a quick settlement, he urged members of the committee to look upon redress as an unprece-dented opportunity to rethink and, more important, to work through the trauma of the wartime uprooting. He admitted that he had suggested to some Japanese Canadians a petition as one way of pressuring the Toronto JCCA Redress Committee to consider other approaches to redress. He also admitted that he had sought the advice of the NAJC president: "I phoned directly Art Miki, asking what am I supposed to do with the petition? It's got over 300 names. They're complaining that they have no way of getting any input into this committee. He said bring it to the [conference] Steering Committee. We'll decide at the Steering Committee what to do with it." Then Fujiwara told everyone at the meeting that he objected to the term "surreptitious" that had been used to describe his actions.

As for voting in favour of the motion passed at the NAJC meeting, to seek $500 million in compensation, Fujiwara explained that another member of the Toronto group, an issei, voted "no but yes in principle ... and since that type of vote could not be allowed, it went as a no." He went on to say that this issei member of the Toronto delegation agreed with the motion but was worried that the figure would cause a "backlash" — echoing Imai's own reason for not seeking individual compensation. "In fact everybody feels that way," Fujiwara said, and he explained:

> You ask for $500 million, and backlash is what everybody's afraid of. That's because of the fact that if you were a Japanese national at the time of 1942 and had to go through all that, that was what everybody was afraid of — a backlash. When we came over here, the niseis, we were afraid of backlash. That's why we kept quiet for 40 years. We're no longer afraid of backlash. We're speaking as Canadians.[4]

Fujiwara and Oki's arguments over the petition consumed considerable time at the meeting and exposed the shifting power relations in the Toronto Japanese Canadian community. Backers of the NRC had often resorted to the argument that despite the criticism of Imai, the "silent majority" continued to support him. This assertion had emotional appeal and was a convenient way to brush off Imai's apparent lack of grassroots community backing. The petition signed by over 300 Japanese Canadians living in Toronto, however, challenged this assumption.

At the meeting, while Fujiwara expressed sympathy for many individuals in Toronto who felt that they were not represented, one of these "many individuals" presented himself unannounced. He identified himself, perhaps in tongue-in-cheek fashion, as one of the "silent majority" and confessed that he had signed the petition because he could think of no other way to have his views heard. Imai, he said, had talked about a questionnaire that the NRC had distributed, but most of the petitioners had not received one to fill out.

When Imai spoke, he dwelled on the "grievance" that Fujiwara had submitted to the NAJC with the petition — possibly a reference to the

---

4   Both George Imai and Jack Oki often warned of a possible "backlash" from white Canadians if Japanese Canadians were to call for substantial compensation. See, for example, Oki's "Comments from the Chair" on compensation in which he stated: "Above all we must take care that our demands are not so 'unreasonable' that the result after expending much effort, time and money over many years is an ignominious 'turn-down' with the resultant tragic 'backlash' of public contempt for the Japanese-Canadian Community."

covering letter that Fujiwara had written on board the plane — because, as he said, he was "the other person [besides Oki] named in this grievance." Then, despite the chair's earlier comment that the issue of the petition would be discussed "at the next meeting," Imai proceeded to cross-examine Fujiwara to determine who had started the petition. The bickering ceased when Fujiwara proposed that he, Imai and Oki should meet later.

But as Oki turned to the next item on the agenda, a member interrupted him by asking for an immediate clarification of the Toronto JCCA Redress Committee's relationship to the NAJC:

> *Comment*: Is George still a member of this committee?
> *Chair*: George is still a member of this committee.
> *Comment*: But he's not associated with the national organization?
> *Chair*: That's an issue that we will come to very shortly.
> *Comment*: I think we have to have that clarified right here, tonight.
> *Fujiwara*: At what point will we bring this up, Mr. Chairman?
> *Chair*: It is item 8 on the agenda.

Although Fujiwara had presented his motion to bring the question of allegiance to the NAJC to a vote, Oki used the agenda, which had been prepared before Imai announced that he was starting a group to oppose the NAJC — to prevent a vote on the motion. The reserve of the committee members deteriorated when they were forced to listen to a lengthy statement of queries and concerns proposed by Henry Ide, which had been accepted as an agenda item at the previous executive meeting on May 28. Addressed to the NAJC council, the statement had been intended for the June 2-3, 1984, council meeting held in Winnipeg to review and ratify the draft of the NAJC's redress brief, but it had been submitted too late. By then, in light of a motion passed at the meeting giving the president the authority to verify what the NRC's status in the NAJC would be, the Ide statement was clearly outdated. But at this meeting it diverted attention from the dissolution of the NRC and from Imai's comments that he had started another organization.

The queries and concerns were familiar ones and were no longer real issues in the NAJC. For example, what about the NRC's position of "acknowledgement now" with compensation later? Where did the $500 million figure come from? There was also the concern that the two largest centres,

Vancouver and Toronto, had voted against the figure — even though one Toronto member, Wes Fujiwara, had voted in favour. These points could have been raised at the NAJC meeting, but by June 27, with the NRC dissolved, the Ide statement had lost its currency. What mattered now was the relationship of the Toronto JCCA Redress Committee to the NAJC. Did the committee support the NAJC or not?

Instead of confronting this question, Imai suddenly moved that Ide's statement be accepted and sent on to the NAJC, a ploy that flustered many people in the room. This led to the expenditure of yet more time on the statement. Meanwhile, Fujiwara's motion hung in the air. All the familiar disputes filtered through the room. At one point a member made an attempt to move toward reconciliation:

> I don't want to waste time but I feel that the discussion is dividing the group, which means the Japanese Canadians. To pursue this in the manner it is being pursued can only widen the gulf. And I don't think that is our intent, as far as the group of people working together. Now I think, Henry [Ide] and this committee have a lot of concerns, and I think a lot of them are very valid. But as being pointed out, there are discrepancies, there are errors. I would like to suggest that we send that back to the committee, and get rid of all these discrepancies and errors and have it come out at the next general meeting that we have as a committee, and at which time we can discuss it really in light of all the corrections. But I think if we vote on George's motion, we're going to create a gulf, and I don't want to see that, because there's too much now already.

Oki agreed that the Ide statement could be accepted "in principle," with errors to be corrected and clarifications to be made by the Executive Committee, but this raised the question of what the changes would be. An undercurrent of mistrust again permeated the room, and, adding to the anxiety, the details of the arguments needed to be interpreted for the Japanese-speaking issei members. Despite the commotion and spontaneous expressions of dissatisfaction with the chair's deference to Imai throughout the evening, Imai called the question on his motion. "I'd like to vote on it now please," he said to Oki. Oki complied. For: 22, against: 14. The motion passed. The emotional barometer rose even higher.

The next item was a report from Rits Inouye, Toronto JCCA president, on the June 2-3 NAJC council meeting, a meeting that neither Imai nor Oki had attended. This report generated a repetition of the familiar argument over the $500 million figure. Inouye finally got to the motion to disband the NRC, which had been passed during the NAJC telephone conference on June 17.

The simple report on this event opened up an animated exchange between Imai and Roger Obata. Imai defended his activities with Collenette by saying that he was following through on the NRC position as presented at the Winnipeg conference in January. Since Miki had stated that he was opposed to Collenette's offer, Imai saw no reason why he should not cooperate with the government, given that it was the NRC, not the NAJC President Gordon Kadota, who had made the presentation to the *Equality Now!* committee. "The response that we gave to the committee," he explained, "was the response from the Winnipeg conference, which was, number one, the apology or acknowledgement, and two, the future negotiations, which was what the committee accepted." Imai then launched into a lengthy explanation of his actions. He had discussed Collenette's projected response (acknowledgement and fund) with the multiculturalism director general, who didn't know the precise figure of the fund, but said the acknowledgement would come as a statement of "regret." Imai continued:

> And then he told me of Miki's objection [to Collenette's offer], and he said can you invite the isseis to Ottawa if the Prime Minister makes a statement. And at that point I said, why did Miki object? He said he objected to the apology as well as to the fund. He said that the fund was not acceptable. I said, well how much is this fund, again. He said he didn't know. I then surveyed six areas, in which I asked if this comes about, would the issei be willing to come out to Ottawa. I did that on behalf of the multiculturalism director general.

According to Imai, there were no "negotiations." The government was acting "unilaterally," and because this was the case, he was simply assisting them at the same time that he was advancing the NRC's position. Whether Imai was rationalizing his actions retrospectively, or was so self-absorbed that he could no longer understand his responsibility, as chair of the NRC, to the NAJC, is difficult to ascertain. Oki, as if on cue, followed up in support of

Imai, saying that the acknowledgement would have been "beautiful," especially for "our parents in nursing homes." He even had with him a copy of the statement that the prime minister would have read had Imai's actions been successful. (A flood of telegrams from Japanese Canadians opposing Collenette's proposal had led to the shelving of the ceremony.) He then proceeded, in defence of the government's language, to read the entire statement.

With so much meeting time taken up by Imai and Oki, and with Fujiwara's motion still on the floor, antagonism toward the chair heightened.

> *Comment*: I think you're out of order.
> *Chair*: Ok, I'm out of order perhaps, but there's a whole lot I wanted to say ...
> *Comment*: Why don't you stick to the motion on the floor.
> *Fujiwara*: It's 11:26.
> *Chair*: We have a motion on the floor.
> *Fujiwara*: Should I read it again?
> *Chair*: No, that's fine. Would you translate that motion? [to the interpreter]

After a few comments, Oki announced that it was getting so late that he wanted to table the motion. Lots of no's erupted — and then the meeting came to an abrupt end, as Imai leapt in:

> *Imai*: I move that we table this motion.
> *Comment*: No way, there's a motion on the floor.
> *Imai*: I moved to table. That takes precedence. We can take a vote on that.
> *Comment*: You might, but we don't.
> *Comment*: You shouldn't even be making any motions.
> *Chair*: Order please! Order! Order please! This resolution can be tabled.
> There's a motion moved and seconded to table this motion. It won't go away,
> I can assure you. It won't go away. I'm going to adjourn this meeting, table
> the motion, adjourn this meeting, and call another meeting.

In an article published in the *Canada Times* on July 3, 1984, Fujiwara told his readers that Oki and Imai had "used the age old trick of 'tabling a motion' to avoid a vote on the motion." Disgusted with what he perceived to be Oki's misuse of the chair's position, he had walked out in protest, accompanied by

Stan Hiraki, Matt Matsui, Kunio Hidaka, Roger Obata and Harry Yonekura. "Through their abrupt departure," the writers of *Japanese Canadian Redress: The Toronto Story* explain, "they were signaling the fact that they had had enough. They had already spent almost a year trying to change the ways of people who acted in the name of the community without consulting the community."

BREAKING AWAY: ESTABLISHING THE "TORONTO CHAPTER"

ON JULY 5, 1984, the follow-up meeting after the walkout began with more discussion of the telephone conference of June 17, during which the NRC had been dissolved. Again, the chair had set up the agenda so that the Fujiwara motion would be delayed. Obata had prepared for the meeting by reminding the chair of the policy on motions to table according to *Robert's Rules of Order*. Obata cited the passage: "if an important question must be settled immediately, and there is no urgency for the assembly to lay aside, a motion to lay the question on the table is clearly dilatory and consequently should be ruled out of order by the chair." Obata wanted Fujiwara's motion to be voted on immediately. Bickering on the interpretation of the passage from *Robert's* followed, and this slid over to the chair's misuse of the agenda to prevent the committee from deciding whether to support the NAJC or not.

Even more confusion was generated when the issei group wanted to place a motion on the floor to have the NRC reinstated. Their fear, it appeared, was that the redress campaign would collapse. Fujiwara then agreed to set his motion aside so that the issei could be informed about the telephone conference. This set off a lengthy, unfocused discussion of the events leading up to that fateful meeting for the NRC. In the process, Fujiwara assured the issei that the redress campaign would continue with the NAJC. The evening dragged on, the antagonism increasing.

Oki again delayed the vote on Fujiwara's motion by steering the meeting to other matters, including a discussion of Ritsuko Inouye's abstention from the vote during the telephone conference. Even though Oki was reminded that the voting was over and that the NRC had already been dissolved, making the question of the vote no longer relevant, Oki insisted that Inouye's abstention had to be addressed before returning to Fujiwara's motion. Tempers flared.

Observer David Suzuki made one last attempt to encourage cooperation before he left. He said he had once believed that the Japanese Canadian community as such had ceased to exist, but he could see in the redress movement "a very fragile beginning of an awareness that there is a community." What pained him, however, was the "you people" attitude displayed by Imai and Oki. As he commented, "Everyone in here is us. I may disagree with a lot of people, including George and Jack, but you are my brothers. I can't help it. This society makes you my brothers." Suzuki went on to speak about the dangers of valorizing the issei generation over the nisei and the sansei, because the latter were "the people who believed in this country and were disillusioned."

More commotion arose as both Imai and Oki responded to Suzuki. After this, still avoiding Fujiwara's motion, Oki called for a motion to determine whether the committee supported the NAJC motion to dissolve the NRC. Obata reminded Oki that the vote had been taken. In any case, because the decision had been made by the NAJC, the issue had to be referred to the Toronto JCCA as a member of the NAJC, and not the Toronto JCCA Redress Committee. But Oki insisted. Stan Hiraki then reminded Oki that he was the vice-president of the NAJC and as such should support the national organization. No response. The frustration level, for some, had reached its peak by this point. Hiraki accused Oki of resorting to delay tactics to prevent Fujiwara's motion from being voted on: "I'm not going to stay here and have you do that again. And I don't think anybody else will adhere to that. How about the rest of us, itadakimasu?"

> *Chair*: I'm calling for a resolution.
> *Hiraki*: I'd like to see you support the NAJC, or not, which is it?

At this moment, Oki allowed a long emotional statement from the issei, in Japanese. It was the same old information — support for Imai and his NRC and opposition to the NAJC's decision. They wanted the NRC to be reinstated. Moans and groans from the audience. The evening deteriorated into further arguments about the NAJC, as Oki allowed Imai to talk at length about the NAJC's lack of representation, ironically adopting the very language of the criticism levelled at his NRC. Again, time ran out on Fujiwara's motion. The meeting adjourned at 11:35. There was no doubt that Imai, Oki and Inouye would never express support for the NAJC, although they must have been aware that a majority on their committee did support it. Otherwise, Oki would not have used his authority as chair to prevent a vote on Fujiwara's motion.

As the Toronto JCCA Redress Committee collapsed, outside the meeting room a large national redress movement was gaining momentum. Within this broader framework, the failure to resolve Fujiwara's motion, the crisis that had caused irreparable divisions in the Toronto JCCA Redress Committee, became the impetus for a new community formation, one that would replace the Toronto JCCA as the representative organization for Greater Toronto.

The seeds of this formation had been planted months before in the group that had spontaneously formed to participate in the NAJC redress movement, the "Concerned Nisei and Sansei." The July 5 meeting of the Toronto JCCA Redress Committee had inspired the group to sponsor a large community forum on redress. Once David Suzuki had agreed to be the keynote speaker, the group began work in earnest on the forum, "Redress: What's Going On?" Held in the auditorium of Toronto's Harbord Collegiate on July 19, 1984, the event drew a crowd of some 500 Japanese Canadians. That evening a petition circulated criticizing David Collenette for allegedly "fostering a course that is factionalizing and causing pain to Japanese Canadians," as cited in Kenneth Kidd's report in the *Toronto Star*. "About half those gathered at Harbord Collegiate signed the petition before a power outage brought the meeting to a halt." The meeting continued in candle-light. (Many suspected, but with no evidence, that the power failure had been an act of sabotage.)

By mid-August 1984, the more coherent and larger "Concerned Nisei and Sansei" began to formulate plans to create a new organization in Toronto. At its inaugural meeting on September 5, 1984, it constituted itself as the Toronto Chapter. The following year this new organization joined the NAJC.

In assisting the Toronto petitioners and in voting for the motion to seek $500 million, Wes Fujiwara helped other Toronto Japanese Canadians to join the NAJC's redress movement. He thus spoke for many when on June 12, 1984, he wrote his passionate letter to the editor, defending the democratic use of petitions by those who felt "disenfranchised and unrepresented at the NAJC" and encouraging his readers to think beyond the local by participat-ing in the work of the NAJC. Redress had become, for the nisei whose rights had been violated in the 1940s, "a concern of national proportions as the issue reached the many scattered Japanese Canadians through the media." Not surprisingly, Fujiwara became the first president of the Toronto Chapter of the NAJC, the organization through which Japanese Canadians in Toronto were catapulted into the national redress movement.

CHAPTER 9

GETTING THE NAJC HOUSE IN ORDER

Forging the Language of Redress

What a cast of characters we were — the courageous, the timid, the totally determined, all making up the army of the quietly passionate. It was a time of high engagement, a time of creating the infrastructures of democracy, a time of rediscovering a sense of community.

— Joy Kogawa

MOVING BEYOND "ACKNOWLEDGEMENT FIRST"

THE DISSOLUTION OF the National Redress Committee (NRC) and the estrangement of George Imai from the National Association of Japanese Canadians NAJC became the occasion for some attacks on Art Miki, president of the NAJC. Vic Ogura, the National Association of Japanese Canadians (NAJC) delegate from Montreal, for example, blasted Miki for not sending the prime minister the letter endorsed at the March 17, 1984, meeting of the NRC — a meeting Ogura had attended as an NRC member but to which Miki had not been invited. According to Ogura, the "timing couldn't have been better" for sending the letter.

Ogura echoed Imai's view that the NAJC had to act promptly, while the political situation was ripe for a quick settlement. But then, in a revealing comment, Ogura wrote: "We knew that the all parties committee on visible minorities was to make a report momentarily and that their recommendations in reference to the Japanese Canadians was [sic] going to be very favourable." Who was this "we"? The NRC had provided no memos to alert the NAJC council to the impending release of a report and to allow them to prepare responses. Moreover, how could anyone be confident that a letter received from the NAJC before the release of *Equality Now!* would have the desired effect? If it did not speak from a well-articulated, coherent position, the NAJC could justly be accused of simply taking advantage of the politics of the moment. Should redress be represented only in this kind of narrow political framework?

Ogura disagreed with Miki's decision to hold off on sending the letter until he got approval from the NAJC council at a meeting scheduled for early April 1984. He lamented the lost opportunity: "What was to be a historical document [that is, the letter] befitting a historical moment had diminuted to a hollow stacatto [sic] on re-processed paper!" And then, in an unusual move, Ogura cited a telegram sent from his Montreal organization to Miki on March 30:

IN HISTORICAL PERSPECTIVE ERRORS OF OMMISION [SIC] ALWAYS BEEN MORE INCRIMINATING THAN ERRORS OF COMMISSION / MONTREAL DEEPLY DISAP-POINTED AND DISTURBED LETTER TO GOVERNMENT NOT BEEN EXPEDITED / UNANIMITY REACHED ONLY AT CEMETARIES [SIC] / YOU HAVE THE MAJORITY VALIDATION FROM COUNCIL / AT THIS JUNCTURE JUDGEMENT IS NOT REQUIRED / IT IS ACTION.

What might have been the consequences of Miki's delay? Would Prime Minister Pierre Trudeau and Multiculturalism Minister David Collenette have been swayed by the letter? What exactly was the "historical moment" perceived by Ogura and other Imai supporters? The government response — Trudeau's rejection of compensation (in early April), followed by Collenette's statement of "regret" with a $5 million foundation for "all

Canadians" and no offer of direct compensation to Japanese Canadians — was undoubtedly in the works well before *Equality Now!* became public. Even Collenette's asking the NAJC for a compensation figure could have been a political ruse to create a stumbling block to negotiation. A large cash figure could easily have been used against the NAJC to portray its members as money-grabbers rather than seekers of social justice. There was no evidence that plans were underway for the federal cabinet to concede to compensation for Japanese Canadians. On the contrary, what was apparent was a strategy to wrap up the redress issue with a vague foundation "for all Canadians."

Trudeau's rejection of redress for Japanese Canadians and Collenette's token gesture came as a great disappointment to many Canadians — including Japanese Canadians — and helped push the NAJC into a struggle to articulate a clear and documented position, one that would both educate the public and rouse Japanese Canadians from their slumber. Moreover, the negative press coverage of Trudeau and Collenette's response was a positive sign. It may even have surprised Imai and Oki to see such a strong critical reaction to the government from some Japanese Canadians. From this perspective, what Ogura described as Miki's "omission" can be understood as a major turning point in the history of the NAJC, its transformation from a loosely organized group of individuals, coming together haphazardly from various places across Canada, into a national council that took on the complex and intimidating work of seeking redress for the injustices of the 1940s.

TRANSFORMING THE NATIONAL ASSOCIATION
OF JAPANESE CANADIANS

IN THE EARLY 1980s, the NAJC was a largely untested organization, even though it carried on the legacy of the National Japanese Canadian Citizens' Association (NJCCA), which had formed in 1947. The association's change of name in 1980 — at a conference called "New Directions" — acknowledged the obsolescence of the founding name with its emphasis on citizenship. In the 1940s, Japanese Canadians were struggling to attain the franchise. But soon after receiving the franchise in 1949 and losing their battle with the Bird Commission at the same time, the sense of purpose in the NJCCA seemed to fade. In fact, after Prime Minister Louis St. Laurent's blunt rejection of its brief asking for further compensation, the NJCCA entered a long dormant period. Except for its sponsorship of a history writing contest in 1958 — as a result of which Ken Adachi was contracted to write an official history of Japanese Canadians, a project that became *The Enemy That Never Was* — the NJCCA as a national association was more virtual than real. There was an attempt to renew it at a conference in 1961, when its membership decided to revise its constitution for changing times. For whatever reason, but perhaps from a lack of goals and vision, the NJCCA did not meet again for over a decade.

Major social changes occurred in the early 1970s. Under the multiculturalism policy announced by Prime Minister Trudeau in 1971, Japanese Canadians came to be viewed in a new light. The "Japanese" affiliations that had relegated them to "enemy" status in the 1940s underwent a reversal as Japanese Canadians were reconfigured as a model minority — exemplary citizens. This about-face gave them the confidence to affirm their relationship with the Canadian nation by celebrating their past. The year 1977 became a focal point, a time to mark their own centennial 10 years after the national centennial. One hundred years before, so it was determined, Manzo Nagano became the first "Japanese Canadian" settler.[1] A newly created Japanese Canadian Centennial Society raised funds, including sizable government grants, to sponsor a number of national events. Ironically, organizing for the centennial provided the impetus for a renewal of the NJCCA.

It was in 1976, at a Japanese Canadian Centennial Society meeting in Toronto, that a handful of members affiliated with the inactive NJCCA changed hats to consider the future, if there was one, for this national association. At the time they had little in common except for their historical awareness of the NJCCA's importance during the late 1940s. But in a prescient way they were prodded to revive the NJCCA by the recently formed Multiculturalism Directorate. The NJCCA had been approached by officials in the directorate who were designing a series of ethnic histories, one of the first initiatives in promoting the new multiculturalism policy. Even though these histories were to be commissioned through the program, the

---

1   The community historian Toyo Takata, author of the popular history of Japanese Canadians *Nikkei Legacy*, has been credited for the idea of the centennial. As Shirley Yamada writes in "The 1977 JC Centennial," it was Takata who, in 1975, "proposed a year long, national centennial commemoration of the arrival of the first immigrant from Japan, Mr. Manzo Nagano (1854-1924)."

government was willing to bend the rules to include Ken Adachi's as yet unpublished history in the series. This would mean not only a large grant to help cover production costs, but federal endorsement as well. Such a seal of approval would give the book a heightened national profile. A report presented by former members of the NJCCA predicted considerable royalties from the sale of the book in the years ahead.

The small group decided that the NJCCA should be resuscitated. Through an informal election process those present agreed that the president elected in 1961, Ed Ide, should retain his position until the next national conference, which would be held in Winnipeg the following year. George Imai became vice-president. Ide stepped down before the conference, and Imai became president.

At the Winnipeg conference in 1977, the question of "reparations" (not "redress" then) led to the creation of a Reparations Committee (later renamed the National Redress Committee), with three members: Gordon Hirabayashi (from Edmonton), Eugene Maikawa (from Hamilton) and Harge Suge (from Ottawa). The guest speaker at the gathering was Norman Cafik, minister of state for multiculturalism. One of the first Ukrainian Canadians to become a federal minister, and conscious of his community's struggle against discrimination, Cafik was sensitive to the injustices endured by Japanese Canadians. He may even have expressed his support for some form of "redress" at the time.

Soon after the 1977 conference, however, a dispute upset relations between Imai and the Reparations Committee, primarily concerning the question of process and form of compensation. As noted earlier, when Imai presented a redress brief to the association's "New Directions" conference in 1980, calling for compensation in the form of a group foundation, his stance was strongly criticized by two members of the national executive, George Tanaka and Roger Obata, and by the Reparations Committee. Gordon Hirabayashi, in particular, objected to the committee's loss of authority and Imai's exclusion of individual compensation. By criticizing Imai, Tanaka and Obata left the impression that he was acting unilaterally.

Nevertheless, the conference held out the prospect of a major renewal of the long-dormant national organization. The name change, from the NJCCA to the NAJC, reflected the postwar demographic profile of local Japanese Canadian groups. There was also hope that the change in the national office site from Toronto to Vancouver, with Gordon Kadota, a Vancouver business-man, as president, would be instrumental in moulding a more inclusive national framework for the NAJC. And despite the controversy over Imai's redress brief, a National Redress Committee was established to seek "redress" for the wartime injustices.

The minutes of the conference record that the National Redress Commit-tee, with Naomi Tsuji as chair, was given the following mandate on redress:

> That a 6 month period be allocated for effective discussion of the issue amongst communities represented. That an assessment be made regarding the consensus of the community following the 6 month period and the NEC [National Executive Committee] be given 6 months after the review of the report back from the redress committee to submit the recommendations to the national council.

Although the rhetoric of a renewed plan for redress was encouraging, the dialogues on redress that were to take place in local communities did not materialize, and the president failed to establish the NEC. Naomi Tsuji later withdrew as chair, apparently for health reasons, and George Imai replaced Tsuji, in effect becoming the NAJC authority on redress. Instead of following through on the process prescribed in the motion, Imai soon began to advocate the position set out in his brief, a position that would be contested in the years ahead.

Even though the NAJC did not develop a redress program, the issue took on a life of its own in federal political circles. Only six months into his term as NAJC president, Gordon Kadota went to Ottawa to make a presentation about the wartime history of Japanese Canadians before the Special Joint Committee of the Senate and the House of Commons on the Constitution of Canada, a committee established to consider reforms to the Canadian Constitution and the Charter of Rights and Freedoms.

THE OTTAWA PRESENTATION TO THE CONSTITUTIONAL COMMITTEE

THE SPECIAL JOINT Committee, made up of 25 members from the Senate and the House of Commons, was set up to receive public input. The NAJC delegation, led by Kadota, appeared on the afternoon of November 26, 1980.

As the voice of Japanese Canadians whose rights had been violated during the 1940s, this group was expected to speak in support of strengthening human rights in the Constitution. But earlier, Kadota had notified NAJC centres that an "acknowledgement" of the injustices "is not our main thrust." Perhaps he felt it was inappropriate to use the occasion to lobby for redress and chose instead to focus on the wartime treatment of Japanese Canadians.

"Our history in Canada," Kadota said as he began his presentation to the Special Joint Committee, "is a legacy of racism made legitimate by our political institutions, and we must somehow ensure that no group of Canadians will be subjected to the whims of political process as we were. We feel that this can only be done by entrenching a Charter of Rights in our constitution, unconditionally entrenching, beyond the reach of Parliament and beyond the reach of provincial legislatures." The experience of the historic injustices was then exemplified in the "life stories" of two well-known nisei activists, Roger Obata and Hide Shimizu.

Hide Shimizu — formerly Hide Hyodo — who was present in the audience, told her story through a written statement read by Obata. She recalled the brutality of legalized restrictions on Japanese Canadians, but also her good fortune in finding a teaching position in an all-Japanese Canadian school in the fishing town of Steveston, B.C.: "They hired me assuming that I could communicate with the children in the Japanese language; but the joke was on them, because I could speak English only." During the mass uprooting, she was instrumental in hastily organizing and coordinating "untrained high school graduates who had to serve as teachers" to educate the children in the B.C. camps. Her own struggle, as Obata elaborated, reached back to prewar efforts to obtain the franchise for Japanese Canadians: she was part of the famous 1936 delegation to Ottawa.

Obata then recounted the devastating effects of uprooting and dispossession on his single mother, living in Prince Rupert, and his personal struggle to "prove" his identity as a "Canadian citizen" by enlisting in the armed forces, once the regulation preventing Japanese Canadians from serving was nullified. He and others enlisted, despite the pressure not to defend a country that had deprived him of his rights, because "we could not accept any kind of discrimination, even in the matter of service in the armed forces for to do so would be to accept a second-class citizens status."

Another member of the delegation, Dr. Art Shimizu, pointed out that

Japanese Americans had been allowed to return to the west coast before the war ended because their citizenship rights were protected by the U.S. constitution. On the other hand, at that same time Japanese Canadians were being deported and dispersed all over Canada because their rights had been arbitrarily revoked through the War Measures Act. If the history of Japanese Canadians was not to be repeated, then the rights of individuals and groups had to be entrenched in the Canadian Constitution. Shimizu was well known among Japanese Canadians as an opponent of the War Measures Act.

Some members of the Special Joint Committee were emotionally affected by the presentation, a clear sign that the Japanese Canadian internment remained a glaring instance of social and personal injustice. In response, John Fraser — who would later, as the House Speaker, assist the NAJC in establishing contacts with politicians in his party — told his own story of being raised in Japan and later encountering discrimination in Canada because of it. He also recalled, in vivid detail, that his father had taken him to the World War I memorial for Japanese Canadians in Stanley Park in Vancouver and urged him to remember the sacrifices of the issei, many of whom gave their lives in fighting for Canada. Fraser's father, who fought alongside the issei during World War I, explained to his son "that what was being done to the sons and daughters of the comrades he fought with was contrary to the very British justice that we thought we were engaged in protecting in the fight against Nazism."

After Fraser's deeply personal comments, Svend Robinson of the New Democratic Party prompted Kadota and his delegation to call for "remedies" — that is, some form of redress — in the way of compensation to those deprived of their rights, and the creation of effective policies to ensure that the same kind of injustices would never be visited on others. Obata responded by reminding the committee of the inadequate compensation provided by the Bird Commission. He informed the committee that the amount was "slightly less than ten cents on the dollar," and elaborated: "We feel that this was really a token compensation only for tangible property losses, and as such I believe that there is much to be argued that the compensation was totally inadequate at this time, and there are steps being taken in the United States this very day to investigate those injustices ... which were very similar to those in Canada."

Although invited to raise the question of redress, Kadota and his delegates were silent on this issue. Understandably, only months after becoming president, Kadota would not have been able to offer a detailed position on redress. Yet the committee members' reactions suggest that some discussion about redress had been circulating behind the scenes in Ottawa (perhaps stemming from Norman Cafik's interest in the issue). And John Fraser's candid identification with the internment of Japanese Canadians, made so much worse by the sacrifices they had made to defend Canada in World War I, demonstrated that some politicians were receptive to an acknowledgement of the injustices. Perhaps they thought that some form of redress could strengthen the fabric of national identity. In a very tangible way, Japanese Canadian internment reinforced the need for a strong Charter of Rights and Freedoms.

REVISING THE NAJC CONSTITUTION

AT THE TIME of the Special Joint Committee's constitutional hearings in November 1980, the NAJC had yet to get its own house in order. As he left Ottawa, Kadota was aware that the first order of business in his own organization, the NAJC, was to revise its constitution, which had not been reviewed since the 1961 conference of the National Japanese Canadian Citizens' Association.

Another three years passed. Then, in the fall of 1983, soon after the Prince Hotel crisis, Kadota asked me to join his NAJC executive committee to assist him and the lawyer Frank Hanano. We distributed a draft of the revision to the NAJC centres in October 1983. After receiving comments, we distributed another draft just in time for the Winnipeg conference in January 1984. Kadota invited me to present our report. Working on the constitution proved to be a rapid initiation into the workings of the NAJC and the difficulties it faced in trying to speak for Japanese Canadians on what was rapidly becoming an irresistible issue.

As I prepared an introductory statement, I became aware of some major changes that had taken place in the NAJC, changes that were the direct outcome of the postwar dispersal. The NJCCA had formed in 1947 in a moment of crisis. The Bird Commission was about to begin its work, and Japanese Canadians had to have a community mechanism to prepare themselves. But even more pressing, in their relocated — or, more accurately, dislocated — condition all over Canada, they desperately needed their own organization to defend themselves against further abuse and to continue to press for the franchise. The first constitution was, given the situation, oriented toward survival as a group and based on a provincial chapter system, with the national office in Toronto, the city that had attracted the largest proportion of nisei in the 1940s.

Once the Bird Commission had slammed the doors on just compensation, most Japanese Canadians resigned themselves to the new places of resettlement. Their future looked more appealing than their immediate past, shaped as it was by rapid economic growth and employment opportunities in the Canada of the 1950s. It was the beginning of a period of quiet assimilation, of becoming socially mobile through education and entry into the professions — in short, of becoming "model citizens." As the children of internment, myself included, learned to see through the (largely white) eyes of their educators and participated in the dominant social and cultural movements of their times, relocated Japanese Canadians forged new — and often fiercely loyal — ties to local groups and networks.

The implications of this change became visible to me while I was working on revising the old constitution. In the report I presented, I wrote:

> During the 1960s and early 1970s, even more so immediately preceding and following our 1977 centennial, a new energy entered our community. The various local communities scattered across Canada began to awaken to some desire to understand their past and to come to grips with the government policies that sanctioned their dispossession, internment, and dispersal from the west coast. It was then that more and more members of our community began to think about the question of redress.
>
> Here we are now, in 1984, gathered together at a national conference hopefully to work out a redress program. The fact that this issue has infused our community with a new life indicates that a major change has occurred since the early 1950s. Over the past three decades, the Japanese Canadians scattered across Canada have developed into local centres with their own identities, which in part reflect regional allegiances, but more so, because of an autonomy arising from a shared history in a given place, such as Winnipeg, Hamilton, or Lethbridge. It is this change that was evident in the

decision of the delegates of the 1980 national conference to adopt an organizational structure based on centres, rather than on a chapter system. This kind of organization acknowledges that authority must come from the centres themselves and the centres, in forming an association, must determine the policies and directions of the national organization. This was why the NJCCA was renamed the National Association of Japanese Canadians at the 1980 conference.

The establishment of the national council in our draft, which is one of the major changes in the revised constitution, is a clarification and a strengthening of the centres as the main legislative body of the NAJC. In the 1953 and 1961 constitutions, this legislative power was vested in the National Conference, attended by "delegates" from centres. Although this was workable then, perhaps necessary, given the communication difficulties, now the NAJC can acknowledge the autonomy of centres in the formation of the NAJC council, which is made up of representatives who are elected or appointed by the centres. If the older format of provincial chapters was necessary to help the community adjust to its dispersal, this new format is necessary to help re-unite in order to ensure a democratic format for redress, the big reason why we're here in Winnipeg.

Although discussion on the constitution was deferred, with further revisions to be handled by a newly formed Constitution Committee, the delegates from 13 NAJC centres first moved to constitute themselves as the NAJC council. By doing so, they established the structure for what would become a much more inclusive national organization that would voice the interests of Japanese Canadians in the redress movement. Here too they would adopt the pyramidal system of apportioning votes, which was based on the number of Japanese Canadians estimated to reside in each NAJC centre.[2]

---

2   The pyramidal system was adopted because of the large discrepancies in the Japanese Canadian population of various centres. The principle was that larger centres such as Vancouver and Toronto should have proportionately more votes, but not enough to be able to control the council together. The following system was worked out at the Winnipeg conference and subsequently adopted as policy: 1 vote for centres with populations under 1,000; 2 votes for centres with populations between 1,000 and 10,000; 4 votes for centres between 10,000 and 15,000; and 5 votes for centres over 15,000. There is a certain arbitrariness in the system. The large spread in the population for 2 votes was justified because the largest centres outside of Toronto and Vancouver consisted of

This was the new organizational structure that President Art Miki inherited in Winnipeg and that he hoped would encourage more Japanese Canadians to participate in the redress issue. In contrast to Imai, who urged a quick settlement to take advantage of the *Equality Now!* report, Miki wanted a more integrated relationship between the NAJC council and the communities it represented in constructing a redress position. The goal was reflected in the agenda of Miki's first NAJC meeting as president.

MAKING A REDRESS POSITION: APRIL IN VANCOUVER

WHEN THE NAJC council assembled in Vancouver on April 7, 1984, anticipation of conflict filled the air. Insiders now recognized that a battle had been brewing within the NAJC between President Art Miki and George Imai and his supporters. Miki resisted the push for "acknowledgement first" and took relentless heat from Imai, Jack Oki and Toronto JCCA President Ritsuko Inouye for doing so. He was determined — for better or worse — to address Collenette's request for a monetary figure. And in a politically astute move, he sought to make the NAJC more democratic by opening space for individuals and groups to make presentations. Observers could also attend. The Plaza 500 Hotel, at the corner of 12th Avenue and Cambie Street, was abuzz with Japanese Canadians who got their first view of the drama created by the redress issue in the NAJC.

The National Redress Committee's controversial letter to Prime Minister Trudeau was on the agenda for council discussion. According to Imai, Miki's inaction was in direct defiance of the NRC, the group he claimed was in charge of redress. According to Miki, as the president of the NAJC — of which the NRC was a subcommittee — he was the voice of his council. He reasoned that this line of authority has been confirmed in a motion at the January meeting requiring the NRC to be accountable to the council through the president and his National Executive Committee.

---

no more than 2,500 people, whereas Vancouver and Toronto clearly had over 10,000. Vancouver and Toronto had very similar population numbers, at least according to the most recent census, but Toronto was given an additional vote because its delegates insisted that the census was inaccurate. The NAJC council, including the Vancouver delegates, accepted this unsubstantiated claim, mainly as a conciliatory gesture to Toronto.

Miki was himself not opposed to taking advantage of the political climate. He could understand the NRC's position that the government of Pierre Elliott Trudeau, according to comments by Multiculturalism Minister David Collenette, appeared willing to offer something to recognize the injustices of the 1940s. He was clearly considering this receptivity when, in his president's report, he highlighted his recent meeting with government officials in Ottawa on February 16-18, 1984. He had gone there to make his first public appearance as the new NAJC president to attend a Conference of Presidents of National Ethno-Cultural Organizations. The occasion also allowed him to meet with Collenette, who "felt that before he could take any proposal [on redress] to cabinet that made reference to compensation, he would like to see a specific figure." The request, Miki reported to his council, led him to conclude: "It appeared that this process of establishing a compensation figure would enhance our position for negotiations."

Imai's strongest and most influential ally, Jack Oki — who was in an awkward situation as both vice-president of the NAJC and chair of the Toronto JCCA Redress Committee — did not attend the meeting, but he sent a letter critical of Miki. To add to the already mounting tension, two grievances from newly formed groups outside the NAJC were also filed, one from Toronto, hand-delivered in the form of a petition by Wes Fujiwara; the other from Charles Kadota of the Greater Vancouver Redress Coalition, contending that the Vancouver Japanese Canadian Citizens' Association, the coalition's vehicle for political access to the NAJC, was actively obstructing the development of a redress campaign.

As the NAJC met in Vancouver, then, the problems of representation were far from resolved. The power struggles between the status quo and emergent voices demanding the fuller participation of Japanese Canadians in redress debates had suddenly become much more apparent. Added to this was the uncertainty of the government's response to the *Equality Now!* report. Was it possible, against all odds, that redress in the form of compensation would be offered?

Few Japanese Canadians, especially in the NAJC, were seeking or expecting full compensation on an individual-by-individual basis. Although this form of redress might ultimately be the most just method in a liberal democracy that favoured property rights, the dollar amounts would run into the billions. Even more difficult, the process of determining precise material and non-material damages — for example, damages for emotional and psychological damage and loss of community — would undoubtedly become bogged down in far too many complexities. Time was closing in on the aging issei and nisei, who would not be able to wait for years and years. What, then, about the $50 million figure proposed by the NRC? Given an estimated 16,000 survivors, this amount, although a significant sum at first glance, was considered far too small to include individual compensation in the range recommended for Japanese Americans by the U.S. commission.

As various figures were debated, the delegates from Ottawa, Tony Nabata and Elmer Hara, upped the ante significantly by assuring their fellow council members that the government was used to large amounts — think, for instance, of the vast sums involved in First Nations land claims agreements. Besides, many were opposed to the NRC's decision not to pursue individual compensation. Here the JCCP Redress Committee presentation spoke for a redress position that combined individual and community compensation, an approach eventually adopted by the NAJC.

THE JCCP REDRESS COMMITTEE PRESENTATION

FOR SEVERAL MONTHS before the Vancouver meeting, a handful of Japnaese Canadian Centennial Project (JCCP) Redress Committee members had already been drafting a redress proposal. In line with the group's longtime interest in the work of the U.S. commission, which favoured individual compensation, we (I was a member of the group) came up with a settlement proposal that included both forms of compensation, individual and community. The decision to seek both forms, rather than one or the other — a choice often presented in the NRC's language — had been gaining popularity among Japanese Canadians in the Vancouver area, and we were voicing what many people already wanted. Our aversion to group compensation alone stemmed from our disagreement with the rationale given for a group settlement in the NRC's paper, "Philosophical Underpinnings of a Reparations Settlement," distributed at the Winnipeg conference: "The actions of the government were not directed at individuals, although individuals suffered, but directed at a group (Japanese Canadians). The settlement is therefore directed at that level." For us, raised as we were in the language of the civil rights movement of the 1960s, redress had to do with the issue of rights. So in our presentation we asked: "Wasn't the unjust treatment of Japanese Canadians the result of the government treating individuals as a group?" And we offered the following conclusion:

> [T]he NRC argument for group compensation ignores the very reason for redress: that the uprooting, dispossession, and dispersal of Japanese Canadians was a gross violation of their individual civil liberties. If we were to forget this fact, any form of compensation would be meaningless ... This is also why we propose that a compensation figure should be calculated in proportion to the number of individuals affected between the period of February 1942 to March 1949. It was during this period that the civil liberties of Japanese Canadians were unjustly suspended through the powers of the War Measures Act.

On the other hand, we were aware that Japanese Canadians had also suffered as a community whose social, economic, and cultural infrastructures had been destroyed in the government's postwar dispersal policy, so much so that Japanese Canadians had never been able to reconstitute themselves as a geographical collective. For this reason, the settlement needed to have some form of community compensation.

We recommended a compensation figure of $725 million: $25,000 for each of the estimated 25,000 Japanese Canadians affected, and $100 million to rebuild the community. And we submitted two resolutions:

1) that the NAJC Council adopt the principle that a compensation figure for redress be based upon a combination of individual and group compensation.
2) that the NAJC Council establish a Redress Brief Committee to draft a compensation package for negotiations with the government.

Although the $500 million figure that was endorsed by the NAJC at the meeting was lower than the amount in our recommendation, we supported the decision, especially because it looked far beyond the NRC in incorporating the principle that individual rights had been violated. For the NAJC, how the $500 million would be used — what forms of compensation would be agreed upon — would be determined by future negotiations and would depend on an assessment of the material effects of internment. First, however, and this was in agreement with the JCCP resolution, a redress brief had to be written to make the "case for redress." George Imai was invited to establish a committee under the NRC to draft the brief. When he declined, a committee had to be formed. Randy Enomoto, a JCCP Redress Committee member, volunteered our group to take the lead, and we were joined by some Sodan-kai members who had already researched Japanese Canadian history. NAJC representative from Ottawa, Tony Nabata, was appointed chair of the Brief Committee.

SHAPING THE LANGUAGE OF THE NAJC BRIEF

THE DECISION TO submit a redress brief to the federal government would have far-reaching consequences for what was, in April, a fragile and only loosely connected NAJC council. Most of its members had had no experience in social and political movements, and they were ill equipped to map out effective strategies for what was rapidly turning into a controversial public issue, even in the mainstream media. It was no longer unusual to hear about the notion of "redress" in local and national news reports.

In NAJC centres all over Canada, Japanese Canadians were being approached for interviews and profiles. Reporters regularly focused on the uprooting as a stripping of rights and on the after-effects of being branded "enemy alien." As this public attention grew, the NAJC sought to overcome decades of inactivity to address the sudden revival of community spirit coalescing around "redress." The difficulty of working out — and through — a democratic process to forge a language malleable and inclusive enough to mould disparate views into a cohesive social movement had no precedent in the community's history. The closest equivalent was the mobilization required to oppose deportation and to prepare for the Bird Commission in the late 1940s. But these were more reactions to government policies, and they arose in the turbulence of uprooting and dispersal. Redress was not a reaction, but an action that depended on the initiative of Japanese Canadians to remake themselves into a collective entity. The weight was on them to create a voice strong and compelling enough to negotiate a meaningful settlement with the government.

The challenge to the NAJC was enormous at the time. Assuming responsibility for a national issue went against the grain of their postwar history. After the Bird Commission, Japanese Canadians had committed themselves to assimilation, a process that rendered them invisible and silent as a collective. They shied away from political controversy and chose to assume the role of a model minority. This behaviour showed that they paid heed to the well-known Japanese injunction, "The nail that sticks out gets hammered down." While their local organizations lost their earlier activist edge, they became informal social clubs, where friends and relatives could meet outside the boundaries of their assimilated lives in white neighbourhoods all over Canada. In the face of this history, all the new "redress talk" generated anxiety and threatened to make them visible all over again. There was always the potential for "backlash," invoked by those who feared that redress would stir feelings of hostility among white Canadians. So much, then, would depend on the ability of the NAJC to make the "case for redress" acceptable not only to the government and the Canadian public generally, but to its own constituency, Japanese Canadians.

In April 1984, when the $500 million figure was endorsed, the NAJC national campaign had not yet begun in earnest. A legitimate discourse for redress had to be constructed, and even determining the substance of the settlement still required considerable discussion. And accompanying the danger of reacting in compromising ways to government overtures was the skepticism and mistrust of government — a legacy of past betrayals. Would this current government be any different from the government of the 1940s? This lack of trust — perhaps a saving grace — also meant that the NAJC had to work on shaping a language of redress that spoke from the perspective of the interned Japanese Canadians. How to do so was not an easy task. Without the economic resources to hire consultants, researchers and writers, the work had to be done from scratch, by volunteers who had little experience in designing a large-scale campaign. Strategies were devised not in the more controlled conditions of backroom designers and planners, but in the heat of unpredictable conflicts and tensions. Learning, by necessity, had to take place through action, not by reference to abstract rules and precedents, and this involved a constant trepidation, made more so by the deeply personal and emotional nature of the great wrong done.

In immediate terms, the internal squabbles that had erupted in the NAJC resulted from organizational weaknesses, but they had deeper roots in the memory of internment. On the one side, there was a desire to contain the anxiety of the past by putting the issue of redress to bed quickly and efficiently. On the other side, there was the daunting and unmapped space of redress as a means to work through the injustices of the past. Whichever way, though, how could Japanese Canadians themselves speak and not, as in the past, be spoken for?

Here the advice of the NAJC's legal adviser, Don Rosenbloom, was invaluable. A Vancouver lawyer with an extensive background in Native land claims, Rosenbloom had become familiar with Japanese Canadian community work through his partner, Michiko Sakata, a founding member of both Tonari-Gumi, a seniors' drop-in centre, and the Japanese Canadian Centennial Project (JCCP), the group that had produced *A Dream of Riches: Japanese Canadians, 1877-1977*. Moreover, Rosenbloom's law firm retained the former B.C. Supreme Court judge Thomas Berger, who had studied Japanese Canadian internment and had written eloquently about the injustices in his influential book *Fragile Freedoms*. Although the NAJC had decided from the outset to speak for itself and not through lawyers and civil libertarians (as in the 1940s), Art Miki also knew that external feedback, reflection and criticism would strengthen and inform the council's deliberations. He invited Rosenbloom to engage in the NAJC's thinking process in order to serve as a sounding board. Rosenbloom offered his thoughts in a confidential letter to the NAJC council, which accompanied his presentation at a meeting to Winnipeg on June 2, 1984.

Coming from outside the community, yet conscious of the volatility of the issue of redress for Japanese Canadians, Rosenbloom brought a thoughtful critical framework to the all-important question of strategy. From his land claims work, he was knowledgeable about the broader social and political ramifications of establishing a redress "claim" to negotiate. As if to mirror the NAJC's uneasiness with an unsubstantiated $500 million figure (other than the U.S. precedent), he cautioned that any figure in the brief could undermine the integrity of the claim. The government — and the media — might jump on the figure itself and represent Japanese Canadians as more concerned with "money" than "justice." Rosenbloom's comments made the NAJC council members much more conscious of the social and political implications of raising money issues prematurely in a public brief. Furthermore, his encouragement to develop a strong redress campaign — reinforced by a strong paper trail — helped to focus the NAJC's language.

The first draft of the NAJC brief was presented at the Winnipeg meeting. Notably, the historical "case for redress" had drawn on the research undertaken by Ann Sunahara in the 1970s. Sunahara, the first independent researcher to examine government papers on the internment of Japanese Canadians, had brought to light incriminating cabinet documents that had been previously inaccessible to the public.[3] In her 1981 book *The Politics of Racism*, Sunahara had used government documents to expose the political opportunism and racism that underlay the policies on uprooting, dispossession, dispersal and "repatriation."

Yet the NAJC's Redress Brief Committee had to reach beyond Sunahara's research findings. To have an impact on both politicians and the media, the brief must present the "voice" of living Japanese Canadians. In other words, it had to present a cogent argument for redress and it had to do so in a language, tone and mode of presentation that would both educate readers and draw them into the drama of redress as a current issue. The language of the brief became a major concern at the June meeting. As media coverage swirled around them because of Collenette's rejection of compensation, NAJC council members worked their way, paragraph by paragraph — sometimes word by word — through the draft copy. At times, the process of making collective revisions on the text must have seemed to be merely an exercise in copy-editing, but decisions made on terminology, vocabulary and intellectual and emotional tone — often with the sharing of personal insights, family stories, and local histories — had a profound effect on the

---

3   In a personal response to my query about the question of accessibility, Sunahara explained: "When I did my research in the 1970s there was no legal right of access to any information in the hands of the government. The Access to Information Act and the Privacy Act did not come into force until 1983. Instead, there was a 'gentlemen's convention' that documents would be made available after 30 years. But even then access was entirely at the discretion of the government of the day, who could impose restrictions on it." She later acknowledged Tom Shoyama, then deputy minister of finance, for enabling her to gain access to the material. At a large redress gathering in Vancouver in August 1984, in talking about the evidence uncovered, she said her "book was made entirely possible because of [Shoyama's] efforts, which got me into the necessary archives ... and I would like at this point to thank him publicly."

writers of the brief. Revisions made and discussed around the council table, while often bringing out conflicting interpretations of the meaning of redress, inculcated a thinking process that was crucial in forging a collective vision, without which a social movement cannot flourish.

For the NAJC, it was also important that the brief argue the "case for redress" using solid documentary evidence from the government's files. The overall effect had to be compelling enough for readers to acknowledge that their government had betrayed democratic principles when Japanese Canadians were stripped of their citizenship rights, uprooted and dispossessed. Yet in light of the historical representation of Japanese Canadians as a racialized minority, the writers had to exercise considerable care to avoid rhetorical pleas — as tempting as such language can be — that would make Japanese Canadians appear to be no more than "victims" seeking compensation from the government. Such a narrative would have set up a "we/they" dichotomy that could result in a dangerous polarization between "mainstream Canadians" (as represented by the government) and "Japanese Canadians" (the beleaguered minority). So the writers identified Japanese Canadians as "citizens"; that is, individuals who were necessarily connected to all other "citizens" belonging to the Canadian nation. These were the "citizens" who were wronged when the democratic system was "betrayed." For this reason, the title of the brief, *Democracy Betrayed: The Case for Redress*, was of critical importance in shaping the language of redress. The word "betrayed" carried highly emotional connotations, and when tied to "democracy," it had the advantage of diverting blame from "individuals" and drawing attention to the horrific consequences of a breakdown in the accountability of the government.

Redress, from this position, becomes a public responsibility that looks forward to a healing of the democratic system — and, by implication, of the nation. By situating violated "citizens" inside the nation, the brief portrayed Japanese Canadians not as "victims" but, more significantly, as the agents of change. Redress is not primarily about reparations for material losses, but a matter of historical truth — the uprooting "had no basis in military necessity" — and justice for the "abrogation of the rights and freedoms of Japanese Canadians." As citizens concerned about the fragility of human rights in a democracy, and as citizens whose "legalized repression under the

War Measures Act" remained an unresolved event in Canadian history, Japanese Canadians "urged" the Government of Canada to "take such steps as are necessary to ensure that Canadians are never again subjected to such injustices" by placing the Canadian Charter of Rights and Freedoms beyond the reach of the War Measures Act.

Simultaneously, to reinforce this approach to redress, a group in Toronto — including some who were aligned with the Sodan-kai — produced a media package to accompany the brief. In 1984 the public knew little of the mass uprooting, but they knew still less of the subjective impact of the injustices. *Democracy Betrayed* was directed primarily at the government. The media package, *The Case for Redress: Information*, offered educational materials to assist reporters and educators to create various approaches to the issue of redress. Of course, the package could also be used in Japanese Canadian communities as a focal point for redress and to stimulate conversation. This compact publication contained a wealth of strategically written and chosen materials. Along with a question-and-answer overview of redress, there were personal biographies, an interview with Joy Kogawa, photos and recent newspaper articles, and a bibliography for further reading on the issues. At the end was a list of Japanese Canadians who could be contacted all over Canada.

Democracy Betrayed was submitted to the federal government in Ottawa on November 21, 1984. From that point on, armed on the one side with an official brief and on the other with a press kit to educate the Canadian public through the media, the NAJC was able to turn outward. In a short but intense period in 1984 — a time of crisis for the NAJC, both with its own National Redress Committee and with the Liberal government, through David Collenette — the association had developed a language of redress to "go public" with its cause.

Yet the cause, though strong in voice and intention, still lacked substance — the kind of public data that would demonstrate beyond doubt that Japanese Canadians had suffered enormous losses because of the internment. How could the NAJC convince Canadians of the legitimacy of the call for redress? Hadn't the Bird Commission already compensated Japanese Canadians for their losses?

THE PRICE WATERHOUSE STUDY

I REMEMBER BEING astounded to hear that some federal government bureaucrats wanted to have Japanese Canadians declassified as a bona fide "visible minority," the euphemism coined by government to designate those who continued to be racialized. It was the term highlighted in the *Equality Now!* report, where redress was recommended. Apparently, recent statistical evidence had shown that Japanese Canadians as a whole enjoyed higher than average incomes. This measure of their upward social mobility was in direct contrast to the lower incomes of other, non-white Canadians. Why, then, should Japanese Canadians be seen as a "visible minority"? And why should they receive redress? From the perspective of the NAJC, redress had nothing to do with need and everything to do with social justice for the abrogation of rights. Nevertheless, the association decided that a study of the social and economic consequences of Japanese Canadian internment would provide objective data to substantiate the severity of the personal and collective losses.

After submitting *Democracy Betrayed* and opening up communication with Jack Murta, the minister in charge of the Multiculturalism Directorate, the NAJC tried — unsuccessfully — to persuade the federal government to sponsor a study of losses based on documents in the National Archives of Canada (now the Library and Archives of Canada), including the meticulous records kept by the Custodian of Enemy Property. Although the NAJC could produce a brief, a comprehensive study of losses was another matter. It was certainly possible to solicit assistance from the pool of Japanese Canadians in various professions, such as law, accounting, sociology and economics, to undertake such a project. Such a project, though, would have a crucial shortcoming. Whatever the credibility of the results, there was a strong likelihood that any report produced by Japanese Canadians would be suspected of bias in their favour. No — if the government would not sponsor it, then the NAJC would have to retain an independent and well-established third party to do the work. Hiring an internationally recognized accounting firm with an impeccable reputation would be the best way to make the case. But the costs of having a study done by such a firm would be prohibitive for an economically deprived organization such as the NAJC, at least in 1984.

In one of many strangely prescient moments that marked the redress movement, the opportunity to retain the highly respected accounting firm of Price Waterhouse came about as a complete but welcome surprise. In the spring of 1985, as Jack Murta turned down the NAJC's request for the government to fund a losses study, Henry Wakabayashi, the vice-chair of the Vancouver JCCA Redress Committee, used his business connections to arrange a meeting between the NAJC and Phil Barter, a senior partner of the firm in Vancouver. The three of us who formed the executive of the JCCA Redress Committee — vice-chair Wakabayashi, secretary Cassandra Kobayashi and myself as chair — attended as representatives of the NAJC.

We began, as planned, by rehearsing our call for redress in *Democracy Betrayed*, our frustration that the federal government had rejected funding for a losses study, and the need for such a study to document the impact of the mass uprooting. Then Barter stopped us short with his memories of close Japanese Canadian friends being shipped away from the coast. He recalled his own awareness of the injustices as he saw off these friends at the train station. We did not have to convince him that the issue of redress had urgency for all Canadians; he said, in a matter-of-fact tone, that he would ask Price Waterhouse to do the study for free. We were all dumbfounded at this generous offer, but we also knew that the lack of a fee could be construed as bias later on. The NAJC should pay a fee, one that a fundraising campaign could cover. We agreed to the figure of $25,000 with a few thousand more for expenses, on the understanding that Price Waterhouse would receive more in the event of an adequate negotiated settlement with the government.

The NAJC, along with many Japanese Canadians, waited with great anticipation for the release of the Price Waterhouse report. The fundraising campaign, which included contributions from city councils in Toronto, Lethbridge and Vancouver, generated a great deal of public attention for what was considered groundbreaking research on the impact of the internment. The Price Waterhouse researchers were able to access crucial government documents from the public archives, including the Custodian of Enemy Property's files, to determine the extent of the material losses resulting from the confiscation and liquidation of properties and businesses. Moreover, while doing so, they would address the limitations of the Bird

Commission, a point that had crucial importance for those who looked upon the commission's results as a further injustice, lacking any semblance of redress. Their study would also examine other issues, such as loss of income and disruption of education.

The Price Waterhouse researchers took one year to complete their study. They released it on May 8, 1986, under the title *Economic Losses of Japanese Canadians After 1941*. In its pages, Japanese Canadians and the Canadian public were told:

> We conclude that the Japanese Canadian community suffered a total economic loss after 1941, of not less than $443 million. This figure is expressed in 1986 dollars.
>
> The total loss is made up of the following elements —
> • Japanese Canadians suffered income loss of $333 million in 1986 dollars as a result of being unable to earn their normal income levels between 1942 and 1949.
> • The community suffered property losses of $110 million in 1986 dollars, principally because the value of property rose quickly between 1942 (when the Canadian Government seized all property belonging to Japanese Canadians) and 1949 (when some of the Japanese Canadians were able to re-enter the property market).

There was further evidence that the substantial losses had been ignored by the government of the 1940s in Price Waterhouse's revelation that the total loss was 40 times the amount paid out by the Bird Commission ($1,200,000, as against $48,167,000 in 1948 dollars). Even where the results were disappointing, Japanese Canadians could take some solace. Losses from the disruption of education were excluded because of the difficulty of accurate calculation, but the report went further and acknowledged that Japanese Canadians themselves skewed the research because they assumed responsibility for the education that had been denied them. The report concluded that they "clearly had their education interrupted," but "it appears they worked hard and succeeded in mitigating any loss they might have suffered in this regard." It shied away from assessing non-economic losses, although it acknowledged that "Canadian courts have awarded damages for non-pecuniary losses" such as "false imprisonment even for a matter of hours."

Even a modest figure of $15,000 per person would have added $325 million to the total.[4] One further area of loss was deemed to be outside the limits of the report: the economic impact of the dispersal process itself, which effectively destroyed the west coast communities of Japanese Canadians. As the authors of the report concede:

> We have not been able to conclude on the value of economic concentration. To do so would require a complex model which would attempt to predict the extent and nature of concentration, and its effects.
>
> We regard this issue as a contingency which, if measurable, would increase the amount of the loss suffered by the community.

Although it was limited in being unable to deal with intangibles such as the loss of community and the violation of rights, the Price Waterhouse report confirmed the NAJC's claim that the social and economic effects of internment were far greater than had so far been recognized by the government. The figures presented in the report dwarfed the token amounts ($5-6 million) that had been offered by politicians. But perhaps most important, the objective results produced by a highly reputable and conservative accounting firm instilled confidence among Japanese Canadians that the quest for redress was just — even a necessary resolution to the injustices of the 1940s.

---

4   The question of compensation for wrongful detention was given urgency in the early 1980s by the publicity surrounding the case of Donald Marshall Jr., who was wrongfully convicted of murder in 1971 and spent 11 years in jail before finally being acquitted in 1983. He received only $270,000 in compensation for being deprived of his freedom for more than a decade in the prime of his life. His case was often the subject of conversation at NAJC meetings.

CHAPTER 10

CONSTRUCTING A REDRESS IDENTITY

History, Memory and Community Formation

Trauma is precisely the open gash in the past that resists being healed or harmonized in the present. It is the prophecy of memories and truths yet to be symbolically, socially, or politically achieved.

— Kyo Maclear

FROM THE GROUND UP: REPRESENTATION AND IDENTITY MAKING

IN THE AFTERMATH of the Prince Hotel crisis in September 1983, questions of authority came to the fore. Who was in charge of the national redress movement: The National Association of Japanese Canadians president? The chair of the National Redress Committee? The NAJC council? What about groups outside the NAJC, such as the Japanese Canadian Centennial Project (JCCP) Redress Committee in Vancouver and the Sodan-kai in Toronto? What authority, if any, did they have to speak for Japanese Canadians?

While these conflicts erupted in the small circles of the NAJC, the vast majority of Japanese Canadians hadn't had the opportunity to think seriously about "redress." The word remained an abstract concept, distant from their everyday lives. Outside the narrow readership of the two Japanese Canadian community newspapers, the *New Canadian* and the *Canada Times*, in which accusations and declarations were hurled about, most were only vaguely aware of the squabbles, for the most part through secondhand accounts in mainstream newspapers.

By the fall of 1984, even while *Democracy Betrayed* was prepared for publication, the concept of redress had not yet surfaced in the consciousness of individual Japanese Canadians. They had long ago severed their connections to a national collective, signified by the National Japanese Canadian Citizens' Association (and its more recent incarnation, the NAJC). The national organization held little relevance for them in terms of identity formation. To the contrary, they often distanced themselves from such an identification, which perhaps only reminded them of their status as the "enemy alien" during the 1940s. As a consequence, and more by default, the NAJC became the enclave of small groups across Canada who identified with its national scope but who were not in touch with ordinary Japanese Canadians scattered all over the country.

The lack of widespread participation meant that the leaders of the NAJC never made the effort to reach a consensus on redress through a grassroots campaign. Had they done so, they would have encountered an explosive undercurrent of unresolved anxieties in the very Japanese Canadians who appeared so absent in their circles. But as redress was invoked as a justice issue in the national media, memories of the mass uprooting stirred up emotions that had been held in check for many decades. It was as if the word itself conjured an awakening of consciousness that brought the past into the present. Soon, large numbers of Japanese Canadians who had been divorced from community associations began to gravitate toward the NAJC in a pattern that took on the contours of a "redress movement." Before such a national movement could gain national recognition, though, the discordant memories of the trauma of incarceration had to be mitigated in more personal ways through direct action.

THE VANCOUVER SCENE IN 1984

MY INITIATION INTO the redress movement from a local perspective came through a surge of interest in redress. It was at one of the community forums organized by the JCCP Redress Committee — this one in Steveston, B.C., the only area in Canada with a sizable concentration of Japanese Canadians — that several nisei, including the well-respected businessman Charles Kadota, openly pledged support for a redress campaign. Getting a movement going, however, was not easy in a community that had kept silent about the wartime history and that used its organizations for maintaining small social clubs and networks. Most of Kadota's generation had long ago ceased concerning themselves with all forms of collective action of a political nature. Their own community association in the NAJC, the Vancouver Japanese Canadian Citizens' Association (JCCA), a parallel association to the Toronto JCCA, resisted the promotion of redress, even to the point of not holding public meetings to air the issue. In a move that resembled the scene in Toronto, but with quite different consequences, a small group of redress advocates, assisted by the JCCP Redress Committee, formed a counter-group, the Vancouver Redress Coalition, to posit an alternative to the Vancouver JCCA.

This instance of social activism — repeated in other communities of Japanese Canadians across Canada — was unexpected by many in the NAJC. Yet here was a vivid reminder that the trauma of the internment years had not been put to rest. In an unplanned but complementary action to those who signed the petition that was handed to Wes Fujiwara in Toronto, the Vancouver Redress Coalition submitted a grievance against the Vancouver JCCA at the NAJC council meeting in Vancouver in April 1984. In this grievance, the coalition accused the Vancouver JCCA of actively preventing a consensus from being formed on the issue of redress, the most pressing issue to face its community since the mass uprooting.

Now, two decades later, the edges have worn off this moment of crisis that marked the Vancouver scene. But then, emotions ran at a fever pitch, and networks of allegiances rapidly formed as the coalition pitted itself against the small group in charge of the Vancouver JCCA, an association that was perceived as the conduit to the NAJC. From the point of view of those who wanted a significant redress settlement, the passivity of the Vancouver JCCA reflected their continued victimization. In other words, their reaction to redress was interpreted as evidence of their fear of backlash and racialized visibility. One incident stands out as a prime example of the politics of representation that raged at the time.

In a strategy similar to that of the Toronto JCCA in the fall of 1983, the Vancouver JCCA sought to contain the explosiveness of redress by establishing its own Redress Committee. The move had been prompted by increasing pressure on the association, especially after the Winnipeg meeting in January 1984 — where the historic resolution to seek redress was passed by the NAJC — to provide leadership for the large population of Japanese Canadians in the Greater Vancouver area. In a form letter, dated March 20, 1984, Ken Matsune, president of the JCCA, invited some 50 individuals to a meeting set for April 1, ironically the 35th anniversary of the date in 1949 when Japanese Canadians were finally allowed to return to the west coast. To a certain extent, the initiative was a concession to those who claimed that the Vancouver JCCA was not reaching out to a broader community, but the concession was limited. Of the group selected, among them a handful from the Vancouver Redress Coalition, 34 invitees did not show up. And not long after the meeting began, a major dispute arose about the question of process and authority. The proposed Redress Committee, to be chaired by President Matsune, was to function only as an advisory body and would therefore not have the power to represent the interests of Vancouver Japanese Canadians in the NAJC.

In opposition, those of us from the Vancouver Redress Coalition recommended that the Redress Committee should be elected from the community at large and that its elected members should then choose a chair to represent Vancouver in the NAJC. A motion was even put forth for the group present to elect an interim chair for the Redress Committee, but when this generated considerable emotional turmoil, it was withdrawn. As the discussion deteriorated, the JCCA members became even more fixed in their position. In this impasse, the Redress Coalition members walked out in protest. Charles Kadota, who then co-chaired the coalition with Tamio Wakayama, was among that group.

From this point on, the Redress Coalition moved away from attempts to work with the Vancouver JCCA and, instead, chose to prepare a slate of candidates to seek election to the board. As board members they could directly take on the responsibility of mounting a redress campaign in

Vancouver. Plans to stand for election were already in place by April 7, when the formal grievance brief was brought to the NAJC council.

The Redress Coalition's brief argued that the Vancouver JCCA had failed to provide adequate representation on redress and called on the NAJC to recognize the coalition as the "representative organization for Vancouver on matters of redress." Much of the pent-up anger of the group was contained in its criticism of the Vancouver JCCA. The brief recalled a bitter JCCA meeting on December 1, 1983. Many Japanese Canadians, eager to learn about redress, had shown up only to be told that it was restricted to recognized community organizations and therefore closed to individuals. "A suggestion to accept nominations from the floor was dismissed out of hand," and this was the backdrop to the meeting on April 1, when once again the JCCA rejected a process of elections for the Redress Committee.

Soon after, the crisis of representation underwent an unusual transformation. By the time the NAJC met in June, in Winnipeg, many members of the Redress Coalition had been elected to the Vancouver JCCA board and Charles Kadota had become the new president. The Redress Coalition, formed in frustration because of the Vancouver JCCA's inactivity, had managed, in a few intense months, to change this major community organization from within. For this reason, the pressure to form another organization, as Japanese Canadians did in Toronto, was avoided and the Vancouver JCCA was able to participate in the national redress movement as an influential presence.

THE VANCOUVER JCCA REDRESS COMMITTEE

BEGINNING IN THE FALL of 1984, a new form of leadership emerged in Vancouver with Charles Kadota as president. As its first order of business, the JCCA board set up a subcommittee to design a procedure to form a Redress Committee with its members, some 25 to 30 in total, elected at large from the Greater Vancouver area. In the first election, which took place in September, a diverse group of individuals came to constitute the first JCCA Redress Committee. I chaired this energetic and tightly knit committee from its inception until the redress settlement in September 1988.

I was hardly prepared for the onslaught of the multilayered work that would be generated in the name of redress. Countering a resistance to political action on the one hand, and the inexperience of all of us on the committee on the other, we had to begin tentatively. We had no master plan other than our belief that seeking redress was an end worth pursuing. Imagining ourselves as participants in a nascent movement, we set up a raft of committees — for fundraising, of course, but also for education, publicity, community events and political activism. Our meeting place, the stark but historically resonant office of the Vancouver JCCA in the Japanese Language School on Alexander Street — the one building that escaped the Custodian of Enemy Property because it was needed for community meetings during the uprooting — was a constant reminder of our history in the city. Meetings inevitably trailed on late into the night as the work piled up, but what I remember most vividly are the stories of internment coming from committee members.

We were a motley mix of young and old, of all generations, including a handful of shin-ijusha (or new immigrants), and we came from highly localized areas of the Greater Vancouver area, some of which, such as the Fraser Valley and Steveston, had fairly large numbers of Japanese Canadians. The language of redress — of the violation of citizenship rights, the loss of community and the trauma of uprooting — became the medium through which a deeper awareness of our collective experience was developed. Despite the serious objective — redress for the wartime injustices — the evenings assumed a social air as Japanese food, brought regularly to meetings by committee members, circulated through the group. Two issei women, Haruko Kobayakawa and Masue Tagashira, both in their 80s, remained with the committee until the redress settlement, and their sushi and manju became legendary in the Vancouver redress movement. Along with the food, they provided an ethic of spirit and vision without which the movement could not have survived.

The former Vancouver JCCA board may have been lax in promoting the issue of redress, but it had already taken root among Vancouver Japanese Canadians, so much so that by the summer of 1984 the anticipation of a large community movement was in the air. To prepare for the JCCA Redress Committee elections, the new JCCA board took advantage of the Powell Street Festival, a large yearly event held on the first weekend in August, to sponsor a redress forum at the Japanese Language School. The program featured high-profile speakers: the broadcaster and geneticist David Suzuki, the author Joy Kogawa, the historian Ann Sunahara and the former editor of the *New Canadian* and acclaimed public administrator Tom Shoyama. On August 3, a sultry summer evening the night before the festival began, more than 500 people crowded into the Japanese Language School to experience the first major public airing of redress by the Vancouver JCCA. The response was electric, more so because at the time the NAJC was embroiled in a public battle with Multiculturalism Minister David Collenette on one side and an internal battle with George Imai's National Redress Committee on the other.

Many nisei came to hear Tom Shoyama. In his presentation, Shoyama admitted that he had "come in from the cold on this question of redress," and he explained the history of his positioning:

> Initially, I, like many of the older Nisei, I'm sure, and similarly perhaps many of the Issei, was rather doubtful or hesitant about trying to open up this issue and to pursue it with our country. Those of us who actually went through that experience recall all too vividly the deep pain, the deep disillusionment, the frustration, the sorrow and the anger that all of us experienced one way or the other. And in some ways I was perhaps in a very unique position to be aware of this, because I travelled across the country. I recall the experiences in Hastings Park, in the ghost towns, on the sugar beet farms, in the road camps in northern B.C. and in northern Ontario, the frustration and the difficulty of younger Nisei who went to the road camps and then to the farm labour camps in southern Ontario. We remember, despite all the assurances from the B.C. Security Commission who were trying to "relocate" us across the country, how many hostile environments, how many hostile critics we had to meet. And the psychic scars of all that, I am sure, have been very, very long lasting, very, very deep.

Shoyama reminded the audience of the deep-seated racism of the times, so common that the mass uprooting had for him, and by implication for other Japanese Canadians of his generation, the air of "inevitability." What, then, had led him to support redress now? He had begun, he said, to see another side of the treatment of Japanese Canadians while reading Ken Adachi's *The Enemy That Never Was*; but it was Ann Sunahara's research in the government's archives, published in *The Politics of Racism*, that turned him around, showing him the "racist motivation" behind the internment. For this reason,

Shoyama concluded, "there is no question that we have not only the right but we have a duty, an overwhelming obligation, to seek redress for the wrongs of 40 years ago." By consenting to the redress movement, Shoyama spoke for many nisei who had been sitting on the sidelines on the redress issue and who subsequently joined in with great passion and commitment.

The Vancouver JCCA Redress Committee, which came into existence the following month through a public election process, could draw on the momentum of the August forum, especially from its guest list. Nevertheless, a difficulty remained. How were we to raise the funds needed to mount a campaign? As luck would have it, President Kadota informed us that he had in his warehouse some 10,000 or more dishes that his company had produced for use by CP Air. Their size apparently had been miscalculated, so they would not sit properly on the airline trays. New dishes (this was before the arrival of plastic) had been produced, but these 10,000 remained in his warehouse. They could be sold, despite the small but visible airline logo on them. It was out of such a modest beginning that the JCCA Redress Committee started selling "redress dishes" for $1 each. In a short time, we raised more than $10,000, a portion of which was forwarded to the NAJC for its national campaign.

The enthusiasm with which many committee members and their friends sold and purchased the dishes turned out to be an instructive process. Was it possible to turn fundraising into a means of drawing Japanese Canadians toward redress? The committee then could raise money and simultaneously strengthen the movement. During one of many brain-storming sessions, the fundraising committee decided to explore the potential of selling copies of an art print by a Japanese Canadian artist. After visiting several Vancouver artists and reviewing their work, they selected *Watari Dori* ("Bird of Passage") by Linda Ohama. A sansei artist whose family had been interned in Emerson, Manitoba, and had resettled in Rainier in southern Alberta, Ohama had created a silkscreen print, part of a series, through which she envisioned the "beyond" of internment in the figure of a crane flying across and over the faintly visible black-and-white family photos invoking their wartime history. In an uncanny way, Ohama's work captured the vision of redress as a vehicle for healing the trauma of the past for all Japanese Canadians. *Watari Dori* was printed in an edition of some 5,000 copies that sold for $30 each, not only in Vancouver but in all

NAJC centres across Canada. Over $50,000 was raised in a process that took the language of redress into the homes of many people who had before been reluctant to express any affiliation.[1]

The ease with which Ohama's *Watari Dori* blended into the proliferating narratives of internment, and the growing popularity of her vision of passage from the past to the future, confirmed the power of redress to conjure and stir up memories of the 1940s. The prospect of a political resolution to the past injustices, in this sense, elicited an abundance of personal stories from people who relived the emotional pain and upheaval that Shoyama recalled. The variations on patterns of displacement, dispossession, confinement and resettlement were seemingly endless, but the core experience of helplessness in being branded "enemy alien" and treated accordingly had nestled deep and often ghost-like in the consciousness of the uprooted. Redress soon took on all the qualities of a collective awakening that was made possible through the medium of stories and the activism it generated. Nowhere was this more apparent than in a community meeting at the Japanese Language School on September 8, 1985. The personal testimonies of three Japanese Canadians exemplified the collective framework for redress.

THE PERSONAL SIDE

"THAT WINTER IT was cold in the shack, no insulation, only one thick paper. The temperature went down to –30 degrees. We had to stay up in turns at night to keep the fire going." So recalled George Miyagawa, an issei, as he softly narrated the hardships that he and his wife, with their three young children, endured during the mass uprooting. In 1942 the Miyagawas were like many peaceful and law-abiding citizens whose private lives had been shattered by the government's decision on February 26 to uproot all people

---

1   There are many stories of heroic efforts made by individuals in the sales of *Watari Dori*. The well-known redress activist Norman Oikawa went door to door to Japanese Canadians in southern Ontario, selling more than 150 copies. Norm Tsuyuki, a member of the Vancouver JCCA Redress Committee, did the same in the Fraser Valley. And Tony Tamayose, another member of the committee, went door to door in Steveston, selling more than 100 prints. Even today, the presence of *Watari Dori* in a Japanese Canadian household invokes memories of the redress movement.

"of the Japanese race." Forced to leave Vancouver on short notice, the Miyagawas felt they had no choice but to sell their grocery business on Davie Street for whatever cash they could get. They ended up in Vernon, B.C., living in substandard housing. George worked at menial jobs simply to survive and to educate his children. The Vernon School Board charged them $6 a month per child — about 20-25 percent of the family income.

In sharing the memory of his desperation to find a house for his family, Miyagawa's words projected the fear and uncertainty — a foreboding — that had rapidly spread through his Vancouver community. A similar sense of that time was expressed by Tom Tagami, a nisei who was 22 years old at the time. Tagami was living on Vancouver Island on April 4 when he and some 400 other Japanese Canadians in the Cowichan District were rounded up like cattle, assembled at Chemainus and sent to Vancouver to be incarcerated in Hastings Park.

Tagami recalled that the atmosphere in the park was always stressful. The food was terrible. Men were segregated from women. The exits were guarded by judo experts working under the direction of Etsuji Morii, chair of the Japanese Liaison Committee, who had been appointed by the B.C. Security Commission. And informants, or "stool pigeons," as they were called, were constantly "snooping around" for those who did not comply with the government's directives. Tagami saw one of these informers "get beaten up." After four months there, Tagami was sent to Slocan, where he remained during the 1940s.

The third speaker, H. Hirota, also a nisei, was 32 years old in 1942 and was working as a fisherman and mechanic in Steveston, B.C. Initially, under threat of imprisonment, he refused to go to a road camp. The RCMP, he explained, would not assure him that his wife and family would be properly cared for. To keep his family together, he eventually went to a sugar beet farm in Alberta. After two years of back-breaking labour there, he had lost $3,000 of his savings just to survive. He had also been forced to sell his three boats at a loss, and while in Alberta, he learned that his house and a building large enough for his garage had been sold. Like many others, he protested the sale, but without success. Hirota noted that he had never trusted the government, even after the RCMP told him his property and belongings would be protected in his absence. Fearing an insecure future, yet having the foresight to realize that he probably would lose everything he left behind, he buried his tools. He later had a friend retrieve them so that he could work as a mechanic in eastern Canada.

The final speaker, Masue Tagashira, an issei and a member of the JCCA Redress Committee, spoke of the frustration and outrage of her late husband, whose extensive business and real estate holdings had been confiscated and liquidated against his protests. In 1942 he was a naturalized Canadian who had emigrated to Canada in 1907, when he was 22 years old. Over a period of three decades he had built his wholesale business, the Heatley Trading Company, into a lucrative operation. He had also acquired houses and properties that were major investments. The Tagashiras resettled outside the "protected area" in Revelstoke, and from there, for many years, her husband tried to prevent the sale of his assets. His protests fell on deaf government ears. Masue Tagashira recalled her late husband's long-held belief that the Canadian government should right the wrongs inflicted on Japanese Canadians. In concluding, she commented: "I appreciate the effort that everybody is putting forward in redress. Mr. Tagashira, while alive, worked toward that goal. Even today, he would have wanted the effort continued and a settlement reached."

The private accounts of Japanese Canadians affected by the government's wartime policies helped to bring home the real impetus behind the redress movement. The injustices experienced were not generalities that could be glossed over merely by the passage of time. They remained in memory, one minute incident after another. George Tsuchiya, speaking as a friend of the Tagashiras in Revelstoke, added that the "injustices that were done to all of us were the prime driving force in Mr. Tagashira's thinking ... and he could see then that unless these things were settled properly, they were going to affect all our lives for the rest of our lives — not just his life or our lives but the lives of the coming generations."

WORKING AS NATIONAL REDRESS COORDINATOR, SPRING 1985

THE DEEPLY CONFLICTED — and dislocated — responses to redress became much more concrete to me when, during the three-month period from February to April 1985, I worked as the national redress coordinator for the NAJC. The growing interest in redress stimulated resonant memories of the wartime uprooting, and often community discussions of its implications for Japanese Canadians would get bogged down in isolated personal stories. While these stories were undoubtedly one of the gifts of redress, there was also the need to construct a more collective language that would bring individual Japanese Canadians together into a movement — a redress movement.

Consequently, the first order of business as the NAJC's national redress co-ordinator was to develop initiatives that would foster a language of redress, or a collective terminology, to give coherence and direction to the redress campaign. This work began with the members of the NAJC council, the individuals who were the main point of contact for Japanese Canadian communities across the country. I was fortunate to have my friend Cassandra Kobayashi, a lawyer, as my assistant. We had worked together on the JCCP Redress Committee and shared similar assumptions about the role of language in constructing a framework to represent the issue of redress, especially in light of the large number of grassroots Japanese Canadians who, for whatever personal reasons, were reluctant to engage in the political process that was intensifying in local areas across Canada. It seemed that the various perspectives, along with an underlying uneasiness about remembering the injustices of the past, had the potential to cause unpredictable divisions unless some means of mediation were devised quickly. Aside from the more practical task of educating the Canadian public, through the media, about the case for redress, we concentrated on three projects that we thought would build the infrastructure to create a more collective language for redress:

- a weekly report distributed to NAJC council members with notes on activities in all areas, information on current media articles and almost "daily" news about the NAJC's dealings with the federal government
- a national newsletter, the NAJC *Newsletter*, published in both English and Japanese, to provide insights into the NAJC, the redress movement and relations with the federal government; such a publication would lessen the need for the NAJC to rely on community-based newspapers such as the *New Canadian* and the *Canada Times*
- a how-to kit for a "house meeting" program to encourage local groups to disseminate news about redress and to attract Japanese Canadians who were not yet connected to redress discussions

For me, the "house meeting" program proved to be the key to understanding the power of narrative to mediate the traumas of the past.

LEARNING TO SHARE STORIES: THE IMPACT OF HOUSE MEETINGS

THE CONCEPT OF "house meetings" arose out of the work Cassandra Kobayashi and I were doing for the Vancouver JCCA Redress Committee. In conversations with friends and relatives during the fall of 1984, committee members had been told that many Japanese Canadians were reluctant, even fearful, of attending public meetings. To counter this problem, we began to organize some meetings in the informal and safe confines of people's homes. These meetings took on the form of social events. With at least two committee members present, a small circle of friends and relatives gathered to listen to the latest redress news, but more importantly to share personal memories of internment, a process that led the participants to reflect on what redress meant to them so many decades later. The JCCA Redress Committee was surprised to find that these meetings had a strong cathartic effect on those present. In sharing memories, people were able to consider the common threads among them in the seemingly infinite variations. It was here that the connections between the personal and the social, the individual and the collective, could become the medium of another identity — what I would call a "redress identity" — produced through the language of redress in the NAJC.

The house-meeting kit that Kobayashi and I designed and assembled was modelled on the success of these small group meetings. It was distributed in the midst of the political stalemate and confrontations with the first Conservative minister of multiculturalism to handle the issue, Jack Murta.[2]

The NAJC submitted its brief, *Democracy Betrayed*, on November 21, 1984, and from then on, it found itself caught in a disheartening language battle with Murta. It erupted after Murta backed down (the NAJC said "reneged") on a negotiation process that had been announced in a jointly

---

2   The original house-meeting kit consisted of the following: a suggested agenda for the meeting, which could be modified to suit specific interests in the group; a chronology of key dates in Japanese Canadian history; a chronology of the redress movement to date; and a selection of current news reports.

issued press release following the December 15 meeting with his representatives in Winnipeg. During January and February 1985, the battle entered the media when Murta threatened publicly to proceed unilaterally with an acknowledgement and his government's proposed "foundation" (the details of which were never spelled out) to "memorialize" the injustices suffered by Japanese Canadians. Negotiations with the NAJC were ruled out, which also meant that no direct compensation would be forthcoming. Murta moved aggressively against the NAJC in his public statements, playing up as well the rear-guard attacks on the NAJC by the Imai- and Oki-run Japanese Canadian National Redress Committee of Survivors. This so-called "Survivors' Group," which had formed on November 21, 1984, the same day the NAJC released *Democracy Betrayed*, had expressed a willingness to accept the government's offer and characterized the NAJC as an "extremist" group motivated only by monetary gain. Up against this double-edged opposition, the NAJC continued to insist on a negotiation process with the federal government, one that would incorporate a study of economic losses using the files of the Custodian of Enemy Property. When Murta refused to endorse such a study, his relationship with the NAJC was strained to the breaking point.

The house-meeting kit, conceived during the dispute between Murta and the NAJC, functioned as an educational device that also heightened the grassroots involvement of Japanese Canadians outside the still relatively small network of the already committed. The house meetings organized around the kit helped to form a bridge between the surfacing of personal memories and the political immediacy of the redress movement. The sharing of internment stories, the main focus of the session, was inextricably wound into the major preoccupation at the time, the political crisis of the NAJC with the federal government. The crisis, then, called for a collective response from those directly affected by the trauma of uprooting and of being branded "enemy alien."

MEDIATING TRAUMA IN THE REDRESS MOVEMENT

IN ONE HOUSE meeting, an adult daughter was dumbfounded to learn that her mother had given birth to her while confined in the filthy livestock buildings at Hastings Park. Why had she not told her before? Her mother said she wanted to protect her daughter from that painful knowledge; but in the advent of redress, she felt that she could disclose this element of her life. In an instant the relationship between mother and daughter changed, and the past as narrated in the framework of redress revealed the effects of trauma.

This revelation was but one in a torrent of memories called forth by the redress movement. The unprecedented disruption of family unity cut deep into the consciousness of those uprooted. Mothers recounted the details of the precise moment that their young sons had been shipped east to work in road camps. Many who were children at the time remembered — as if it were the day before — the shock of removal from school, their education terminated as they went from being "Canadian" to becoming a figure "of the Japanese race." There were memories of lonely and fearful train rides as women, children and the elderly — without fathers and husbands — were sent to bleak "ghost towns" in the B.C. interior. Overnight, places like Slocan City, Sandon, New Denver, Popoff and Lemon Creek became sites of incarceration, called "relocation centres" by the government. In fact, much of the pain had been covered over by euphemisms — especially the term "evacuation," used by the government to identify what was in actuality "internment" and "dispossession."

But as the stories of the lingering emotional legacy of internment became more public — as these did in 1984 — there was an opening for horrific instances of brutal losses: of a baby dying in the hands of a mother in the freezing confines of a chicken shack on a sugar beet farm in Alberta; of a fisherman beaten to death on his boat; of many elderly women and men suddenly losing their will to live in the camps; of deaths that could not be mourned because of restrictions on movement; of relentless uncertainties; of the inability to determine why this violence against Japanese Canadians was non-negotiable. An issei redress activist, Haruko Kobayakawa, already in her 80s when she worked on the JCCA Redress Committee in Vancouver, spoke for many when, during an interview, she recalled the reactions of her deceased husband: "He always used to say he was a native-born Canadian and had looked upon Canada as his homeland, but even at that he was treated like a man who, after having his legs and arms cut off, was thrown out into the freezing snow. He felt helpless. He often talked about that and what a terrible injustice it was."

The sustained condition of helplessness, braided with a sense of betrayal, produced a trauma that would continue decades after the period of incarceration. All of the stories were unmistakable signs that the violations leading to the social and psychological degradation of Japanese Canadians were still held in memory, as if sustained in an arrested state of mourning. As Maryka Omatsu writes of her father, who carried his worn registration card in his wallet until his death: "It's as if the clock stopped in January 1942." In the death of the prewar identities and communities, and in the death of trust in the rights of citizenship, the trauma of the past still awaited some meaningful closure.

But what is this notion of trauma for Japanese Canadians? How are we to conceive of its constitution and its subsequent effects during their dispersal, a dispersal in which the identity of "Japanese Canadian" would be marked by a reduction to "Japanese" as the face of the "enemy alien"? The paradox would be that this "Japanese Canadian" in the postwar years would enter the dominant (white) Canadian nation, eventually becoming a model minority — more "Canadian" than Canadian. These model citizens would simultaneously retain, in the folds of their memories, their historical connections to the experience of being marked.

Cathy Caruth and other theorists of trauma have pointed out that trauma is not simply a subject's psychological distortion of some overwhelming event, or an unconscious reaction to the event. Trauma needs to be recognized as the symptom of a failure to contain, comprehend or otherwise assimilate the event through existing avenues of knowledge and perception. It is this failure to mediate the event that constitutes the syndrome identified, in medical terms, as "post-traumatic stress disorder" (PTSD) and acknowledged by the American Psychiatric Association in 1980. Caruth explains this condition:

> While the precise definition of post-traumatic stress disorder is contested, most descriptions generally agree that there is a response, sometimes delayed, to an overwhelming event or events, which takes the form of repeated, intrusive hallucinations, dreams, thoughts or behaviors stemming from the event, along with numbing that may have begun during or after the experience, and possibly also increased arousal to (and avoidance of) stimuli recalling the event. This simple definition belies a very peculiar fact: the

pathology cannot be defined either by the event itself — which may or may not be catastrophic, and may not traumatize everyone equally — nor can it be defined in terms of a *distortion* of the event, achieving its haunting power as a result of distorting personal significances attached to it. The pathology consists, rather, solely in the *structure of its experience* or reception: the event is not assimilated or experienced fully at the time, but only belatedly, in its repeated *possession* of the one who experiences it. To be traumatized is precisely to be possessed by an image or event.

The sense of being "possessed" is a crucial element of trauma, and binds the person affected to the event through a delayed response. In this condition, the event remains immediately "real" over time because it is always in a state of incompletion — in process — and not resolved in a distant past. Traumatized persons are then attached to the "symptoms" of a history that haunts them precisely because it continues to possess them. They "carry an impossible history within them, or they become themselves the symptom of a history that they cannot entirely possess."

The "impossible history" carried by Japanese Canadians was not a history constructed on principles of objectivity and verisimilitude, but history as lived took on the contours of a catastrophic event. This crisis assumed the force of trauma in taking shape "in the collapse of its understanding." As we have seen, even a well-educated nisei such as Tom Shoyama, editor of the *New Canadian* during the mass uprooting, who was supposedly kept informed of the government's rationale for removal, was taken aback by the archival evidence uncovered by Ann Sunahara.

Although the authorities issued official rationalizations for the policies that stripped Japanese Canadians of their rights, those directly affected by the policies had no access to knowledge of the behind-the-scenes political decisions. In the thousands of censored letters now resting in the Library and Archives of Canada, none are more reflective of the cloud of unknowing and anxiety that surrounded groups of Japanese Canadians during the internment than the letters (many of them never reaching their destinations) that described the responses to the "repatriation" and "dispersal" orders of 1945. Japanese Canadians were asked to declare their so-called "intent" after the war on a form that was distributed by RCMP officers and was described as a survey only: either go to Japan — which meant the loss of citizenship for many — or settle "east of the Rockies." For those who had been confined in the B.C. camps for three years already, many of whom thought they had been "good citizens" by obeying the uprooting policy in the first place, these orders were not at all about "choice," the language of the government. These people were being drawn into a power politics that severed their ties to their pre-internment identities and that would thrust them into social spaces (in either Japan or Canada) where they became stateless figures. As one Japanese Canadian, in a letter dated April 15, 1945, wrote:

> Isn't it pitiful this situation of us? I mean Nisei! We're a people without a country. We're not wanted here, we're not suited to Japanese customs, gosh what a pickle! If we go east, we're called Japs and shunned — if we go to Japan, they'll consider us something like "hakujin" [white person] because we're born and educated out here in America.

Even the emotionally resilient nisei writer Muriel Kitagawa found herself struck by a psychological numbness associated with trauma, in a letter to her brother Wes Fujiwara: "Last ruling forbids anyone — even Nisei — to go anywhere in this wide Dominion without a permit from the Minister of Justice St. Laurent, through Austin C. Taylor of the B.C. Security Commission here. We go where they send us."

The phrase "even Nisei" shows that Kitagawa is upset by the announcement saying "Canadians" would not be exempt from mass removal, as the government had earlier promised. The loss of agency and the denial of her national identity set up a psychic disorientation in Kitagawa:

> Honest Wes, I don't know where all to start talking. Things happen so fast, so sudden; so much has happened — that I'm in a daze — (and thankful for it) and nothing affects me much just now except rather detachedly. I mean — everything — I must wake up — yet I know it's real — there's no sadness when friends of longstanding disappear overnight — either to Camp or somewhere in the Interior. No farewells — no promise at all of a future meeting or correspondence — or anything. We just disperse. Uncle Fred's going to Westbank — I hope — to work in a Nursery. Eddie's cousin went to Camp — . We're hit so many ways at one time that if I wasn't past feeling I

think I would cry. This curfew business is horrible. At sundown we scuttle into our holes like furtive creatures. We scan the papers to look for the time of next morning's sunrise when we may venture forth. The gov't has requisitioned the Livestock Bldg and the Women's Bldg at Hastings Park to house 2,000 Japs pending removal. Men (white) pictured blithely filling ticks with bales of straw (for mattresses to sleep on the floor I presume) and putting up makeshift partitions for toilets, wash basins, etc. etc. Here the lowly Japs will be bedded down as per livestock in stalls, perhaps open for display to a morbidly curious crowd of "whites," or maybe closed around under police guard, I don't know. The Nisei will be "compelled" (news report) to volunteer in the Labour Gangs. The worse the news from the Eastern Front, the more ghoulish becomes the public. We are the billy-goats and nanny-goats and kids — all the scapegoats to appease a damfoolish few who don't figure that our presence here is the best security for this Coast.

Kitagawa's letter reveals a tension between the intent to inform — that is, to give an accurate account of the latest "news" to her brother — and the awareness of a split in consciousness whereby she has become strange to herself. In a "daze" she finds it difficult to attend to events around her — yet she is "thankful" for this state. Her numbed detachment — a symptom of dissociation — makes everything seem unreal and real at the same time, or unreal in its stark reality. In this mental space, the "real" is seen as a fatalistic outcome in the disintegration of her personal, familial and community relations. The movement of Japanese Canadians to unknown places is envisioned as the removal of "lowly Japs" and "scapegoats" who are reduced to objects of the white gaze. "We just disperse," Kitagawa says, as the social violence that is destroying her life unfolds. In her eyes, Japanese Canadians (herself included) are turned into "furtive creatures." The image already prefigures her internalized identity as "enemy alien," accompanying, if not constituting, the traumatic state in which the white public comes to appear "ghoulish" in its determination to police their bodies. In the daze, Kitagawa can recognize fragments of the mass uprooting, but she does not know about the political machinations that have come to dominate her perceptions. The credibility of her subjectivity is thereby undermined by a "collapse of understanding." It is as if she were saying, "I can't believe what is happening to me/us," and her inability to believe her situation, from this point on, seems destined to create internal disturbances in her postwar memories of the uprooting.

Many Japanese Canadians did not have the language to account for the unspeakable monstrosities that manifested themselves internally as shame and guilt for being singled out, ostracized and labelled the "enemy alien" within the social body of their own country. They reverted to such common phrases as "blessing in disguise" (that is, the uprooting forced them to leave the limited sphere of their west coast communities and made it possible for them to assimilate) and "shikata ga nai" (translated as "it can't be helped" — the uprooting was an event that simply had to be endured as an aspect of wartime hysteria) to mediate a past that refused resolution. And, most tellingly, they continued to frame their history as "the evacuation," the euphemism that sublimated the violence inflicted on them. Such linguistic compromises both enacted and reinforced the government's own propaganda and formed the limits within which Japanese Canadians' memories would be constructed. It was these limits that would be exposed and transfigured by the language of redress.

MOBILIZING THE LANGUAGE OF REDRESS:
SEEKING AN ACKNOWLEDGEMENT

IN THE DECADES following the lifting of restrictions on April 1, 1949, Japanese Canadians had managed to carve out — quietly and modestly, for the most part — social spaces for themselves. They came to be respected because of their strong belief in the work ethic and education and because they embodied such positive social values as trustworthiness, loyalty and cooperativeness. Dispersed demographically throughout central and western Canada as a result of government policy, they had become much less visible as a group and were generally accepted as individuals wherever they settled. This also meant that, small in numbers as they were (less than 50,000 by the 1980s), Japanese Canadians were relatively well known because of their widespread distribution. Why, then, rock the boat now? Why dreg up the past when Japanese Canadians had assimilated so well?

The model-minority syndrome may have led to a feeling of acceptance by (white) Canada, but the cost for Japanese Canadians was the unresolved awareness that wartime policies had betrayed their trust in the very democratic principles they thought should have been upheld for them as Canadian citizens. Thus, although their hyphenated identity, as "Japanese Canadians" within the framework of a dominant multicultural ideology, provided some consolation in aligning them with other "ethnic" groups, the betrayal could not be resolved. That is why redress, especially in the form of a negotiated settlement, struck such a discordant note in them, one that had the power not only to disturb their complacency but to rechannel the traumatic memories of the past into a new formation, a "redress movement," which could allow for a collective narrative to be shaped.

So how did this process come about when Japanese Canadians had distanced themselves so much from the events of the 1940s? The boundaries of the model-minority syndrome are always tenuous — tenuous in that its formation depends on a group's acquiescence to dominant social spaces in which they have already been constructed as a minority or, put another way, where they have already been minoritized. For Japanese Canadians this construction occurred directly, in being racialized as the "enemy alien" in their own nation. They would have had to remake themselves through a denial, often conscious, of the very inequalities that sustained the illusion of equality in the social system. But the effects of traumatic memory do not have time limits; they produce a legacy that continues to call out, however silently, for acknowledgement — for that "telling" moment. Muriel Kitagawa voiced this conundrum long before, in the late 1940s, already pointing toward a future resolution:

> Time heals the details, but time cannot heal the fundamental wrong. My children will not remember the first violence of feeling, the intense bitterness I felt, but they will know that a house was lost through injustice. As long as restitution is not made, that knowledge will last throughout the generations to come ... that a house, a home, was lost through injustice.

Redress could not have been imposed as an abstract concept, or if it were — for instance, through a unilateral action by the government — it would have become yet another facet of the unspoken trauma, yet another cover-up. What was required for memory to be transformed was a new language, spoken in the enabling spheres of reception. The memory theorist Laurence Kirmayer, commenting on the process of remembering traumatic events, has argued that the "context of retelling is crucial to the nature of memory." Memory and what is remembered are never simple reflections of a past event that "really" happened, but are "highly selective and thoroughly transformed by interpretation and semantic encoding at the moment of experience." The objects and events that appear in memory are themselves produced by the act of remembering, and thus are created in the subjectivity of the rememberer. This is not to say that the events and objects are not "real" (that is, based on the material elements of experience), but that what is called to memory, in that calling, is always a narrative construct tied to the present. A memory is not, as Paul Antze and Michael Lambek, the editors of *Tense Past*, point out, a "pregiven object of our gaze" but more an "act of gazing." It is in this act that the particulars constituting what is remembered come to be produced. Memory functions as a process of consciousness through which the past is transformed, or translated, through images generated under present conditions of experience. As a dynamic process, it consists of three interacting components: the subject who is remembering, the past that is remembered and the present conditions in which the remembering occurs. The third component is often neglected, on the assumption that memory is primarily a neutral window on one's past, and not itself governed by a consciousness engaged in remembering.

The conditions of "memory acts" are unpredictable, but they are identified through the most critical point of enactment — what Daniel Schacter, in *Searching for Memory*, has described as a "retrieval cue." This cue is the sign or complex of signs that work together to instigate the process of remembering, which, in turn, leads to the struggle to have these signs make sense in the form of narratives. Cues then generate a field of memories that transform the past into images experienced in the moment of remembering. As Schacter writes:

> The stored fragments [of events and things] contribute to the conscious experience of remembering, but they are only part of it. Another important component is the retrieval cue itself. Although it is often assumed that a retrieval cue merely arouses or activates a memory that is slumbering in

the recesses of the brain, I have hinted at an alternative: the cue combines with the engram [a unit of memory] to yield a new, emergent entity — the recollective experience of the rememberer — that differs from either of its constituents.

Among its many effects, the term "redress" could be said to have functioned as a potent "retrieval cue" that produced a powerful influx of memory constructs for those who had undergone uprooting and dispossession. But faced with a growing media preoccupation with the personal dimensions of that history, many shied away from telling their stories. This reluctance to make their memories public often concealed a lingering fear that voicing the injustices would stimulate a backlash from mainstream Canadians and even from federal authorities. At the first public meeting for Japanese Canadian seniors in Vancouver in 1984, for instance, the audience learned that rumours were circulating among seniors that the government might cut off the pensions of those who stood up for redress. This mistrust in the government, fuelled by their memories of racist violence and censorship in the past, compelled many seniors, and even younger Japanese Canadians in communities across the country, to stay clear of public gatherings where they might be seen as "ungrateful" or "resentful" citizens. It was precisely in response to these fears that the phenomenon of "house meetings" became a crucial component of the NAJC's redress campaign in 1984.

REDRESS EMBODIED

DURING THE DRAMATIC awakening of consciousness among Japanese Canadians in 1984 and 1985, "redress" became a term embodied. It went from being an abstraction tied to the future to a more immediate word signifying the connection of a traumatic (that is, unresolved) past to the present narrative of seeking a political resolution. But concurrently — and here the power of memory becomes evident — the stories constituted the vehicle of a new identity, a redress identity that came to life in the new context of a social and political movement. It was a revolution akin to the shift from memory as "a monument visited," in the words of Pierre Nora, to memory as a "context, a landscape inhabited." In other words, the language of redress allowed for the dislocation of a past that was fixed in its irresolution, and this opened up a contemporary social space in which the historical violations could be seen as resolved in an imagined future.

In the process of sharing stories, individuals who have experienced trauma are able to see the personal in relation to an imagined collective. And when tied to a collective movement, the act of remembering allows those possessed by history, as Cathy Caruth writes, to "bear witness to a past that was never fully experienced as it occurred. Trauma, that is, does not simply serve as a record of the past but precisely registers the force of an experience that is not yet fully owned." For Japanese Canadians, the enactment of memory through the activist framework of redress then became an interventionist cue — or more, a common horizon — through which they could take some ownership of their traumatic history.

As a medium, language has the power to create group coherence and identity. The forging of terminology, definitions and concepts is not only a means of disseminating information, but also the means through which individuals already marked by signs of difference can mould themselves into a more collective entity. The power of that collective entity — and its collective "voice" — will subsequently depend on the extent to which its members can relate to each other through the language that gives shape to their common horizon. This common horizon, articulated on the basis of a common cause, can be a powerful focal point for action. For Japanese Canadians in particular, the movement to redress the violations of the 1940s resulted in the expansion of an identity formation to incorporate the more inclusive language of "citizenship" and "human rights" that constitutes the liberal democratic values of the Canadian nation. In this process, the vast field of memories — in all their singular configurations — took on social significance as a representation of Japanese Canadian subjectivity. Redress as the basis of citizenship and rights provided the framework within which the struggle of Japanese Canadians could be read as a national issue — one that called for a "settlement" by the federal government, the authority responsible for the violations.

The apparent clarity of this position, of course, needed to be measured against the pervasive memories of anger, confusion and outrage that saturated the perceptions of Japanese Canadians. The government's abusive policies had catastrophic effects on every aspect of their lives, so much so that the subjective manifestations were multiform and highly varied from person to person. In such a situation, an ambiguous concept of redress would not have unified them; rather, it would have divided them further. Redress for what, for instance? For property loss alone, the most obvious basis? Income loss? Loss of education? Psychological and emotional damage? Material hardships? The breakup of the family? The destruction of community facilities and businesses? Wrongful incarceration? And who merited redress? Only those who were uprooted? Only adults? Only those who owned property? Everyone?

Here, the call for an "official acknowledgement" in the House of Commons of the injustices endured by Japanese Canadians took on central importance as an objective. Here, Japanese Canadians could find a common horizon.

In Joy Kogawa's *Obasan*, Aunt Emily says to Naomi Nakane, "None of us ... escaped the naming. We were defined and identified by the way we were seen." Aunt Emily implies that the marking of all Japanese Canadians, regardless of citizenship, as "of the Japanese race" supplanted the more nuanced social identities that had existed prior to the mass uprooting. In the language of racialization they were remade as the monolithic "enemy alien" in the very Canadian nation with which they identified as citizens. The "naming," which limited the production of counter-narratives by Japanese Canadians who were "identified by the way we were seen," would then be internalized as both a point of origin and a boundary. An apology — not an acknowledgement — for the violation of rights, four decades later, would then simply reproduce the "victim" position of Japanese Canadians: they would be seen to be on the receiving end of a political gesture that released the state from further accountability. In this interaction, the group doing the apologizing would retain the dominant position. And such a gesture would likely have reinforced the hierarchical context, invoking a pathos instead of attaining what concerned Japanese Canadians the most in their call for justice: the public recognition that their racialization as "of the Japanese race" had named them out of existence as Canadian citizens.

The critical theorist Judith Butler, in *Excitable Speech*, has aptly commented that "we do things with language, produce effects with language, and we do things to language, but language is also the thing that we do." As a language act, seeking an "acknowledgement" helped to situate the discourse of redress in the public realm in a crucial way. By implicating the very political and administrative system that had made possible the racialized abrogation of rights, it would enact the recognition, by the federal government, that democracy itself had been "betrayed" by the internment of Japanese Canadians. In this process, the individual pain and suffering of Japanese Canadians can be displaced so that their victimization can become a matter of "citizenship" rights, a more inclusive condition that transforms their internment into a "Canadian" experience.

We now begin to understand the discursive distances the NAJC had travelled between 1984, when the public squabbles with Murta erupted, and 1986, when a position paper on a redress settlement was issued at a national meeting in Winnipeg. Then the main components of the 1988 settlement — acknowledgement, individual and community compensation, a foundation to fight racism, the rescinding of the War Measures Act and measures to exonerate those who had been wrongfully charged under the Act — were formulated and submitted to the federal government as the context for further negotiations. The question of compensation had been settled through a community questionnaire distributed earlier in the year. The clarity and coherence of the position paper, now supported by a broad-based "collective voice" of Japanese Canadians, was quite astounding, given the state of the NAJC only two years before.

The historical experience of a powerlessness that rendered people unable to defend themselves from the wartime violations led the NAJC to dwell on two important principles, both of which are consistent with democratic modes of solving disputes: a process of negotiation and a settlement based on a legitimate accounting of material losses. The collective position of Japanese Canadians, on the other hand, would be determined by another acceptable mainstream mode: the questionnaire. These three elements would come to form the critical pillars of the NAJC redress movement, but without the mobilization of memory in the construction of a "Japanese Canadian redress identity," none of the elements would have made sense.

In May 1986, the NAJC made public its position paper, which contained the major components of the redress agreement later reached with the federal government. By this time, the language of redress had cohered around the principle of citizenship and the violation of citizenship rights.

It was the very limits of this language — the focus on redress based on the rights of citizenship — that provided the commonality to unite otherwise disparately related "Canadians of Japanese ancestry."

CHAPTER 11

THE POLITICS
OF THE PROCESS

Encounters of the Federal Kind

*A sense of incompleteness gnaws at me. I need to feel right about my country.
I need this to happen while I am still around to appreciate it. What would
finally ease the bitter memories and deep hurts that simmer inside me is for
the government in Ottawa to take the high road in producing a Redress settlement. It should not only satisfy Japanese Canadians but also assure all
Canadians that, despite temporary aberrations, our country guarantees that
the rights and privileges of citizenship cannot be taken away, for whatever
reason.*

— Frank Moritsugu

THE GARDEN PATH, OR FAUX PAS?

ON DECEMBER 15, 1984, at the request of the federal government, the National
Association of Japanese Canadians (NAJC) council members assembled at
a downtown hotel in Winnipeg to meet with a special three-person

committee that had just been set up by the Conservative government's new secretary of state for multiculturalism, Jack Murta. The head of this delegation, Doug Bowie, assistant deputy minister for the secretary of state, introduced Orest Kruhlak as the regional director, Secretary of State, Pacific Region, and Anne Scotton as a member of the Corporate Policy Group in his department. They had been asked to talk with the NAJC and to advise the minister. Murta either could not attend or had decided not to. The NAJC was assured that this committee was authorized to represent him.

In a cautiously worded opening statement, Doug Bowie set out his understanding of the "motivations" propelling the redress issue. He talked in familiar terms about the importance of "justice" in the official acknowledgement, and he went further — a sign that he sympathized with the position of Japanese Canadians — to share his awareness of the limits of an "apology." "It's not just enough to apologize," he said. "There has to be a full, complete acknowledgement of what was done. An apology is too simple, too easy. It's more fundamental than that. That is so important to your community because there are many of you who do not feel reconciled with Canada because of what took place, and you would like the opportunity to be able to come to some reconciliation. That's the sense that I have picked up and tried to understand." Bowie went on to express his belief in the value of process and the necessity for Japanese Canadians to agree with the resolution. He also recognized "different views of compensation." But then he turned to the current political situation, pointing to the pressures on his minister to resolve the issue quickly. There was also the "problem of backlash," related mostly to the "difficulty with the individual compensation issue generally," though he was quick to qualify that a recognition of potential "backlash" in no way meant the government would "back away because of that." In a somewhat uncanny way — though Bowie may have been briefed on this — he echoed some concerns that the elderly had expressed about the potential for a "backlash" to redress. It was difficult to tell whether he had invoked this "problem" as a warning or as a sincere gesture of sympathy.

In any case, the warmth of Bowie's comments, which implied the willingness of the government to make concessions, came as a surprise. "We need to have you tell us what it is that you feel should be done," he told the NAJC council, supposedly speaking on behalf of his minister. What was happening? Had Jack Murta undergone some miraculous change of mind?

Had some political therapists been hired to rewrite the script on Japanese Canadians? The trust barometer — the deeper measure of "just and honourable" — was already fluctuating uncertainly, but no one seated around the large tables wanted to break the spell, at least for the moment. In the margins of Bowie's statement were vague references to the "time frame" for a resolution — a time that seemed to extend somewhere between "now" and perhaps "never."

Expanding on the theme of "healing" that Bowie had alluded to, Orest Kruhlak spoke about the value of what were termed community "visitations." These were described as tours by government representatives, and presumably the minister, through some of the more isolated communities, such as the former internment sites of Greenwood and New Denver in B.C., where elderly Japanese Canadians continued to live. These "visitations," according to his logic, would allow the government to "listen" to those who experienced the injustices, and this information could then become part of Canadian history. A number of NAJC council members replied that such "visitations" — which would no doubt be seen as "hearings" by the media and by Japanese Canadians themselves — were unnecessary. Had not the government already recognized that the treatment of Japanese Canadians was unjust? Why did this need to be confirmed? In any case, the "visitations" could easily become media spectacles, with individuals under pressure to provide public testimonies about their personal suffering. Moreover, the appearance of government officials would be disturbing to many Japanese Canadians. Bowie said that the meetings could be "private," with no reporters. They would be valuable for the government, he explained: "We want to understand and we want to be able to allay some of the fears that we have not done a good job of seeing what the situation is."

While it was difficult to determine the government's motivation in asking for the visitations, one point seemed clear: Bowie had prepared himself for this session. He had isolated NAJC concerns and was openly attentive to what he perceived to be the demands of Japanese Canadians. He emphasized his personal endorsement of the issue, and in his demeanour he presented himself as a go-between whose advice to his minister would extend his commitments here. And in what was the largest concession, he also announced his government's move away from the Trudeau argument that redress would mean that all historic injustices would have to be addressed, as far back as the expulsion of the Acadians. "But we've turned that corner," and the government was now prepared to address specifically what happened to Japanese Canadians. In short, redress had risen on the government's agenda, and because of this shift, heavy pressures had been exerted daily on Bowie's minister to deal with it quickly. The change was signalled in Bowie's offer to Art Miki to have the NAJC script the acknowledgement with the government: "Art, I can tell you right off the top that we would have no difficulty at all in recommending to the minister that you [the NAJC] be intimately involved in helping us write the joint resolution in the House."

The radical shift in mentality and the much softer and gentler approach — "we're listening" — had a strange ring to it. How did Bowie's language register on the trust scale? Could he actually be representing Murta's views, or was he coming on too strong, giving away too much?

THE LEAP INTO THE POLITICAL MAELSTROM:
THE JACK MURTA ERA

ONLY A FEW weeks before, Jack Murta had caused conflicts through his actions and words. On November 22, 1984, one day after the release of *Democracy Betrayed*, he was quoted in the *Globe and Mail* using language derived from a meeting with Jack Oki, George Imai and their Toronto Japanese Canadian Citizens' Association (JCCA) supporters, a group that had just declared its opposition to the NAJC — indeed, it had chosen November 21 to do so, in an effort to publicly embarrass the NAJC. "The older Japanese Canadians," Murta concluded from this single meeting, "the ones who were actually involved in the uprooting for the most part, don't want compensation." Perhaps he was briefed badly by his aides, or was simply speaking out of his own perceptions; more slyly, he may have been testing the waters to see whether the politicization of a "division" among Japanese Canadians would undermine the NAJC's stability enough for him to move ahead unilaterally. The underlying assertion — that in seeking compensation the NAJC was misrepresenting the views of the Japanese Canadians who had been interned — could not be read as other than a manoeuvre on Murta's part. This was confirmed at his meeting with NAJC representatives a few days later, on November 26, in Winnipeg. There he began by saying that the government intended to deal with redress quickly, as early as before Christmas. He had already made statements to the press that he was prepared to move "unilaterally" — without the participation of the NAJC.

In a personal interview, Kruhlak recalled that he had advised the government to view the NAJC as the legitimate voice of Japanese Canadians. Perhaps, when Murta took office, the existing files on Japanese Canadians in the multiculturalism office were influenced by George Imai's connections. In other words, Murta may have been given the impression that the Imai forces were more powerful than they were. This could explain why he met with Imai, Oki and their partisan issei group in Toronto, then emerged with the statement that "older Japanese Canadians" did not want compensation. As it turned out, as Jack Murta admitted in a personal interview, the Imai group was finally not a significant force for him: "It's always great to have a group ... agreeing with what you're saying, but they were never broadly based enough that it was an issue."

My own notes from this meeting record the details of the tensions between the minister and the NAJC — tensions that were replayed in later years with Murta's successors, Otto Jelinek and David Crombie:

- Murta was told that his comment in the newspaper that the majority of elderly Japanese Canadians do not want compensation is incorrect. Some issei are not vocal because they are afraid of backlash, but in private discussions and small group meetings, they have supported compensation. Murta did not comment on this point, though it was surprising to hear that he thought there were only about 3,000 victims still alive.
- Murta said that the government was against individual compensation. He was reminded of the example of the recent case in Nova Scotia, in which a man [Donald Marshall] was compensated $270,000 for false imprisonment; the government of Nova Scotia could have set aside funds to establish a halfway house to rehabilitate such victims, but decided on individual settlement as the most just and meaningful form of compensation. No amount of money can give back to this victim the eleven years he spent in prison, but the monetary compensation is an attempt to redress that wrong.
- Murta was also told that the injustices suffered by Japanese Canadians were a direct result of the violation of their individual rights and

freedoms. Redress must therefore acknowledge them as individuals, not simply as members of an ethnic group. We pointed out that Japanese Canadians place a high value on citizenship, so that recognition of individual rights is extremely important to them.

So what had happened? Was Murta advised by cabinet, or by the prime minister, to open talks with the NAJC? Had his hard-line approach been softened by the flurry of protest letters denouncing his threat to act "unilaterally" and calling on him to negotiate with the NAJC? His own absence at the December 15 meeting was curious. What was his strategy in using a special committee of hand-chosen government administrators to act as the go-between?

The meeting with Bowie, Kruhlak and Scotton continued without any serious disputes. The first priority was to issue a press release to announce what had transpired at the meeting and what agreements had been reached. In a spirit of cooperation, the release was jointly drafted with the following statement:

> December 15, 1984: At the request of the Minister of State for Multiculturalism, Jack Murta, senior officials of the Federal Government met today with Council members from across Canada of the National Association of Japanese Canadians to design a consultation process to allow Federal Government officials to recommend a course of action on redress for Japanese Canadians.
>
> A full and frank discussion was undertaken establishing a negotiation process between the NAJC and the Federal Government.
>
> Discussion has started on:
>
> 1. the timeframe for the process of negotiation
> 2. the wording and content of the official acknowledgement of the injustices suffered by Japanese Canadians
> 3. the amount and nature of compensation
> 4. the steps that should be taken to prevent the re-occurrence of such injustices
> 5. the possibility of a series of meetings with Japanese Canadian communities across the country.

The wording of the release, Bowie reported soon after, had been approved by Murta. In preparation the NAJC council immediately set up a Negotiation Committee to replace the recently formed Strategy Committee. The negotiation process might start as early as January 1985. Official photographs were taken of the NAJC council with Bowie, Kruhlak and Scotton. Could it all be this simple?

That evening the members of the NAJC council openly celebrated what they took to be a major breakthrough with the government. Our legal advisor, Don Rosenbloom, was contacted by speakerphone and given an account of the discussions. Later we all waited excitedly for the CBC national news. As the announcer described this historic meeting on redress, we all gasped at the image looming behind him: barbed wire coiled around the Japanese flag, a graphic portraying the rising sun. The CBC, "our" national news source, had it all wrong, and the Canadian public was having the wartime misrepresentation confirmed for them: those seeking redress are "Japanese," not "Canadian." Imagine the impact, had the Canadian flag been enclosed in barbed wire! It was an omen.

The negotiation process, announced so clearly and explicitly in the press release, ended abruptly. At the first sessions, on January 4 and 12, 1985, the newly formed NAJC Negotiation Committee was hurled into a linguistic turnaround. We learned that there would be no "negotiations" — which apparently had never been intended by the government — but only "consultations." There would be no "compensation" — which apparently had never been intended by the government — but only "memorialization." And there would be no flexible time frame: redress discussions had to be concluded by the end of the month. The outraged response from the NAJC led to an extension until February 20. At that time, with or without the agreement of the NAJC, the government would deal with the issue on its own.

And what was the government willing to do? Even though Murta never presented an offer in writing, the substance of his comments clearly resembled the Liberal offer of the year before: an acknowledgement of the injustices and a $6-10 million educational trust fund for all Canadians. The fund was to be considered not as "compensation" but as the government's "memorialization" of the wartime internment. Direct compensation was off the table — or had never been on it in the first place.

Had Bowie misunderstood his mandate? Or had Murta erred in not checking with cabinet before endorsing the press release? Had there been some intervention behind the scenes to kill the agreement? Suddenly, with no warning, the NAJC found itself seemingly cornered. What to do in the face of this terrible setback? Overnight, the optimism pervading the December 15 meeting vanished, and in place of the prospects for a negotiated settlement were all the familiar signs of betrayal.

Kruhlak recalled that the mandate he, Bowie and Scotton had been given was clear, and that Murta had approved the wording of the press release. Murta, for his part, recalled that the government — that is, cabinet — wanted a quick solution to the redress issue, with a minimal price tag. Prime Minister Brian Mulroney, in challenging Trudeau in the House of Commons, had made a public commitment prior to the previous federal election. He couldn't very well ignore that commitment, but redress was considered more a political "problem" than an urgent social issue, so it was something the government wanted to put behind it as quickly and efficiently as possible. In other words, redress had a high rating as a campaign promise, but there was little, if any, support for a monetary figure beyond what was allowable in the modest budget for the multiculturalism programs. And some government insiders feared that any form of direct compensation to Japanese Canadians would set a precedent for others to come forward with redress claims — Chinese Canadians for the head tax, Ukrainian Canadians for internment during World War I and Italian Canadians for internment during World War II.

Then again, in early 1985, after the Conservative government was elected in a landslide victory over the Liberals, most politicians and administrators in Ottawa would not have thought that redress had to be resolved with the agreement of Japanese Canadians. Kruhlak confirmed this assumption. Of course, they were not opposed to a token settlement that could be used to bolster the government's human rights profile, but direct compensation had little support. After all, Japanese Canadians were a very small and apparently unorganized group, with few allies and no political clout, so a lack of action would have no serious political consequences. The redress issue would soon pass away.

For its part, the NAJC had no choice but to fight back, despite its lack of financial resources and, at the time, effective political connections. As if struck by lightning, the group had no time to surrender to despair. It acted immediately to handle the crisis. Thus what had initially appeared as the concluding phase of redress turned out to be the beginning of a long political struggle that continued for four more years. It was in this often unpredictable process that the NAJC learned to negotiate its way through the labyrinth of the federal political system.

In the most determined response to the government's handling of redress to date, the NAJC accused Murta outright of betraying the trust embodied in the December 15 press release. He was also betraying the pre-election commitment made by Prime Minister Mulroney that a Conservative government would "compensate Japanese Canadians." In a lengthy letter, dated January 18, 1985, NAJC President Art Miki reconstructed the history of this betrayal, citing the agreements reached with the minister's special committee, headed by Doug Bowie, and the commitment made to the negotiation process. The letter, widely circulated in the national media, presented the NAJC position in both real and strategic terms. Yes, we were hurt and outraged, but we were learning quickly — and in the heat of the moment — that vocal opposition in itself would not further our cause. We needed to establish a much more compelling public presence. We needed, in short, to create a redress "voice" that would not only generate political attention but also have national appeal for its advocacy of human rights.

Acting in consultation with our legal advisor, Don Rosenbloom, we drafted the letter as both a political and a public document — the first of many documents that would mark the paper trail of the movement. Here we presented our call for "negotiations" and challenged the minister, and by implication the government, to keep his word. This accounts for the modulated tone of the letter, forceful in expressing outrage, yet insistent in setting out the terms of an acceptable political process. One crucial passage set into play a mediating language for future encounters with the government:

> Let it be clearly understood that we reject any negotiation process that imposes deadlines, not to mention one that imposes an unrealistic deadline of just over 60 days from the very date the government announced its willingness to negotiate with our community.
>
> For 40 years the Government of Canada has shown little interest in righting the wrongs committed on our people during and after World

War II. Although we applaud the announced intentions of the present federal administration in wanting to negotiate a settlement with us, we deplore the pressure that suddenly within 60 days we must come to an agreement on the many complex questions surrounding a prospective settlement. To suggest that issues of compensation for the losses suffered by our community, constitutional and statutory amendments to ensure that this type of incident never happens again, pardons for criminal records imposed under the War Measures Act, reinstatement of Canadian citizenship to members of our community who were illegally deported from Canada, and a host of other complex questions, can all be dealt with within this limited time frame, is naive and unrealistic.

When the NAJC went public with its letter to Jack Murta, we were certain the government would retaliate in some form. Soon after, the February 20 deadline for agreement was rescinded, and we learned that the wheels had been set in motion for a unilateral parliamentary resolution by the end of January. Thrown again into a state of emergency, the NAJC Negotiation Committee made the first of many treks to Ottawa (we were reminded, of course, of the 1936 trek to seek the franchise) to lobby the key political players. In January 1985, those players were in the opposition parties, starting with John Turner of the Liberals and Ed Broadbent of the NDP.

Significantly, it was during this first trek that the NAJC's founding principle of future negotiations was articulated, and soon functioned as a touchstone for an unfolding campaign. A settlement not approved by the NAJC, we told both the Liberals and the NDP, would never be acceptable. Through the work of two multiculturalism critics, Sergio Marchi (Liberal) and Ernie Epp (NDP) — MPs who supported redress in the years ahead — the NAJC met with the Liberal caucus on January 28 and with the NDP caucus on the following day. Both Turner and Broadbent emerged from the meetings to make press statements endorsing the principle that a settlement had to meet with the approval of the NAJC. What a relief. Now a unilateral resolution by the Conservatives would not have all-party support.

Shockingly, even while the NAJC met with Turner and Broadbent, the government moved to a final stage. During our meeting with Broadbent, we all learned that a motion on redress, pending in just a few days, had at that very moment been handed to the NDP caucus for discussion. Surely,

Broadbent said, the NAJC had a copy of this. When we said no, and that we had no idea of what the government had in mind, Broadbent showed us his copy of the acknowledgement. Had the NAJC not come to Ottawa, we realized, the motion may very well have received all-party support. Broadbent himself was visibly moved that we had intervened at this precise moment. And when we examined the wording of the acknowledgement, we were astounded to see the very language that we had strongly rejected in our first meeting with Bowie's committee, before the crisis with Murta. We explained to Broadbent that the NAJC had submitted a proposed acknowledgement that had been ratified by the association. Another version was drafted through a negotiation process between Bowie's committee and the NAJC Negotiation Committee, but that one was never agreed upon because talks with Murta had terminated. The version slated for the official ceremony in the House of Commons was the government's first version, which had been rejected by the NAJC. It was little more than a reworking of the "regret" statement prepared by the office of David Collenette the year before. It focused not on the specific nature of the injustices inflicted on Japanese Canadians, but on the "regret" that certain groups in Canadian history were treated badly. The NAJC version, which we gave to Broadbent, highlighted the racist policies and actions that resulted in the violation of citizenship rights.

Broadbent was horrified by the government's crass political manoeuvring. Suddenly the ante had been upped on redress.

Without all-party backing, there was no point to a parliamentary acknowledgement. The government had been exposed and the national media zoomed in on redress, rapidly heightening the importance of the issue. For Murta, the language battle with the NAJC turned into a spiralling descent into a public maelstrom that he could no longer control. For the NAJC, despite the disappointing disruption — even abrupt halt — in the negotiation process, the language of redress was spreading in all directions. In addition the NAJC had managed to get the opposition parties to reject any unilateral settlement and to urge the government to negotiate with the NAJC.

In the confrontation with Murta, the acknowledgement itself, which seemed to be only a matter of words, became the symbolic centre of a growing national redress movement. The task that lay ahead, though obviously complicated and uncertain, was clearer. For the issue of compensation to assume more urgency, the NAJC had to place on record some estimate of the losses resulting from uprooting and dispossession. While any compensation figure would finally still be a "symbolic" amount, to be "just and honourable," should it not have some relationship to the losses? After all, the government's $6 million was merely an arbitrary sum pulled from the air.

The NAJC, in a gesture of reconciliation, recommended to Murta that they jointly commission an independent study of losses based on the files in the government's archives, particularly the files belonging to the Custodian of Enemy Property. Murta said no — and called off further discussions.

Nevertheless, the apparent impasse — and this became a pattern as the redress movement gained momentum — forced the NAJC to develop a political language that reflected the emerging voice of Japanese Canadians. As a direct consequence of the January 1985 crisis, the NAJC formulated a position for achieving the goal of a negotiated settlement. At the council meeting in Calgary immediately following the crisis, on February 2-3, 1985, three requests were made in a letter to Prime Minister Brian Mulroney:

1. that a redress settlement must be acceptable to the NAJC and our community and would include as one package the wording and content of the Acknowledgement, monetary and non-monetary compensation;
2. that the government will discuss with the NAJC amendments to the War Measures Act and the Charter of Rights and Freedoms to ensure that Canadians are protected from the injustices suffered by Japanese Canadians; and
3. that discussions on compensation be deferred until the feasibility of a socio-economic study of the wartime treatment of Japanese Canadians is assessed, as was agreed to by the government's representatives.

Rather than accept closure — that is, rather than react to Murta's withdrawal from the process — the NAJC continued on the assumption that negotiations were in process. The decision to seek "one package," though, was a sign that every aspect of a proposed settlement had to be negotiated. There would be no acknowledgement until the NAJC "program" was completed.

As the months passed, Murta said on occasion that his door was still open for further talks with the NAJC, but his words had little substance.

Clearly he had no room to negotiate a substantial settlement, and perhaps he assumed that the NAJC would simply run out of steam.

During my flight to Ottawa on January 27, 1985, I noted my anxieties as I pondered the fragile political moment:

> It's pretty clear now that the government set up that meeting with Doug Bowie, Orest Kruhlak, and Anne Scotton, to define the NAJC's position and to dilute public pressure supporting JCs. As Orest K. said at the January 12 meeting in Winnipeg, the government never ever intended to negotiate with the NAJC. They were setting us up for the January 4 announcement (from Kruhlak) that a deadline would be imposed.
>
> The JCs are such a vulnerable group, with internal divisions, animosities, etc. which cut through our quest for redress. The government has had a long period of dealing with JCs via double standards, so it comes easily for them. Murta in private meetings bullies us and uses intimidation tactics to try to coerce us into accepting/complying with the government's decisions. The JCs have nothing other than the rightness of their position. This is their strength, but their weakness is their awe before the power of government. Once the government threatens to act to discredit JCs, they tend to buckle and give in to their fears that continued challenge to authority will bring retaliation and censure from the white community and its government, forgetting that the struggle for justice does involve risk and the need to maintain the purity of the position against the external pressure to compromise away the inner perspective of the community — last evening at a house meeting, of being forced to endure the barbarism of Hastings Park, the barbarism of living in chicken shacks in the beet fields of Alberta, and the countless stories of personal lives cut off in the midst of living. Lost dreams, and the searing sense of betrayal, held in, but present in the stories.

On Murta's side, his inability to resolve redress may have cost him his position, or so we thought at the time. He went from the multiculturalism portfolio to tourism, and this change may have led to his withdrawal from political life. Years later, reflecting on this period, he said that everyone wanted redress put to rest quickly, but at the time there was little awareness of the depth of public support for Japanese Canadians, particularly because of the sympathetic image of the NAJC that was rapidly developing in the media. As he put it, "The will was there but the sensitivity at that time wasn't there." By implication, the decision to squash the agreement announced in the press release was made in cabinet. Murta had apparently gone far beyond the limited range that his government had in mind for redress.

Murta himself may have been taken aback by cabinet's censorship of the December 15 press release. At the meeting to form the special committee, Kruhlak recalled, the government had already decided on an acknowledgement and a $6 million education trust fund as "redress" for Japanese Canadians. Both Bowie and Kruhlak advised against an imposed resolution with an offer that the NAJC had already rejected from David Collenette. What was required, at this critical moment, was a process that offered more flexibility, a wider range for discussions on compensation, and more participation from the NAJC. Apparently Murta agreed with them: he allowed for the December 15 meeting with the NAJC council, which concluded with an agreement that incorporated the key terms "negotiation" and "compensation." But he attempted to disavow both words in January, substituting "consultation" and "memorialization." Between the press release and the beginning of January, in other words, key players in the cabinet were sufficiently disturbed by the implications of the terms to close the door on any further public exchanges with the NAJC. If the fallout from the commitments evident in the press release could be managed, the redress issue could still be put to rest with a token offer: acknowledgement and $6 million for an educational fund. Murta admitted that had he gone to cabinet to ask for a large sum of money, he would "have been thrown out." He ended up feeling alone with the issue: on the one side, a cabinet opposed to direct compensation, and on the other, what he saw as a Japanese Canadian community directing all of its antagonism toward him. The public drama that erupted around him, though, was a catalytic force in propelling the issue of redress into the national news.

REFINING THE ABILITY TO SAY "NO THANKS": THE OTTO JELINEK EXPERIENCE

OVER THE NEXT two years, until the summer of 1987, the NAJC engaged in a series of public encounters with Jack Murta's successors, first Otto Jelinek (1985-86) and then David Crombie (1986-87). The offers varied slightly, but the issue of negotiations toward direct compensation to Japanese Canadians was never part of the government's agenda. "Consultation" continued to be the approach, as both ministers attempted, through various tactics, to manipulate the NAJC into compliance. It was as if the NAJC were caught in a flawed script that was replayed with only cosmetic variations. Appearances changed, but the form remained the same.

Out of the turmoil and the sheer physical effort required to remain attentive to the government's schemes — which meant constantly reading the clues given — the NAJC gained in public stature. If the script appeared to have been determined by the ministers who represented the government, the authority that could resolve redress at any level, the NAJC took on the role of the "citizens wronged," whose own perspective had to be respected. The dynamic of this interchange produced a focal point that gave the NAJC a necessary stability in the midst of political uncertainties. This was the power to say no, even when all the forces of political expediency were against such an uncompromising position. The principle was tested many times with Jelinek and Crombie.

Otto Jelinek, who replaced Jack Murta as secretary of state for multiculturalism in the summer of 1985, brought a much less friendly and even a cold and hard-edged approach to government encounters with the NAJC. Perhaps that tactic was adopted to demonstrate government authority. Gone was the sympathetic approach through government bureaucrats — the approach of Doug Bowie, who was always more available and who had a genuine awareness of the historic value of redress. Apparently that approach had been judged a failure with Murta, and Bowie bore much of the blame for the language of the December 15 press release. Jelinek chose to work directly through his political staff, among whom there seemed to be little concern for the subjective positioning of Japanese Canadians. Communication took on a more formal look in public interchanges. Redress was still a priority for the govenment, as Jelinek would say, but the problem for him as a politician was how to deliver the package to the government without "negotiations" and "compensation." The implication was that Murta had faltered, and finally failed, because he had been inconsistent and too flexible with the NAJC. What was needed was a tough and determined stance — no more conciliatory gestures.

Jelinek opened with a slight increase in the amount offered for the educational trust fund, from $6 million to (perhaps) $10 million, depending on some corporate or provincial contributions (his theme as the new minister was "multiculturalism means business"). The foundation would have some Japanese Canadians on its board of directors — a proposal that was supposedly an advance on Murta's offer — but it was still intended as a "global" settlement for "all Canadians." There would be no direct compensation to Japanese Canadians. The offer had no appeal whatsoever to the NAJC, since the foundation was merely a vaguely described government body that would "memorialize" the internment. We were still engaged in the same discourse we had had with Murta, and with Collenette before him.

Clearly Jelinek did not set out to be creative. He was recycling Murta's position, but in his tactics he adopted the public image of a no-nonsense minister who had been called in to do what his predecessor had failed to do. Sadly, more for the government than for the NAJC, he lacked some insights into the history of Japanese Canadians — insights that he could easily have gained from the brief *Democracy Betrayed*. This lack, which may have reflected the shortcomings of his own staff, made him an unpredictable speaker in his comments on redress. Redress for him seemed to be simply a political issue, not a human rights issue that struck to the core of Canadian democratic values. It was Jelinek, for instance, who met with some NAJC representatives in Winnipeg, including the well-respected nisei veteran Harold Hirose, and opened the meeting by announcing that he understood exactly what Japanese Canadians had gone through because, as a Hungarian refugee to Canada, he too was an immigrant. The quick-witted Hirose clipped back: "That's our problem — we aren't immigrants, we were born here." The irony seemed to escape the minister.

Our sporadic talks ("non-talks" is more accurate) with Jelinek went on during the fall of 1985. Again it seemed that we were being dragged along, month after month, as the government skirted Prime Minister Mulroney's pre-election promise to "compensate" Japanese Canadians. We read this move as a stalling tactic to provide the government with time to undermine the NAJC's campaign.

Murta had been burned when he attempted to use Imai and Oki's Japanese Canadian National Redress Committee of Survivors or the "Survivors' Group" to discredit the NAJC. Jelinek took the much harsher position of publicly refusing to acknowledge the NAJC as the representative organization for Japanese Canadians. Instead he sought to undermine their authority by simply going around them. Redress, he rationalized, was an issue that went beyond the NAJC, so he undertook a broader process of "consultations" with other Japanese Canadian groups as well as the so-called "public at large," primarily a euphemism for meeting with hand-picked people and organizations.

Right from the outset, Jelinek moved to an extreme that Murta had shied away from. By presuming to talk with a broad range of Canadians, Jelinek could politicize redress in the context of a national ethnic constituency and then manipulate this context to promote a view of the NAJC as unrepresentative of Japanese Canadians. This was a tactic through which he could also make use of the "Survivors' Group." All along, Imai and Oki had been making overtures to the federal government to settle with them because their "Survivors' Group" shared the government's position. In the Jelinek phase, they presented their group as the model minority, made up of those who professed to be moderates and who rejected individual compensation as selfish and radical.

In a way it was predictable that the "Survivors' Group" got on track with a receptive Jelinek. This complicity brought back, for many Japanese Canadians, bitter memories of the mass uprooting, when the government took advantage of community divisions to defuse dissent and critique. Perhaps Jelinek thought that an alliance with the "Survivors' Group" would help to turn public opinion against the NAJC. Since redress concerned all Canadians, Jelinek could argue, the NAJC was only one element in the resolution of the issue. And as the minister, he had the authority to negotiate with the whole of Canada — which in effect meant those who agreed with the government's position, including the "Survivors' Group." Even Jelinek's appointed (and therefore partisan) Canadian Multiculturalism Council came out with a resolution that agreed with the government's offer. This now-defunct CMC was itself a government construction, made up of individuals who were loosely supposed to reflect "ethnic" constituencies; but appointments to the CMC were largely a matter of party affiliation. That is why Jelinek's claim that the CMC represented specific ethnic groups was contested by the more community-based organizations in the Canadian Ethnocultural Council (CEC). The NAJC belonged to the CEC. NAJC President Art Miki was part of its executive. Even though the CEC depended on government grants, it was independent enough to come out in support of the NAJC's representative authority.

During the Jelinek period of "negotiations," rumours constantly circulated that the minister was contacting influential individuals from various ethnic communities to gain support for his government and that he was resorting to coercive tactics, such as the threat of cutbacks in grants to groups that aligned themselves with the NAJC. By transporting redress into the national spaces of ethnic politics, however, Jelinek himself became the unwitting vehicle of a dramatic rise in public attention. Media coverage escalated, and soon controversies were breaking out in several arenas of the public sphere simultaneously.

Jelinek's failure to respect the NAJC and his hard-edged language when he spoke about redress earned him the title of the "Rambo" minister. He was seen as a government official with so little sensitivity toward Japanese Canadian history that his only intent was to railroad redress to a government-imposed closure. In a repeat performance, the NAJC had to respond to Jelinek's resolve to settle redress with a unilaterally imposed resolution by the end of January 1986. The minister placed on the table the same package that had been offered by his predecessor, except that he said he would try to add another $3-4 million, perhaps consisting of contributions from Canadian businesses. Once again, the NAJC Strategy Committee, the new name of the Negotiation Committee after the negotiation process with Murta had deadended, organized a lobbying trek to Ottawa. Once again, endorsements from the Liberals and the NDP were confirmed. But this time contacts were made with a handful of sympathetic Conservative MPs — for example, with John Fraser, then Speaker of the House — and meetings with national labour unions and newspaper editors were productive. The government again backed down from a unilateral action on settlement.

By early 1986, aided to some extent by Jelinek's politicization of the issue, redress seemed to have taken on a national narrative of its own. On one side was the NAJC, representing Japanese Canadians who were struggling to unify a community dismantled by policies that enforced assimilation. On the other side was the federal government, through its political agent, threatening to close off redress because Japanese Canadians were not unified. The drama was not lost on the media. As Jelinek's reputation as a minister incapable of handling redress grew, Japanese Canadians began to come under media scrutiny. All the elements of a spectacle became apparent in media representations that dwelled on the so-called "split" in the community.

In one of the most dramatic instances, *Ottawa Citizen* reporter Dan Turner, who had been covering redress, wrote a feature-length piece dramatizing the so-called community split. On one side in his construct was the author Joy Kogawa, who spoke in favour of the NAJC; on the other was X, an unidentified Japanese Canadian — whom many readers suspected to be George Imai — who opposed the NAJC. Turner sets up a drama in which the voices of Kogawa and X function as opposites in a divided community. Kogawa, endorsing the NAJC's call for a negotiated settlement, looks upon X as a compromised figure who cheapens the suffering of Japanese Canadians by supporting the government's position. X refuses to be identified but is described as a "passionate supporter of the 'Survivors' Group'" who have "received favorable attention from both Murta and Jelinek," presumably because they are against individual compensation. X believes Japanese Canadians should blend in, and so supposedly supports the government's policy of enforced assimilation. He refers in a positive way to the notion of the social "melting pot." But then Turner introduces a twist in the drama. X does not want to make demands on the government because, according to his perceptions, the "majority" of Japanese Canadians were loyal to Japan. The article ends with Kogawa suggesting that X may have another motive for questioning the loyalty of Japanese Canadians. "What does he want to destroy?" she asks, and the article ends on this question. Readers are left hanging while the plight of Japanese Canadians takes on the aura of a melodrama. Although this kind of heightened media attention may have propelled Japanese Canadians into mainstream public spheres, it also threatened to turn redress into a social spectacle, a spectacle that could have undermined the community's collective power to act on its own behalf.

Fortunately the tactics Jelinek had adopted — often to exacerbate the tensions among Japanese Canadians — were beginning to lose their effectiveness by the spring of 1986. The chair of the Canadian Multiculturalism Council, purportedly speaking as a "Ukrainian Canadian," was criticized by members of the Ukrainian Canadian Committee, which was a member of the Canadian Ethnocultural Council. Other individuals on the CMC were also taken to task by national organizations, such as the Chinese

Canadian National Council, for taking a partisan position against the NAJC. And in a major turnaround, the Canadian Jewish Congress, which had initially come out in favour of the government's foundation to "memorialize" Canadian injustices, reversed its position and supported a negotiated settlement with the NAJC. Indeed, it was during the Jelinek tenure that the seeds were planted for what later emerged, in the fall of 1987, as the National Coalition for Japanese Canadian Redress.

But another event eroded Jelinek's credibility even more severely: the release, on May 8, 1986, of the Price Waterhouse report, *Economic Losses of Japanese Canadians After 1941.* This report, completed during the year the NAJC engaged in public confrontations with Jelinek, had an immediate impact. It dramatically substantiated the NAJC's claim that the social and economic effects of internment were far larger than recognized by the government. The figures presented by the Price Waterhouse researchers — not less than $443 million in 1986 dollars — dwarfed the token amounts, in the range of $5-6 million, offered by the federal government.

Thus, when Otto Jelinek responded to the report by stating that the figures were irrelevant for the government's settlement package, his words began to sound hollow.[1] How could the government ignore a report from Price Waterhouse? Rather than having to argue with Jelinek in public, the NAJC could use the report's findings as tangible evidence of the real alienation — documented in the media — that had developed between Japanese Canadians and the minister who was in charge of finding a means to settle the redress issue. But even more important, the dissemination of the losses study was instrumental in building more community coherence. Resistance to Jelinek was thereby transformed in positive ways, through the growing involvement of grassroots Japanese Canadian organizations — from church groups to bowling clubs to garden associations — who felt

---

1   The media took Otto Jelinek to task for downplaying the importance of the Price Waterhouse report. In one typical editorial, "The Jelinek Waltz," the *Globe and Mail* supported compensation related to the calculation of economic losses: "Those interned during the Second World War have a special case to make ... They have documents showing they were victims of racism and records itemizing the losses they suffered when the government sold their property for a fraction of its value." The editorial concluded: "If the Mulroney Government is truly reluctant to 'set a precedent' for compensating such groups, any apologies it gives or symbolic foundations it finances will mean nothing."

compelled to demonstrate to the "Canadian public" that the minister's perceptions had gone awry in not recognizing the NAJC as a representative authority on redress.

By May 1986, the month the Price Waterhouse report was released, the NAJC was also able to turn the most critical corner of the redress movement. That month, at a council meeting in Winnipeg, we finally announced a position on the three areas that would subsequently constitute the redress settlement:

- an official acknowledgement of the injustices suffered by Japanese Canadians
- measures to prevent a recurrence of the injustices
- compensation in both an individual and a community form

REFINING THE ABILITY TO SAY "NO THANKS": THE DAVID CROMBIE ERA

WHEN IT WAS announced that Jelinek would be replaced as multiculturalism minister, no one was surprised. There was a sense of relief and even optimism that he would be replaced by the minister of Indian affairs, David Crombie, the polar opposite of Jelinek: affable, informal and supposedly a friend to ordinary people (a reputation he had built as the former "friendly" mayor of Toronto). Crombie was known to many Toronto Japanese Canadians, and over the years he had made some contacts in the community. Had the government changed its position? Would Crombie be the one to "negotiate" with the NAJC?

With the appearance of David Crombie as the new minister in charge of redress, the government circle shrank even more. If Murta spoke through his administrators and Jelinek through his political staff, Crombie wanted to speak directly to the NAJC, one on one, with only his advisor, Ron Dearing, privy to discussions. And right from the outset, he created an image of himself as completely different from Jelinek. He claimed a deep understanding of the citizenship issue behind redress, unlike his counterpart Jelinek, who had come to Canada as an immigrant.

Art Miki, Roger Obata and I first met David Crombie informally (seemingly a strategy on his part) in a steak house in central Toronto, just off

Yonge Street, where he reserved a private room. There it was evident that his approach would be to handle redress personally; and to counteract the negative press surrounding his predecessor, he wanted to establish a publicly amicable relationship with the NAJC. But he needed time to immerse himself in the issue, and this meant reading the relevant publications on Japanese Canadian history and seeking views from many Japanese Canadians. Like the seasoned politician that he was, he fondly referred to the Japanese Canadian who owned the laundry he frequented and to his friendship with the well-known architect Raymond Moriyama. He wanted to understand redress from the "inside," so that he could, as a minister, come up with a settlement that would be agreeable to both Japanese Canadians and the Canadian public. He cautioned us, though, that he would have to work within government limits. In meetings he often invoked two metaphors to describe the constraints on him as a politician: the "leash" and the "footprint." The former was only so long and the latter was only so big, and though he would not say what these metaphors meant in monetary terms, he was clear that the measurements were fixed by cabinet.

In sharp contrast to the NAJC's meetings with Jelinek — who at times had not even looked directly at us but communicated only through his aides — a meeting with Crombie was always a friendly, "call-me-David" kind of session. Sympathy has a contagious quality, and many Japanese Canadians began to develop a faith in the more open process of "consultations" that he initiated. The NAJC Strategy Committee, on the other hand, already jaded by disappointments with Jack Murta and Otto Jelinek, waited patiently to see whether Crombie would recommend to his cabinet the process of "negotiations" that had been announced back in December 1984. Crombie had received the NAJC's position paper released in May 1986, and he had been briefed on the Price Waterhouse report, but he consistently refused to respond to either — until, as he kept insisting, he had the opportunity to *personally* understand all aspects of the issue.

The waiting game lasted for nine months. During this period Crombie talked with individual Japanese Canadians and read material on Japanese Canadian history. By early 1987, five months after his first meeting with the NAJC, as he continued his tight-lipped tour through Japanese Canadian centres, it was already apparent that he would not come through for the NAJC. It was all starting to resemble another political ploy — more elaborate, to be sure, but more of the same. In a trip to Vancouver, for instance, he agreed to meet with the active members of the JCCA Redress Committee at the old Japanese Language School on Alexander Street. There he listened to senior members of the community articulate the importance of recognizing individuals in the settlement and the need to negotiate with the NAJC. In his response, he was noncommittal and evasive, and the only hope he could offer was a sunny disposition. By then, though, the once-hopeful Japanese Canadians were getting ready for another letdown.

From this perspective, Crombie was the most dangerous "negotiator" of all. Because he was handling the issue personally, the NAJC could no longer appeal to the bureaucry for assistance and clarification. The only doorway to the minister was through his advisor, Ron Dearing. While Crombie never officially acknowledged the NAJC as the legitimate authority, his candour and personal manner opened up the community to him. We had vigorously resisted Jelinek's intrusion into our affairs, so the NAJC gave Crombie privileged status — a status that made Japanese Canadians more trusting of him.

Through our growing experience with politicians, I began to see Crombie's strategy as a Trojan horse move. By meeting with Japanese Canadians here and there across Canada, he was gaining their trust, which was making them relax, making them believe that something significant was finally being done. In that sense he was always dangling a carrot in front of us. He even told the Strategy Committee that he would discuss his position with them before submitting his proposal to cabinet.

That discussion never occurred. Instead, one day in March 1987 he sent the NAJC a now-infamous letter, in which he outlined his position advocating a community fund of $12 million but no individual compensation. He had taken the concept of the fund further than all the previous ministers. This fund, $2 million more than Jelinek's, would be given to the Japanese Canadian community. Here, then, was the community fund desired so much by the Imai-Oki "Survivors' Group." Crombie made much of the concession he made — control of the fund — which made the figure a form of compensation. But the figure represented only a paltry amount, once it was calculated in terms of the estimated 25,000 people whose rights had been abrogated. That was the extent of his "leash" and "footprint," he explained, but there was no evidence to show that Crombie had ever tried to convince cabinet to negotiate a settlement with the NAJC. It was clear that the concept of individual compensation had been rejected all along. We were back in the same political scene as we had been with Jelinek. Our "no thanks" to Crombie, it turned out, was the final phase of our campaign.

When in June 1987 the NAJC had its final meeting with David Crombie to say "no thanks" to his offer of $12 million for a community fund, we parted with considerable tension because we believed that he had led us down the garden path. After some nine months of apparently studying and consulting — these were his terms — we learned that he had never had any intention of considering individual compensation, the major stumbling block for his predecessors. Instead he was trying to break down the will of the NAJC so that the $12 million offer would appear to be the final offer. By clear implication, if we said no to his offer, the NAJC would receive nothing from the government. But in saying no, the NAJC had arrived at a very delicate, yet significant level of the broader negotiation process.

Although in a narrow perspective the NAJC had apparently nowhere else to turn, two key things had occurred when talks with Crombie broke off. First, the government had finally said no publicly to the principle of individual compensation (up to this point, it had refused to take a position), which meant that the onus was on Crombie to articulate his rationale. Now he would have to be on the defensive. How could he explain his rejection, in principle, of the human rights issue raised by his no? The view that compensation should be in a community form alone, because Japanese Canadians were interned as a community, would not stand up to public scrutiny. Second, the government cut off discussions with the NAJC after we had said no to its final offer. In effect, this action on its part was a clear sign that the government had failed to resolve the redress issue after Prime Minister Mulroney had made a pre-election commitment to "compensate" Japanese Canadians. Significantly, the government would have to deal with a point of honour — of keeping one's word.

The end of the Crombie period, however, was a uneasy moment for our community. I remember that many individuals were thrown into despair. They started to doubt the value of individual compensation and to think that we had "lost" $12 million. Some started to grumble that perhaps the NAJC Strategy Committee was being too unreasonable. Still others thought the redress movement would now collapse.

One question, though, lingers even now. Why did Crombie finally decide to offer so little? There were strong indications that the U.S. settlement package would be successful, despite rumours that President Ronald Reagan would use his presidential veto powers. In our meetings, Crombie declared his belief that U.S. redress would not go through — though, of course, his motive for saying so could have been more strategic than real. In fact, my own greatest fear was that Crombie would offer an amount far lower than the NAJC's expectations, but high enough that the Japanese Canadian community — tired of waiting so long — would be seduced into accepting it. A figure such as $75-100 million, for instance, would in all likelihood have brought pressure on the NAJC to agree.

In our final session with Crombie in the summer of 1987, we presented a proposal to create annuity plans for individuals over a period of 10 years. The proposal was prepared in consultation with Price Waterhouse accountants, and the total was in the range of $150 million. Crombie did not even give the proposal a serious response. It then became clear that he personally did not support individual compensation, and that his view was entrenched. There was no flexibility for him to reconsider the justice issue of recognizing the individual basis of the human rights violations. His belief that Japanese Canadians should not receive individual compensation may have blinded him to the political scene in the U.S. and around him in Canada, too, where public support for individual compensation had grown.[2]

I had a theory, shared with only a few close friends, that I had developed after the disappointments with Murta and Jelinek, and during Crombie's months of stalling. I thought that we would eventually succeed, but only after we had reached that darkest point where we, as a community, thought that we would not achieve a negotiated settlement with the government. Following our bitter separation with Crombie, a thread of hopelessness ran through the community as many people felt that we could no longer maintain the intensity of the campaign. Our last chance at a settlement seemed to be gone. Some who had previously supported individual

---

2   A poll undertaken by Environics Research Group early in 1986 revealed that 63 percent of Canadians surveyed supported some form of redress for Japanese Canadians who were interned. Of these, "71 percent said each individual who was unfairly treated should receive financial compensation."

compensation were willing to accept the $12 million community fund, and they doubted that the NAJC had been right in its unequivocal rejection of Crombie's offer.

Here, then, was that point of darkness. But I remember going back to Vancouver with a great sense of relief after we had reached an impasse with Crombie. We no longer had to hope that he would do something. More significantly, he had done us a great service by taking a position against individual compensation. Overnight, the press and media, civil rights leaders, and ethnic-minority organizations began to think about Crombie's position on the rights of individuals. The real issue — the issue of acknowledging individuals — had finally surfaced, and we were at last in a position to press for support on this principle.

It was then that we formulated plans for what came to be called the National Coalition for Japanese Canadian Redress. Up to the time of Crombie's rejection of the NAJC's position, ethnic-minority communities and many other Canadians were reluctant to endorse the NAJC's position outright, preferring instead to support the principle of a negotiated settlement. But now that negotiations with the government had been terminated by Crombie, these groups and individuals were freer to back the NAJC's call for individual compensation. Even the newspapers and other media started to talk about the importance of individual compensation as a basic democratic principle. Like a miracle, what had seemed to be a dead end turned out to be an opening.

Meanwhile, in September 1987, a major event occurred in the U.S. when the House of Representatives ratified redress for Japanese Americans. Although we in Canada were still uncertain about our situation, a few of us in Vancouver celebrated that milestone. It seemed to make redress inevitable in Canada.

THREE VANCOUVER VISITATIONS

JACK MURTA CLARIFIES THE TERMINOLOGY

IT WAS ONE of those gala affairs common in multicultural circles during the 1980s. The minister of state for multiculturalism arrives in town to announce grant recipients, hand out cheques and promote multicultural ideology, usually to a large crowd of invited guests from ethnic organizations and multicultural associations, and affiliated individuals. The Negotiation Committee of the NAJC was still reeling from the bombshell relayed at the first "negotiation" session that the government would not negotiate, and this devastating message came with the threat that the minister would impose his symbolic settlement (an acknowledgement of injustices endured by Japanese Canadians and a $5 million foundation for "all" Canadians) whether the NAJC agreed or not. When Murta flew into Vancouver in January 1985 for his public appearance at the Bayshore Inn, the NAJC committee felt that his ultimatum hovered over our heads, and there seemed little to do other than generate some support for the NAJC at the event.

As NAJC representatives, Don Rosenbloom, Cassandra Kobayashi and I were asked to hand-deliver a letter from the NAJC to Murta calling on him to return to the "negotiation" process that had been announced in our joint press release of December 15, 1984. At the outset of the event, Cassandra and I quietly circulated in the crowd, handing out copies of the letter to select people in many Vancouver ethnic-minority communities to let them know of our impasse with the minister. Most of them knew about the redress issue through media reports and were sympathetic to the NAJC's cause. Later in the evening we were summoned by Murta's aide to a hotel room, where we could present the letter to him directly.

As we entered the large suite, we could see Jack Murta seated at a large table. It was my first meeting with him. We waited while he scanned the NAJC's letter, and then we talked about the NAJC's concerns — specifically the rejection of "negotiations" and, by implication, the rejection of "compensation." In the back-and-forth conversation, Murta clung to his political terms: that for the government, "negotiation" meant "consultation," and "compensation" meant "memorialization." In other words, while he may actually have used the words, at no time did the government ever intend to "compensate" Japanese Canadians through a "negotiation" process. When we pressed him to honour the commitments made in the press release, which he had endorsed, he became visibly agitated and reacted by invoking the power of government and the fragility of "redress" — an issue, he said, that could easily be snuffed out by government indifference or opposition.

While Murta talked, I had the vision of a towering skyscraper whose height could not be determined from our perspective on the sidewalk. He talked about the impossibility of ever expecting individual compensation from the government, implying that Japanese Canadians should be grateful for his current offer of an acknowledgement and a foundation. We held our ground, but left the meeting with the impression that Murta had already been ordered by his superiors to take a hard line with the NAJC. Later, I discovered the further sting of political machinations, when he returned to Ottawa and supposedly told some reporters that we were asking for over $300 million in compensation. This misrepresentation had further ramifications when I was subsequently attacked in the Japanese Canadian press for demanding such an outrageous amount from the government. Such is the power of the language of political authority over some Japanese Canadians.

The possibility that the minister was playing hardball politics with us was not taken into consideration. The Miki who was accused by the minister was blamed for bringing shame onto Japanese Canadians.

The potential for such duplicity in public representations of supposedly "personal" actions stayed with me throughout the redress movement. In retrospect, the January meeting in that hotel room provided further evidence of Murta's defensiveness and destabilization as a politician who was slowly losing control of an issue that was burgeoning outward even as he tried harder and harder to contain its power over him. On the other hand, the attack from within a community newspaper signalled the need to develop a collective language for redress that would enable Japanese Canadians to respond more critically to statements made by federal politicians and bureaucrats.

OTTO JELINEK MEANS BUSINESS

IN AN UNCANNY repetition of the political visit by Jack Murta, his successor Otto Jelinek also came to Vancouver to court the "ethnic" vote. He too arranged a lavish affair at the Bayshore Inn to announce his views on multiculturalism and to mingle with representatives of ethnic organizations in the Vancouver area.

Jelinek had risen in popularity to become a politician largely through his reputation as a figure skater. Having come to Canada as a refugee, he projected the image of a self-made man who had risen to power through determination and a strong will. In contrast to the more amiable figure of Murta, Jelinek adopted a stern public pose, especially toward Japanese Canadian redress. He appeared unapproachable. Though we invited him to meet with Japanese Canadians in the area formerly called "Japantown," around Powell and Alexander Streets, we weren't surprised that he did not reply.

Cassandra Kobayashi and I attended the reception at the Bayshore on December 2, 1985, where Jelinek spoke to a large audience about getting multiculturalism down to the streets, by which I suppose he meant down to "ordinary folks," but his language was unconvincing. It was the familiar political use of multiculturalism to promote Canadian unity, but with no commitment to real change in the status quo. Frustrated that we had not been able to get him to meet with some of the elders from the Japanese Canadian community, I asked him in the question period why we had not seen him on the streets where Japanese Canadians had lived before they were uprooted and dispossessed. I hoped to remind him that he had chosen not to meet with us.

Before I knew it, Jelinek appeared to lose his temper, accusing me of unfairly negotiating with him in public. We got into a heated verbal exchange that was picked up by a reporter. The debate lasted only a couple of minutes. Worried that I had offended the minister, and therefore was jeopardizing future redress talks — though we had already reached a stalemate with him — I backed away.

I thought for certain that the news report on the event would cast a dark shadow on the redress movement. As one of its spokespersons, I would likely be criticized for disrupting what was supposed to be a celebration of Canadian multiculturalism, and this could turn the public against us. Sure enough, the altercation was the subject of a reporter's account and an editorial in the *Vancouver Sun*. What a surprise, though, to encounter two totally unexpected phenomena: the story published the day after the event identified me by name and ran with a photo of my brother Art, who was identified only as "Miki"; and the editorial on the following day, "Sorry — Now Get Lost," ascribed my comments to "NAJC President Art Miki" and chastised the minister for not agreeing to meet "face-to-face" with the Japanese Canadian community. In short, Jelinek was to blame! The editorial began by pointing out that the minister was being "awfully clumsy in his handling of the sensitive issue of redress for the mistreatment of Japanese Canadians during the Second World War," and concluded that the prime minister might have to "take the job out of his [Jelinek's] hands and get someone more diplomatic to do it." What a relief for me. But how to explain Art's presence at the meeting in Vancouver? Art, who was a schoolteacher at the time, said that someone from his school board in Transcona, Manitoba, had seen the photo and thought that Art had skipped his classes without notifying his employers.

Jelinek continued to bring a sense of strangeness to the political process. At one point during our public disputes with him, this time in Ottawa, we planned a press conference. He had been making statements, based primarily on his meetings with the Japanese Canadian National Redress Committee of Survivors headed by Imai and Oki, that older Japanese

Canadians were not interested in direct monetary compensation. To counter this allegation — obviously a political ploy — we decided to undermine Jelinek's credibility by exposing his lack of cultural knowledge of elderly Japanese Canadians, especially the behaviour of the issei generation. In his statement to the press gallery, Art began by explaining that although elderly Japanese Canadians would never openly state that they wanted individual compensation, privately they were in favour of this form of redress. At this moment, the whole gallery suddenly — and dramatically — emptied out. Had Art said something wrong? Before we could figure it out, someone yelled out that the U.S. space shuttle had just exploded. It was January 28, 1986.

BRIAN MULRONEY "REMEMBERS" A MEETING

PRIME MINISTER MULRONEY made a rare visit to Vancouver on March 7, 1986. Amid the media hype and the discontent voiced by protestors outside the downtown hotel where a press conference was about to take place, Cassandra Kobayashi and I made our way through the crowd. We entered the conference room, where apparently only the press were allowed, and seated ourselves in anticipation. The prime minister opened with a prepared statement saying that he was grateful for the views received from labour and business leaders — views that would be helpful in an upcoming meeting in Washington and a major trade trip planned for the Far East in May, beginning in Japan and South Korea.

Cassandra and I were both nervous and fearful, imagining ourselves as "crashers" of the conference, since our only tie to the press was our largely self-appointed role as "reporters" for the NAJC newsletter. With all the security guards hovering around Mulroney and the possibility of any disruptive questions from the large group of reporters present, we thought that our question on redress would get us removed from the space without a response. Our strategy was simply to insert an intervention into this mainstream event — an unexpected question that would highlight, even if only momentarily, the presence of redress as a political issue. After the prime minister handled two brief questions very easily, I rose anxiously, introducing myself as a member the NAJC and congratulating his government for its intention to resolve the redress question. I then asked him to meet with the NAJC to mediate its current differences with the minister of multiculturalism,

Otto Jelinek. At the time of this press conference, Jelinek had already adopted an autocratic stance toward the NAJC.

As one of his guards immediately began to move toward me, the prime minister, no doubt sensing the need for tact in what could have turned into a disruptive moment, gestured to show that he wanted to answer the question. And then he did:

> I think one of the regrettable days in the House of Commons came when the then Liberal prime minister of Canada, in response to a question from me, as leader of the Opposition, said on behalf of the Liberal government that he had no intention of ever resolving this matter in regard to Japanese Canadians, and that was a very unfortunate situation, and that's what we inherited. We have moved it along to the point where, contrary to that, I think, quite regrettable statement of opinion, that I took the view with my colleagues that there ought to be an apology in the House of Commons. I agree that there ought to be certainly an important symbolic recognition of that by the creation of an institute on racial justice to ensure that this kind of situation never occurs again.

Then, more to the moment, he said that Jelinek "met with your brother today, did he not?" The "meetings" with Jelinek were usually bizarre. Art Miki had once bumped into Jelinek at the Winnipeg airport, and that accident was later described by Jelinek as a "meeting." When the NAJC did meet with him in Ottawa, the atmosphere resembled a straitjacket. We received his ultimatums, we courteously said "no thanks" and the meeting ended abruptly. By March 1986, after months of icy confrontations, the NAJC had lost all confidence in Jelinek. So what was this meeting "today"?

Here we switch to the perspective of my brother in Winnipeg. Art was in an important educational meeting that day in his position as principal of an elementary school, when suddenly two men appeared and insisted on speaking to him immediately. They represented "Minister Jelinek," they said, and he needed to meet with Art that day. But Art was scheduled for an interview on redress with the CBC to begin shortly — at 3 p.m. He was told that when the interview ended, a taxi would be waiting for him to take him to the Fort Garry Hotel, where he would see Jelinek. Assuming that the meeting was important, Art phoned Harold Hirose, a member of the NAJC

Executive Committee, to join him. At the hotel, at about 5 p.m., they were ushered into a room. Jelinek entered, greeted them and then promptly departed. After they had waited for some time, Jelinek reappeared, only to say that nothing had changed in his view of redress. That was the extent of the meeting. Art was flabbergasted. What was going on? It was only later, when we talked about the press conference statement by Mulroney, that it dawned on us that Jelinek, who had no intention of meeting with Art, must have been informed that Mulroney had already announced the meeting, so a "meeting" had to be concocted.

CHAPTER 12

THE REDRESS SETTLEMENT

Negotiations with the Nation

After the settlement happened, someone asked me: "How do you feel now that redress has happened?" I told that person I felt as if a huge weight had been taken off my shoulders, a huge weight that had been there for more than 40 years. I no longer felt like a second-class citizen. I felt like a first-class citizen for the first time.

— Wes Fujiwara

FINALLY, NEGOTIATING FACE TO FACE

"PACK A CLEAN white shirt," National Association of Japanese Canadians President Art Miki told me over the phone on August 23, 1988. The NAJC's Strategy Committee had been summoned to a meeting with the latest multiculturalism minister, Gerry Weiner. "That's what I was told by the government contact," he said. We had often imagined — and even joked about — receiving this call from Weiner's office, and here we were, at that moment. It was the first genuine sign that the government had finally come around to accepting a process of negotiation with the NAJC. Our flight to Montreal, Weiner's hometown, had to be kept secret, so we were advised.

On the flight, Cassandra Kobayashi and I were thrilled that a settlement could be imminent, after so many years of strenuous work in the redress movement. To pass the time, we engaged in a mock interview in which we played out our mistrust in the scene that awaited us. With no information about the substance of the secret session, our speculations included the fear that we were being lured into a trap. Perhaps the government simply wanted to get redress off its agenda, but at the lowest cost possible, especially in light of the U.S. Civil Rights Bill of 1988 that had been signed into law by President Ronald Reagan on August 10.[1] At best, we thought, Weiner would offer individual compensation in the $10,000 range (a far cry from the NAJC's recommended $25,000), with a similarly reduced community fund (from the NAJC's $50 million). During our years in the movement we had often shared the anxiety that the government would offer an amount much lower than the NAJC's request but high enough that the Strategy Committee would be under pressure to accept, simply to end the anxious waiting of Japanese Canadians, many of whom had grown impatient with the lengthy delays.

In Montreal, the Strategy Committee, which included our legal advisor Don Rosenbloom, was guided through a series of inner passageways in the Ritz-Carlton Hotel. We walked — "trooped" might be more accurate — through hallways and up back steps to enter a room with a large table. The stealth of our movements had created an air of drama and anticipation. We were ushered to the side of the table facing the door. Once we were seated, Gerry Weiner appeared. We had met with him in Winnipeg a few months before, so we had expected him to be present. But we were completely taken by surprise when, behind Weiner, in walked Lucien Bouchard. He had recently been appointed — amid some controversy — the minister for the secretary of state by his longtime friend, Prime Minister Brian Mulroney. In all the years the NAJC had been struggling to negotiate a redress settlement,

---

1   The news from the U.S. was that President Reagan opposed the Civil Rights Bill and would exercise his right to veto it, in defiance of majority support in both the Senate and the House of Representatives. The House of Representatives passed the bill in September 1987, and the Senate passed it in the spring of 1988. And when the time came, Reagan consented to it.

we had never met with any minister other than the minister of state for multiculturalism, a junior ministerial position in the office of the secretary of state. To us, Bouchard's presence instantly signalled a positive change in the federal government's approach — but then again, when we recalled our disappointing encounters with four previous government ministers, we knew that this might be yet another manoeuvre.

Bouchard wasted no time. Once seated, he announced that a settlement was "now or never," and that the government had come to accept the principle of individual compensation. He and Weiner were prepared to negotiate and wanted to work out an agreement at this meeting, no matter how long it took. Then he stated — in a matter-of-fact tone, as if we had been moving toward this moment all along — an opening offer of $15,000 individual compensation for each Japanese Canadian interned during the 1940s. Just like that — after we had been told repeatedly, by successive ministers, that the principle of individual compensation would *never* be accepted by the government.

I flashed back to our final meeting with David Crombie. With a vehemence that disclosed an emotional edge to his usual friendly manner, he had rejected this principle. When I suggested that the exclusion of individual compensation from any settlement would be an "insult" to the enormity of the injustices endured by Japanese Canadians, he expressed anger at our position, leaving the impression that the $12 million community fund he had offered would be the best we could expect from the government. Now I wondered whether he could have convinced the prime minister, as it appeared Bouchard and Weiner had done, to work out an agreement with the NAJC.

Bouchard made no reference to the other components of the NAJC's proposed redress settlement. The Strategy Committee responded by saying that his opening offer fell short of the NAJC's figure, but at least there was room to begin negotiations. We agreed to set aside the figure for individual compensation and to work through the other components of the settlement first. At this point Bouchard said he would be available by phone at any time during our negotiation session with Weiner and his staff. Then he exited abruptly.

Apparently Bouchard had the clout to convince Prime Minister Mulroney that redress had to be settled through negotiations with the NAJC, and that, to be acceptable to Japanese Canadians, an agreement had to incorporate individual compensation in a range close to that set out by the NAJC. Later we learned in unofficial conversations with government staff that Bouchard, when he examined the redress file, could not believe that Japanese Canadians had not been compensated. In one decisive act, Bouchard had seemed to accomplish what the three Conservative ministers before Weiner had sworn to us was impossible. To his credit, we knew that Weiner, who was passionate about the human rights focus of the issue, favoured a negotiation process. We could only conclude that he was fortunate in forging an alliance with Bouchard, a minister who had the necessary personal ties to the prime minister.

In his brief account of redress in *On the Record*, Bouchard says that redress had special importance for him when he first reviewed the files of the secretary of state. Summarizing the injustices faced by Japanese Canadians, and acknowledging that the monies received through their material dispossession "had been used to pay for the camps" in which they were confined, he had concluded: "I could see in this the proof that there was no political structure in Canada, federal or otherwise, that would be safe from arbitrary decisions and abuses of civil liberties." He goes on to say that the "opponents" of redress in Ottawa continually pointed to the "terrifying precedent" it would set, primarily because Japanese Canadian dispossession "was not the only skeleton in the federal closet." There was the head tax levied on Chinese Canadians, the internment of Ukrainian Canadians and the "arrest, without proof, charges, or trial, of 453 Québécois, which a federal law had authorized during the October Crisis." He implies that in the face of some resistance, perhaps from his own cabinet colleagues, he had asked the prime minister — who wanted a redress settlement before the forthcoming election — to have Gerry Weiner negotiate with the NAJC. This action would explain his presence at our meeting in Montreal.

The Strategy Committee began negotiations with Gerry Weiner and his staff the next morning at another location, the Delta Chelsea Hotel. Two days and 17 hours later — at 10:56 p.m. on my watch, as I noted — we had worked out all the elements in what became the redress agreement of September 22, 1988. The moment was captured in Cassandra Kobayashi's photograph of a handshake across the table between Art Miki and Gerry Weiner. The agreement included $21,000 for each individual Japanese

Canadian whose civil rights had been violated between 1942 and April 1, 1949, the day when the last of the restrictions on movement was lifted. This figure was $1,000 more per person than the recommended figure for Japanese Americans, and the difference was meant to signify, albeit symbolically, the more severe treatment of Japanese Canadians. Another $15 million would be used to establish a "community fund" that included $12 million for community projects and $3 million to implement the settlement. The agreement also offered pardons, upon application, for those convicted under the War Measures Act during the same period, as well as Canadian citizenship to those who had lost it through deportation — an offer extended to their offspring, who would otherwise have been born in Canada. The call to dismantle the War Measures Act, an important component of the NAJC's demands, had lost its relevance by August 1988. Not long before, the government had repealed the Act and replaced it with the Emergencies Act.

After the Montreal negotiation session, the Strategy Committee entered a long period of waiting. Sworn to secrecy, we were told to wait until the government could find the opportune moment for the official announcement after the House of Commons reconvened in September. As the days passed in September, we lived with an omnipresent fear (at least I did) that the agreement could be nullified by unforeseeable political manipulations in cabinet or in the prime minister's office.

The controversy raging at the time was the proposed free trade agreement with the United States. This agreement would prove to be a crucial sign of major shifts in the social and political landscape of Canada following Japanese Canadian redress. For several days in September, we held our breaths while the free trade issue was hotly debated in the House of Commons. Then there was a hiatus — and finally, September 22, 1988, was proclaimed the official date for the ratification of the redress agreement.

ON THE ROAD TO BECOMING "CANADIAN"

IF THE 1977 centennial of Japanese Canadians was a critical turning point in the formation of the redress movement, changes in the boundaries of their identity were evident some years before. By the early 1970s, the wartime group whose members had been stripped of their rights because they were "of the Japanese race" found themselves in quite different social relations with other Canadians. No longer considered "enemy aliens" who had to be expunged from the nation, they had emerged as an exemplary minority, still racialized but now seen through a new concern called "multiculturalism." What had happened?

From once having used the language of race in an attempt to maintain the purity of its English and French colonial origins, the Canadian nation and its governments had to adjust to a new climate of respect for human rights, which had become prominent in the wake of the civil rights movement. In more pragmatic terms, it had to manage a new politics of cultural difference, as various groups challenged the status and power of English and French Canadians. This situation was complicated by the unusual decline in the numbers of European immigrants at a time when more immigrants were needed in the labour force. Eva Mackey in *The House of Difference* describes the social conditions then:

> During the 1960s the government made several attempts to de-racialize the immigration selection process, and yet still maintain control and selectivity. The Conservatives changed the selection criteria, replacing ethnicity and country of origin with questions about skills, education and training. By 1967 [the year of the Canadian Centennial], the economic boom was in full swing and the demand for skilled labour was high; yet European sources for that labour were dwindling. Changes were made to immigration law, now to be set up on a point system, which allowed in Asian and other Third World skilled immigrants. By the mid-1970s more immigrants came from the Third World than from Europe.

The unprecedented demographic shift — ironic, in light of the determination to limit and even prohibit immigration from Asian countries throughout the century — meant that Japanese Canadians, a relatively small group, were seen as part of an expanding population of "Asian Canadians" and thus as one of the elements in the federal government's efforts to manage cultural difference.[2] It would not be long before Japanese Canadians

---

2   I use the term "Asian Canadian" for convenience here, but am aware of its limits. At the time only a handful of people, mostly activists and some writers and artists, would have thought of such an identity formation. It was more common for various groups to distinguish themselves from each

would be seen as one of the "visible minorities" (the federal government's euphemism for those racialized as not-white) and, as such, one of the target groups of a proliferating series of multicultural policies.

This turnabout was strange for Japanese Canadians — at least it was for me. As if overnight, the "Japanese" associations that had been anathema in the early postwar years took on a new currency. By then, in my family — and I believe the pattern holds elsewhere — the trauma of dispersal had been written over by the story of B.C. as our "other" past. It was through this layering that the process of assimilation into (white) Canada had produced a narrative of new lives — a narrative in which to grow children. For my family, the new car, the new house in the developing west end of Winnipeg, and the excursions to enjoy picnics and concerts became the trappings in which the uprooting took on the hazy gauze of something to be put to sleep. In the mythical east — in this case, the prairies and Ontario — lay the geographical sites where identities could be reinvented into a transparent "Canadianness," which meant acceptance and invisibility for Japanese Canadians in a (white) nation that had formerly rejected them.

Once the power of the Japanese-speaking issei waned, and the drive to assimilate supplanted the anxiety of mass dispersal, the west coast became a place to avoid — at least for the many Japanese Canadians who chose not to return. My childhood memory was shaped by an ambivalent relationship to the west coast: on the one hand, in family stories it was portrayed as a lush landscape, with fruit trees forever dangling with apples, peaches and pears, its streams and rivers teeming with salmon, incomparable beaches and sunsets; on the other hand, it was remembered as a place rife with white supremacists, its media hysterical in their call to expel all "Japs," and its politicians constantly mouthing "Yellow Peril" slogans. Both representations were extremes, but they were intriguing enough to draw me to Vancouver when I decided to leave Winnipeg in 1967. My parents feared that I would be the object of racist violence.

---

other, as for instance, Chinese Canadians and Japanese Canadians, a situation that reflected a lack of perceived commonality and even animosities stretching far back in time. The term did not become part of a collective cultural struggle until the late 1980s, perhaps signified most vividly by the exhibit curated by Paul Wong, *Yellow Peril Re-Considered* (1990). One earlier instance is the publication *Inalienable Rice*, edited collaboratively by a small group of Chinese and Japanese Canadian writers, the nucleus of which would help initiate the Asian Canadian Writers Workshop.

What I found in Vancouver were only remnants of racism toward Japanese Canadians, but even these remnants were quickly disappearing as the city began to reflect the growing presence of Asian Canadians. The cultural sphere was also changing in the new language of "ethnicity" and "cultural difference." But this change was not without its disruptions for Japanese Canadians. The politics of identity that marked the 1970s brought an unprecedented paradox into their lives. After two decades of enduring the pressure to assimilate in what has been called an "anglo-conformity" era, a language of multiculturalism now encouraged them to value their history and to affirm the generational linkages that tied them together. From being social pariahs in the 1940s, "Japanese Canadians" were now reborn as model "citizens," whose rapid upward social mobility in the aftermath of the mass uprooting demonstrated their loyalty to the nation.

This representation was the one foregrounded in Prime Minister Lester B. Pearson's speech at the opening of the Japanese Canadian Cultural Centre in Toronto, on June 7, 1964. The Cultural Centre was a monument to the re-establishment of Japanese Canadians, the concrete evidence that they had "recovered" from the trauma of the mass uprooting. Yet Pearson's language — despite his praise for Japanese Canadians — is carefully guarded. In his comments, "Canadians of Japanese ancestry" were seen as producing "the Japanese way of life" on the west coast. And when Pearson spoke about internment, he used language that echoed what many Japanese Canadians would have understood as the "blessing in disguise" myth. In this myth, the internment was a "blessing" because it forced Japanese Canadians out of their ethnic ghettos on the west coast and enabled them to enter mainstream Canada. One paragraph is especially revealing:

> In 1942 ... following the unhappy outbreak of war between our two countries, the coastal area of British Columbia was declared a protected area. People of Japanese origin were required to leave. That action by the Canadian government — though taken under the strains, and fears and pressures of war — was a black mark against Canada's traditional fairness and devotion to the principles of human rights. We have no reason to be proud of this episode, but it had one compensation. Relocation brought to the attention of other parts of Canada the strong character and the fine qualities of *our Japanese citizens and settlers.* Their self-reliance and energy

and their varied contribution to Canadian development were a revelation to the rest of Canada. Perhaps even more important, the distribution — even though forceful — over the whole country undoubtedly hastened the full integration of Japanese Canadians into Canadian life.

Some years later, on October 25, 1976, another Liberal prime minister, Pierre Elliott Trudeau, also extended an acknowledgement of the unjust treatment of Japanese Canadians. But this time it would be offered, not in Canada to the Japanese Canadians who were directly affected, but in Japan to the Japanese government. Beside the obvious lack of tact, Trudeau's speech showed that the "Canadians of Japanese ancestry" who, to Pearson, had been integrated into Canadian society, in Trudeau's eyes were still "Japanese." (Trudeau would later take a position against compensation, and perhaps his perception of Japanese Canadians as "Japanese" explains his thinking.)

Trudeau began by highlighting the 1977 centennial but mistakenly identified the first settler, Manzo Nagano, as a "nisei" rather than "issei." Moreover, he assumed that Nagano had been "born in Japan in that momentous year [100 years before, in 1877] in British Columbia." Nagano was recognized by Japanese Canadians as the first Japanese settler in Canada. After referring to the "record of intolerance in Pacific Canada in the decades around the turn of the century," Trudeau addressed the mass uprooting:

> No more exemplary was the decision taken by the federal government in the heat and fright of World War II to evacuate Japanese Canadians inland from coastal communities and to deprive so many of their civil rights.
>
> In the past 30 years, however, the record has been a much happier one. In that period Nisei have been accepted with enthusiasm into Canadian communities and have demonstrated again and again their talents and their skills. In the highest ranks of business, academia, and the public service are found persons with Japanese names. A number of them are so well known as to be virtual national celebrities.

Then, in what was either a serious faux pas or a simple misreading of history, Trudeau went on "to thank Japan, on behalf of all Canadians, for the contribution made to Canada by the men and women of Japanese origin who have shown through their courage, their tenacity, their industry, and their skills what gifted Canadians they are. Their contribution to Canada is out of all proportion to their numbers and we are grateful to them for their many qualities."

In both of these public acknowledgements, first by Pearson in Toronto and later by Trudeau in Tokyo, Japanese Canadians were portrayed according to the dominant discourse of the political centre. In neither case was there an attempt to understand the position of the Japanese Canadians whose rights had been violated. Pearson was intent on restoring the image of Canada as the upholder of human rights, and in this sense he considered the erasure of the "black mark" to have been accomplished in the assimilation of Japanese Canadians into the body of the nation. In his logic, their dispersal — "even though forceful" — created the opportunity to prove themselves worthy of Canadian citizenship. Thus, the "unhappy" war had a happy ending. Pearson covered over the personal and collective suffering that was the more direct consequence of the mass uprooting and dispossession, and he failed to recognize the government policy of having those interned pay for their own internment through the forced liquidation of their properties, businesses and belongings. And even though he began by identifying Japanese Canadians as "Canadians," as his speech continued they reverted to being "Japanese." Notably, in this shifting language, they could never be considered unqualified "Canadians." The reference to "full integration" remained a fantasy that reconfirmed the dominance of the (white) majority, the group on whose behalf Pearson spoke.

Trudeau, on the other hand, paid more attention to personal merit and achievement, measuring the rise of Japanese Canadians in terms of an upward class mobility — a good liberal principle — that allowed a few to become "national celebrities." But for Trudeau, as for Pearson, "Canada" as a nation was not accountable for the racialized actions through which Japanese Canadians became "enemy aliens" and were dispossessed. Instead, their incorporation into the nation and their acceptance "with enthusiasm" by (white) Canadians became the achievement of the "nisei" themselves, who "demonstrated again and again their talents and their skills." It was this achievement, rather than any change in the social and political values of the government, that resulted in their social integration into the nation.

Tellingly, in both statements, the model "Japanese Canadian" citizens were made visible in the representational boundaries of the prime ministers' assumptions. In the process, the Canadian nation was not only protected from scrutiny but was imagined as the receptacle of former "strangers" who, in being assimilated, had been remade as "citizens" of a liberal democracy. The decision to uproot and intern "Canadians" who had not committed any crimes against the state was made, for Pearson, "under the strains, and fears and pressures of war," and for Trudeau, "in the heat and fright of World War II." The myth that the internment was simply the end product of wartime "hysteria" elided the more calculated actions of the cabinet of Mackenzie King, particularly the plan to remove Japanese Canadian communities from the west coast through policies that prescribed dispossession, dispersal and deportation. In the cabinet's reasoning, the destruction of these communities was, in the long run, good for Japanese Canadians because it enabled them to enter Canadian society — as if they had been on the "outside" of it before. Japanese Canadians had been "inside" the nation for more than a century.

Although the redress agreement negotiated by the NAJC in 1988 would not have been achievable within the discourse of the unofficial acknowledgements offered by Pearson and Trudeau, the socially sanctioned status of Japanese Canadians opened up surprising new possibilities for their identity formation in the 1970s. This change, in turn, led in the 1980s to an empowerment process unprecedented in their history. Once their wartime treatment was seen as a "black mark" in Canadian history, the injustices they had endured began to call for more social and political recognition. Such recognition could even strengthen national coherence, particularly in demonstrating the capacity of the liberal nation to address its racist past. In a strange twist, as the new politics of difference threatened to destabilize Canadian nationalism in the late 1970s and early 1980s, the "Japanese Canadian example" took on a political visibility through which Canadian citizenship, and thus the nation, could be strengthened. It was out of this recent history that the power — as well as the language — of redress assumed the force of a social movement that would win the approval of mainstream Canadians.

REDRESSING THE JAPANESE CANADIAN SUBJECT

THE FEDERAL MULTICULTURALISM policy of 1971 led to the establishment of a Multiculturalism Directorate in the office of the secretary of state (now the Department of Canadian Heritage). New funding for groups who were identified as the "other Canadians" — that is, other than the two founding groups, English and French Canadians, and non-Natives — resulted in the growth of national ethnic associations and the move toward a recognition of ethnic alliances. The Canadian Ethnocultural Council, a national organization that received funding from the federal government and that consisted of a major coalition of national ethnic associations, was formed in this context. The NAJC, one of its members, received CEC endorsement throughout the redress movement. As these associations shaped their own interests to align with federal government expectations and funding guidelines — guidelines that then included very attractive operating grants — certain individuals came to be recognized by government officials and politicians as representatives of their "communities," even though some of these individuals had little contact with a grassroots community as such. Far too often, these ethnic "leaders" assumed the role of "culture brokers" who became government advisors and participated in the politics of multiculturalism, often seeking funds through their political connections. It was in this climate that George Imai was known by administrators and politicians in the Multiculturalism Directorate, and most likely this recognition helped him secure the large redress grant from the directorate.

From the perspective of the language of multiculturalism, the decision by Japanese Canadians to mark 1977 as their centennial year was understandable. What better way to reclaim their history in Canada than to assume the national narrative of immigration, settlement and community building that had received great attention during the Canadian centennial year only 10 years earlier? This was the social milieu in which the Japanese Canadian Centennial Project (JCCP), of which I was a member, came together in the early 1970s. In our photo exhibit *A Dream of Riches: The Japanese Canadians, 1877-1977*, which toured Canada during the centennial year and was published in book form a year later, we sought to break the silence of the past and to narrate Japanese Canadian history through its photographic traces.

Given the public image of Japanese Canadians as the model minority, the chances were less than slim that the principle of individual compensation would have been considered seriously by the federal government. The political solution — the one that could bring the maximum ideological benefits to the government with the minimum economic cost — would be some form of memorialization. Such a government policy would have been a benign but socially effective way to counter the growing calls for redress for other injustices — prominent among them the internment of Ukrainian Canadians in World War I and the Chinese Canadian head tax. The opportunity came with the *Equality Now!* report, but the government, through its then multiculturalism minister, David Collenette, responded with a meagre proposal to establish a "justice institute" with a grant of $5 million to memorialize the internment of Japanese Canadians.

It is revealing that before Collenette became involved, the question of redress had been considered part of the mandate of Mark MacGuigan, the minister of justice. In a news article in June 1983, MacGuigan acknowledged that his government had been thinking of some form of redress for Japanese Canadians. MacGuigan is cited as saying: "The government is generally looking at the matter." He referred to "an exchange of letters" between his government and Japanese Canadians. There were also rumours, proven to be true but which the NAJC could not verify at the time, that MacGuigan had ordered an economic-losses study of Japanese Canadian internment. Unfortunately, because cabinet documents are inaccessible to the public for a lengthy period of time, the substance and conclusions of this study were kept secret for years.

In 1990, two years after the redress settlement had been reached, *Vancouver Sun* reporter Kevin Griffin followed up on a failed attempt by a colleague to access the study in 1983. He applied to the federal Access to Information officer to get permission to examine government documents pertaining to the redress settlement. In 1992, after several attempts and complaints, Griffin was sent a package of documents from the Department of Justice. In the 665 pages he received, the MacGuigan report was noted, but all of its specific details and relevant discussions about redress were excised under the authority of Section 69 (1) of the Access to Information Act. Despite the irritating blanks, enough information remained visible to verify that, as early as 1983, the government was concerned about the potential for substantial compensation should the redress movement gain momentum. The Department of Justice was also closely monitoring developments in the United States subsequent to the U.S. commission's recommendation of $20,000 compensation for each Japanese American incarcerated. In one memo, dated June 20, 1983, J. N. LaBarre, executive assistant to the deputy minister in the Department of Justice, wrote to B. L. Strayer, assistant deputy minister, Public Law, saying that the minister "has requested to know how the amount of compensation recommended by the U.S. Commission on Wartime Relocation and Internment of Civilians (see attached clippings) compares to the amount of compensation paid in the past by the Canadian government to individual Japanese Canadians relocated during World War II." Inquiring whether "the internal review of the Japanese-Canadian question" has been started, he added: "We should also report to the Minister fairly soon on whether we have set out a work plan, and we should also institute an approach towards the review of the considerable Justice files relating to Japanese-Canadians."

Although the comments relating to the economic-losses study were removed from the documents, it is likely that the figures would have been in the range of those in the Price Waterhouse study undertaken by the NAJC in 1985. What is also significant is that the government advisors were working in anticipation of a response to the redress recommendation in the *Equality Now!* report — a report that focused on systemic forms of racism preventing non-white Canadian subjects, identified as "visible minorities," from gaining equal access to opportunities and resources. The conjunction of the experience of racism and the violation of rights made the "Japanese Canadian example" a central part of the report, and perhaps resulted in transferring the issue of redress from the Department of Justice to the Multiculturalism Directorate in the office of the secretary of state. If prior to the release of *Equality Now!* the minister of justice, Mark MacGuigan, was deemed the relevant minister, after the report the authority began to reside with the minister for multiculturalism, David Collenette. Whether the move was strategic or pragmatic is difficult to ascertain, but what it did was re-situate the consideration of redress in government circles on apparently more tenuous grounds.

At the NAJC's November 1985 meeting in Toronto, council members debated the question of which minister should be approached to negotiate redress. On one side were those who felt that since redress was a justice issue, we should meet with the minister of justice, not with the minister of multiculturalism, as we were doing at the time. As long as our "case for redress" was considered only as a multicultural issue, we would be treated only as a group, not as individuals. After all, we wanted to stress the violation of individual rights. On the other side were those who recognized the power of multiculturalism discourse in bringing to prominence the issue of redress for Japanese Canadians. Because it was seen as a multiculturalism issue, the NAJC had managed to establish strong connections with politicians, the media and many powerful ethnic-minority groups in Canada. Moreover, any attempt to open the doors to the Department of Justice might disturb the momentum that had already been built up through the movement. The NAJC decided to stick with the Multiculturalism Directorate, assuming that the Department of Justice would nevertheless be involved in any negotiated settlement.

On the government's side, it may have appeared feasible and politically efficient, as early as the spring of 1984, to respond to *Equality Now!* with a proposal intended to close the redress issue at the same time. Prolonging the issue, in light of the U.S. commission's position in favour of individual compensation, would mean a more costly settlement in the future. Collenette's response, as evident in the speaking notes dated June 1984, prepared for him by his advisors, was to avoid redress through a carefully worded refusal to issue an "acknowledgement" (which would have been an admission of responsibility for redress) and the gesture to establish a "justice institute," not for Japanese Canadians but for all Canadians. Collenette's comments, however, shed light on the contradictory implications for Japanese Canadians of the eventual settlement in 1988.

The Government of Canada:

I.   Regrets that at times throughout our history Canadians representing minority communities have been victims of discrimination and intolerance;

II. Expresses its regret regarding the deprivation and hardship suffered by most members of the Japanese-Canadian community during the Second

World War and in its immediate aftermath, and in particular by the Issei generation;

III. Takes pride that the Canadian Charter of Rights and Freedoms in the Constitution Act, 1982 now affords members of minority communities protection against the recurrence of such treatment.

In addition, the Government will establish with a $5 million endowment, a trust to be known as "The Canadian Foundation for Racial Justice." This foundation will serve as a continuing and dynamic memorial to the courage and perseverance of the Issei generation of the Japanese-Canadian community, and support initiatives developed by concerned Canadians to combat systemic racism in our society. The Foundation will be a charitable organization, at arms-length from Government with a Board of Directors composed of highly respected Canadians, representative of our racial diversity.

Clearly the government wanted to avoid responsibility for redress. It is highly possible that legal advisors in the Department of Justice warned against the use of the term "acknowledgement" or even "apology" and strongly advised the use of the noncommittal, non-accountable "regret." The statement also elided the specific aspects of Japanese Canadian internment through the vague and general "throughout our history," which neutralized the wartime experiences of still-living Japanese Canadians. And when their "community" was mentioned, no reference was made to the violation of their citizenship rights, the confiscation and sale of their properties, the use of monies they received to pay the costs of their own incarceration, their forced dispersal after the war, and their deportation by the thousands to postwar Japan.

In singling out the "Issei generation," the statement denied that the majority of those interned were Canadian-born nisei. These were the citizens who bore the full force of "democracy betrayed": they believed in Canadian democracy and acted accordingly, some of them serving with distinction in the Second World War. Even more disturbing, the example of Japanese Canadians allowed the government to "[take] pride" that the past injustices would not be repeated in the future. The implication was that the mass uprooting, though unfortunate, had enabled the nation to improve itself, and that the "hardship and deprivation" of Japanese Canadians belonged to a past that could be put to rest because of the new Canadian Charter of Rights and Freedoms. Therefore, it was, then, logical that the government would set up a monument to its own redeemed state; in the form of some amorphous "memorial" foundation that would "combat systemic racism in our society." At the same time, the government was "proud" of its new consciousness that would protect "members of minority communities." Although the statement admitted to "systemic racism in our society," for the Japanese Canadians who were praised for their "courage and perseverance" but whose wartime internment was glossed over, such language was both familiar and disappointing. What remains ironic, however, is the apparent political intent of the statement to read the injustices inflicted on Japanese Canadians into a supposedly renewed Canadian nation. It is this intent, and the hollowed-out language it produced, that gave redress its compelling social and political value.

By continuing to call for a process of negotiations, the NAJC was able to withstand the pressure to accept a token settlement. The government eventually came to accept the principle of individual compensation, despite public proclamations by a series of ministers that this was impossible. Now, two decades later, it is clearer just how dependent the 1988 redress agreement was on the language of citizenship and human rights. As a social justice issue, redress drew from the language of the civil rights movement of the 1960s and 1970s. The internment itself was transformed in the process, from what had been conceived as an unfortunate consequence of wartime hysteria to a major instance of injustice in the country's backyard. It was this injustice that had to be redressed. This point became the rallying cry of the large National Coalition for Japanese Canadian Redress that mushroomed into existence in the fall of 1987 in the aftermath of Crombie's rejection of individual compensation. The coalition, a broad cross-section of Canadians — well-known politicians, labour and union leaders, civil rights advocates, community and religious organizations, educators, writers and many other publicly recognized individuals — soon proved that Japanese Canadian redress had become a national story. This backing of mainstream "citizens" became the prelude to the Ottawa redress rally in April 1988. In a highly uncharacteristic mobilization of Japanese Canadians, a large proportion of whom were seniors, this event turned out to be the last one in the redress campaign. Gerry Weiner, the fourth Conservative federal minister to take on the redress portfolio, showed up to speak at the rally, his first public appearance in his new role. Four months later, in August, he endorsed the government's historic agreement with the NAJC.

SETTLEMENT DAY

AT THE PACKED PRESS conference immediately following the official signing of the redress agreement between NAJC President Art Miki and Prime Minister Brian Mulroney, on September 22, 1988, Miki spoke about the timing of the settlement. He did so less in relation to the causal language of politics, than in the spiritual language of an event that is both inside and outside of time — through the subjective trajectory of the Japanese Canadians he spoke for:

> As far as our community is concerned, I think that we have to realize that there's a time and a place when things happen, and sometimes you have to wait for it. And we waited patiently, and many of us have worked on this together for that long [four and a half years] without giving up hope that someday there would be a time and a place. And I think that the time and the place happens to be here today.

The patience that Miki emphasized referred to the long period of public negotiations with five federal ministers — Collenette, Murta, Jelinek, Crombie and finally Weiner — all of them part of the political machinery through which redress arrived at a "time and place." For Miki, a larger vision was confirmed in the long time that was taken to achieve the settlement for Japanese Canadians. The persistence of their belief that a "just and honourable" redress agreement must be negotiated with the NAJC had enabled them to "wait patiently" for the right moment to arrive. No one in the press gallery responded to the subjective dimension of Miki's comment, its relationship to the Japanese Canadians who had engaged in such a strenuous movement. Instead, a reporter immediately pounced on the more restricted understanding of time and place. By accepting the redress settlement, he asked Miki, "Do you think you're being used at all for political purposes and does that bother you?"

I remember being astonished by the question, from a supposedly not-naive reporter in the press gallery. Hadn't the redress movement been, from the moment the NAJC submitted its brief *Democracy Betrayed* to the federal government on November 21, 1984, undertaken as a political movement? In negotiating a settlement package that corresponded to the NAJC's list of demands, hadn't the NAJC engaged in a political exchange? Although the question did not appear to spring from any ill will toward Miki or the NAJC, raising the issues of "being used" and being "bothered" seemed to be an attempt to elicit the "guilt" that Miki had earlier stated was dispelled through the settlement. It was as if the reporter were speaking from — and in that moment speaking for — a social sphere that had identified the Japanese Canadians represented by Miki as the "model minority" who were being "used" by the political system. But hadn't Japanese Canadians, through the NAJC, "used" the political system to negotiate a redress agreement?

From the perspective of the political moment, a skeptical observer might conclude that the government too benefited from the redress settlement. It could take credit for resolving a major human rights issue and simultaneously affirm the multicultural discourse that gave the nation coherence. My astonishment at the reporter's question revealed my own distance from its mundane intention; perhaps it was no more than an off-the-cuff remark by a reporter who was simply trying to be provocative. There was no follow-up question, and its deeper ramifications vanished in the other questions following.

What the memory brings back for me now, or what it exposes, are the disjunctive spheres of symbolic meanings that were not so obvious to me on that day. In the public celebratory moment of that "time and place," a political resolution had been achieved. The violations inflicted on Japanese Canadians during and after World War II were officially ameliorated by a parliamentary acknowledgement and the comprehensive redress agreement signed with the NAJC. This was the gist of the discourse around human rights and citizenship articulated by both Art Miki and the federal government representative, the minister for multiculturalism, Gerry Weiner. But when Miki went on to thank everyone who supported Japanese Canadians, he did so on behalf of all Japanese Canadians, saying to those present, "for us this is a great day."

By invoking the collective "us," Miki, as president of the national organization for Japanese Canadians, had in mind all those whose rights were violated in the 1940s, and perhaps even further back, to all those, issei and nisei, who had been disenfranchised in the early years of settlement. This "great day" was the culmination of a long history of struggle, reaching back many decades, and coming just in time for the aging members of the community. In contrast, the reporter's question about being "used" was situated only in contemporary politics, a time in which "Japanese Canadian uprooting" had become the hot topic. In "being proud to be here today" and being "proud to be a Canadian," Miki spoke out of a long history in which to be "Japanese Canadian" was to be marked as an excluded figure in the Canadian nation.

In the crossing of these times, however — the historical resonances governing Miki's language and the media-based conception of time held by the reporter — we can begin to unravel the complexities of the broader sphere of negotiations operative in the redress agreement. It would be simple enough to say that redress would have had a much deeper significance for Japanese Canadians than a reporter at a press conference could be expected to understand. But the misunderstanding apparent in his question to Miki, as spontaneous as it may have been at the time, returns us to the question of redress as a gift and the complications that this question reveals.

THE MOMENT OF ACKNOWLEDGEMENT:
DISSONANCE AND HARMONY

LOOKING BACK TO the redress movement and settlement, the social theorist Kirsten Emiko McAllister clarifies its reciprocal nature. For such an action to happen, she says, there needed to be a congruency in the language of redress between a general liberal discourse founded on citizenship status and the Japanese Canadian subjects whose social and political identity had been founded on the racialized exclusion from this discourse. To cross this divide — a decades-long divide that had painfully harboured the bundled nerve-ends of dislocated memories — those Japanese Canadians who sought redress, McAllister argues, "realized that it was politically necessary to write themselves into the nation's public sphere. They needed to be seen as Canadian citizens whose parents and grandparents were also Canadian as opposed to new immigrants, Asians, Japanese, or the Yellow Peril."

To "write themselves" into the Canadian nation, Japanese Canadians, especially the NAJC, mobilized the power of language. By telling the story of the wartime internment in the framework of redress, the NAJC found a public medium in which individuals who had been wronged could come to speak through a collective voice. Without this voice, they could not have negotiated the necessary social and political space for redress to take on visibility — and thereby to assume a strong enough presence to call forth a response from those who hold the reins of political power.

In the process, Japanese Canadians were themselves formed by the call for redress. They shaped their unredressed identity out of the racialized national boundaries that had disenfranchised them since the issei first arrived in Canada, and that had led to their incarceration during the war as the "enemy" within. To read themselves into that nation as "citizens," they had to situate themselves in the narrative of nation building as a collective of "citizens" to which they belonged through the rights and responsibilities of citizenship.

In this historically rich sphere, the reporter's question about being used was both out of sync with the spirit of Miki's language and a vivid reminder of the more immediate limits of the settlement. In reading themselves into the nation as the agents of redress, the Japanese Canadians who were now named "Canadians of Japanese ancestry" in the agreement signed by the NAJC were also incorporated into the nation as subjects who had been redressed. While they enjoyed the euphoria of their achievement, the nation, represented by the prime minister and the House of Commons, was symbolically redeemed by its acceptance of redress. In this interchange, the "Japanese Canadian" identity that was constituted by a history of injustices at the hands of the nation was given up as a gift to the nation and therefore ceased to exist in the conditions of its desire for a resolved future.

In the 16 years since the redress settlement, Canada has undergone major changes. The heightened language of citizenship rights that was heralded in the 1988 redress settlement seems to have lost much of its currency, though new meanings of citizenship may be emerging as the borders of nations become zones of conflict and contradictory loyalties. The distance from 1988 to the present can be measured through the free trade debates that raged that year, in the midst of the final phase of the redress movement. It was only when there was a pause in the debates, on September 22, that the government moved quickly to organize the official announcement of the agreement. What became the Free Trade Agreement (FTA) and later the North American Free Trade Agreement (NAFTA) signalled the rapidly ascending power of globalizing processes that brought in their wake the neoliberal values of transnational corporations. The preoccupation of forging a national identity based on citizenship values was soon eclipsed by the arrival of a "new" economy in which the social and cultural formations of the nation in the Cold War era were increasingly seen as obsolete.

The destabilization of national identity in Canada was always a threat in the postwar period, but up until 1988 the efforts to produce and maintain a sense of national coherence had worked, to an extent. And here, yes, despite the relative insignificance of Japanese Canadians as a political presence — with a population of only 50,000 in 1988 — their call for redress could be of "use" in giving value to Canadian citizenship. In the 1980s alone, the question of redress, as we have seen, was raised at the hearings on the repatriation of the Canadian Constitution and its Charter of Rights and Freedoms (1982), was incorporated into the recommendations of an all-party task force on the effects of racism in Canada, *Equality Now!* (1983) and was associated with the passage of the Multiculturalism Act (1988). In short, the Japanese Canadian redress movement was implicated in major government initiatives that attempted to strengthen national identity at a time when its hold was rapidly loosening. Redress, in the limited political context of this moment, might encourage a revaluation of Canadian citizenship at a critical juncture in the federal government's efforts to mediate the emergence of the new global economy.

In his study of Canadian nationalist formations in *A Border Within*, Ian Angus begins by recognizing that the forces of globalization have "finished the English Canadian left-nationalist politics" and, along with it, the identity politics that was so prominent in previous decades. As he explains, "Throughout the period since the end of the Second World War until recent changes in both political culture and intellectual orientation that may be associated with the Free Trade Agreement and the North American Free Trade Agreement, 'identity' was the key term through which the will to maintain, or develop, an independent Canada was expressed." Without this "key term" as a mediating vehicle of public discourse, questions of equity, racism and cultural difference begin to be measured, not in relation to citizenship values, but in relation to the neoliberal agenda of global capitalism, wherein self-interest supersedes the collective good. In retrospect, then, Japanese Canadian redress was woven into a complex negotiation process — an event that redeemed the nation at a time of shifting formations and that brought to political resolution the historical injustices endured by Japanese Canadians.

THE NAJC DELEGATES in the guest gallery, after being told not to express themselves, defied parliamentary convention by standing to applaud when the prime minister issued the official acknowledgement. In this brief moment, they entered into an unprecedented exchange with the Canadian nation and simultaneously underwent a historical transfiguration with far-reaching implications. When they rose to clap their hands, they were no longer the same "Japanese Canadians" who had sat down in the guest gallery. In receiving the gift of redress from a nation that had stripped them of their rights in the 1940s, they also gave the gift of redress to a nation that had acknowledged the injustices they suffered as a consequence of that action. The receivers had become the givers. So what had happened to the receivers? When Japanese Canadians achieved their settlement — this "dream of justice," in the language of their movement — they gave their wartime experience as a gift to the official history of the nation. And in a reciprocal process, the "Japanese Canadian" identity that was forged in its negotiations with the Canadian nation, an un-redressed identity that was so intimately connected to the condition of "enemy alien," was released from its historical boundaries. The 20th-century history that had been carried in the living bodies of Japanese Canadians for over many decades had to be resolved — it was one of the givens in their negotiations with the nation — but in the singular event of redress, that history had to be surrendered. From that time on, "Japanese Canadian" entered a post-redress condition of new transformations and limitations.

The redress agreement of September 22, 1988, will remain a significant moment in the record of late 20th-century Canadian history, an unusual achievement by a small group of citizens who, because of a nation's violation of their citizenship rights, launched a movement to negotiate an acceptable settlement with the federal government. As impressive as this moment was, it meant much more for the Japanese Canadians named in the agreement, those "Canadians of Japanese ancestry" whose call for justice reached back a long time, to Tomey Homma's demand that his name be placed on the voters' list. The pride in citizenship that NAJC President Art Miki affirmed on September 22, 1988, although set in the quotidian sphere of the press conference following the settlement, reached beyond the moment — back and forth — to mediate long-standing issues of exclusion and alienation from the nation. When he told the press gallery, "for us this is a great day," he invoked the collective memory of all Japanese Canadians who had struggled against the restrictions placed on them throughout the 20th century. Many voices spoke through Art Miki's voice that day.

REFERENCES

Note: When a source for a document is not provided, the document comes from the author's personal papers.
BCSC = British Columbia Security Commission
DEA = Department of External Affairs
DL = Department of Labour
RCMP = Royal Canadian Mounted Police
NJCCA = National Japanese Canadian Citizens' Association
NAJC = National Association of Japanese Canadians

PREFACE

xii   *"exhibit unquestioned support for ..."* Roy L. Brooks, "The Age of Apology" 6.

INTRODUCTION

1   *"It is not enough ..."* Muriel Kitagawa, *This Is My Own* 286.

3   *"to require by order ..."* Cited in Ken Adachi, *The Enemy That Never Was* 217.

4   *"Mr. Speaker, nearly half..."* Cited in Roy Miki and Cassandra Kobayashi, *Justice in Our Time* 143.

4   *"On this date [May 19, 1942] ..."* BCSC Papers, RG 36/27, Volume 9, File 204, LAC.

6   *"it was sort of like slaves ..."* Manitoba Japanese Canadian Citizens' Association, *The History of Japanese Canadians in Manitoba* 9.

7   *"There are some nightmares . . ."* Joy Kogawa, *Obasan* 194.

9   *"a) $21,000 individual redress ..."* Cited in Miki and Kobayashi 138–9.

10   *"procedures to ensure ..."* "Highlights of the *Emergencies Act*," published by the Government of Canada; accessed July 23, 2003, www.ocipep.gc.ca/info_pro/

fact_sheets/general/PDF/english/L_high_emer.pdf.

11   *"I do appreciate the support ..."* Transcribed from a tape of the press conference, NAJC, Ottawa, September 22, 1988.

CHAPTER I
FRAMED BY RACE: A CANADIAN KNOT

13   *"Mythologies or national stories ..."* Sherene H. Razack, "When Place Becomes Race" 2.

14   *The Nisei educator Ted Aoki, speaking ...* Ted T. Aoki, "In the Midst of Slippery Theme-Words" 4–5.

15   *"It was," he concluded, "historically ..."* Forrest E. La Violette, *The Canadian Japanese and World War II* 43.

16   *"the day after he presented ..."* Ad Hoc Committee, *Japanese Canadian Redress: The Toronto Story* 77.

17   *In a brief introductory note, Hidaka says ...* All citations from Hidaka's study refer to Kunio Hidaka, *Legal Status of Persons of Japanese Race in Canada*, unpaginated.

17   *As a result, with the exception ...* For a well-documented history of Japanese Canadians' involvement in both world wars, see Roy Ito's *We Went to War*.

19   *"My principle objection to them ..."* Cited in W. Peter Ward, *White Canada Forever* 107.

19   *"In the minds of whites ..."* Ward 117.

20   *"on the participation of trade unions ..."* Michael Barnholden, "Anti-Asian Riot" 3.

21   *"With the 8,125 Japanese who entered ..."* Adachi 70.

21   *"would be several hundred ..."* Cited in Roy Miki and Scott McFarlane, *In Justice* 66.

21   *"By nightfall," Adachi writes, "when police ..."* Adachi 74.

22   *"signalled the virtual cessation ..."* Ninette Kelley and Michael Trebilcock, *The Making of the Mosaic* 152.

22   (footnote): *"The* Komagata Maru *arrived at ..."* Cited in Miki and McFarlane 72.

23   *"agreed to restrict the number ..."* Adachi 81.

23   *"belonging to any race deemed unsuitable ..."* Cited in Kelley and Trebilcock 137.

24   (footnote): *And whereas the standard of living ...* Cited in Adachi 141.

25   *"gave white groups the power ..."* Kay J. Anderson, *Vancouver's Chinatown* 25.

25   *Although Anderson focuses on ...* Anderson 37.

25   *"The main thing was this lack ..."* Cited in Japanese Canadian Centennial Project, *A Dream of Riches* 38.

26   *"The Naturalization Act, passed ..."* Andrea Geiger-Adams, "Writing Racial Barriers into Law" 3. A shorter version of Geiger-Adams' paper, "Pioneer Issei: Tomekichi Homma's Fight for the Franchise," is available in *Nikkei Images*, a publication of the Japanese Canadian National Museum.

26-7   *"The residence within the province ..."* Cited in Adachi 54; emphasis added.

27   *"From the time of William III ..."* Cunningham and Attorney-General for British Columbia v. Tomey Homma and Attorney-General for the Dominion of Canada,

On Appeal from the Supreme Court of British Columbia, Number 45 of 1901, House of Lords and Privy Council, December 17, 1902.

27-8 (footnote): *"that the doctrine it invoked ..."* Geiger-Adams 8.

28 *"We are relieved from the possibility ..."* Cited in Adachi 54.

28 *"The 200 men go not only ..."* Cited in Japanese Canadian Centennial Project, *A Dream of Riches* 40.

28 *"54 were killed ..."* Japanese Canadian Centennial Project 40.

28 *"We recognize the deadly ..."* Cited in Roy Ito, *We Went to War* 72–3.

29 *"passed by a margin ..."* Ito, *We Went to War* 73.

29 *"I cannot help thinking ..."* Cited in Adachi 156.

29 *"The [Marine and Fisheries] Department's ..."* Government of British Columbia, *Report on Oriental Activities Within the Province* 19.

29 *"By 1925,"* Adachi writes, *"the Department ..."* Adachi 142.

30 *"federal minister did not have ..."* Adachi 144.

30 *"A vote for any* CCF *candidate ..."* Cited in Adachi 182.

31 *"that clause XI of section 4 ..."* Government of Canada, *Minutes of Proceedings and Evidence, Special Committee on Elections and Franchise Acts, 1936.*

31-2 *"We have come to plead ..."* *Minutes of Proceedings and Evidence* 200.

32 *"the process of Canadianization ..."* *Minutes of Proceedings and Evidence* 201.

32 *"be like fish out of water ..."* *Minutes of Proceedings and Evidence* 200.

32 *"My colleagues here and I ..."* *Minutes of Proceedings and Evidence* 204.

32 *"anxious to serve Canada ..."* *Minutes of Proceedings and Evidence* 206.

33 *"of service to Canada by ..."* *Minutes of Proceedings and Evidence* 207.

33 (footnote): *"The Japanese American Citizens League ..."* Leslie T. Hatamiya, *Righting a Wrong* 140–41.

33 *"I found in Japan ..."* *Minutes of Proceedings and Evidence* 208.

34 *"Hundreds of young boys and girls ..."* *Minutes of Proceedings and Evidence* 210.

34 *"You all speak English ..."* *Minutes of Proceedings and Evidence* 212.

34 *"that the delegation presented ..."* *Minutes of Proceedings and Evidence* 215.

34 *"to know that these conditions ..."* *Minutes of Proceedings and Evidence* 221.

34 *"Why do you not agitate there ..."* *Minutes of Proceedings and Evidence* 216.

34 *"I think that is a most ..."* *Minutes of Proceedings and Evidence* 216.

35 *"When that day comes ..."* Thomas Reid, "Opposing Oriental Franchise in the Province of British Columbia" 10.

35 *"As a matter of fact ..."* Reid 13.

36 *"this dominion is primarily ..."* *Minutes of Proceedings and Evidence* 239.

36 *"it is British Columbia to-day ..."* *Minutes of Proceedings and Evidence* 240.

CHAPTER 2
REGULATING JAPANESE CANADIANS:
RACIALIZATION AND THE MASS UPROOTING

39 *"The sound policy and the best ..."* Mackenzie King's speech, in *Hansard*, is reproduced by Ken Adachi in *The Enemy That Never Was* (431–33). All citations are

from Canada, House of Commons, *Debates*, Volume VI, August 4, 1944, 5915–18.

40 *But regulated by the War Measures Act* ... For a discussion of the federal government's use of the War Measures Act in its treatment of Japanese Canadians and other Canadians, see Ann Sunahara, "The Abuse of Emergency Law in Canada: Is It Inevitable?"

42 *"United States policy appears* ..." Draft Memorandum, June 15, 1943, DL Papers, RG 27, Volume 655, File 23–2–11–1 pt. 1, LAC.

43 *"classified as a 'jap-hater'* ..." Sunahara, *The Politics of Racism* 105.

43 *"a decision made in January* ..." Interdepartmental Committee on Enemy Interests in Canada and Canadian Interests in Enemy Occupied Territories, undated, DL Papers, RG 27, Volume 655, File 23–2–11–1 pt. 1, LAC.

43 *"The Custodian has been vested* ..." Cited in Adachi 427–28; emphasis added.

43 *"as a protective measure* ..." From Order-in-Council PC 1665; cited in Adachi 426.

43 *"In property liquidation no distinction* ..." Interdepartmental Committee on Enemy Interests in Canada and Canadian Interests in Enemy Occupied Territories, undated, DL Papers, RG 27, Volume 655, File 23–2–11–1 pt. 1, LAC.

44 *"only a token uprooting* ..." Sunahara, *The Politics of Racism* 61.

45 *"'If I fail at this* ...'" Sunahara, *The Politics of Racism* 61; citing J. Tanaka, from an interview.

45 *"Official notices for removal* ..." Sunahara, *The Politics of Racism* 62.

45 *"It has just boiled down* ..." Muriel Kitagawa 90.

45-6 *"The first steps taken* ..." Editorial, *New Canadian*, March 3, 1942.

47 *"determination to co-operate with* ..." Japanese Canadian Citizens' Council, Minutes, March 29, 1942, NJCCA Papers, MG28 V7, Volume 1, File 1–2, LAC.

48 *"Mr. Murphy," their release said, "will also* ..." Japanese Canadian Citizens' Council, Minutes, March 31, 1942, NJCCA Papers, MG28 V7, Volume 1, File 1–2, LAC.

49 *"only other option* ..." Telegram, Austin Taylor, March 4, 1942, BCSC Papers, RG 36, Series 27, Volume 2, File 31, LAC.

51 *"'Evacuation' is the process of* ..." Raymond Y. Okamura, "The American Concentration Camps" 97.

51 *"security and defence* ..." Order-in-Council, PC 1665, March 4, 1942.

52 *"But these almost reassuring* ..." Adachi 252.

52-3 *"It was an evacuation* ..." Kogawa, *Obasan* 118.

53 *"victims of the cruel* ..." Canada, BCSC, *Removal of Japanese from Protected Areas* 2. Unless otherwise indicated, all citations are from 2.

53 *"It may be said that the foregoing* ..." Canada, BCSC, *Removal of Japanese from Protected Areas* 218.

54 *"unamenable disposition of mind* ..." Canada, BCSC, *Removal of Japanese from Protected Areas* 18.

54 *Documents in the B.C. Security Commission* ... BCSC Papers, RG36/27, Volume 16, File 613, LAC.

CHAPTER 3
IN DEFENCE OF RIGHTS: THE NISEI MASS EVACUATION GROUP

57   *"If Canada is supposed to be ..."* Robert K. Okazaki, *The Nisei Mass Evacuation Group and P.O.W. Camp* 101 6.

57   *"the evidence against him ..."* *Vancouver Sun*, October 30, 1948; cited in Ken Adachi 338.

58   *"On the first night in Vancouver ..."* Adachi 232.

59   (footnote): *The term is used to describe ...* Minutes, Japanese Canadian Citizens' Council, April 15, 1942, NJCCA Papers, MG28 V7, Volume 1, File 1–2, LAC.

59-60 *"Japanese began their disturbance ..."* "Jap Riot," *Vancouver Sun*, May 14, 1942.

60   *In Ottawa, Minister of Labour ...* *Vancouver Sun*, May 14, 1942.

60   *"failed to report to ..."* *Vancouver Sun*, May 14, 1942.

61   *"Our people have been disposed ..."* "Japs Are Poor Sportsmen, Indeed!" *Vancouver Sun*, May 14, 1942.

62   *"carried out to satisfy ..."* Okazaki x.

62   *"to show the present and future ..."* Okazaki vi.

62   (footnote): *His reclamation of the subjective ...* Readers who are interested in post-redress publications should consult Art K. Miki's *The Japanese Canadian Redress Legacy*, an account of all the projects funded by the Japanese Canadian Redress Foundation, the foundation established to administer the community fund that was part of the NAJC's redress agreement with the federal government.

62   *"Mass Evacuation ..."* Okazaki 6.

63   *"It is ... alleged that he ..."* BCSC Papers, RG36/27, Volume 16, File 613, LAC.

63   *"for this morning was not held ..."* Minutes, Japanese Canadian Citizens' Council, March 26, 1942, NJCCA Papers, MG28 V7, Volume 1, File 1–2, LAC.

64   *"That any person of the Japanese race ..."* BCSC Order No. 5, RCMP Papers, RG 18, Volume 3568, File C3129–1–5, LAC.

64   *"prosecutions and mass appearance ..."* S. T. Wood, Commissioner RCMP, to Louis St. Laurent, Minister of Justice, March 27, 1942, RCMP Papers, RG 18, Volume 3568, File C3129–1–5, LAC.

64   *"to go to-night."* Minutes, Japanese Canadian Citizens' Council, March 29, 1942, NJCCA Papers, MG28 V7, Volume 1, File 1–2, LAC.

65   *"Out from the next boat ..."* Okazaki 6.

65   *"I am envious of the ..."* Okazaki 4.

65   *"An issei woman, whose ..."* Harry Yonekura, "POW 348, Camp 101, Angler" 44. See also his essay, "The Courage to Resist: Angler and the Nisei Mass Evacuation Group" 20.

65   *"I knew that I could ..."* Yonekura 45.

66   *"140 west coast boys ..."* Robert (Yukio) Shimoda, Unpublished Diary, Robert Y. Shimoda Papers, University of British Columbia.

66   *"worked all night on ..."* Shimoda, Unpublished Diary.

66 *"state of anxious Japanese families ..."* Tameo Kanbara, "The Origin of Mass Group," np.

66-7 *"That we should be evacuated ..."* Copy of pamphlet provided to the author by Tameo Kanbara.

68 *"Honourable Sir ..."* Reproduced in Muriel Kitagawa, *This Is My Own* 39.

68-9 *"cold hearted doing job ..."* Shimoda, Unpublished Diary.

69 *"reported that Commissioner Mead ..."* Minutes, Japanese Canadian Citizens' Council, April 15, 1942, NJCCA Papers, MG28 V7, Volume 1, File 1–2, LAC.

71 *"individual movement of Japanese ..."* Ian Mackenzie to Austin Taylor, March 5, 1942, BCSC Papers, RG 36/27, Volume 2, File 31, LAC.

71 *"Legally, of course, the Nisei ..."* Ann Sunahara 66.

72 *"to the breaking up of ..."* S. T. Wood to H. L. Keenleyside, DEA, May 1, 1942, RCMP Papers, RG18, Volume 3568, File C3129–1–5, LAC.

72 *"British subjects, of Japanese ..."* S. T. Wood to Louis St. Laurent, Minister of Justice, March 27, 1942, RCMP Papers, RG18, Volume 3568, File C–3129–1–5, LAC.

72 *"Section 11 Order in Council ..."* A. MacNamara to Austin Taylor, March 27, 1942, RCMP Papers, RG18, Volume 3568, File C–3129–1–5, LAC.

73 *"to detain them [in reference ..."* C. H. Locke to A. M. Harper, April 14, 1942, BCSC Papers, RG36/27, Volume 2, File 53, LAC.

73 *"If they are interned under ..."* A. M. Harper to RCMP Commissioner Mead, April 24, 1942, BCSC Papers, RG 36/27, Volume 2, File 53, LAC; emphasis added.

74 *"Under Regulation 22, these ..."* D. C. Saul to Officer Commanding, RCMP, Vancouver, April 22, 1942, BCSC Papers, RG36/27, Volume 2, File 53, LAC.

75 *"in collaboration with the Security ..."* S. T. Wood to Commanding Officer, RCMP, Vancouver, April 30, 1942, BCSC Papers, RG36/27, Volume 2, File 53, LAC.

76 *"INTERNMENT OPERATIONS REQUIRE ..."* J. Barnes to F. J. Mead, May 14, 1942, BCSC Papers, RG36/27, Volume 2, File 53, LAC.

77 *"July 5th, 1942 ..."* BCSC Papers, RG 36/27, Volume 3, File 59, LAC.

78 *This position was endorsed by Mead ...* F. J. Mead to A. MacNamara, July 24, 1942, BCSC Papers, RG 36/27, Volume 2, File 53, LAC.

78 *"I feel that it is useless to keep ..."* F. J. Mead to Austin Taylor, August 1, 1942, BCSC Papers, RG 36/27, Volume 2, File 53, LAC.

78 *"weaken our position ..."* W. A. Eastwood to J. Shirras, August 3, 1942, BCSC Papers, RG 36/27, Volume 2, File 53, LAC.

78 *"without the slightest deviation ..."* J. Shirras to F. J. Mead, August 4, 1942, BCSC Papers, RG 36/27, Volume 2, File 53, LAC.

78 *He argued that they could help ...* See Yonekura, "The Courage to Resist" 22–23.

79 *"Life is very tense now ..."* Okazaki 14.

79 *"had agreed to become guinea ..."* Okazaki 17.

79-80 *"I was awakened early by ..."* Okazaki 19.

80 *"turned a fire hose on ..."* "Soldiers Bar Japanese from Immigration Building Area."

80 *"We grabbed the fire hose ..."* Okazaki 21.

80 *"denied that plaster had ..."* "Soldiers Bar Japanese from Immigration Building Area."

80-1 *"We obliterated the marble ..."* Okazaki 21–22.

81 *"riot was suppressed without ..."* "Jap Riot."

81 *"A tear gas canister was fired ..."* Okazaki 22.

81 *"Down on the street, the ..."* Okazaki 22.

82 *"a place called Yellowhead ..."* Ujo Nakano, *Within the Barbed Wire Fence* 14.

82 *"You see, these inmates were what were known ..."* Nakano 44–45.

83 *"out-spoken gambariya ..."* Nakano 66.

83 *"Primeval forest ..."* Nakano 71.

84 *"Since gambariya like M numbered ..."* Nakano 94.

84 *"while far from a microcosm of ..."* W. Peter Ward 114.

84 *"were imprisoned between March ..."* Ward 123.

84 *"outlaws and trouble-makers ..."* Kanbara, "The Origin of Mass Group," np.

85 *"are carefully nursing what they ..."* D. C. Saul to F. J. Mead, October 12, 1943, RCMP Papers, RG18, Volume 3564, File C–11–19–2–13, LAC.

85 *"would not care to see a lot of Japanese ..."* F. J. Mead to A. H. Brown, Deputy Minister, DL, October 15, 1943, RCMP Papers, RG18, Volume 3564, C–11–19–2–13, Volume 2, LAC.

85 *They were warned by internment camp officials ...* See Report to Under-Secretary of State for External Affairs, Pedro E. Schwartz, October 19, 1943, DEA Papers, RG 25, Volume 2937, File 2966D–40 Pt 1, LAC.

CHAPTER 4

DISPERSED: DISPOSSESSION AND RELOCATION

87 *"We are the billy-goats and ..."* Muriel Kitagawa, *This Is My Own* 96–97.

87 *"at the end of the year, the centers ..."* Commission on Wartime Relocation and Internment of Civilians, *Personal Justice Denied* 49.

88 *"that an admittedly loyal American citizen ..."* *Personal Justice Denied* 239.

88-9 *"for the security, defence, order ..."* Cited in Ken Adachi 419.

89 *At the critical federal cabinet meeting ...* See Ann Sunahara, "The Decision to Uproot Japanese Canadians," *The Politics of Racism* 27–48.

90 *"justly treated ..."* From MacKenzie King's official statement, cited by Forrest E. La Violette 47–48.

91 *Even the Co-operative Commonwealth Federation (CCF) party ...* For an analysis of the CCF's failure to support Japanese Canadians at the moment of uprooting, see Werner Cohn's "The Persecution of Japanese Canadians and the Political Left in British Columbia, December 1941-March 1942."

91 *"No Japs from the Rockies ..."* Cited in NAJC, *Democracy Betrayed* 13.

91 *On April 14, only six weeks after ...* See Sunahara, *The Politics of Racism* 101–5.

92 *"I believe that from these lands ..."* Ian Mackenzie to T. A. Crerar, December 7, 1942, Ian Mackenzie Papers, MG27IIIB5, Volume 25, File 70–25C, LAC.

92 *"Japanese in Vancouver ..."* "Jap Troubles Here Soon to Be Dispelled."

93 *"If it is humanly possible for a member ..."* Austin Taylor to A. MacNamara, April 4, 1942, DL Papers, RG27, Volume 174, 614.02: 11–1, Volume 4, LAC.

93   *"Mr. DesBrisay of the* B.C. *Security Commission ..."* Japanese Situation in British Columbia, DL Papers, RG27, Volume 169, File 614. 02: 11, Volume 1, LAC.

94   *"I am entirely in favour of this purchase ..."* Cited in Sunahara, *The Politics of Racism* 109.

94   *"Departmental policy to distribute the Japanese ..."* F. J. Mead to A. MacNamara, March 30, 1943, DL Papers, RG 27, Volume 169, File 614.02:11 Volume 1, LAC.

95   *"to inquire into the provision made ..."* Report of the Royal Commission Appointed Pursuant to Order-in-Council, PC #9498, January 14, 1944, BCSC Papers, RG36/27, Volume 34, File 2202, LAC. All subsequent citations from the report refer to this document.

97   *"Government involvement ..."* Mona Oikawa, "'Driven to Scatter Far and Wide'" 59.

98   *"policy of firing all women ..."* Oikawa 55.

98   *"another of these Japanese haters ..."* Report from Tashme by the Citizenship Defence Committee Toronto, May 2, 1946; cited in Oikawa 61.

98   *"whirlwind five-day tour ..."* Adachi 266.

98-9 *"This house, bought out of slender ..."* Kitagawa 182–83.

99   *"The proposed liquidation is of course ..."* Cited in Kitagawa 184.

99   *"Who would have thought that ..."* Kitagawa 185.

99   *"very principle for which ..."* Kitagawa 185.

100 (footnote): *"incredibly enough ..."* Adachi 231.

100 *Meanwhile, in Kaslo, site of one ...* For further details on the work of the Japanese Property Owners Association, see Adachi 322 ff. and Sunahara, *The Politics of Racism* 107 ff.

100 *"filed a petition against ..."* Adachi 322.

100 *"under instructions from the Secretary ..."* Cited in Adachi 322.

101 *"the Custodian was not a servant ..."* Adachi 323.

101 *"Hon. J. T. Thorson, minister ..."* Sunahara, *The Politics of Racism* 109.

102 *So it was that Irene (Kato) Tsuyuki ...* Roy Miki and Cassandra Kobayashi, *Justice in Our Time* 49.

102 *"government, which he had trusted ..."* Irene Tsuyuki, "The Second Uprooting" 41.

102 *At least that was the subtext of the Dispersal Notice ...* This Dispersal Notice, dated March 12, 1945, is reproduced in Miki and Kobayashi, *Justice in Our Time* 48.

104 *"the point whether some words ..."* Supreme Court of Canada, 1946, 267.

104 *"the equivalent of a statute ..."* Supreme Court of Canada, 1946, 274. For a more detailed account of the Japanese Canadian deportation issue, see Adachi 307–18, Sunahara 136–40 and Edith Fowke *They Made Democracy Work* 12–25.

104-5 *In 1945, the Japanese Canadian population...* The figures for population and deportation are taken from Audrey Kobayashi, *A Demographic Profile of Japanese Canadians and Social Implications for the Future* 6–7.

105 *"The government policy of forced ..."* Kobayashi 9.

106 *The most prominent of these alliances ...* For a history of the Co-operative Committee on Japanese Canadians from the perspective of its participants, see Fowke.

106 *"and expressed their willingness to co-operate ..."* Fowke 9.

107-8 *"When the meeting voted ..."* Cassandra Kobayashi and Roy Miki, *Spirit of Redress* 133. For the story of Japanese Canadians who enlisted in both wars, see Roy Ito's *We Went to War,* for comments on the meeting to which Obata refers, see 195 ff.

108 *"survey of 1,800 evacuees in ..."* Adachi 324.

108 *"forbade the congregation ..."* Manitoba Japanese Canadian Citizens' Association, *The History of Japanese Canadians in Manitoba* 40.

109 *"mutual co-operation ..."* Report of the First Ontario Convention May 25 and 26 1946, Kunio Hidaka Papers.

CHAPTER 5
NOW YOU SEE IT, NOW YOU DON'T:
THE PERILS OF THE BIRD COMMISSION

111 *"Apologists for the government argue ..."* NAJC, *Democracy Betrayed* 18.

112 *"fair price ..."* Comments by Prime Minister King cited in Edith Fowke 25.

112 *On April 17, 1947, just after ...* Cabinet Committee on Japanese Questions, Agenda and Minutes 1945-48, Raymond Ranger Papers, RG27, Volume 3026, LAC. All the minutes of the CCJQ have been kept intact in the papers of Raymond Ranger, who worked in the Privy Council. There were 11 meetings noted in Ranger's papers, beginning on September 12, 1945, and ending on January 15, 1948.

113 *"to investigate claims made ..."* Agenda, CCJQ, April 17, 1947.

113 *"the amount of compensation that in his opinion ..."* Agenda, CCJQ, April 21, 1947.

113 *"that, by reason of the failure of the Custodian ..."* Minutes, CCJQ, April 21, 1947.

114 *"It is probable that thousands of claims..."* Agenda, CCJQ, April 21, 1947.

114 *"that if the terms were not broadened ..."* Fowke 28.

115 (footnote): *The NJCCA handled 1,100 of ...* See Ann Sunahara, *The Politics of Racism* 155.

115 *"to take advantage of the Commission ..."* Statement by the Co-operative Committee on Japanese Canadians, September 19, 1947, Kunio Hidaka Papers.

116-7 *"Some time between April ..."* Sunahara, *The Politics of Racism* 153.

117 *"I am satisfied ... that the very ..."* Cited in Ken Adachi 328.

118 *"not accepted our representations ..."* National JCCA Bulletin #1, September 17, 1947, Kunio Hidaka Papers.

118 *"public support ... to get the ..."* National JCCA Bulletin #1, September 17, 1947, Kunio Hidaka Papers.

118 *"Most claimants ..."* Adachi 326.

119 *Again, the NJCCA agreed with ...* See Executive Secretary's Report, Minutes of the National Executive Committee, NJCCA, February 8, 1949, Kunio Hidaka Papers.

119 *"desired to know whether..."* Meeting of the National Executive Committee, February 8, 1949, NJCCA Papers, MG2, V7, Volume 2, File 28, LAC.

120 *"Settlement Proposal from ..."* Special Emergency Meeting of the National Executive Committee, Minutes, April 10 and 11, 1949, NJCCA Papers, MG2, Volume 2, File 28, LAC. Unless indicated, all subsequent citations from the minutes for this meeting refer to this document.

123 *"R. [Roger] Obata felt that Mr. Brewin's ..."* Notes on the National Executive Committee Meetings Held May 10, 1949, NJCCA Papers, MG2, Volume 2, File 28, LAC.

124 *"In 1919, I purchased property ..."* Notes on the National Executive Committee Meeting Held May 12, 1949, NJCCA Papers, MG2, Volume 2, File 28, LAC.

125 *"rough justice ..."* Cited in Adachi 331.

126 *"to press the Government for ..."* Letter from Senji Takashima to George Tanaka, September 12, 1950, Kunio Hidaka Papers.

128 *"that the dispersal and assimilation ..."* Peter T. Nunoda, "Co-operation and Co-optation" 18. Readers interested in an in-depth study of the internal political history of Japanese Canadians, up to 1951, should consult Nunoda's well-documented Ph.D. dissertation, "A Community in Transition and Conflict: The Japanese Canadians, 1935-1951."

128 *"to the benefit of some ..."* Nunoda 32.

128 *"while Tanaka sat silently by ..."* Nunoda 25.

129 *"After a year's experience with ..."* "Submission to the Prime Minister and Members of the Government: In the Matter of Japanese Canadian Economic Losses Arising from Evacuation," National Japanese Canadian Citizens' Association Brief, September 22, 1950.

130 *"The government appointed a ..."* Minutes, JCCA NEC Meeting, October 16, 1950, NJCCA Papers, MG28 V7, Volume 2, File 29, LAC.

130 *"the Japanese [sic] in Canada ..."* Cited in Sunahara, *The Politics of Racism* 145.

131 *"(a) To bring to the attention..."* Final Meeting of the Toronto Claimants' Committee, May 28, 1951, Kunio Hidaka Papers.

INTERLUDE
THE CALL FOR JUSTICE IN MOOSE JAW

133-4 *"Who is the Custodian of ..."* Muriel Kitagawa 250.

134 *"consisted of requisitioned buildings ..."* Jesse Nishihata, "Internment of Japanese Canadians, 1941-1946" 8.

135 *"this group as the initial group ..."* A. H. Brown, DL, to F. J. Mead, Commissioner RCMP, June 8, 1946, DL Papers, RG 27, Volume 646, File 23–2.2–9–2, Saskatchewan, LAC.

135 *"the ten men occupied ..."* Nishihata 10.

135 *"When a sharp drop in temperature ..."* Nishihata 12.

136 *"Democratic rights of Canadian ..."* Cited in Adachi 342.

136 *"alleged to have drawn a knife ..."* RCMP Papers, RG27, Volume 646, File 23–2–3–9–2 pt 2, LAC.

136 *"Hirokichi Isomura found a ..."* Roy Ito, *We Went to War* 57.

137 *"Summoned before a Security Commissioner ..."* Roy Miki and Cassendra Kobayashi 44.

137 (footnote): *"54 Japanese Canadians had died ..."* Ito, *We Went to War* 70.

137 *"Uazusu [sic] Shoji, who ..."* Fowke 26.

137 *"promptly declined, claiming ..."* Adachi 324.

137 *"mentally cock-eyed holdouts..."* Nishihata 8.

138 *"Who was responsible for ..."* *New Canadian*, June 7, 1947; cited in Adachi 341.

138 *"The government took us out ..."* Cited in Adachi 342.

CHAPTER 6
SETTING THE WHEELS IN MOTION: THE JCCP REDRESS COMMITTEE

139 *"What is redress ..."* Japanese Canadian Centennial Project, Redress Committee, *Redress for Japanese Canadians* np.

139 *In 1945, just as the war was coming ...* "Information Sheet" for *Of Japanese Descent*, August 1945.

142 *"the status of speaking subjects ..."* Christopher E. Gittings, *Canadian National Cinema* 70.

145 *"recommend appropriate remedies ..."* Commission on Wartime Relocation and Internment of Civilians, *Personal Justice Denied* 1.

146 *"The Centennial was a year ..."* Roger Obata, "NAJC — Its Ups and Downs" np.

149 *"would affirm that they were ..."* Michael T. Kaufman, "A Case of Honor in Canada."

149 *"The trauma of the Second ..."* Stanley Meisner, "Why Vancouver Lacks a Little Tokyo."

149- *"to see what support exists ..."* Steve Berry, "Japanese-Canadians Demand
150 Apology and Pay."

150 *"personal redress ..."* Commission on Wartime Relocation and Internment of Civilians, *Personal Justice Denied: Summary and Recommendations of the Commission on Wartime Relocation and Internment of Civilians* 28.

150 *"The promulgation of Executive Order 9066 ..."* Commission on Wartime Relocation and Internment of Civilians, *Personal Justice Denied: Report of the Commission on Wartime Relocation and Internment of Civilians* 18.

151 *"Japanese Canadian community ..."* Joe Serge, "Japanese Canadians Seek $50 Million for War Uprooting."

151 *"came to me as a surprise ..."* Personal Interview with Gordon Kadota, July 18, 1995.

152 *"I know this issue well ..."* Jim Fleming, "The Way to Right Wrongs."

154 (footnote): *"arriving at a mutual decision..."* Roy Ito, "Sodan Kai," *Japanese Canadian Redress: The Toronto Story* 104. Ito lists its main members: "Along

with Shin Imai, Marcia Matsui and Maryka Omatsu, the core group of founding members included Connie Sugiyama (a corporate lawyer), Jesse Nishihata, Ron Shimizu, David Fujino, Joanne Sugiyama, Jim Matsui, Joy Kogawa, Roger Obata and Frank Moritsugu."

158 "*an accurate and meaningful* ..." Victor Ujimoto to the Multiculturalism Directorate, June 16, 1983; from the personal papers of Gordon Kadota.

159 "*consisting of regional representatives* ..." From the author's personal notes written at the conference.

160 *Kadota recalled that he never saw* ... Personal Interview with Gordon Kadota.

160 "*Since the 1980 Conference* ..." National Redress Committee Report, September 3, 1983.

161 "*came from the minister's office* ..." Personal Interview with Art Miki, November 9, 1989.

CHAPTER 7

NINETEEN EIGHTY-FOUR: DEFINING THE REDRESS MOVEMENT

163 "*So much experience in such* ..." Shirley Yamada, "A Visit to My Childhood" 122. Yamada's essay is a narrative of a bus tour for Japanese Canadians through the B.C. internment camps, May 18-22, 1987.

164 "*walked out partly to protest* ..." Mark Suzuki, "Resignations."

165 "*Do they not realize that we* ..." Shizue Takashima, "An Open Letter."

165 "*There are people who at first felt* ..." Bryce Kanbara, "The Complex Redress Issue."

166 *With such a strong history of activism* ... For an excellent history told through the eyes of the community, see Manitoba Japanese Canadian Citizens' Association, *The History of Japanese Canadians in Manitoba*.

167 "*[T]he NAJC seeks official acknowledgement* ..." Unless otherwise indicated, citations from this NAJC meeting are from the conference minutes, prepared by Gordon Kadota, and tapes of the conference made by Wes Fujiwara.

168 "*In consequence of the abrogation* ..." NAJC, *Democracy Betrayed* 24.

168 *Setting themselves up as a moderate group* ... For the perspective of the Japanese Canadian National Redress Committee of Survivors, see their article, "Another Serious Division in Toronto J.C. Redress Action"; see also the response from the Toronto Chapter, NAJC, "Silent Majority Should Speak Up," in the same issue of the *New Canadian*.

169 (footnote): "*a depreciatory image of themselves* ..." Charles Taylor, "The Politics of Recognition" 75.

172-3 "*After 6 years, the Committee* ..." National Redress Committee Report, September 3, 1983.

173 "*the people of our community* ..." President's Report.

173-4 "*The current Reparation Paper was prepared* ..." National Redress Committee, "Reparations Paper."

175 "*make the issue of redress politically* ..." National Redress Committee,

"Reparations Paper."

175 *"They fear it may renew resentment ..."* Joe Serge, "Japanese Canadians Seek Redress for Wartime Losses."

176 *"the issue is to determine ..."* National Redress Committee, "Philosophical Underpinnings of a Reparations Settlement."

177 *"What appears to be the best ..."* National Redress Committee Questionnaire.

177 *"exchange of letters ..."* Paul Gessell, "Internees Get Hope of Redress."

177-8 *"The Parliament of Canada should ..."* Canada, Special Committee on Visible Minorities in Canadian Society, *Equality Now!* 62.

178 *Given Imai's ties with Jim Fleming ...* The acknowledgements in *Equality Now!* mention "the contribution of the Honourable Jim Fleming whose concern and foresight led to the formation of this Committee." The Special Committee on Participation of Visible Minorities in Canadian Society was officially established on June 27, 1983. It held hearings across Canada in the fall of 1983 and released its report to the public in March 1984.

178 *"Members were deeply moved ..."* *Equality Now!* 61.

178 *"In late January, 1984, The National ..."* *Equality Now!* 62.

179 *"come up with some kind of ..."* Minutes 29.

179 *"a political thing. Let's ..."* Minutes 31.

179 *"We are a minority group that is ..."* Transcribed from a tape of the conference.

179 *"It appears that the old ..."* From a memo, "Seeking Acknowledgement of Injustices — First," dated November 30, 1983.

180-1 (footnote): *"could range anywhere from ..."* From a transcript of an interview in the NAJC Papers in Winnipeg.

181 *"full compensation ..."* "Japanese Canadians to Seek Compensation."

181 *The dispute hinged on their opposition ...* Letter from Ritsuko Inouye and memo from George Imai, NAJC Papers, Winnipeg.

181 *The critical March 17 meeting ...* Information from this meeting drawn from tapes made by Wes Fujiwara.

183 *"people whose ancestors in ..."* Cited in John Gray, "PM 'Not Inclined' to Compensate Interned Japanese Canadians."

184 *Why else would he, in 1976 ...* Trudeau's statement is reproduced in Roy Ito, *We Went to War* 286.

184 *"The Government will be discussing ..."* Memo from George Imai, April 17, 1984, NAJC Papers, Winnipeg.

185 *In a vote taken during ...* Information drawn from a tape recording of this conference call, June 17, 1984.

CHAPTER 8

THE TORONTO CAULDRON: COMMUNITY CONFLICT
AND THE FOUNDING OF THE "TORONTO CHAPTER"

187 *"We have been hurt by what ..."* Transcribed from a tape of a redress meeting at the home of Stan and Marjorie Wani Hiraki, June 24, 1984.

189 *The answer to this question ...* This account of the redress movement in Toronto is derived from research materials that include documents, reports and tapes of several critical community meetings. Readers interested in the history as told through the eyes of several of the key players in the Toronto struggle should consult *Japanese Canadian Redress: The Toronto Story.* This book is a collection of essays written by members of the Ad Hoc Committee, a group formed to tell the story of the redress movement in Toronto.

190 *"apology ..."* Report on the Issei Meeting; from the personal papers of Harry Yonekura.

191 (footnote): *"in the heart of downtown Chinatown ..."* Ad Hoc Committee 125.

191 *"to carry on as the active ..."* Report of the Toronto JCCA Redress Committee, January 12, 1984; from the personal papers of Harry Yonekura.

192 *"community agreement ..."* Minutes of the Executive Committee Meeting of the Toronto JCCA Redress Committee, January 15, 1984; from the personal papers of Harry Yonekura.

193 *"a proviso that future negotiations ..."* Minutes, Toronto JCCA Redress Committee, January 11, 1984. Interestingly, this motion was made by Wes Fujiwara when he first became involved in redress. He soon changed his position.

194 *"I don't think we should confine ..."* Transcribed from the tape of the Toronto JCCA Redress Committee meeting, March 28, 1984. All subsequent citations from this meeting are transcribed from this tape.

199 *The motion to disband the NRC ...* For a report on the dissolution of the National Redress Committee, see Regina Hickl-Szabo, "Japanese Committee on Redress Dissolved."

199 *"Imai said he plans to continue ..."* Brian McAndrew, "Split Leaves 2 Groups Claiming to Speak for Interned Japanese."

199 *"Recently there has been an ..."* Copy of this motion from the personal papers of Harry Yonekura.

200 *It all began for him when one ...* Unless otherwise noted, much of the content of this account of Fujiwara's redress experience comes from personal conversations with the author.

202-3 *"We, the undersigned Japanese Canadians ..."* From the petition submitted to the NAJC.

204 *A hostile unsigned article ...* See "Opposition."

204 *"doctor-member of the Sodan ..."* "Broken Promises."

205 *"I phoned directly Art Miki ..."* Transcribed from a tape of a meeting of the Toronto JCCA Redress Committee, June 27, 1984. All subsequent citations from this meeting are transcribed from this tape.

206 (footnote): *"Above all we must take care ..."* "Comments from the Chair"; from the personal papers of Harry Yonekura.

210 *"used the age old trick of ..."* Wes Fujiwara, "Toronto JCCA Redress Committee Splits."

211 *"Through their abrupt departure ..."* Ad Hoc Committee, *Japanese Canadian Redress: The Toronto Story* 137.

211 *"if an important question must ..."* Transcribed from the tape of the Toronto JCCA Redress Committee meeting, July 5, 1984. All subsequent citations from this meeting are transcribed from this tape.

213 *"fostering a course that is factionalizing..."* Kenneth Kidd, "Federal Moves Upset Japanese Canadians."

213-4 *"disenfranchised and unrepresented ..."* Wes Fujiwara, "Letter to the Editor."

CHAPTER 9
GETTING THE NAJC HOUSE IN ORDER:
FORGING THE LANGUAGE OF REDRESS

215 *"What a cast of characters we ..."* Joy Kogawa, "Epilogue," *Japanese Canadian Redress: The Toronto Story* 352.

216 *"timing couldn't have been ..."* Vic Ogura, "The Fine Art of Peaking."

218 (footnote): *"proposed a year long, national ..."* Shirley Yamada, "The 1977 JC Centennial," *Japanese Canadian Redress: The Toronto Story* 83.

218 *It was in 1976, at a Japanese Canadian ...* Information about this meeting comes from "The Minutes of the Seventh National Japanese Canadian Citizens' Association Conference," Prince Hotel, Toronto, May 22-24, 1976, as well as from discussions with Gordon Hirabayashi and Bryce Kanbara, both of whom were present.

219 *At the Winnipeg conference in ...* Minutes of the 1977 NJCCA conference, Winnipeg.

220 *"That a 6 month period be allocated ..."* Minutes of the NAJC conference, Vancouver, 1980.

220 *The NAJC delegation, led by Kadota ...* On the preparations undertaken for Gordon Kadota's appearance, see the first-hand account written by Edy Goto and Ron Shimizu, "On the NAJC Presentation to the Special Joint Committee on the Constitution: An Entrenched and Inviolate Charter of Rights." For details of the presentation, see Canada, Special Joint Committee of the Senate and of the House of Commons on the Constitution of Canada, *Minutes of Proceedings and Evidence, November 26, 1980*, np. All citations from the NAJC presentation are taken from this text.

221 *During the mass uprooting, she ...* For an excellent collection of stories about teaching in the B.C. camps, see *Teaching in Canadian Exile*, by Frank Moritsugu and the Ghost Town Teachers Historical Society. This publication is dedicated to Hide Hyodo Shimizu, whose work as a teacher is profiled in the chapter "The First Japanese-Canadian Teacher" (31–38).

222 *Shimizu was well known among ...* For Art Shimizu's view of the Act at the time, see his "Abolition of the War Measures Act as Part of the Restitution Request Package."

224-5 *"During the 1960s and early 1970s ..."* Taken, with some modifications, from the Minutes of the NAJC Council meeting, Winnipeg, January 21, 1984.

227 *"felt that before he could take ..."* President's Report, NAJC meeting, Vancouver, April 7-9, 1984.

228 *For several months before the Vancouver ...* The proposal began as a brainstorming session, October 18, 1983, to compose a JCCP position paper. The group consisted of Randy Enomoto, Fumiko Greenaway, Martin Kobayakawa, Ken Shikaze, Mayu Takasaki, Tamio Wakayama and the author.

228 *"The actions of the government were not directed ..."* National Redress Committee, "Philosophical Underpinnings of a Reparations Settlement."

229 *"[T]he NRC argument for group compensation ..."* JCCA Redress Committee presentation, NAJC meeting, Vancouver, April 7-9, 1984.

230 *NAJC representative from Ottawa ...* Writing the brief, *Democracy Betrayed: The Case for Redress,* turned out to be a collective effort with contributions from numerous individuals connected to the NAJC. The following are listed as members of the Redress Brief Committee at the back of the publication: Tony Nabata (Chair), Charlotte Chiba, Randy Enomoto, Fumiko Greenaway, Elmer Hara, Allan Hoyano, Shin Imai, Roy Miki, Maryka Omatsu, Ken Shikaze, Ann Sunahara, Mayu Takasaki and Tamio Wakayama, with contributors Harold Hirose, Gordon Kadota, Joy Kogawa, Art Shimizu and Victor Ujimoto.

233 (footnote): *"When I did my research in the 1970s ..."* E-mail correspondence with the author, January 10, 2003.

233 (footnote): *"book was made entirely possible because ..."* Ann Sunahara, "Redress and Government Documents" 11.

234-5 *"had no basis in military ..."* NAJC, *Democracy Betrayed* 24.

235 *At the end was a list of Japanese Canadians ... The Case for Redress: Information* was designed and produced by Jim Matsui, Shirley Yamada, Kerri Sakamoto, Ken Noma and David Fujino.

238 *"We conclude that the Japanese Canadian ..."* NAJC, *Economic Losses of Japanese Canadians After 1941* 1.

238 *"clearly had their education ..."* NAJC, *Economic Losses of Japanese Canadians After 1941* 20.

238 *"Canadian courts have awarded ..."* NAJC, *Economic Losses of Japanese Canadians After 1941* 21.

239 *"We have not been able to ..."* NAJC, *Economic Losses of Japanese Canadians After 1941* 28.

CHAPTER 10

CONSTRUCTING A REDRESS IDENTITY:

HISTORY, MEMORY AND COMMUNITY FORMATION

241 *"Trauma is precisely the open ..."* Kyo Maclear, *Beclouded Visions* 11.

245 *"representative organization for Vancouver ..."* Brief to the NAJC Council, April 7, 1984, Vancouver Redress Coalition.

246 *Two issei women, Haruko Kobayakawa and Masue Tagashira ...* For biographical information on these two incredibly influential women on the JCCA Redress Committee, see "Haruko Kobayakawa" in Roy Miki and Cassandra Kobayashi, *Justice in Our Time* 54, and "Masue Tagashira" in Nancy Knickerbocker and Stephen Bosch, *First Canadians* 44–50.

247 *"come in from the cold on ..."* Tom Shoyama, "Redress and the War Years" 32–33.

247-8 *"racist motivation ..."* Shoyama 34–35.

249 *"That winter it was cold in ..."* The description of and citations from this meeting draw from an article written by the author, "The Personal Side of Redress: Four Japanese Canadians Tell Their Stories."

252 *a national newsletter, The NAJC Newsletter ...* Four issues of the NAJC *Newsletter* were published while Cassandra Kobayashi and I ran the National Co-ordinator's office. When our term ended, the newsletter moved to Toronto and eventually became the national Japanese Canadian newspaper, *The Nikkei Voice*.

254 *Murta moved aggressively against the NAJC ...* See the article issued by the National Redress Committee of Survivors, "Another Serious Division in Toronto J.C. Redress Action."

255 *"He always used to say he was ..."* Miki and Kobayashi, *Justice in Our Time* 54.

256 *"It's as if the clock stopped ..."* Maryka Omatsu, *Bittersweet Passage* 43.

256 *"post-traumatic stress disorder ..."* Cathy Caruth, *Trauma* 3.

256-7 *"While the precise definition of post-traumatic..."* Caruth 4–5.

257 *"in the collapse of its understanding ..."* Caruth, *Trauma* 7.

257 *In the thousands of censored letters now resting in ...* These censored letters are collected in the "Intercepted Letters" files, DL Papers, LAC.

258 *"Isn't it pitiful this situation of ..."* Cited in Muriel Kitagawa, *This Is My Own* 50.

258 *"Last ruling forbids anyone ..."* Kitagawa 96.

258-9 *"Honest Wes, I don't know where ..."* Kitagawa 96–97.

261 *"Time heals the details, but ..."* Kitagawa 229.

262 *"context of retelling is crucial ..."* Laurence J. Kirmayer, "Landscapes of Memory" 178.

262 *"highly selective and thoroughly transformed ..."* Kirmayer 176.

262 *"pregiven object of our gaze ..."* Paul Antze and Michael Lambek, *Tense Past* xii.

262 *"retrieval cue ..."* Daniel L. Schacter, *Searching for Memory* 70.

262-3 *"The stored fragments [of events and things]..."* Schacter 70.

263 *"a monument visited ..."* Pierre Nora, cited in Paul Antze and Michael Lambek, *Tense Past* xiii.

264 *In the process of sharing stories, individuals ...* For an excellent discussion of the power of sharing stories to mediate the effects of trauma, see Judith Herman, *Trauma and Recovery*.

264 *"bear witness to a past that was ..."* Caruth 151.

265 *"None of us ... escaped the naming ..."* Joy Kogawa, *Obasan* 118.

265 *"we do things with language ..."* Judith Butler, *Excitable Speech* 8.

CHAPTER 11
THE POLITICS OF THE PROCESS:
ENCOUNTERS OF THE FEDERAL KIND

269 *"A sense of incompleteness gnaws at ..."* Cited in Roy Miki and Cassandra Kobayashi, *Justice in Our Time* 61.

269 *December 15, 1984, at the ...* Unless otherwise indicated, all citations from this meeting are transcribed from the tapes made by the NAJC, December 15, 1984, Winnipeg.

272 *"The older Japanese Canadians ..."* "Murta Won't Discuss Redress for Internees But Apology 'Likely'."

273 *In a personal interview, Kruhlak recalled ...* Personal interview with Orest Kruhlak, June 22, 1992.

273 *"it's always great to have a group ..."* Personal interview with Jack Murta, July 12, 1991.

274 *"December 15, 1984: At the request ..."* This press release is reproduced in Miki and Kobayashi 82.

276 *Kruhlak recalled that the mandate he ...* Personal interview with Orest Kruhlak.

276 *Murta, for his part, recalled ...* Personal interview with Jack Murta.

276 *And some government insiders feared ...* To understand the importance of redress for these groups, see the testimonials in Miki and Scott McFarlane, *In Justice.*

276 *Kruhlak confirmed this assumption ...* Personal interview with Orest Kruhlak.

277 *He was also betraying the pre-election ...* See Richard Cleroux, "Compensate Internees for Unfair Treatment, Mulroney Urges PM." In this article Brian Mulroney, in response to Prime Minister Trudeau's rejection of redress, is quoted as vowing, "If there was a Conservative government I can assure you we would be compensating Japanese Canadians."

277-8 *"Let it be clearly understood that we ..."* Art Miki, NAJC President to Jack Murta, January 18, 1985.

280 *"1. that a redress settlement ..."* Art Miki, NAJC President to Prime Minister Brian Mulroney, February 2, 1985.

282 *"The will was there but the sensitivity ..."* Personal interview with Jack Murta.

282 *At the meeting to form the special committee ...* Personal interview with Orest Kruhlak.

282 *"have been thrown out ..."* Personal interview with Jack Murta.

287 *"passionate supporter of the ..."* Dan Turner, "Redress, War Role Split Japanese Canadians."

288 (footnote): *"Those interned during the Second ..."* "The Jelinek Waltz."

293 (footnote): *"71 percent said each individual who was ..."* Deborah Wilson, "Poll Indicates Ottawa, Public at Odds."

INTERLUDE
THREE VANCOUVER VISITATIONS

298 *"NAJC President Art Miki ..."* "Sorry — Now Get Lost." See also "Jelinek Drawn into Argument."

300 *"I think one of the regrettable days ..."* Transcribed from a tape of Prime Minister Brian Mulroney's press conference, March 7, 1986, Vancouver. My special thanks to the reporter, whose name I do not know, who generously gave me her tape recording of the press conference.

CHAPTER | 2
THE REDRESS SETTLEMENT: NEGOTIATIONS WITH THE NATION

303 *"After the settlement happened, someone ..."* Cited in Kevin Griffin, "Redress Helped Japanese Forgive."
304 *Our flight to Montreal, Weiner's ...* For another account of the negotiation session in Montreal from a member of the Strategy Committee, see Roger Obata, "Justice at Last."
306 *"had been used to pay for the ..."* Lucien Bouchard, *On the Record* 191–92.
308 *"During the 1960s the government made ..."* Eva Mackey, *The House of Difference* 53.
310 *"anglo-conformity ..."* Augie Fleras and Jean Leonard Elliott, *The Challenge of Diversity* 71.
310-11 *"In 1942 ... following the unhappy outbreak ..."* Cited in Ken Adachi, 434; emphasis added.
311 *"born in Japan in that momentous year ..."* Trudeau's speech is cited in Roy Ito, *We Went to War* 286.
314 *"culture brokers ..."* Personal interview with Art Miki.
315 *"The government is generally looking at ..."* Paul Gessell, "Internees Get Hope of Redress."
316 *"has requested to know how the amount ..."* J. N. LaBarre to B. L. Strayer, June 20, 1983; from the Access to Information documents received by Kevin Griffin.
317-8 *"The Government of Canada ..."* David Collenette, Speaking Notes on the Government's Response to the Report of the Special Parliamentary Committee, *Equality Now!*, Multiculturalism Canada, June 1984; from the Access to Inform-ation documents received by Kevin Griffin.
319 *The coalition, a broad cross-section of Canadians ...* The story of the National Coalition for Japanese Canadian Redress and the Ottawa rally is told in Roy Miki and Cassandra Kobayashi, *Justice in Our Time* (108–132). There, as well, the individuals and groups who formed the Coalition are thanked and acknowledged (114–15).
320 *"As far as our community is concerned ..."* All citations from the press conference are transcribed from a tape of the NAJC press conference, September 22, 1988, Ottawa.
322 *"realized that it was politically necessary ..."* Kirsten Emiko McAllister, "Narrating Japanese Canadians In and Out of the Canadian Nation" 88.
324 *"finished the English Canadian ..."* Ian Angus, *A Border Within* ix.
324 *"Throughout the period since the end ..."* Angus 3.

WORKS CITED

Adachi, Ken. *The Enemy That Never Was: A History of the Japanese Canadians.* Toronto: McClelland and Stewart, 1976.

Ad Hoc Committee; Momoye Sugiman, ed. *Japanese Canadian Redress: The Toronto Story.* Toronto: HpF Press, 2000.

Anderson, Kay J. *Vancouver's Chinatown: Racial Discourse in Canada, 1875-1980.* Montreal: McGill-Queen's University Press, 1991.

Angus, Ian. *A Border Within: National Identity, Cultural Plurality, and Wilderness.* Montreal: McGill-Queen's University Press, 1997.

Antze, Paul, and Michael Lambek, eds. *Tense Past: Cultural Essays in Trauma and Memory.* London and New York: Routledge, 1996.

Aoki, Ted T. "In the Midst of Slippery Theme-Words: Living As Designers of Japanese Canadian Curriculum." *Designing the Japanese Canadian Curriculum.* Conference Report, Appendix C, 1992. 1–18.

Barnholden, Michael. "Anti-Asian Riot." Unpublished paper.

Berger, Thomas R. *Fragile Freedoms: Human Rights and Dissent in Canada.* Toronto: Clarke, Irwin and Company, 1981.

Berry, Steve. "Japanese-Canadians Demand Apology and Pay." *The Province,* December 28, 1982.

Bouchard, Lucien. *On the Record.* Trans. Dominique Clift. Toronto: Stoddart, 1994.

British Columbia. Legislative Assembly. *Report on Oriental Activities Within the Province.* Victoria, B.C., 1927.

"Broken Promises." *Canada Times,* May 18, 1984.

Brooks, Roy L. "The Age of Apology." *When Sorry Isn't Enough: The Controversy over Apologies and Reparations for Human Injustice.* Ed. Roy L. Brooks. New York: New York University Press, 1999. 3–11.

Butler, Judith. *Excitable Speech: A Politics of the Performative.* New York: Routledge, 1997.

Canada. British Columbia Security Commission. *Removal of Japanese from Protected Areas: Report of British Columbia Security Commission.* Vancouver: British Columbia Security Commission, 1942.

Canada. Department of Labour. *Royal Commission into Provisions Made for the Welfare and Maintenance of Persons of the Japanese Race Resident in Settlements in the Province of British Columbia.* Mimeographed. 1944.

Canada. House of Commons. *Debates (Hansard), Volume VI, 1944.* Ottawa: 1945. 5915–18.

Canada. Special Committee on Elections and Franchise Acts. *Minutes of Proceedings and Evidence.* Ottawa: 1936, 1937.

Canada. Special Committee on Visible Minorities in Canadian Society. *Equality Now!: Report of the Special Committee on Visible Minorities in Canadian Society.* Ottawa: Queen's Printer, 1984.

Canada. Special Joint Committee of the Senate and of the House of Commons. *Minutes of Proceedings and Evidence, November 26, 1980, Issue No. 13.* Ottawa: 1980.

Canada. Supreme Court. "In the Matter of a Reference As to the Validity of Orders in Council of the 15th Day of December, 1945 (PC 7355, 7356 and 7357), in Relation to Persons of the Japanese Race." *Supreme Court of Canada.* Ottawa: 1946. 248–77.

Canadian Broadcasting Corporation. "A Call for Justice." *The Journal.* 1982.

Caruth, Cathy, ed. *Trauma: Explorations in Memory.* Baltimore and London: Johns Hopkins University Press, 1995.

Chinese Canadian National Council. "It Is Only Fair! Redress for the Head Tax and Chinese Exclusion Act." *In Justice: Canada, Minorities, and Human Rights.* Ed. Roy Miki and Scott McFarlane. Winnipeg: National Association of Japanese Canadians, 1996. 64–70.

Cleroux, Richard. "Compensate Internees for Unfair Treatment, Mulroney Urges PM." *Globe and Mail,* May 16, 1984.

Cohn, Werner. "The Persecution of Japanese Canadians and the Political Left in British Columbia, December 1941-March 1942." *B.C. Studies* 68 (Winter 1985-86): 24–51.

Commission on Wartime Relocation and Internment of Civilians. *Personal Justice Denied: Report of the Commission on Wartime Relocation and Internment of Civilians.* Washington DC: U.S. Government Printing Office, 1982.

Commission on Wartime Relocation and Internment of Civilians. *Personal Justice Denied: Summary and Recommendations of the Commission on Wartime Relocation and Internment of Civilians.* San Francisco: Japanese American Citizens' League, 1983.

Daniels, Roger, and Sandra C. Taylor; Harry H. L. Kitano, ed. *Japanese Americans: From Relocation to Redress.* Revised Edition. Seattle and London: University of Washington Press, 1991.

Editorial, *New Canadian*, March 3, 1942.

Enomoto, Randy, ed. *HomeComing '92: Where the Heart Is*. Vancouver: NRC Press Publishing, 1993.

Fleming, Jim. "The Way to Right Wrongs." *Toronto Sun*, January 31, 1985.

Fleras, Augie, and Jean Leonard Elliott. *The Challenge of Diversity: Multiculturalism in Canada*. Scarborough, Ontario: Nelson Canada, 1992.

Fowke, Edith. *They Made Democracy Work: The Story of the Co-operative Committee on Japanese Canadians*. Toronto: Co-operative Committee on Japanese Canadians, nd; c. 1951.

Fujiwara, Wesley M. "Letter to the Editor." *Canada Times*, June 12, 1094.

Fujiwara, Wesley M. "Toronto JCCA Redress Committee Splits." *Canada Times*, July 3, 1984.

Geiger-Adams, Andrea. "Pioneer Issei: Tomekichi Homma's Fight for the Franchise." *Nikkei Images* 8.1 (Spring 2003): 1–6.

Geiger-Adams, Andrea. "Writing Racial Barriers into Law: Upholding B.C.'s Denial of the Vote to its Japanese-Canadian Citizens *Homma v. Cunningham*, 1902." Unpublished Essay.

Gessell, Paul. "Internees Get Hope of Redress." *Vancouver Sun*, June 1, 1983.

Gittings, Christopher E. *Canadian National Cinema: Ideology, Difference and Representation*. London and New York: Routledge, 2002.

Goto, Edy, and Ron Shimizu. "On the NAJC Presentation to the Special Joint Committee on the Constitution: An Entrenched and Inviolate Charter of Rights." *Asian Canadians: Regional Perspectives*. Ed. K. Victor Ujimoto and Gordon Hirabayashi. Proceedings of *Asian Canadian Symposium*, Halifax, May 23-26, 1981. 380–98.

Gray, John. "PM 'Not Inclined' to Compensate Interned Japanese Canadians." *Globe and Mail*, April 3, 1985.

Griffin, Kevin. "Redress Helped Japanese Forgive." *Vancouver Sun*, October 8, 1992.

Hatamiya, Leslie T. *Righting a Wrong: Japanese Americans and the Passage of the Civil Liberties Act of 1988*. Stanford, California: Stanford University Press, 1993.

Herman, Judith. *Trauma and Recovery: The Aftermath of Violence — from Domestic Abuse to Political Terror*. New York: Basic Books, 1997.

Hickl-Szabo, Regina. "Japanese Committee on Redress Dissolved." *Globe and Mail*, June 19, 1984.

Hidaka, Kunio. "Legal Status of Persons of Japanese Race in Canada: A Preliminary Investigation." Unpublished, c. 1942.

House of Lords and Privy Council. *Cunningham and Attorney-General for British Columbia v. Tomey Homma and Attorney-General for the Dominion of Canada, On Appeal from the Supreme Court of British Columbia, Number 45 of 1901*. House of Lords and Privy Council, December 17, 1902.

Inalienable Rice: A Chinese and Japanese Canadian Anthology. Vancouver: Powell Street Revue and the Chinese Canadian Writers Workshop, 1979. 58–64.

Ito, Roy. *We Went to War: The Story of the Japanese Canadians Who Served During the First and Second World Wars*. Stittsville, Ontario: Canada's Wings, 1984.

Ito, Roy. "Sodan Kai." *Japanese Canadian Redress: The Toronto Story.* Ed. Momoye Sugiman. Toronto: HpF Press, 2000. 103–120.

Jamal, Sherazad, and Zool Suleman. "When the Ship Came In ... Remembering the *Komagata Maru.*" *In Justice: Canada, Minorities, and Human Rights.* Ed. Roy Miki and Scott McFarlane. Winnipeg: National Association of Japanese Canadians, 1996. 71–72.

"Jap Riot." *Vancouver Sun,* May 14, 1942.

"Jap Troubles Here Soon to Be Dispelled." *Vancouver Sun,* April 4, 1942.

Japanese Canadian Centennial Project. *A Dream of Riches: The Japanese Canadians, 1877-1977.* Vancouver: Japanese Canadian Centennial Project, 1978.

Japanese Canadian Centennial Project, Redress Committee. *Redress for Japanese Canadians.* Vancouver: JCCP Redress Committee, 1982.

Japanese Canadian National Redress Committee of Survivors. "Another Serious Division in Toronto J.C. Redress Action." *New Canadian,* December 21, 1984.

"Japanese Canadians to Seek Compensation." *Globe and Mail,* January 24, 1984.

"Japs Are Poor Sportsmen, Indeed!" *Vancouver Sun,* May 14, 1942.

"Jelinek Drawn into Argument." *Vancouver Sun,* December 3, 1985.

"Jelinek Waltz, The." Editorial. *Globe and Mail,* March 8, 1986.

Kanbara, Bryce. "The Complex Redress Issue." *New Canadian,* October 4, 1983.

Kanbara, Tameo. "The Origin of Mass Group." Unpublished Translation by Tatsuo Kage. Published in Japanese in the *New Canadian,* May 4, 1976.

Kanbara, Tameo. "HomeComing Presentation." Unpublished Translation by Tatsuo Kage, 1992. Unpaginated.

Kaufman, Michael T. "A Case of Honor in Canada: Redress for Its Japanese." *The New York Times,* November 22, 1982.

Kelley, Ninette, and Michael Trebilcock. *The Making of the Mosaic: A History of Canadian Immigration Policy.* Toronto: University of Toronto Press, 1998.

Kidd, Kenneth. "Federal Moves Upset Japanese Canadians." *Toronto Star,* July 20, 1984.

Kirmayer, Laurence J. "Landscapes of Memory: Trauma, Narrative, and Dissociation." *Tense Past: Cultural Essays in Trauma and Memory.* Ed. Paul Antze and Michael Lambek. London and New York: Routledge, 1996. 173–98.

Kitagawa, Muriel. *This Is My Own: Letters to Wes and Other Writings on Japanese Canadians, 1941-1948.* Ed. Roy Miki. Vancouver: Talonbooks, 1985.

Knickerbocker, Nancy, and Stephen Bosch. "Masue Tagashira." *First Canadians.* Vancouver: Asia Pacific Initiative, 1990. 44–50.

Kobayashi, Audrey. *A Demographic Profile of Japanese Canadians and Social Implications for the Future.* Ottawa: Department of the Secretary of State, 1989.

Kobayashi, Audrey. "The Japanese-Canadian Redress Settlement and its Implications for Race Relations." *Canadian Ethnic Studies* 24.1 (1992): 1–19.

Kobayashi, Cassandra, and Roy Miki, ed. *Spirit of Redress: Japanese Canadians in Conference.* Vancouver: JC Publications, 1989.

Kogawa, Joy. *Obasan.* Markham, Ontario: Penguin, 1983.

Kogawa, Joy. "Epilogue." *Japanese Canadian Redress: The Toronto Story.* Ed. Momoye

Sugiman. Toronto: HpF Press, 2000. 351–53.

La Violette, Forrest E. *The Canadian Japanese and World War II: A Sociological and Psychological Account.* Toronto: University of Toronto Press, 1948.

Mackey, Eva. *The House of Difference: Cultural Politics and National Identity in Canada.* Toronto: University of Toronto Press, 2002.

Maclear, Kyo. *Beclouded Visions: Hiroshima-Nagasaki and the Art of Witness.* Albany: State University of New York Press, 1999.

Makabe, Tomoko. *The Canadian Sansei.* Toronto: University of Toronto Press, 1998.

Manitoba Japanese Canadian Citizens' Association. *The History of Japanese Canadians in Manitoba.* Winnipeg: Manitoba Japanese Canadian Citizens' Association, 1996.

McAllister, Kirsten Emiko. "Narrating Japanese Canadians In and Out of the Canadian Nation: A Critique of Realist Forms of Representation." *Canadian Journal of Communication* 24 (1999): 79–103.

McAndrew, Brian. "Split Leaves 2 Groups Claiming to Speak for Interned Japanese." *Toronto Star,* June 19, 1984.

Meisner, Stanley. "Why Vancouver Lacks a Little Tokyo: An American Compares Notes on Race Dispersal." *Vancouver Sun,* March 19, 1983.

Miki, Arthur K. *The Japanese Canadian Redress Legacy: A Community Revitalized.* Winnipeg: National Association of Japanese Canadians, 2003.

Miki, Roy. "The Personal Side of Redress: Four Japanese Canadians Tell Their Stories." *Greater Vancouver Japanese Canadian Citizens' Association Bulletin* 27.10 (October 1985): 16–18.

Miki, Roy, and Cassandra Kobayashi. *Justice in Our Time: The Japanese Canadian Redress Settlement.* Winnipeg and Vancouver: National Association of Japanese Canadians and Talonbooks, 1991.

Miki, Roy, and Scott McFarlane, ed. *In Justice: Canada, Minorities, and Human Rights.* Winnipeg: National Association Japanese Canadians, 1996.

Moritsugu, Frank, and the Ghost-Town Teachers Historical Society. *Teaching in Canadian Exile: A History of the Schools for Japanese-Canadian Children in British Columbia Detention Camps during the Second World War.* Toronto: Ghost-Town Teachers Historical Society, 2001.

"Murta Won't Discuss Redress for Internees But Apology 'Likely'." *Globe and Mail,* November 22, 1984.

Nakano, Takeo Ujo, with Leatrice Nakano. *Within the Barbed Wire Fence: A Japanese Man's Account of His Internment in Canada.* Toronto: University of Toronto Press, 1980.

National Association of Japanese Canadians. *Democracy Betrayed: The Case for Redress.* Winnipeg: National Association of Japanese Canadians, 1984.

National Association of Japanese Canadians. *The Case for Redress: Information.* Winnipeg: National Association of Japanese Canadians, 1984.

National Association of Japanese Canadians. *Economic Losses of Japanese Canadians After 1941.* Winnipeg: National Association of Japanese Canadians, 1986.

National Redress Committee of Survivors. "Another Serious Division in Toronto

J.C. Redress Action." *New Canadian*, December 21, 1984.

Nishihata, Jesse. "Internment of Japanese Canadians, 1941-1946." Unpublished Essay.

Nunoda, Peter T. "Co-operation and Co-optation: Nisei Politics, 1943-1950." Unpublished Essay, 1993.

Nunoda, Peter T. "A Community in Transition and Conflict: The Japanese Canadians, 1935-1951." Ph.D. Dissertation, University of Manitoba, 1991.

Obata, Roger. "NAJC — Its Ups and Downs." *NAJC Leadership Conference Report*. Winnipeg: National Association of Japanese Canadians, 1989. np.

Obata, Roger. "Justice at Last." *Japanese Canadian Redress: The Toronto Story*. Ed. Momoye Sugiman. Toronto: HpF Press, 2000. 291–304.

Ogura, Vic. "The Fine Art of Peaking." *New Canadian*, April 27, 1984.

Of Japanese Descent. National Film Board for the Department of Labour. 16 mm, 22 minutes, August 1945.

Oikawa, Mona. "'Driven to Scatter Far and Wide': The Forced Resettlement of Japanese Canadians to Southern Ontario." MA Thesis, Department of Education, University of Toronto, 1986.

Oiwa, Keibo. *Stone Voices: Wartime Writings of Japanese Canadian Issei*. Montreal: Véhicule Press, 1991.

Okamura, Raymond Y. "The American Concentration Camps: A Cover-Up Through Euphemistic Terminology." *Journal of Ethnic Studies* 10.3 (1982): 95–109.

Okazaki, Robert K. *The Nisei Mass Evacuation Group and P.O.W. Camp 101: The Japanese-Canadian Community's Struggle for Justice and Human Rights During World War II*. Trans. Jean M. Okazaki and Curtis T. Okazaki. Scarborough, Ontario: Self-published, 1996.

Omatsu, Maryka. *Bittersweet Passage: Redress and the Japanese Canadian Experience*. Toronto: Between the Lines, 1992.

"Opposition." *Canada Times*, May 11, 1984.

Razack, Sherene H. "When Place Becomes Race." *Race, Space, and the Law: Unmapping a White Settler Society*. Ed. Sherene H. Razack. Toronto: Between the Lines, 2002. 1–20.

Reid, Thomas. "Opposing Oriental Franchise in the Province of British Columbia." Unpublished Brief, March 4, 1937.

Schacter, Daniel L. *Searching for Memory: The Brain, the Mind, and the Past*. New York: BasicBooks, 1996.

Serge, Joe. "Japanese Canadians Seek $50 Million for War Uprooting." *Toronto Star*, February 14, 1983.

Serge, Joe. "Japanese Canadians Seek Redress for Wartime Losses." *Toronto Star*, August 27, 1983.

Shimizu, Art. "Abolition of the War Measures Act as Part of the Restitution Request Package." *Inalienable Rice: A Chinese and Japanese Canadian Anthology*. Vancouver: Powell Street Revue and The Chinese Canadian Writers Workshop, 1979. 69–72.

Shoyama, Tom. "Redress and the War Years." *Redress for Japanese Canadians: A Community Forum*. Vancouver: Japanese Canadian Citizens' Association

Redress Committee, 1984. 32–37.

Silversides, Ann. "No Apology for Internments." *Globe and Mail*, June 22, 1984.

"Soldiers Bar Japanese from Immigration Building Area." *Vancouver Daily Province*, May 14, 1942.

"Sorry — Now Get Lost." Editorial. *Vancouver Sun*, December 4, 1985.

Sunahara, Ann Gomer. *The Politics of Racism: The Uprooting of Japanese Canadians During the Second World War.* Toronto: James Lorimer & Company, 1981.

Sunahara, Ann. "Redress and Government Documents." *Redress for Japanese Canadians: A Community Forum.* Vancouver: Japanese Canadian Citizens' Association Redress Committee, 1984. 11–17.

Sunahara, Ann. "The Abuse of Emergency Law in Canada: Is It Inevitable?" In *Justice: Canada, Minorities, and Human Rights.* Ed. Roy Miki and Scott McFarlane. Winnipeg: National Association of Japanese Canadians, 1996. 7–22.

Suzuki, Mark. "Resignations." *Canada Times*, September 16, 1983. Also published under the initials "MS" with the title, "Three Members Threaten Resignation," in *New Canadian*, September 23, 1983.

Takashima, Shizue. "An Open Letter." *Canada Times*, November 1, 1983. Also published in *New Canadian*, November 11, 1983.

Takata, Toyo. *Nikkei Legacy: The Story of Japanese Canadians From Settlement to Today.* Toronto: NC Press, 1983.

Taylor, Charles. "The Politics of Recognition." *Multiculturalism: A Critical Reader.* Ed. David Theo Goldberg. Oxford and Cambridge: Blackwell, 1994. 75–106.

Toronto Chapter, National Association of Japanese Canadians. "Silent Majority Should Speak Up." *New Canadian*, December 21, 1984.

Tsuyuki, Irene. "The Second Uprooting: Exiled to Japan." *HomeComing '92: Where the Heart Is.* Ed. Randy Enomoto. Winnipeg: National Association of Japanese Canadians, 1993. 40–41.

Turner, Dan. "Redress, War Role Split Japanese Canadians." *The Citizen*, Ottawa, February 22, 1986.

Van Der Kolk, Bessel A., and Onno Van Der Hart. "The Intrusive Past: The Flexibility of Memory and the Engraving of Trauma." *Trauma: Explorations in Memory.* Ed. Cathy Caruth. Baltimore and London: Johns Hopkins University Press, 1995. 158–182.

Ward, W. Peter. Afterword. *Within the Barbed Wire Fence: A Japanese Man's Account of His Internment in Canada.* By Takeo Ujo Nakano, with Leatrice Nakano. Toronto: University of Toronto Press, 1980. 109–126.

Ward, W. Peter. *White Canada Forever: Popular Attitudes and Public Policy Toward Orientals in British Columbia.* Montreal: McGill-Queen's University Press, 1990.

Wilson, Deborah. "Poll Indicates Ottawa, Public at Odds." *Globe and Mail*, April 11, 1986.

Wong, Paul, ed. *Yellow Peril Reconsidered.* Vancouver: On Edge, 1990.

Yamada, Shirley. "A Visit to My Childhood." *Spirit of Redress: Japanese Canadians in Conference.* Ed. Cassandra Kobayashi and Roy Miki. Vancouver: JC Publications, 1989. 115–22.

Yamada, Shirley. "The 1977 JC Centennial." *Japanese Canadian Redress: The Toronto Story*. Ed. Momoye Sugiman. Toronto: HpF Press, 2000. 83–93.

Yonekura, Harry. "The Courage to Resist: Angler and the Nisei Mass Evacuation Group." *HomeComing '92: Where the Heart Is*. Ed. Randy Enomoto. Winnipeg: National Association of Japanese Canadians, 1993. 20–24.

Yonekura, Harry, with Blanche Hyodo. "POW 348, Camp 101, Angler." *Japanese Canadian Redress: The Toronto Story*. Ed. Momoye Sugiman. Toronto: HpF Press, 2000. 40–51.

ARCHIVAL COLLECTIONS

British Columbia Security Commission Papers, Library and Archives of Canada (LAC) (formerly the National Archives of Canada)

Department of External Affairs Papers, LAC

Department of Labour Papers, LAC

Ian Mackenzie Papers, LAC

Kunio Hidaka Papers, Japanese Canadian National Museum

National Association of Japanese Canadians Papers, Winnipeg

National Japanese Canadian Citizens' Association Papers, LAC

Raymond Ranger Papers, LAC

Robert Y. Shimoda Papers, Special Collections, University of British Columbia

Royal Canadian Mounted Police Papers, LAC

PERSONAL INTERVIEWS

Gordon Kadota, July 18, 1995

Orest Kruhlak, June 22, 1992

Art Miki, November 9, 1989

Jack Murta, July 12, 1991

INDEX

access to information, 117, 160, 233, 315
Adachi, Ken, 217
Anderson, Kay J., 24–25
Angler P.O.W. camp, 133, 134–35
Angus, Ian, 324
Aoki, Ted, 14
Asiatic Exclusion League, 20
assimilation, 39–42, 309–10

backlash, fear of, 167, 168, 175–76, 206, 263, 270
Banno, Chutaro (Edward), 31, 32
Barter, Phil, 237
British Columbia Security Commission (BCSC), 3, 69; & favouritism, 54–55, 63; & legality of internment, 72–74, 76; policy of family breakup, 64–67, 70–72, 77
Bird Commission (Royal Commission on Property Claims), 111, 113–27
Bouchard, Lucien, 304–6
Bowie, Doug, 270–72, 283
Brewin, Andrew, 103, 115, 118–23, 126, 128

Broadbent, Ed, 7, 278–79
Butler, Judith, 265

Cabinet Committee on Japanese Questions (CCJQ), 112
Cafik, Norman, 219
A Call for Justice, 142–43, 146, 147–48
Canada Times, 164
Canadian Ethnocultural Council (CEC), 285–86, 314
The Canadian Japanese and World War II, 15
Canadian Jewish Congress, 288
Canadian Multiculturalism Council, 285, 287, 288
Cartwright, J. R., 103
Caruth, Cathy, 256–57, 264
CBC (Canadian Broadcasting Corporation), 142–44, 146, 147–48, 275
CCF (Co-operative Commonwealth Federation), 30, 136
CCJC. See Co-operative Committee on Japanese Canadians
censorship, 69

ABOUT
THE AUTHOR

Roy Miki was born in Manitoba in 1942, six months after his family had been uprooted from their home in Haney, B.C., and sent to work on a sugar beet farm in Ste. Agathe, Manitoba. A sansei, or third-generation Japanese Canadian, Miki was one of the leading figures in the redress movement.

A poet, editor, writer and teacher, Miki is a well-known literary figure in Canada. He has published a number of books, including *Justice in Our Time: The Japanese Canadian Redress* (1991), co-authored with Cassandra Kobayashi, *Broken Entries: Race, Subjectivity, Writing* (1998), and *Surrender* (2002), which received the Governor-General's Award for Poetry. He is also the editor of *Pacific Windows: The Collected Poems of Roy K. Kiyooka* (1997), which received the 1997 poetry award from the Association of Asian American Studies, and more recently, *Meanwhile: The Critical Writings of bpNichol* (2002).

Miki lives in Vancouver and teaches at Simon Fraser University.